CONSTRUCTION SAFETY AND HEALTH MANAGEMENT

CONSTRUCTION SAFETY AND HEALTH MANAGEMENT

Edited by

Richard J. Coble

Jimmie Hinze

Theo C. Haupt

Prentice
Hall

Upper Saddle River, New Jersey
Columbus, Ohio

Cataloging in Publication Data

Construction safety and health management / edited by Richard Coble, Jimmie Hinze,
Theo C. Haupt.

      p. cm.

   Includes bibliographical references.

   ISBN 0-13-087173-7

    1. Construction industry—Safety measures.   2. Construction industry—Health aspects.

I. Coble, Richard J. II. Hinze, Jimmie.   III. Haupt, Theo C.

HD7269.B89 C66 2000

624'.068'4—dc21

00-024995

Vice President and Publisher: Dave Garza
Editor in Chief: Stephen Helba
Executive Editor: Ed Francis
Production Editor: Christine M. Buckendahl
Design Coordinator: Diane Lorenzo
Cover Designer: Jeff Vanik
Cover photo: FPG International
Production Manager: Pat Tonneman
Electronic Text Management: Marilyn Wilson Phelps, Karen L. Bretz, Melanie N. Ortega
Marketing Manager: Jamie Van Voorhis

This book was set in Zapf Calligraphic 801 by Prentice Hall and was printed and bound by Victor Graphics. The cover was printed by Victor Graphics.

10 9 8 7 6 5 4 3 2 1
ISBN 0-13-087173-7

PREFACE

The construction industry continues to be the industrial sector responsible for the most occupational accidents, injuries, and fatalities. Many reasons have been postulated for the poor safety record of construction. These reasons have included:

- the uniqueness of the products of construction with respect to form, size, and purpose;
- the fragmented nature of the industry;
- the nature of the construction safety legislative and regulatory framework;
- the lack of continuity in the composition of project teams;
- separation of design from the construction process;
- divergent objectives of the major contracting parties;
- lack of integration into the project schedule;
- compressed work schedules;
- inadequate and inappropriate safety education and training programs;
- lack of commitment by management to safety in the workplace;
- subjection to economic cycles;
- changing governmental priorities and policies;
- constantly changing physical work environments;
- impact of natural phenomena such as weather and climatic conditions; and
- unfavorably high supervisor-worker ratios.

Despite all of these seemingly negative influences, construction safety is still achievable. Virtually all the hazards prevalent in construction can be identified, reduced, or, at a minimum, totally eliminated. The improvement of safety and health in construction is, therefore, still a necessary goal for all the participants in the construction process—from project inception through to the final demise of the facility through demolition at the end of its usefulness.

This text is a contribution toward the effort to improve safety performance in construction. It has been produced from a selection of the papers presented at the University of Florida in the United States during the Rinker Eminent Scholars Lecture series on Construction Safety and Health from August through December 1998. Each of the scholars has earned an international reputation for their work in specific areas of construction safety. The chapters in this book are produced specifically for all participants in the construction process, university and college students, and others who have more than a passing interest in producing an industry that is safe for all. The many techniques and approaches presented in the book are practical and can be implemented with ease by any construction participant.

Boyd Paulson, in his chapter on safety programs for volunteer-based construction projects, suggests that volunteer organizations and their workers seem ignorant about safety hazards and safe procedures, which are well understood in conventional sectors of the industry. There are more similarities than differences between volunteer and conventional construction. Best practices will produce improved safety results in either environment.

Costs are incurred whenever an accident occurs on a project. Jimmie Hinze, in the chapter covering investing in safety versus incurring the costs of injuries, suggests that a distinction must be made between the cost of safety and the cost of injuries. He discusses the level of certainty of the occurrence of cost. However, quantifying the costs of injuries and the investment being made in safety is not a simple or easy task. The influence of the investment in safety or injury occurrence is discussed.

In their chapter on scheduling for construction safety, Richard Coble, Brent Elliott, and Michael Adair postulate that integrating safety into every aspect of the construction process is something that must first start with the project schedule. They describe the use of safety software to identify safety needs, integrate safety databases into the schedule, and provide field access to this information.

Steve Rowlinson deals with human factors in construction safety in his chapter. He discusses the roles of the men and women who manage the construction company, those who manage the construction project, and those at the sharp end of the industry, who are exposed to the risk. Issues of training, the nature of workers and their preparedness for work, and the role of management are covered.

Amarjit Singh presents the results of research studies into falls and fall protection in his chapter on innovative fall protection for construction workers on low-rise roofs. Falls are a major cause of accidents and injuries in construction. The variables of feasibility, simplicity, economy, flexibility, passivity, and protection need to be optimized when determining the most suitable fall protection system to be implemented. He suggests that prefabrication systems are highly feasible, protective, and simple.

In their chapter on safety and health teambuilding, John Smallwood and Theo Haupt argue that team building and the development of a teamwork ethic can contribute to the achievement of improved safety performance on construction projects. The roles and contributions of stakeholders as well as several strategies, systems, and processes are presented to demonstrate the effectiveness of teambuilding, team-based structures, and team-work in achieving adequate safety and health performance.

Kent Davis suggests that there are many striking similarities between construction quality and safety, which include the scope, causes, and effects of associated problems. In his chapter on the implications of the relationship between construction quality and safety, he describes several contrasts, including the typical failure scenario and the presence of a "third party" in safety. Taken together, quality and safety losses represent a major unnecessary source of expenditure in construction. The application of existing safety research knowledge might be used to improve quality.

The design profession has not been an active participant in the safety effort. This is the view of John Gambatese, expressed in nis chapter on designing for safety. He argues that the lack of designer involvement in worker safety has been attributed to their educational focus, limited experience in addressing construction site safety, restricted role on the project team, and a deliberate attempt to minimize liability exposure. He suggests that the design community should consider adopting the philosophy that their scope of work includes designing for construction safety. Implementation of this knowledge represents a proactive effort to reduce worker injuries and fatalities and will ultimately create a safer construction workplace.

Ronald Sikes, Tan Qu, and Richard Coble describe the approach of an owner to safety in their chapter, "An Owner Looks at Safety." In particular, the responsibilities, rights, and expectations of owners are examined. The benefits in terms of avoidance of human suffering and in the realization that safety is good business will far outweigh the perception of increased risk through undertaking to act responsibly.

In her chapter on the health consequences of working in construction, Marie Haring Sweeney suggests that construction workers die at a greater rate than the general public from chronic diseases, such as chronic lung diseases (asbestosis, chronic bronchitis, and emphysema). Construction workers are also at high risk for musculoskeletal disorders, particularly of the back and shoulder, noise-induced hearing loss, dermatitis and other skin disorders, and eye injuries. All these problems are preventable when the right information and preventative strategies are available and utilized.

It is hoped that this book will help in the all-out war against accidents, injuries, and fatalities in the construction industry and produce a safer industry. The words of Barbara De Woody of Universal Studios, Florida, that "safety is everyone's business" ring truer today than ever before. They need to ring louder still!

The editors acknowledge the contributions of every scholar in the fight to improve safety and health in construction. Without the efforts of Boyd Paulson, Jimmie Hinze, Richard Coble, Brent Elliott, Michael Adair, Steve Rowlinson, Amarjit Singh, John Smallwood, Theo Haupt, Kent Davis, John Gambatese, Ronald Sikes, Tan Qu, and Marie Haring Sweeney, this book would not have been produced. Thank you, too, to the thousands of warriors who wage war daily to keep construction safe.

—*Richard J. Coble, Jimmie Hinze, and Theo C. Haupt, editors*

ABOUT THE AUTHORS

Richard J. Coble

Richard J. Coble is an associate professor in the M.E. Rinker Sr., School of Building Construction and the director of the Center for Construction Safety and Loss Control at the University of Florida. He has extensive hands-on experience in construction, having undertaken several major construction projects throughout the U.S.A. His major research interest is in safety and health in construction, and he has recently been conducting investigative studies into workman's compensation fraud. He has shown a strong research interest in the area of automating the construction foreman, which is integral to scheduling safety into all aspects of the construction process. He is currently the international director of CIB W99, which is an international consortium of construction safety experts. He has published widely in the area of safety and health.

Kent Davis

Kent Davis has been in the Division of Engineering, Department of Construction Management at John Brown University since 1977. His major research interest is in construction quality and to that end, he has done leading edge studies in quantifying quality measurement systems. He has received several prestigious awards and authored many journal articles. He is a certified Professional Constructor, registered Professional Engineer, and a member of American Institute of Constructors. He currently teaches a construction course in safety and quality.

Brent Elliott

Brent Elliott is a doctoral candidate at the University of Florida. His research interests include scheduling for construction safety and automation of the construction foreman. He has published several papers in the area of construction safety as well as presented several conference papers.

John Gambatese

John Gambatese is a professor at the University of Nevada. He has done cutting edge research into the area of designing for safety and has developed 500 ways in which safety can be incorporated into the building process. He has developed a methodology wherein designing for safety can be achieved without compromising design and increasing liability. He has published several authoritative articles on the subject.

Theo Haupt

Theo Haupt is a lecturer at the Department of Construction Management and Quantity Surveying at Peninsula Technikon, Cape Town, South Africa. He has served as the chairperson of the Western Cape branch of the South African Institute of Building (SAIB). He remains a National Council member of SAIB and enjoys membership in Architects and Surveyors Institute, Chartered Institute of Building, and Commonwealth Association of Surveying and Land Economics. His research interests include infrastructure policy and delivery in the context of developing countries. However, he is presently engaged in doctoral studies at the University of Florida, where his focus has been on construction safety issues. He has published several safety related articles and conference papers.

Jimmie Hinze

Jimmie Hinze is the director of the M.E. Rinker Sr., School of Building Construction at the University of Florida. He has been involved in the construction industry with particular interest in the field of safety and health since the early 1970s. He is a strong proponent of the view that safety should be incorporated into every subject on construction. He has worked extensively with OSHA in conducting several research studies. He has authored several books and journal articles on safety and health issues as they relate to construction. His book, entitled *Construction Safety*, is considered one of the most practical and comprehensive texts in the field of construction safety.

Boyd Paulson

Boyd Paulson is the Charles H. Leavell Professor of Engineering in the Civil and Environmental Engineering Faculty at Stanford University, where he has been since 1974. His research and teaching interests are in the design and construction of affordable housing, computer applications in construction, equipment and methods for construction field operations, and international construction. His interest in affordable housing and working with untrained workers has led to his interest in safety training development for volunteer workers. He has authored two books and more than 90 papers. He is involved in several national professional and government service activities and has received several prestigious and international honors and awards.

Tan Qu

Tan Qu is a doctoral student in the College of Architecture at the University of Florida. His research interests include wireless communication, robotics, and automation. He has published articles and conference papers in this area.

Steve Rowlinson

Steve Rowlinson is a chartered civil engineer and works in the Department of Real Estate and Construction at the University of Hong Kong. His main fields of research interest are construction safety, construction project management, and the application of visualization (virtual reality) to these fields. He is Director of the Construct IT Center in Hong Kong as well as a consultant to the Hong Kong Housing Authority and Hong Kong Government Works Bureau on site safety matters. Steve has authored more than seven books, eight refereed international journal papers, and several consultancy reports. He has recently published a book on construction safety, which is widely used throughout the Pacific Rim.

Ronald W. Sikes

Ronald Sikes is the head of Safety and Business Affairs at Universal Studios, Florida, and is responsible for all legal, safety, and business matters. He is a lawyer by training and is a member of the Florida Bar with a specific interest in construction. He was previously a construction attorney at Walt Disney World, where he was involved with all aspects of the construction process. Currently he is responsible for the $2.5 billion new theme park at Universal Studios in Orlando.

Amarjit Singh

Amarjit Singh is a professor at the University of Hawaii and is an accomplished researcher into productivity and safety with respect to hazardous areas of construction, such as blasting, and aspects of residential construction with a specific interest in roofing safety. He has done considerable research, the results of which is widely published and considered a standard in many of the unique areas that he has studied. He has also brought scheduling with an emphasis on safety and productivity to a new level of excellence.

John Smallwood

John Smallwood is currently a senior lecturer in Construction Management at the University of Port Elizabeth. He is currently president of the South African Institute of Building (SAIB) and enjoys membership of the Institute of Safety Management (IoSM) and the Ergonomics Society of South Africa (ESSA). His research interests include construction management generally, but, more specifically, construction health and safety, in which he has published widely both nationally and internationally. He chairs various regional and national committees and forums.

Marie Haring Sweeney

Marie Haring Sweeney is a manager with NIOSH heavily involved with the construction industry. An epidemiologist by education, she has provided considerable leadership in the areas of health issues in the construction industry and to this end has taken this research to a new level. She has been a keynote speaker at many national and international conferences around the world and is involved with many of the leading health-related researchers because NIOSH falls under the Centers for Disease Control and Prevention (CDC).

BRIEF CONTENTS

CONTENTS

CHAPTER 1

Safety Program for Volunteer-Based Construction Projects   1

Boyd C. Paulson, Jr.

CHAPTER 2

Incurring the Costs of Injuries Versus Investing in Safety   23

Jimmie Hinze

CHAPTER 3

Scheduling for Construction Safety   43

Richard J. Coble

Brent R. Elliot

CHAPTER 4

Human Factors in Construction Safety—Management Issues   59

Steve Rowlinson

CHAPTER 5

Innovative Fall Protection for Construction Workers on Low-Rise Roofs   87

Amarjit Singh

CHAPTER 6

Safety and Health Team Building   115

John Smallwood

Theo C. Haupt

CHAPTER 7

Implications of the Relationship Between Construction Quality and Safety   145

Kent Davis

CHAPTER 8

Designing for Safety   169

John A. Gambatese

CHAPTER 9

An Owner Looks at Safety   193

Ronald W. Sykes

Tan Qu

Richard J. Coble

CHAPTER 10

Health Consequences of Working in Construction   211

Marie Haring Sweeney

David Fosbroke

Linda M. Goldenhar

Larry L. Jackson

Kenneth Linch

Boris D. Lushniak

Carol Merry

Scott Schneider

Mark Stephenson

SAFETY PROGRAM FOR VOLUNTEER-BASED CONSTRUCTION PROJECTS

Boyd C. Paulson, Jr.
Department of Civil and Environmental Engineering
Stanford University

ABSTRACT

Volunteer-based construction produces thousands of new homes and other structures every year in the United States. However, in some cases volunteer organizations and their workers seem ignorant about safety hazards and safe procedures that are well understood in conventional sectors of the industry. While it may not be clear even to senior safety officials how state and federal regulations apply to work done by unpaid volunteers, there should be little dispute that such work should be done as safely as any.

This chapter first provides background about the scope and nature of volunteer-based construction organizations. They range from small local groups to one of the nation's largest home builders. Next, it reviews both organizational and procedural aspects of safety programs and comments on how these apply to volunteer work. Basically, almost all principles apply similarly, though there are some unique aspects of volunteer construction that make application more difficult.

This chapter contains a study of a 24-unit condominium development, with buildings two to three stories high, constructed almost entirely by volunteers. Its safety program was derived from those of leading commercial and industrial construction companies and helped maintain a safe environment for some 6,000 volunteers who participated in the work. Volunteers worked on foundations, framing, roofing, siding, electrical, mechanical, landscaping, insulation, drywall, painting, and various other trades. We compare its organization, supervision, schedule, costs, and quality to a similar project built next door by another developer working with an experienced general contractor. We then describe the project's safety program in some detail, and discuss problems encountered and results achieved in implementing the program. Finally, we consider what lessons from the volunteer work apply well to conventional construction.

There are far more similarities than differences between volunteer and conventional construction. Those who work on both types can see and learn from the cross-connections. Conventional work develops higher levels of skill and more advanced procedures in coping with safety on more complex projects. Volunteer construction keeps us focused on basic issues that may become obscured in larger projects. Similar best practices will produce similarly improved results in either environment.

KEYWORDS

construction; planning; residential building; safety; volunteer work

INTRODUCTION

Each year, non-profit, volunteer-based charitable organizations perform a large amount of construction work in the United States and abroad. Examples that often make the TV news or feature in newspapers include the construction and renovation of new and existing homes for low-income people, installation of computer networks for schools, construction and remodeling of churches, renovation of community centers, development or rehabilitation of playgrounds, and restoration of historic buildings. However, these news stories too often include pictures that inadvertently display what most responsible contractors would consider blatant and sometimes dangerous safety violations. It appears that some photographers even put themselves at risk to get a dramatic shot of a daredevil act to illustrate the stories. It seems that well-intended efforts too often are accompanied by ignorance of laws and good practices related to construction safety.

This chapter will first describe the nature of volunteer and self-help construction and then indicate the extent to which existing safety knowledge applies to that environment. It will then describe a 24-unit condominium project where a Habitat for Humanity affiliate in California designed a safety program that drew extensively on commercial building standards. Following this will be an explanation of the safety program itself and an evaluation of its results. Finally, we will explore the implications of this volunteer construction safety experience for the conventional building industry.

THE NATURE OF VOLUNTEER-BASED CONSTRUCTION

Volunteer construction, as its name implies, depends mainly on the efforts of unpaid workers to build or renovate structures. Closely related is self-help construction, primarily found in housing, where support organizations guide and help finance families and individuals who mainly depend upon their own labor to build their homes.

The nation's leading non-profit builder of affordable ownership housing, Habitat for Humanity International, is now 15th among over 100,000 U.S. home builders (Professional Builder 1998). Habitat annually builds over 2,000 homes in the U.S. and twice that in other countries. Its prospective homeowners typically commit 500 hours of "sweat equity" to their homes. Volunteers from nearby communities provide many times that amount. Another organization, Christmas in April, rehabilitates thousands of homes and other structures every spring using volunteer labor and contributed materials from business and community organizations. Religious and community groups not only build homes but also churches, playgrounds, and other facilities. Numerous other non-profits operate with funds from the U.S. Department of Agriculture's (USDA) Rural Housing self-help program, which relies primarily on prospective owners to contribute a minimum of 35 hours per week for about 8 to 10 months, or about 1,400 hours. In both Habitat and Rural Housing, this labor is the "down payment." Combined with zero or low interest rates, these programs are often the only feasible home ownership option for the low- and very-low-income people they serve.

Most programs are local or highly decentralized. Habitat has over 1,400 local affiliates in the U.S. alone, and builds most of its units in over 50 other countries. They range from purely volunteer small-town and rural affiliates that struggle to raise funds via pancake breakfasts and similar means for a house or two a year, to professionally staffed urban affiliates with multimillion-dollar budgets. The USDA program works in rural areas and in communities with populations of less than 10,000. In California alone, it works with 11 regional non-profit developers.

These programs rely primarily upon people with little or no construction experience to do the building work and staff committees, but the larger programs also employ experienced professionals to coordinate the development process and oversee construction. Both hire subcontractors for some skilled specialty work. At this grass-roots level, there is often more goodwill than knowledge about how to translate the goals into action. Nevertheless, in building relatively modest single-family detached homes (typically 1,100 sq. ft. or 100 m² for a 3-bedroom unit), both programs have an excellent track record for quality construction at costs well below those of comparable structures in their local markets.

In urban metropolitan areas, where affordable housing needs are often more acute than in rural areas, land costs for a small single-family lot in an average neighborhood can exceed the $60,000 complete cost typical of self-help homes in rural areas. Permits and impact fees can add over $10,000 more per unit. To keep costs affordable, developers must look to higher density forms of housing, such as town homes, condominiums, apartments, etc. But such buildings become more complex structurally, especially in hurricane and seismic areas, have stricter requirements for acoustic isolation, often require fire sprinklers, and may involve structured parking. Elevators may even be required in mid-rise structures to satisfy tougher regulations for accessibility. Safety needs in building such projects become even more complex when working with volunteers.

The lessons to be reported in this chapter are not confined to the self-help environment. Indeed, the world of "zero-cost" unskilled labor simply amplifies some basic principles of planning and management that apply to any type of design and construction project. Safety is no exception.

APPLICABILITY OF SAFETY RESEARCH AND PRACTICE

In the past three decades, safety has been a major focus of industry, government, and academia. Inspired by the leadership of Clarkson Oglesby in the late 1960s and early 1970s (Oglesby 1989), and documented in books such as those by Levitt and Samelson (1993) and Jimmie Hinze (1996), proven best practices, implemented by many companies, have led to significant decreases in accidents, deaths and injuries. Recently, the Construction Industry Institute showed that its member companies that have adopted such proven safety practices have dropped their accident rates to less than 50% of the industry average (Jortberg 1998).

Basic components and principles found in such safety programs were summarized in Barrie and Paulson (1992, pp. 395–412). This section will further condense their main observations based on work done by others and comment on the applicability in volunteer work.

Implementation

Regarding the overall implementation of a safety and health program, Barrie and Paulson summarized the many parallel functions as follows (p. 402):

Personal or behavioral factors:
- Worker: training, habits, beliefs, impressions, educational and cultural background, social attitudes, and physical characteristics
- Job environment: attitudes and policies of the employers and the managers, supervisors, foremen, and coworkers on the project

Physical factors:
- Job conditions: dictated by hazards inherent in the work being performed, as well as by health hazards arising from methods and materials and the location of the job
- Mechanical hazard elimination: use of barriers, devices, and procedures to shield workers physically from hazardous areas or situations (trench shields, chain guards, etc.)
- Protection: use of such equipment as hard hats, safety glasses, respirators, earplugs, seat belts, roll bars, and other devices to protect the individual's health and safety

All these factors are essential to a well-rounded safety program. Traditionally, major company safety expenditures as well as government regulatory programs have been aimed mainly at the physical factors. Studies have shown, however, that roughly 80% of all industrial accidents result from unsafe acts in the accident chain, and not just from unsafe conditions. This finding implies that there should be much heavier emphasis on the personal and behavioral side rather than solely on the physical aspects. Given the lack of training and experience found in volunteer workers, this finding is at least as important in that environment.

It is important to emphasize that both the behavioral and the physical sides must be developed simultaneously in an effective safety and health program. This summary will thus present each in turn and comment on their application in volunteer construction. The following section will summarize the findings of four research studies giving policy guidelines at levels from worker to top management. A subsequent section will touch on the physical aspects of construction safety.

Behavioral Approaches to Safety and Health

The studies summarized below were based on extensive survey work conducted in the field with the aid of construction companies, labor organizations, insurance companies, and their employees at all levels. Four separate but interrelated studies focused on (1) top management, (2) superintendents and project management, (3) foremen, and (4) workers.

Guidelines for Top Managers

Dr. Raymond E. Levitt (1993) led the study of top managers. He found that top managers whose companies have the best safety records generally take an active and positive leadership role. They know the safety records of all field managers and use this knowledge in evaluating them for promotion or salary increases. They talk about safety on job visits, in the same way that they talk about costs and schedules. In many cases, their cost accounting systems encourage safety by allocating safety costs to a company account and allocating accident costs to projects. These managers expect supervisors to have detailed work planning to ensure that equipment and materials needed to perform work safely are at hand when required. They insist that newly hired employees receive training in safe work methods. They also make good use of safety awards and recognition programs for good results at crew and supervisory levels. Finally, they have active and respected safety departments that have strong field interactions.

There is nothing in Levitt's findings that does not apply equally well in volunteer construction. Executive directors of non-profit organizations that use volunteer construction labor are often even more thinly spread across diverse activities than busy construction executives in the profit-oriented sector. Nevertheless, executive directors who put safety at the top of their list know that volunteer recruiting, fund raising, community relations and their central missions of building affordable housing will quickly run aground if their organization acquires a reputation for unsafe work practices. In this respect they are even more vulnerable than conventional profit-oriented construction organizations, where some still see safety program costs as a trade-off.

Guidelines for Supervisors

Dr. Jimmie Hinze (1976) conducted the middle-management study. His findings, the summary of which was paraphrased in Barrie and Paulson, show that middle managers can reduce injuries significantly by establishing rapport with foremen and workers. They orient new workers to the job and acquaint them with other job personnel. They give particular attention to the new workers in their first few days of employment. They show respect for the ability of foremen, but also accept the fact that foremen are not immune to error. They keep safety priorities ahead of those for cost and schedule. They actively support job safety policies, for example, by including safety as a part of job planning and conducting regular safety meetings. They accept responsibility for and take initiative in eliminating unsafe conditions and unsafe activities from the job. Furthermore, Hinze found that top management can help supervisors reduce job accidents by personally stressing the importance of job safety through their informal and formal contacts with field supervisors and by stressing safety in meetings held at the company level.

Because some of these findings indicate that pressures on cost and schedule should be reduced, it is notable that these studies also showed that safe supervisors, foremen, and workers can also be among the most productive. This puts to rest the myth that schedules and budgets must be traded off against safety and health.

Guidelines for Foreman

The foremen study was the primary focus of research social psychologist Dr. Nancy Morse Samelson (1977). She sought answers to the question: How do highly effective (both safe and productive) construction foremen manage their crews? The answers: They handle the new worker differently, ask more questions and ask less threatening ones. They watch new workers carefully until the workers meet expectations for safe behavior. They stay calm and do not get frustrated when work is not going well, and they continue to work with and teach people rather than show anger or resignation. Their approach to safety is different. They integrate safety into the job with personal work rules rather than having a set of safety admonitions. They are neither safety "nit-pickers" nor are they unaware of safety violations—they are in between.

In the volunteer environment, supervisors may be either paid staff or they may be volunteers themselves. The foreman level very often corresponds to volunteer team leaders. Volunteers in these roles may only be on the project once a week or less, typically on a Saturday after a week's work in another profession. While the principles outlined by Hinze and Samelson are at least as important in the volunteer construction environment, and indeed can be implemented similarly with paid supervisory staff, they are more challenging to put into practice under the casual relationships with supervisors and team leaders who also are volunteers. However, the desirable skills and characteristics the researchers identified are not unique to construction supervisors. Volunteers can bring them ready-made from other walks of life. It is also probable that the type of good-natured people who volunteer for community service activities are more likely to have these qualities in greater abundance than people as a whole. The important thing is to identify these people and motivate them to assume these important leadership responsibilities and do so on a repeat basis.

Guidelines for Workers

The study of construction workers was conducted by Lance deStwolinski (1969). His objective was more to identify characteristics of safe and unsafe workers than to prescribe a set of guidelines. These characteristics can then be used by management in selection and in tailoring supervision and assignments to recognize the needs and limitations of individuals. In particular, the following characteristics are danger signals regarding workers who may be more prone to accidents:

1. The worker with abnormal time loss (absenteeism)
2. The worker whose time losses tend to occur on Mondays or days after payday
3. The individual who requires the most supervision to produce normally
4. The worker working in isolated areas
5. The worker with problems from home, skirmishes with the law, and the like
6. The individual who acts abnormally to attract attention (e.g., dress, hair style, hot rodders)
7. The worker whose attitude changes with the time of day and the day of the week
8. New workers with less than one year of service or those with more than 10 years' service
9. Any individual whose name "crops up" frequently in any unfavorable light (e.g., absent, sick, frequently leaves job site)
10. The worker whose personal appearance changes noticeably (watch for sudden change in gait, color, or actions)

Here, it would appear at least, volunteer work may significantly differ from such stereotypical types of construction, where substance abuse, aggressive behavior, and other antisocial characteristics have been major problems for some workers in the industry. Most of the people who regularly volunteer for community service activities are much less likely than society at large to have characteristics such as 1, 2, 5, 6, 9, and 10, in particular. Of course, compared to skilled journeymen, most volunteers will indeed have a lack of experience and need extra supervision; that is the nature of the business. But most volunteer workers are also intelligent, mature, responsible, and highly motivated.

Sometimes personnel problems such as those described in deStwolinski's list arise unexpectedly. For example, in the condominium project to be described later in this paper, two of the three initial supervisors themselves exhibited many of the 10 troublesome characteristics. The kindly executive director of the Habitat affiliate may have been trying to solve too many societal problems at once by giving these supervisors a chance to straighten out troubled lives, but eventually they had to be terminated for the safety of others around them. Thus, volunteer construction, for all its noble aspirations and successes, must also be vigilant regarding the human issues identified by deStwolinski.

But volunteer construction organizations can also build more than structures. Occasionally volunteer groups will come from programs for troubled youth, parolees, or others trying to find a bridge from unfortunate past experiences, and then indeed supervisors must be alert for risk factors. But even here there are opportunities for success. One of the most notable examples of volunteer construction—and human reconstruction—is the Delancey Street Foundation in San Francisco (Stehle 1995). This is a complex and elegant structure consisting of residential, training, office, and retail components that was built almost entirely by the former convicted felons whose lives it was designed to rehabilitate. Each worker went there voluntarily and received only shelter, food, and clothing in return. Today, some 500 people live in the Delancey complex, participate in its job training, staff the Foundation's diverse businesses housed in the building complex, counsel recent arrivals, and indeed manage the organization itself. All but the founder, Dr. Mimi Silbert, have backgrounds that led to incarceration. At least one who became a successful general contractor and numerous skilled craftsmen got their start on new lives here. Like the Delancey Street neighborhood in New York that was a way station for new immigrants to the United States, construction has long been a way station for the upwardly mobile. At San Francisco's Delancey Street Foundation, the analogy has taken on a new dimension.

Physical Approaches to Safety and Health

The physical aspect of construction safety requires proper equipment and procedures, regular and knowledgeable inspection, and good planning. This section derives from Barrie and Paulson (1992, pp. 407–409), where components were summarized as follows:

1. Education and training in correct methods and procedures
2. Provision and proper utilization and application of good-quality, well-maintained tools and equipment, both for construction operations and for mechanical elimination of hazards; examples include roll-over protection on earthmoving equipment, and noise-level controls
3. Enforced use of approved equipment for personal protection: hard hats, seat belts, earplugs, etc., as required by specific operations
4. Good housekeeping on the job site

Clearly, it is beyond the scope of this chapter to attempt the type of detailed elaboration contained in safety manuals. Suffice it to say that detailed knowledge of this type is fundamental to an effective program in construction safety and health. In volunteer work, however, some peculiar situations can arise. For example, people who have not worn hard hats before react in different ways. Some are reluctant to mess up hair-dos carefully coifed for this outing with their group, while others are happy to be the "weekend warriors" of construction. In spite of advance mailings, some show up in shorts and sleeveless shirts to do composition roofing, for example, or install fiberglass insulation in ceilings. Peninsula Habitat has a "lost-and-found" box of abandoned clothing to rescue these unknowing people from abraded knees, sunburn, and itchy skin. In general, if supervisors emphasize the dangers and consequences of improper use of power tools, falls from roofs, ladders and scaffolds, falling objects, etc., the vast majority of volunteers readily accept the cautions and safety procedures that are given to them. The biggest danger is supervisors who feel they can skip this important aspect of volunteer orientation and leave people ignorant of common construction safety hazards.

Inspection

Good in-house inspection by personnel authorized to implement changes is increasingly common these days, in part as a matter of self-defense against OSHA fines. In some companies with outstanding safety programs, the "job-safety coordinator" is the first step up to line supervisory ranks. Other companies make good use of experienced inspectors provided by insurance companies. In some cases this approach either directly or indirectly affects insurance premiums. Others, including Peninsula Habitat, have benefitted from OSHA's own consultation service. Regardless of the motivation, the trend toward objective and qualified inspection of work sites is a good one, and it has been a long time in coming. Inspection has always been an essential part of an effective safety and health program.

It is essential that the inspectors themselves be experienced in construction operations, and that they be objective, fair, and practical in their recommendations and directives to project managers and supervisors. Few things can discourage a safety program more quickly than conspicuously ignorant and inexperienced inspectors who compensate with missionary zeal for what they lack in knowledge. However, given that we can have intelligent and objective inspectors, it is also important that they have the authority, either directly or through recommendations backed by higher management, to see that safety and health standards are maintained on job sites. All of this applies equally well to the inspection of volunteer construction operations. It is the fortunate volunteer organization that has a qualified safety professional among its regular volunteers.

Preplanning

Thorough and conscientious preplanning is essential to economy, efficiency, and high productivity in almost all construction operations; safety and health considerations should be an integral part of this process. Safety-conscious professionals should participate in the development of standard procedures and should review job-operation plans for considerations such as the following:

1. To verify that the method selected does indeed adhere to recommended and required standards and regulations for safety and health

2. To be certain that the correct tools and equipment will be available for the work, including the necessary personal protection gear

3. To express reservations about supervisors or workers who lack the skills that will be needed, and to suggest remedial training procedures where appropriate

4. To anticipate hazards inherent in the work and recommend precautionary steps for dealing with them

Preplanning of this type, with competent supervision to see that the plan is indeed executed, is one of the best methods to assure not only high levels of safety and health, but high production and quality as well. It is doubly important in volunteer construction, where inexperience and the short duration of most people's stays make it essential to analyze work, break it down to bite-sized elements, and task out teams with goals they can accomplish productively, safely, and with high quality. Lacking plentiful and experienced journeymen and subcontractors to move the job along, managers and supervisors of volunteers must be exceptional planners, organizers, and supervisors—and have the patience of Job to see their plans fulfilled.

EXAMPLE CONDOMINIUM PROJECT

Non-profit self-help builders already are building multi-family structures, with varying degrees of success and failure, in or near Chicago, Seattle, San Francisco, Washington, D.C. and elsewhere. The primary source of information for this chapter is a 62-unit condominium and apartment project recently completed in California. Total cost was approximately $8,000,000, including land, design, permits and fees, developer overhead, etc.—about $130,000 per typical three-bedroom unit in an overheated California market where comparable units now cost $300,000 and up.

In this project, 24 ownership units were built by a self-help developer new to this type of construction, and 38 rental units were constructed by an experienced non-profit developer and contractor. Both the developer and contractor for the apartment side are among the best of their type in the United States, so the benchmark for comparing the self-help approach is about as demanding as it could be for this type of work. The author has also visited self-help multi-family projects of similar and even greater complexity that have been completed or are under-way in other cities, and discussions with their developers and managers have revealed similar findings to those to be described here, so this is not an isolated example.

Built on approximately 3 acres (1.2 hectares) of land at a density of 20 units per acre (20 units per hectare), both sides of the project had stacked flats and two-story town houses built over one-story flats in two- and three-story buildings of six to eight units each. Figure 1–1 is a site plan; Figure 1–2 shows two elevation photos; and Figure 1–3 is a floor plan for a three-bed-room flat. The ownership side also had a four-unit building and 24 garages organized into six four-bay buildings. The apartment side had an office and community center. While far from high-rise structures, the buildings had Zone 4 seismic structural design details for wood-frame housing, met California's stringent Title 24 energy code, had numerous details to assure acoustic isolation, and were fully sprinklered. The site is fully landscaped, has an automated irrigation system, and includes two children's playgrounds. The project was designed by an award-win-ning architect who, to help get the project approved by a demanding architectural review board and planning commission typical of California's cities, made no concessions to the simplicity of construction typically found in single-family homes designed for self-help construction.

Project Organization

The project was a three-way joint effort between a non-profit multi-family apartment devel-oper, a local affiliate of Habitat for Humanity, and a local non-profit community organization. The first two shared costs of design, permitting, and site development, then proceeded inde-pendently with the structures. The community organization facilitated planning and approvals and helped with fund-raising.

The apartment developer had an in-house professional staff to get the project through design and permitting, then contracted with a construction management (CM) firm for con-struction. The CM had a part-time home-office-based project manager and a full-time site super-intendent, but otherwise subcontracted all construction work to numerous specialty firms.

The Habitat affiliate's executive director provided input to planning and design, then hired site staff to plan and supervise volunteer work and to manage subcontractors. The site staff looked to a volunteer construction committee for assistance in planning, estimating, pro-curement, and policy guidance for safety, subcontracting, labor relations, and related field mat-ters. Site development (grading, compaction, underground utilities, and access roads) was sub-contracted, but most of the building work was done by volunteers.

Technical and Managerial Oversight

The apartment developer employed architects, planners and experienced construction people to work with the design consultants and the CM's professional staff. The architectural consul-tant coordinated the work of other consultants for civil, structural, mechanical, plumbing, elec-trical, and landscape design. The CM and Habitat's executive director (previously an indepen-dent designer-builder) provided constructibility and valuable engineering input during design. The CM's project manager and site superintendent developed the construction schedule for the 38 apartment units and coordinated the scheduling and oversight of numerous specialty subcontractors to perform the work. Tools, equipment, labor, materials, trade expertise, and craft supervision were the responsibility of subcontractors.

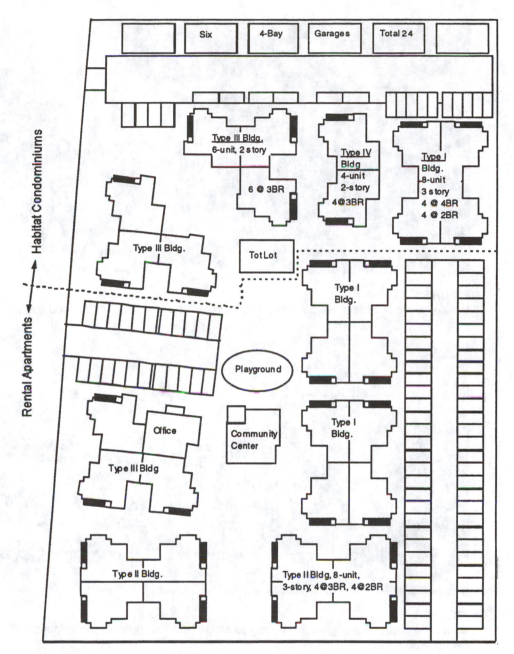

FIGURE 1–1
Site plan.

The Habitat site staff varied over the project, but generally included a project manager (a registered engineer), construction supervisor (a licensed contractor), and foreman (a journeyman carpenter) to plan and supervise volunteer work and to manage subcontractors. As the project wore on, up to four AmeriCorps and two VISTA volunteers joined the team for up to a year each.[1] Knowledgeable volunteer "regulars" assisted the site staff as team leaders for inexpe-

---

[1]Like many other non-profit organizations, Habitat benefits from the very low-cost services of the extraordinary people—typically recent high school or college graduates—who volunteer a full year of their lives for public service under the federal government's VISTA and AmeriCorps programs. For two years, Peninsula Habitat had two VISTA volunteers to assist with office administration and four AmeriCorps volunteers to assist in the field, and had smaller numbers before then.

FIGURE 1–2A
View of six-unit building (six one-story flats, three on first floor, three on second floor).

FIGURE 1–2B
View of eight-unit building (four two-story four-bedroom townhouses above four one-Story two-bedroom flats).

rienced volunteer groups. Some regulars were industry professionals, such as the retired commercial electrical contractor whose knowledge and people skills enabled volunteers to perform most aspects of electrical work, and a skilled finish carpenter whose teams installed cabinets and trim. Others learned their skills simply by working almost every weekend and then were willing to lead others. Examples included Silicon Valley software and electronics engineers, a prospective homeowner who became a journeyman carpenter as a result his experience, and another worker who far exceeded her 500-hour obligation and became especially effective in leading fiber-cement lap-siding teams.

Work Force Organization and Supervision

The apartment construction was typical of San Francisco Bay area residential building. The CM, a "merit-shop" organization with respect to labor relations, issued low-bid subcontracts to a

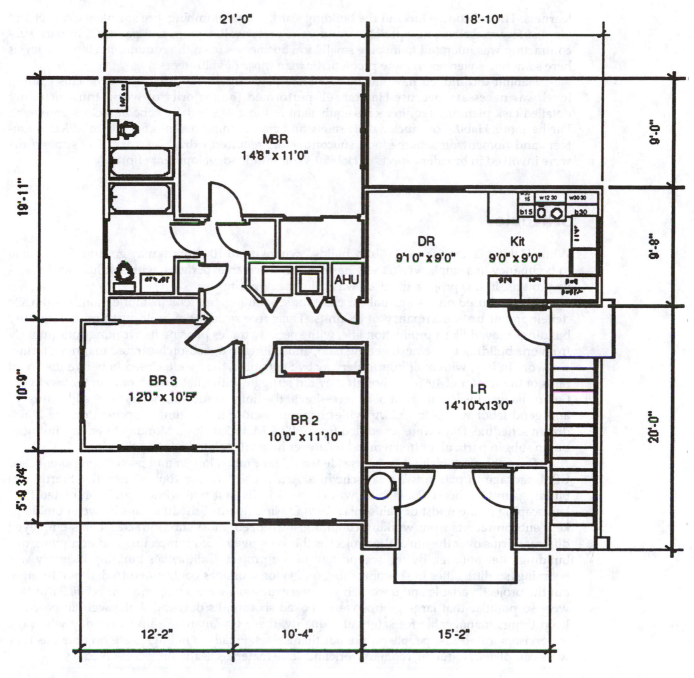

FIGURE 1–3
Floor plan for three-bedroom flat.

mixture of union and non-union specialty firms. Workers thus ranged from skilled union-trained journeymen to relatively unskilled people driven by piece-work production incentives. The CM made some effort to include local people to teach them construction job skills. The CM effectively orchestrated all of this to maintain schedule and budget.

Habitat's project was very different. It performed most building work and some site work (lighting, landscaping) with its own volunteer forces and its prospective homeowners. Approximately 6,000 volunteers and more than 100 owner family members participated in site construction. Typically anywhere from 10 to 100 people were on site on any given day. Most volunteers had no prior experience with construction, but the majority were highly intelligent and motivated professionals and students from California's Silicon Valley area, and they were quick learners. The subcontractors did the building slabs, rough plumbing, fire sprinklers, carpet and vinyl, a few miscellaneous specialties, and parts of drywall, taping, and painting. In part, subcontracting was intended to involve small local businesses from the community, but skill levels here sometimes were even more problematic than those of volunteers.

Habitat did indeed have far more on-site paid supervision than the CM. This staffing level was necessary because Habitat self-performed the majority of work (thus including detailed task planning requirements equivalent to those of specialty subcontractors' foremen). Furthermore, Habitat conducted daily safety and craft training sessions for the unskilled volunteers and homeowners. Some local subcontractors required extra assistance. The supervisors were involved in broader aspects of Habitat's community development efforts.

Schedule

While Habitat is famous for its "blitz builds," where up to 100 homes may go from floor frame to occupancy in a single week, there has not been such an experience with self-help multi-family projects. In this project, the story was quite the opposite.

The CM used only a manual bar chart for scheduling, but took just nine months from site development until occupancy of 38 units. Their five residential buildings and community buildings moved like a production line, with specialty trades phasing in, working continuously from one building to the next, getting paid, and exiting in a well-orchestrated manner. Starting site work in July, with buildings underway by September, they were closed in before the worst rains of the winter of 1995-96, though they did struggle with final landscaping in that wet year. California was just coming out of its recession at the time, so subcontractors were still "hungry" and good labor was plentiful. Activities happened close to the times specified on the hand-drawn schedule. Days were scheduled from 7:00 A.M. to 3:00 P.M., Monday to Friday, but non-union subs in particular often worked whatever hours it took to maintain the schedule.

From the start, Habitat knew its side would take much longer and used a computer-based CPM package to plan a two-year schedule. Actual construction took 32 months. Starting its buildings in October 1995, Habitat was exposed in its first two winters and completed final landscaping in the midst of California's 1998 El Niño floods. Schedule gaps between buildings kept subcontractors from working continuously. Indeed, most subcontracted items employed different firms over the life of the project as the job moved from completing and occupying one building after another. By the second half of the project, California's building industry was booming, so difficulties in subcontracting and labor shortages contributed to delays. Throughout the project, variable and uncertain volunteer turnouts were a major factor. While Saturdays were so popular that large groups were booked six months out, and limits were imposed to keep things manageable for safety and quality, there was many a rainy weekday when the supervisors found few people on site but themselves. Finally, buildings were occupied as they were completed, reducing room to work and store materials as the project evolved.

Costs and Quality

As expected, volunteer labor made many tasks much less expensive (e.g., framing, electrical, drywall, etc.). Quality, as judged by city inspectors and other impartial and knowledgeable observers, was superior to that of similar market-rate housing, let alone low-income projects. Habitat upgraded some specified products to more durable materials and installed them at or above code standards. The standing joke in Habitat organizations is that volunteers pound so many nails that if a Habitat house ever did burn down it could be sold for scrap metal! Twenty-seven homes standing almost alone and relatively unscathed in South Florida amidst the devastation following Hurricane Andrew in 1992 show that the effort pays off (Fuller 1995). Best intentions notwithstanding, the long schedule dragged out supervision costs, and both interrupted schedules and Peninsula Habitat's decision to pay union wage scales made subcontractor costs per unit higher than the rental side. The bottom line was that Peninsula Habitat's first venture into multi-family housing came in about even in costs per housing unit when compared with the subsidized rental project next door. The latter was built by an experienced non-profit developer (about 4,000 units to date) and a respected and professional general contractor who specializes in this type of work. In California's high-cost market, units on both sides of this project sold or rented for about half of equivalent market-rate condominium and rental units not far away. Because home buyers benefited further from Habitat's zero-interest mortgage policy,[2] ownership in this development costs less even than the adjacent subsidized rentals and builds 100% equity with every dollar paid (in contrast to conventional mortgages where most dollars go to interest in the early years).

It was in this environment that a safety program for unskilled construction volunteers was conceived and implemented.

VOLUNTEER SAFETY PROGRAM[3]

Although cumulatively it is the largest sector of the construction industry, residential building is also the most fragmented. Hundreds of thousands of firms compete as builders, suppliers, subcontractors, developers, and consultants to construct relatively small structures. Whether for these or other reasons, many firms in the residential sector are notorious for ignorance or lax attitudes when it comes to safety. Even in the San Francisco Bay area, where the construction industry prides itself on its skilled labor force and professionalism in building, there are noticeable differences between safety on larger commercial and industrial projects and that on even large tracts constructed by residential builders.

In its condominium project, Peninsula Habitat knew that this effort would pose far more risks than its previous single-family homes. Furthermore, they knew that their past supervisors, all with residential backgrounds, lacked the sophistication of the area's commercial and industrial builders. Therefore, before construction began, Peninsula Habitat set out to develop a formal safety program that would be suitable for its volunteers and would be closer to the best non-residential standards expected locally. Fortunately, the San Francisco Bay area has several large contractors that have excellent safety programs and outstanding safety records that consistently rank among the best in the nation. One of these is Rudolph and Sletten (R&S), which does a wide variety of general building, including housing, and is especially well known for its work on the complex technical facilities of Silicon Valley's electronics, computer, and biotechnology industries. They made available all of their safety materials. Their "Code of Safe Practices" and 35-mm safety slide set used for worker orientation were simplified and adapted to the needs of the Habitat project. A copy of Peninsula Habitat's Code of Safe Practices, included at the end of this chapter, gives insight into the priorities deemed most essential for typical one-day workers. This is the type of technical and physical knowledge found to be most applicable in residential work—R&S materials also go on to deal with such matters as the toxic materials handling needed for clean rooms, biotech firms, etc.

---

[2]Habitat's zero-interest mortgage policy is based on several biblical prohibitions against charging usury to the poor, most notably Exodus 22:25—"If thou lend money to any of my people that is poor by thee, thou shalt not be to him an usurer, neither shalt thou lay upon him usury." Typical Habitat families are the working poor, falling near what the federal government defines as "very low income," which is at or below 50% of the mean for their area. As their "down payment," these families are expected to put 500 hours of their own labor toward their home—about 20% of the overall volunteer effort. All proceeds from their payments go into the "Fund for Humanity," 100% of which is supposed to go toward building more homes.

[3]Parts of this section and the next draw from "Safety Program for Volunteer Construction Workers," the author's paper given at the 2nd International Conference on Implementation of Safety and Health on Construction Sites, CIB Working Commission W99, in Honolulu, Hawaii, March 24–27, 1999.

Desiring to continue with supervisors who had been involved on previous single-family homes, Peninsula Habitat foresaw a need to give them safety training. Another large local firm, DPR Inc., which works in markets similar to R&S but does so nationwide, included Habitat's construction supervisors and staff in its own in-house OSHA-certified ten-hour safety course. At no cost they not only provided instruction to each participant, but also gave each trainee the state and federal safety manuals and their own in-house safety course and reference materials. Furthermore, it was most beneficial for Habitat's supervisors to see just how seriously and professionally truly high-end firms such as DPR and R&S integrate safety into their mainstream operations on a wide variety of projects. The firms sometimes build housing, but their main market ranges from luxury office remodels to extremely complex $2-billion electronics plants.

Once the supervisory situation settled down (there were problems initially, to be discussed later), the pattern on Habitat's condominium project became as follows.

- Before arriving on site, volunteers and groups who signed up in advance received an orientation letter that, among other things, told them what to wear, how to get to the site, and asked them to read the Code of Safe Practices. The purpose was to distinguish between this type of fun group activity (it is indeed fun to build) and more familiar group experiences, such as weekend softball games, picnics, etc., and to get their attention directed toward safety issues that pertain to construction.

- Upon arrival on site, either a supervisor or a volunteer coordinator met each person and had him or her sign in. If this was their first day on site, they also filled out an information and waiver form. On subsequent visits, they simply acknowledged when they signed into the log book that they had previously filled out the waiver. While nobody at Habitat seriously expected that the waiver form would exempt the organization from liability in case of an injury accident, signing the waiver form further directed the volunteers' attention toward safety and also provided information for Habitat's volunteer data base.

- When most people were present, and usually at the planned time, volunteers got together in a four-bay garage (completed early and set aside for this purpose) for a 30-minute orientation and training session. Here they received some background about Habitat's program and the role of this project in its community, heard a 15-minute overview of safety guidelines with emphasis on those applicable to the day's work, and then were divided into teams that would perform specialized tasks. Volunteers who arrived too late for the safety orientation (somewhat understandable when people are giving up a day at no pay) usually were kept together and did not start work until supervisors gave them a second iteration of the safety part of the orientation.

- Team leaders (mostly regular volunteers or AmeriCorps volunteers) then took their respective teams to the next four-bay garage, where tools and safety supplies were kept. They made sure the volunteers were properly equipped for the tasks they were to perform (all had hard hats; earplugs, tool belts, glasses, and gloves were normally needed as well). Tools in hand, volunteers reported to their work stations in the buildings under construction. At this point the team leader gave further instruction regarding the technical requirements of the tasks, demonstrated the methods to be used, and reinforced specific safety rules and procedures that applied here.

- Only at this stage, about an hour after arrival, were the volunteers ready to start climbing their own personal steep learning curves in the six hours that remained to accomplish a good day's work. Typically, they would spend the morning on a few production iterations of their task (tying reinforcing steel, framing a small wall, hanging a few sheetrock panels on the ceiling, pulling electrical circuits, running a heating duct, etc.). They usually could do three times as much work in a similar amount of time by the end of the day—if they still had the energy to do so. Very often they developed such enthusiasm in doing what they learned that it would be difficult to get them to stop work at the 4:00 P.M. clean-up time.

At the end of the day, after they cleaned up, the volunteers usually spent a few minutes admiring and discussing their work and that of others, then went away for a month, a year, or more. The process started all over again the next morning—more new people, more new things to learn—and it continued that way until 24 families were in their new homes.

This was not a formula for high production, and it was a difficult operation to supervise. Some 6,000 different people had worked on site by the time the project was completed. While some groups came as often as monthly, most were once a year or just once overall. Each volunteer had to be trained in both construction tasks and in safety. Nevertheless, this volunteer building approach got the job done relatively safely and with quality results. The next section will discuss some issues and problems that arose.

PROBLEMS AND RESULTS

As experienced professionals know, even the most complex projects often have their greatest challenges in the organization and people involved. This was no exception.

Surprisingly, the volunteers—even though they numbered in the thousands—were seldom a significant problem once one understood their needs and limitations. This type of activity attracts some of the kindest, most community-spirited and well-meaning people one could hope to know. Working in such groups is its own reward. Most were intelligent, enthusiastic, eager to learn, and willing to follow instructions. Occasionally a high-school group got a little rambunctious and needed to settle down. At times someone started using a power tool without being checked out first. Every now and then someone would have climbed to the top of a three-story roof on a 6 in 12 pitch only to realize that they really felt frightened and should not be there, and needed reassurance to get back down and move to another task. As volunteers go, perhaps a larger problem was groups that insisted on bringing too many people, or to only come for half a day, but these problems normally were handled in the home office. On site, perhaps the main hazard was an occasional home handyman or engineer from another field who convinced site staff that he knew it all already and then proceeded to give conflicting instructions to fellow volunteers. But all in all, these were not the main issues.

The initial crew of three site supervisors (nominally a superintendent and two foremen) had been involved in varying degrees supervising or working on the nine single-family homes Peninsula Habitat had built prior to starting the condominiums. While each had some post-secondary education, they were up-from-the-ranks residential construction craftsmen—two carpenters and a cement mason—and had years of experience with traditional ways of doing things. When working with small groups and little stress building one single-family home at a time, they seemed to have worked well with volunteers and were well liked. Apart from a volunteer who fell from a ladder and broke his arm in one of those homes, they did not say much about safety on those jobs. Nevertheless, they agreed that the larger project was more of a challenge and two went to DPR's 10-hour OSHA course.

However, in the early months of the project it became evident that these supervisors were unlikely to change much from their years of working "the way it is always done on these jobs." They mainly were paying lip service to the safety program and seemed to think themselves personally exempt from the requirements observed by the volunteers, such as wearing hard hats. The superintendent delegated the safety orientation to a regular volunteer and it only happened when that volunteer was on site. One foreman, who brought an antiquated and poorly maintained forklift, along with an old dump truck and loader, as part of his hiring "package," was clearly of the hard-driving "cowboy" school of high production at all costs. After his brakes and engine failed and his forklift rolled back to do $2,000 damage to a volunteer's car, he received a warning and promised to do better. Shortly thereafter, when trying to move and place a 40-foot-long by 10-foot-high double truss over a second story, it fell over—pinning his fellow foreman and toppling already-placed trusses like dominos, with the last two falling off the end of the building—fortunately with nobody standing below. He had been in a hurry and tried to skid along the tops of opposite walls with just four people. He was contrite, but blamed the results of the collapse on a knot in a 1x4 brace that prevented the previously set trusses from taking the blow when the big truss came down on them. His goal was noble, he said—to finish the wing by the end of the day before more securely bracing the truss system. Contrition notwithstanding, he was terminated at that point.

The other two supervisors soldiered on, but their planning in general was as seat-of-the-pants style as their safety and the project fell further and further behind. The superintendent, a good and decent man at heart, pledged to get safety up to par. But he gave priority to cost and production. An example was that he only had enough scaffolding to work from one or two sides of the building at a time, and tried to move it around so that it was under the roof decking and shingling work areas. One day, when the chairman of the construction committee came up on the roof, he noticed a crew of four volunteers rolling out felt paper near the lower edge of a section of pitched roof. There was nothing between them and a 20 foot (6 meter) fall to hard concrete below. Eleven feet is the height at which 50% of such falls become fatal. The chairman immediately pointed this out to the superintendent, who was just over the ridge, snapped a quick photo to make the point, and stopped the operation. The project remained closed for two weeks while the construction committee and home office staff tried to come up with a better way of managing this site. While this was the most serious situation observed, the pattern was typical of others at that stage. During this shut-down time, the superintendent concluded that it was best for himself and for the project that he resign rather than try to leave the old ways behind to work in the new system—a sad but probably necessary conclusion.

But his resignation left the project in the hands of the remaining foreman. He proved to be the most problematic of all, but for reasons less directly related to safety. Fortunately, a structural engineer and a contractor, who had first come to the project as volunteers with their church group, came to the organization with an offer to take on the supervision. There were three more difficult months of personnel problems with the remaining foreman. He proved unwilling and unable to work with the new team, berated volunteers, harassed prospective owner families, accused city inspectors of collusion, and eventually wound up badgering city hall and picketing the site even while on paid leave. But that is another story. The two new men saw the project to completion and have continued on with subsequent Habitat projects.

It was at that stage when the scenario of orientation and training described above really began to become effectively implemented. Indeed, the two new supervisors had wonderful people skills and seemed to have what it took to work with the extraordinary professionals and community-minded citizens who take time from their busy lives in Silicon Valley to volunteer. These volunteers know that their work in turn helps some of their less fortunate neighbors achieve the dream of home ownership in a high-priced market where this dream would otherwise be nearly impossible. Hundreds of people leaving their neat middle-class suburbs to cross over the Bayshore Freeway to volunteer their time in a town where many caution their children not to go has helped build broader community understanding, particularly regarding the impact of high housing costs on poor people. The project, like similar efforts around the world, built much more than new housing.

Candidly, by the standards of an R&S or DPR, Peninsula Habitat's organization still has a way to go to improve its safety program. The condominium project was not accident free. One volunteer, without having been checked out, tried ripping a board on a table saw. It jammed (ironically, in the safety guard), kicked back into her chin, knocked her over and sent her to the clinic for a couple of stitches. Another volunteer, one of the loyal regulars, was walking along the top of a 6-inch curb instead of down on the driveway; she tripped, fell, and broke her arm. While not a construction accident as such, it happened on site. The other significant accident was a volunteer who got out on the second-floor joists ahead of the floor decking, slipped, partially fell through, and incurred a doctor visit to treat the resulting bruises and abrasions. Other than these injuries, lesser cuts and slivers were treated with on-site first aid equipment. No doubt at R&S and DPR, any of the three significant injuries mentioned here would have received management attention and probably would have cost the site crew their monthly safety commendation, so again there is little cause for celebration. But at the end of the job there was some sense of relief if not satisfaction in seeing 6,000 amateurs through a challenging project without anything worse having happened.

IMPLICATIONS FOR THE CONSTRUCTION INDUSTRY

At first, many people familiar with the construction industry think that volunteer construction must be as different from regular construction, say, as Disneyland's "Frontierland" is from the 19th century American west. Some think of volunteer home building as a kind of amusement park for weekend volunteers. But in some ways, volunteer construction is more like a kind of magnifying glass that enlarges and to some extent dramatizes—even to the point of caricature—some of the major issues and problems that face the construction industry every day. In other ways, it is like a teaching laboratory, where experiments are often designed to put the focus on key parameters and the results of making changes stand out clearly without as much "noise" to confuse the basic issues. Volunteer construction is not an experiment, of course, but problems and successes do stand out clearly.

Examples of principles and concepts that apply well in both volunteer and conventional construction include the following:

- Learning curves occur in all kinds of construction, and happen whether or not a task begins with skilled workers. In volunteer work they start at an earlier stage of the curve, and the improvements become readily evident in a few iterations. Safe practices are an important part of the learning process and must be learned rapidly.

- Modern management concepts (Theory Y, TQM, Meyers-Briggs, etc.) have emphasized the importance of understanding people in getting good results in business. Even in construction, the "yeller and screamer" tough-guy approach to management is no longer acceptable in most successful companies. Nevertheless, particularly in a recession, employees working for pay will put up with some level of abuse. In the volunteer world, treating people disrespectfully, making them feel their time is unproductive as a result of poor planning or supervision, or not commending them for tasks well done, will lead directly (they do not come back) and indirectly (they tell their friends) to diminishing work force turnouts and lost donations. Treat people well, build up an esprit de corps, let them know the importance of their work, provide competent leadership, teach new skills, show quality results, and they will come back rain or shine to be a willing part of the process.

- Most contractors appreciate the importance of planning at both the task and the project levels, but many are too busy "fighting fires" to put enough time into it. Skilled craftsmen, good subcontractors, and others can help mask the effects of such deficiencies. The results of poor planning in volunteer work are immediately evident:
  - several people watching just a few work when tasks are over-manned or not enough work is planned
  - people waiting to proceed until the supervisor gets back from the store with missing tools or materials
  - people queued up around the supervisors asking questions about steps in procedures and figuring out objectives that were neither put in writing nor explained clearly

- The problem of rework, while closely related to planning, deserves its own spotlight. In part it results from errors and omissions in design documents left unresolved by requests for information (RFIs). More often, however, rework results from inadequate planning and supervision. Given the large numbers of willing but unskilled workers who often turn up on volunteer sites, rework can quickly get out of control if supervisors do not have everything figured out in advance. To avoid rework, supervisors must break the work down into bite-sized pieces, communicate clearly what must be done, and monitor the work in progress. A supervisor who can manage and be effective in this environment may find conventional construction to be easier.

Safety lessons in volunteer work parallel those in conventional construction, but perhaps are even more readily clear.

- Supervisors of volunteers must assume that their workers may not recognize hazards that may seem obvious; nor should supervisors in conventional work make this assumption.
- Safety should be an integral part of planning, training, and supervision in both environments. In volunteer work it is an everyday necessity. This is also the way top-peforming construction companies treat safety.
- Neither side should cut corners on safety equipment and procedures.
- The indirect costs of accidents and industrial health problems far exceed the direct costs. The loss of volunteer and community support can be far more devastating to a volunteer organization than the resulting medical and insurance costs. Top contractors are well aware of similar implications for their bottom line.
- Comparatively small investments in safety yield very large direct and indirect benefits in return.

As this was written, Peninsula Habitat had three single-family homes under construction and was about to start a 10-unit townhouse project. The author had recently returned from a 10-month sabbatical and was happy to find that the supervisors had maintained similar safety standards and positive attitudes rather than slip back to lower standards just because they were building single-story homes. These were probably the only fully scaffolded one-story frame homes in the area, but that is the type of measure they take to keep lots of good people safe and healthy—and indeed to live up to the law as it is written. There have been no significant accidents or injuries subsequent to those mentioned for the condominium project. In some respects, this amateur volunteer outfit is ahead of much of the residential building industry. But it still has much to learn from the industry's leaders.

CONCLUSION

Taken as a whole, there are far more similarities than differences between volunteer and conventional construction. Those who work on both types can see and learn from the cross-connections. People are foremost. Without the full understanding and cooperation of those in charge, even the best-designed safety program will be of little value. Conventional construction—especially on larger and more complex projects—develops higher levels of skill and more advanced procedures in coping with more difficult situations. Volunteer construction keeps us focused on basic issues that may become obscured in more complex projects. Similar best practices will produce similarly improved results in either environment. With continuing efforts, it should be feasible even for volunteer-based construction organizations to aspire to and achieve the lofty goals set by, and the commendable safety results obtained by, the leading firms in the commercial and industrial building sectors.

REFERENCES

Barrie, D. S. & Paulson, B. C. (1992). *Profe~ional Construction Management*, 3rd Ed. Chapter 17: Safety and Health in Construction. New York: McGraw-Hill Book Co.

CalOSHA (1995). *State of California Construction Safety Orders.* Anaheim, California: BNi Building News.

deStwolinski, Lance W. (1969). *A Survey of the Safety Environment of the Construction Industry.* Technical Report No. 114. Stanford, Calif.: Stanford University, Dept. of Civil Engineering.

Fuller, Millard (1995). *A Simple, Decent Place to Live.* Dallas, Texas: Word Publishing.

Gibson, Lydia (1998). "How Safe Are Your Houses?" *Professional Builder.* (63) 3: 71–74.

Hinze, Jimmie (1976). *The Effect of Middle Management on Safety in Construction.* Technical Report No. 209. Stanford, Calif.: Stanford University, Dept. of Civil Engineering. 4–6.

Hinze, Jimmie (1996). *Construction Safety.*

Jortberg, Robert F. (1998). *An Assessment of the Impact of CII.* Austin, Texas: Construction Industry Institute, University of Texas at Austin.

Levitt, R. E. & Samelson, N. M. (1993). *Construction Safety Management*. New York: John Wiley & Sons.

Office of the Federal Register (1995). *Code of Federal Regulations*, Part 1926 (Occupational Safety and Health Standards for Construction). Washington, D.C.: National Archives and Records Administration.

Oglesby, Clarkson, Parker, Henry, and Howell, Gregory (1989). *Productivity Improvement in Construction*. Chapter 12: Safety and Environmental Health in the Construction Industry. New York: McGraw-Hill Book Co.

Professional Builder (1998). "The Giant 400." (63) 6: 128.

Rudolph & Sletten, Inc. (1995). "Code of Safe Practices." Foster City, CA.

Samelson, Nancy M. (1977). *The Effect of Foremen on Safety in Construction*. Technical Report No. 219. Stanford, Calif.: Stanford University, Dept. of Civil Engineering.

Stehle, Vince (1995). "Vistas of Endless Possibility." *The Chronicle of Philanthropy*. (8) 2.

Peninsula Habitat for Humanity

Code of Safe Practices

1010 Doyle Street, Suite #6
Menlo Park, CA 94025

Phone: (650) 324-2266
Fax: (650) 324-4375
E-mail: Penhabitat@igc.org

The following are our site safety rules. Before you start to work, we will request you read or attend a briefing on these safety rules and abide by them and any additional safety requirements of this project. They are intended for your personal safety and for the safety of those around you.

I. IN GENERAL

1. All persons shall follow these site safety rules and take the time necessary to do their work in a safe manner. Failure to cooperate and comply with these rules could result in your being requested to leave the site.
2. All persons immediately shall fix safety hazards within their authority or notify their team leader, Habitat supervisor, or Job Safety Coordinator of the hazard. While the hazard exists, please warn those nearby.
3. All personnel will attend safety meetings when offered, where instructions will be given for the prevention of injuries. Your feedback on safety issues is welcomed.
4. Report all injuries or suspected injuries promptly to you team leader, Habitat supervisor, or Job Safety Coordinator, for arrangements to be made for medical treatment or first aid if necessary. Even splinters can cause dangerous infections.

II. PERSONAL PROTECTION

1. Wear clothing appropriate for construction work:
   a. Do not wear loose-fitting clothing. Shirt (minimum "tank top" or as specified)
   b. Wear a shirt (minimum "tank top" or as specified). Long pants are recommended.
   c. Work or hiking boots are recommended; steel-toed boots are best. No sandals please.
2. Hard hats <u>must</u> be worn at all times, unless otherwise directed.
3. Eye protection (i.e., safety glasses) must be worn when exposed to flying/falling particles, splashing chemicals, and harmful light rays. This includes use while operating power tools, hammering, chiseling, painting, and similar tasks.
4. Additional personal protective equipment such as face, ear, hand, knee and foot protection; dust masks and respirators; and safety belts are to be provided as necessary for your safety. When you need this equipment, ask for it from your team leader, Habitat supervisor, or Job Safety Coordinator.
5. Do not wear musical headphones. They can impair warnings and other communications.

III. COMMON SENSE

1. No alcohol or drugs are permitted on site; do not work under their influence.
2. No one shall work while his/her ability or alertness is so impaired by fatigue, illness, medication, or any other reason that might cause him/her or others to be injured.
3. Horseplay, scuffling, and other similar disruptive acts often lead to injury and are prohibited. Personnel engaged in such acts will be required to leave the site.
4. No task requires running. Walk, do not run.
5. Be aware of work going on around you. Stay clear of suspended loads and traffic areas when possible. Give others room to work and be aware when power tools are in operation.
6. Make sure you have a clear area behind you before swinging sledge hammers or other tools or materials.
7. Know and respect your personal limitations. Don't lift anything or perform any task with which you are uncomfortable. There will be plenty of other tasks available for you to do.
8. If there is other equipment operating on the job site, take personal responsibility to stay clear. Always assume that the operator does <u>not</u> see you.

Habitat for Humanity's Code of Safe Practices

This document was adapted from a policy used by Rudolph & Sletten, Inc., Foster City, CA.

9. Read and follow the health and safety precautions on the containers of chemical products, paint, etc. before you use them. For additional product safety information, please ask the site supervisor.

IV. POWER TOOLS

1. <u>NEVER</u> underestimate the potential for harm resulting from misuse of a power tool. Injuries are swift, unexpected and often severe. Be deliberate and focused in handling power tools, and <u>STOP</u> before you take a shortcut.

2. You must be pre-qualified, or "checked out," by the appropriate personnel before operating any power tool. Wear appropriate eye, ear and hand protection when using power tools.

3. Make sure that all guards and other protective devices are in their place and properly adjusted on all tools and equipment before using. If the guard is missing, the equipment is defective and must not be used.

4. Make sure your power cords are in good condition (no exposed inner wires or spliced cords), that plugs have a ground pin when so designed (3 prongs), and that the prongs are not loose.

V. WORKING AT HEIGHTS

1. Always check a ladder's condition before you use it. Take damaged ladders out of service, tag them, and report them to your team leader, Habitat supervisor, or Job Safety Coordinator.

2. Support all ladders on a stable surface. Straight ladders require a 3-foot overlap at landings and a tie-off. Inclination should be about four-to-one (vertical-to-horizontal).

3. Arrange your work so that you are able to use both hands and face the ladder when climbing or descending; don't rush it. Only one person should be on a ladder at a time.

4. Don't work off the cap or the back of a step ladder. Move the ladder rather than over-reaching for the last bit of work.

5. Before working on a scaffold, check that it has good footing, proper bracing, and full planking, properly overlapped; a railing is required at heights of 7-1/2 feet above the surface below. Report damaged equipment.

6. When railings are not practical, personnel working at unprotected heights above 7-1/2 feet must wear a safety harness with the lanyard tied to a substantial anchorage.

7. Avoid "jump down" shortcuts; use stairs, ladders, ramps, and walkways.

8. Never work in an elevated position above vertical rebar, stakes, etc. unless these protruding objects are properly covered. When working over 6 feet in elevation above these hazards, the use of railings or a safety harness is required.

9. Never take down guardrails or uncover holes without the authorization of the site supervisor.

10. Do not throw materials, debris, or other objects from a building until proper precautions (a spotter, barricades, etc.) are taken to protect others from the falling objects.

VI. CLEAN JOBS ARE SAFE JOBS

1. Do not block stairs or aisles with scaffolds or debris any longer than is necessary.

2. Do not leave loose materials on stairs or in aisles, which create a slipping or tripping hazard. Clean-up oil, grease, or other material spills immediately.

3. Bend over or remove protruding screws or nails in your used materials, crates, etc.; stack materials in an orderly manner and place debris in debris containers or piles.

4. In general, clean up after yourself and put tools and materials back where they belong when finished with them.

INCURRING THE COSTS OF INJURIES VERSUS INVESTING IN SAFETY

Jimmie Hinze, Associate Dean
College of Architecture
University of Florida

INTRODUCTION

Costs are incurred whenever an accident occurs on a project. Those costs can be quite dramatic when the accident involves an injury. Most analyses of the actual costs of injuries acknowledge that there are costs related to human suffering, but virtually no attempt is made to quantify those costs. The only times that these costs are quantified on a regular basis are in various courts of law when lawsuits are resolved.

COST OF SAFETY VERSUS COST OF INJURIES

A distinction must be made between the cost of safety and the cost of injuries. While the difference may appear quite obvious, there are characteristics of each which must be understood. One particular characteristic of interest is the level of certainty of the occurrence of the cost. This is perhaps the single major difference that exists between these costs that so drastically influences managers. This level of certainty of occurrence is readily understood.

The costs associated with injuries consist of the direct and indirect costs of injuries. These will be described in greater detail later. Nonetheless, these are costs that are incurred as a consequence or result of the occurrence of accidents in which injuries are sustained. In other words, in the absence of injuries, there are no injury costs. This is a certainty. What is not certain is whether or not there will be an injury. On the other hand, the costs of safety are those which are incurred as a result of an emphasis being placed on safety, whether it be in the form of training, drug testing, safety incentives, staffing for safety, personal protective equipment, safety programs, etc. These are costs that are a certainty for any implementation of some facet of the safety program. The dilemma, on the surface, is that safety efforts will cost a given amount of money, while the costs of injuries are incurred only if there is an injury. Thus, should funds be spent on safety when there might be no injuries even if there are no expenditures on safety? This is a game of probabilities.

Figure 2–1 illustrates the relationship of the cost of injuries and the cost of safety. The hypothesis is that injury occurrence (consequently injury cost) will be high when there is a low emphasis on safety and that injury occurrence will be low when the emphasis on safety is high. From an economic perspective, there appears to be an optimal level of emphasis to be placed on safety. From a practical point of view, this level is rarely achieved with the emphasis generally being far below the optimal. This is because of the "gambler" point of view. The dollars spent on safety cannot be directly measured against the injuries that did *not* occur. Perhaps some modeling effort could generate a likely number of injuries in the absence of safety expenditures. Even then, tremendous or gross approximations will need to be made to estimate the costs of the injuries that might have occurred. These are all uncertainties that make it difficult to sell the need to make expenditures on safety on a purely economic basis. It is important that an emphasis on safety be recognized or even be accepted as being a principle means by which injuries can be reduced. If this is not accepted, the allocation of funds to the safety effort may fail to produce results simply because there is insufficient commitment to the safety effort.

The issue of probability is illustrated further in Figure 2–2. This shows, in simple terms, the various outcomes related to emphasizing safety and incurring injuries. For example, if efforts are expended on safety, the probability of sustaining high costs associated with injuries becomes relatively small. However, if safety is not emphasized, the chance of sustaining a high cost of injuries is markedly increased and the probability of sustaining no injuries is small. These probabilities are difficult to quantify but they help to conceptualize the relationship

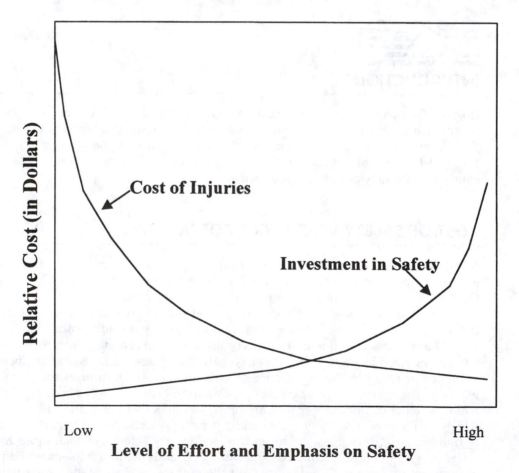

FIGURE 2–1
The relationship of the cost of injuries and the investment in safety.

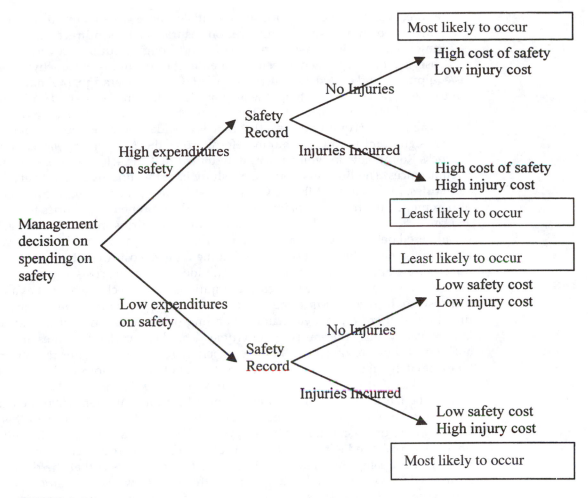

FIGURE 2–2
Relationship of the emphasis on safety to injury occurrence.

between a commitment to safety and the occurrence of injuries. The factor that is most influential when the safety emphasis is low is the assumption that no injuries will occur. The reality of the process is quite simple: If safety is emphasized, the occurrence of injuries can be expected to be low and, conversely, if no emphasis is placed on safety, the occurrence of injuries can be expected to be high. If this fundamental premise is accepted, it is not a difficult decision to commit funds toward a safety objective.

There are two routes in the decision tree that lead to results that would not be predicted as being likely occurrences. One is that good safety performance can occur without emphasizing safety. This is an all too common attitude that exemplifies the idea that safety and injury occurrence is not related or that injuries are truly chance occurrences and management can do little to alter or influence safety performance. The other unlikely path in the decision tree is that injuries will occur despite an emphasis being placed on safety. Of course, this can occur if the safety emphasis is not thorough in its coverage or if certain aspects of the hazards on a project go ignored.

THE TRUE COSTS OF INJURIES

The true costs of injuries can be characterized in many ways, but the most typical means used in recent years in the construction industry has been to express the indirect costs as a function of the direct costs. The direct costs are essentially those costs incurred due to any injury that are reimbursed by workers' compensation insurance. The indirect costs are all other costs resulting from the injury that are not recovered through insurance coverage. Most of the indirect costs can be categorized as being related to the cost of lost productivity, damaged materials/equipment, and added administrative effort. Over 50 years ago, the indirect costs of injuries were determined to be four times the magnitude of the direct costs by H. W. Heinrich (1941), an employee of Traveler's Insurance. That number has been broadly accepted in safety circles as being valid, but it is questionable if that ratio is as widely accepted outside of the area of safety.

A significant report, commonly referred to as the A-3 Report, was issued in 1982 by the Business Roundtable in which it was determined that the 4:1 ratio was still valid under given circumstances. The Business Roundtable study based its findings on a detailed examination of 49 injuries. In the early 1990s, the Construction Industry Institute (CII) culminated a study that also examined the true costs of injuries. That study examined 834 injuries that were reported by 185 projects, constructed by more than one hundred firms in 34 different states. This was a broad-based detailed study that determined that the indirect costs of medical case injuries were about the same as the direct costs and that the indirect costs of restricted activity/lost workday injuries were approximately twice the magnitude of the direct costs.

It is questionable if the true costs of injuries should be characterized as a ratio of the indirect costs to the direct costs. If the indirect costs are expressed in terms of the magnitude of the direct costs, there must a clear understanding of the actual magnitude of the direct costs. Unfortunately, this criterion is not often met. The direct costs of injuries are certainly retrievable, but if they are obtained, they are generally received long after the injury has occurred. Unfortunately, all too often these direct costs are not given serious review. This probably stems from the fact that the insurance carrier will pay for the direct costs. The impact of these costs will not be felt directly by the employer until at least a year later, when the cumulative direct costs are reflected in the experience modification rating (EMR). Because of this time lag and a lack of a clear understanding of the link of the direct costs with the EMR, many employers are not overly concerned with the magnitude of the costs that are associated with injuries. Another problem with using the ratio of indirect costs to direct costs is that the direct costs of similar injuries will vary considerably due to the differences in workers' compensation benefits paid and the medical costs. Thus, the ratio will vary for the same injury, sometimes quite dramatically, from state to state.

The costs of injuries can be expressed in actual dollars and this would certainly be more readily understood than a ratio. Unfortunately, costs expressed in monetary terms lose their significance and value over time. Inflation can drastically distort the true costs of injuries when expressed in monetary terms. Such monetary costs of injuries will also vary considerably due to regional variations in the costs of labor. An injury on a project where workers are paid little over the minimum wage will differ dramatically from areas where average hourly wages exceed $20 per hour. Whenever possible, costs should be expressed in terms of lost productivity. Productivity impacts are probably more constant over time than are monetary units, and they are well understood. In addition, this measure is not sensitive to differences in geographic regions.

INDIRECT COSTS RELATED TO MEDICAL CASE INJURIES

The indirect costs of injuries will be described in detail. Note that most measures of these will be in terms of worker hours or administrative hours. The data source on which this information is based is the same as the CII study described earlier. While the cost data were collected in the early 1990s, the value of the information is still considered valid when expressed primarily in labor hours. The costs will first be discussed for medical case injuries and then for restricted work/lost workday injuries. The data included information on 582 medical case injuries and 247 restricted work/lost workday injuries. It should be noted in this study that all participants did not make estimates of lost productivity for every category of lost productivity. The values are thus based on the information that was made available.

The Injured Worker

Whenever an injury occurs, there is an immediate impact on the ability of the injured worker to be productive. The worker will generally be taken by someone to receive treatment and then, depending on the nature of the injury, will return to work. If the injury occurs in the afternoon hours, the worker may simply receive treatment and not return to work that day since the end of the workday is near or past. The worker would then return to work the next day. From the data collected from 582 medical case injuries, the lost productivity of the injured worker on the day of the injury was 3.7 hours. It was also estimated that the worker, due to the injury, would lose an average of an additional 8 hours of productive work. This lost productivity would stem primarily from lost work time resulting from follow-up care provided by a medical professional. Upon returning to work, it was further estimated the injured worker might not be as productive as was the case prior to the injury. Of the medical case injuries where the productivity was adversely impacted (for 23% of the injuries), it was estimated that, on average, the next 48 hours of work were worked at a production level that was 67 percent of the level maintained prior to the injury.

Worker Assisting the Injured Worker

It is a common practice that another worker assists the injured worker in obtaining medical treatment. The bulk of this time is consumed in driving the injured worker to the nearest medical treatment facility, waiting until the treatment is complete, and driving the worker back to the job site. Naturally, this time is not significant when medical stations are located on the job site. When the injured worker is driven to receive medical treatment, the time that is typically involved until the assisting worker can return to work is about three hours. Note that a company vehicle is often used for this purpose. While the actual cost of the vehicle use will vary, it was estimated that this vehicle cost was about $44 for each injury. In this study of injury costs, this equates to an hourly vehicle cost that is about the same as the average hourly wage of the workers on site.

Crew Productivity

Whenever an injury occurs, the injured worker receiving treatment will impact the crew. The crew is forced to work shorthanded. Obviously, this results in a crew that is not as productive as it was prior to the accident. In the study, it was estimated that for 84% of the medical case injuries the crew productivity was compromised. This often resulted in a crew of five being reduced to a crew of four. It was estimated that the crew productivity was approximately 94% of the pre-accident level and that this was sustained over a period of about 50 hours. This equates to a loss of 12 hours of worker time (0.06 x 50 hours x 4 workers) per injury.

Workers Idled by Watching

Injuries are the result of accidents that are disruptive to the steady flow of work. This disruption attracts the attention of other workers who are in the vicinity of the accident, but who are not directly impacted by the accident. Nonetheless, these workers, by their close proximity to the accident will often have their attention diverted from their work to the accident. This distraction may be brief, but it may impact a large number of workers. For example, 30 workers in the vicinity may stop working for 10 minutes each to observe the events that follow an accident. Such a disruption of the work of other workers was noted for 86% of the medical case injuries. Furthermore, it was estimated that this disruption equated to a total loss of about 5 hours of production work time.

Damaged Materials/Equipment

When workers are injured, it is common for the injury to be associated with damage to some of the construction materials and/or construction equipment. Naturally, this cost will vary widely depending on the nature of the work being performed at the time of the injury and the nature of the accident itself. It was estimated that, in 92% of the medical case injuries, some type of material/equipment damage was sustained. When such damage occurred, an average of about two worker hours was required to repair the damages. In addition to repairing the damage, additional worker time may be required to restore conditions to their pre-accident level. Such added work was estimated to exist for 93% of the medical case injuries and amounted to an estimated two hours of additional worker time. In addition, it has been estimated that the cost of replacing damaged materials and/or equipment averages about $100 per accident (Brown 1988). These costs can certainly vary widely, but this amount can serve as a conservative estimate.

Replacement Worker

When a worker is injured and promptly returns to work, it is not common for a replacement worker to be hired. Even so, a replacement worker may be required until the injured worker does return. It was found that a replacement worker was needed for 93% of the medical case injuries. Since these workers are generally asked to "fill a slot" for a short while, until the injured worker returns, the cost is not severe. It was estimated that the replacement worker, possibly shifted temporarily from another crew, was able to work at about 98% of the level of the injured worker prior to the accident. If the injured worker returns to work in three hours, essentially 0.06 hours of productive work are lost due to the inexperience of the replacement worker. While this is the value estimated by the participants in the study, it is likely that the true loss is greater.

Supervisory Assistance

It is essential that each injured worker receive prompt treatment. Whenever an injury occurs, it is important for someone to take charge of the situation in order to ensure that such treatment is promptly acquired. Supervisory personnel are generally the individuals that have this responsibility. This individual will subsequently be expected to have primary input in completing the necessary forms and reports. It was estimated that approximately 2.7 hours of supervisory time were consumed for each medical case injury. This would include time to assess the immediate circumstances, ensure that first aid treatment is provided, designate a worker to take the injured worker to receive medical treatment, and subsequently to make the necessary adjustments in the crew to reflect changes in the crew makeup. The supervisor will commit an additional amount of time after the worker has been removed from the site to obtain medical treatment. This time, devoted primarily to investigating the accident, has been estimated to be about 1.5 hours. The completion of required reports will consume added time and this was estimated to be about 1.3 hours.

Other Impacts

While most medical case injuries are not dramatic in the global sense, some may attract the attention of OSHA compliance officers or media personnel. While most medical case injuries did not attract such attention, it was reported that OSHA compliance officers would be on site for about one hour to discuss circumstances specifically related to the accident. Media personnel generally were on site for about two hours.

Summary of Indirect Costs Related to Medical Case Injuries

It has been noted several times that not all types of costs will be incurred for every medical case injury. Furthermore, the costs will vary a great deal. Nonetheless, some average values have been accumulated from the CII study that are helpful in identifying the various cost components of the impacts of medical case injuries. These costs are summarized below:

- Injured worker:
  - 3.7 productive hours lost on the day of the injury
  - 8 productive hours lost subsequent to the day of the injury
  - 4 hours lost productivity (productivity level at 90% for 8 hours for crew of 5)

- Transporting the worker:
  - 3 productive hours lost on the day of the injury
  - 3 hours of vehicle time and mileage

- Crew costs:
  - 12 hours lost by a crew of 5 reduced to a crew of 4

- Workers idled by watching:
  - 5 hours of other workers' time

- Damaged materials/equipment:
  - 2 hours of worker time to repair the damage
  - 2 hours of additional time to restore conditions
  - $100 to replace damaged materials/equipment

- Replacement worker:
  - 0.06 hours of lost productivity

- Supervisory time:
  - 2.7 hours to assist injured worker and respond to the situation
  - 1.5 hours to investigate the accident
  - 1.3 hours to complete reports

- Other impacts:
  - 1 hour impact of OSHA compliance officers
  - 2 hour impact of media personnel

Assume that a medical case injury occurs and incurs the impacts noted above, but is not associated with a replacement worker, any regulatory visit or any media attention. The total impact can be expressed in terms of the worker hours for the injured worker (15.7 hours), the assisting worker for transportation (6 hours), the crew (12 hours), the idled workers (5 hours), material/equipment damage (4 hours), and supervisory time (5.5 hours). This comes to 42.7 worker hours and 5.5 supervisory hours. If workers on a project are paid at a rate of $12 per hour, the material/equipment damage is estimated at $100, and the supervisor's salary is $20 per hour, the total indirect cost of a medical case injury can be estimated to average $722 for this particular project.

INDIRECT COSTS RELATED TO RESTRICTED WORK/LOST WORKDAY INJURIES

The Injured Worker

For restricted work/lost workday injuries, the cost components are similar to the medical case injuries with minor differences.

Worker Assisting the Injured Worker

It should be recognized that the restricted work/lost workday injuries are generally more serious in nature than are the medical case injuries. Thus, the assistance may be more extensive and possibly relate to life-threatening injuries if prompt care is not provided. The need to get the injured worker to medical treatment may be more serious for these injuries. Another difference is that with the restricted work/lost workday injuries the injured worker will generally not be returning to the job site on the day of the injury. Even if there is a medic station on the job site, additional medical attention will generally be required to obtain a full diagnosis of the extent of the injuries and to obtain the services of specialized professional personnel.

Crew Productivity

Whenever a restricted work/lost workday injury occurs, the injury will have a definite impact on the crew, as the worker will not return to that crew in the immediate future. The crew will be forced to work shorthanded for a while or with a replacement worker. Whether working short-handed or with a new member of the crew, the productivity will be compromised in most instances.

Workers Idled by Watching
All accidents seem to attract the attention of other workers, but naturally the more serious ones will probably create a larger distraction for the other workers.

Damaged Materials/Equipment
Damage to construction materials and/or construction equipment may or may not be associated with any injury, regardless of the seriousness of the injury.

Replacement Worker
For the restricted work/lost workday injuries, a replacement worker is more often required.

Supervisory Assistance
The nature of the supervisory assistance for the restricted work/lost workday injuries is similar to the assistance provided to medical case injuries, but more attention may be on achieving a prompt dispatch of the injured worker to obtain medical care.

Other Impacts
Only a few restricted work/lost workday injuries are sufficiently dramatic or severe to attract the attention of OSHA compliance officers or media personnel. While media visits and OSHA visitations were rare, it was reported that OSHA compliance officers would be on site for about four hours to discuss circumstances specifically related to restricted work/lost workday injuries. Media personnel generally were also on site for about four hours.

Summary of Indirect Costs Related to Restricted Work/Lost Workday Injuries

The types of costs for the average restricted work/lost workday injury were similar to those noted for medical case injuries. The impacts did vary between these types of injuries. While considerable variation was noted, some average values have been accumulated from the CII study. The averages represent conservative estimates derived from the CII data. The costs associated with typical restricted work/lost workday injuries are summarized below:

- Injured worker:
  - 6 productive hours lost on the day of the injury
  - 60 productive hours lost subsequent to the day of the injury
  - 10 hours lost productivity (productivity level at 84% for 90 hours)

- Transporting the worker:
  - 4 productive hours lost on the day of the injury
  - 4 hours of vehicle time and mileage

- Crew costs:
  - 8 worker hours lost by a crew working below optimal level

- Workers idled by watching:
  - 6 hours of other workers' time

- Damaged materials/equipment:
  - 5 hours of worker time to repair the damage
  - 5 hours of additional time to restore conditions
  - $100 to replace damaged materials/equipment

- Replacement worker:
  - 10 hours of lost productivity due to new worker
  - 4 hours to train the replacement worker

■ Supervisory time:
  - 4.2 hours to assist injured worker and respond to the situation
  - 8.5 hours to investigate the accident
  - 3 hours to complete reports

■ Other impacts:
  - 10 worker hours of impact of OSHA compliance officers
  - 4 hour impact of media personnel
  - 10 hours related to planning and handling losses

Assume that a restricted work/lost workday injury occurs and incurs the impacts noted above, but does not attract a regulatory visit or any media attention. The total impact can be expressed in terms of the worker hours for the injured worker (76 hours), the assisting worker for transportation (8 hours), the crew (8 hours), the idled workers (6 hours), material/equipment damage (10 hours), and supervisory time (15.7 hours). This comes to 108 worker hours and 15.7 supervisory hours. If workers on a project are paid at a rate of $12 per hour, the material/equipment damage is estimated at $100, and the supervisor's salary is $20 per hour, the total indirect cost a restricted work/lost workday injury can be estimated to average $1710 for this particular project.

RECAP ON INDIRECT COSTS

The indirect cost estimates that were presented were derived from a CII study that consisted of several hundred injuries. Even with the large data base, much variability was noted. The averages shown for the different cost categories were determined without incorporating the outliers from the data. Thus, some costs were noted to be extremely high for some of the cost categories. For example, replacement workers were reported by some crews to reduce crew productivity to 70% of the pre-injury level for extended periods. The time to repair damages was also reported to be very high for some injuries, e.g., some reported that more than 100 worker hours were required to repair accident damages. These estimates should be acknowledged as being representative of typical costs only, i.e., the estimates are conservative.

It should also be noted that these indirect costs represent *indirect field costs* only. The CII study determined that an allowance for liability claims costs should be included in these costs to more accurately reflect the true indirect costs. It was determined that these claims costs could be estimated as being about 38% of the indirect field costs of medical case injuries and 7.8 times the indirect field costs of restricted work/lost workday injuries. With these factors taken into consideration, the example indirect injury costs would now be estimated as being $996 for the medical case injury and $15,048 for the restricted work/lost workday injury.

It should be evident why the indirect costs have been expressed primarily in terms of worker hours. The cost impacts will vary considerably for firms paying wages that are only slightly above the minimum wage when compared with firms paying wages that exceed $20 per hour. Nonetheless, the indirect costs can be computed for the field costs as long as the hourly wages are known or can be estimated with accuracy.

Accuracy in estimating is a constant concern. Despite this, the costs of injuries will often be underestimated. It is difficult to compute a value that expresses pain and suffering in monetary terms. The adverse impact on a family is also difficult to estimate, especially for restricted work/lost workday injuries when the uncertainty of returning to work can present a very worrisome dilemma. The impacts of injuries on a firm are also difficult to assess with accuracy. Perhaps a single injury does not have a notable impact, but when coupled with several other injuries, the firm may be excluded from the select bidders list of a primary client. Such costs can be quite high, but difficult to relate in monetary terms. The goodwill or general reputation of a firm can also be adversely impacted by a series of widely publicized injuries. This may result in the inability of the firm to attract quality craft workers. This impact may be quite severe, but may never be linked to a single injury. Other related costs will also be incurred.

INVESTMENT IN SAFETY

The term *cost of safety* has negative connotations, so a preferable phrase would be "investment in safety." The word *investment* has an inherent connotation of a return or eventual benefit, generally assumed to be greater than the original invested sum. This may appear to be a matter of semantics, but it is probably more than that. To view the commitment of funds for safety as an investment rather than an operational cost requires a cultural change. Expenditures for safety must be viewed as a means to improve the bottom line, and, naturally, to reduce the incidence of injuries. That is, safety must be viewed differently than it has in the past.

Safety is multifaceted, consisting of the many ways that can result in its attainment. Unfortunately, no single safety task can take the place of all others. Some safety efforts are more effective than others in impacting safety performance. It would be expedient to promote especially those that are known to be particularly influential. This chapter will not attempt to isolate all the relative merits of the different components of a safety program. The most salient ones will be discussed and only general comments will be made about their ability to favorably impact safety performance. To isolate the costs of the different types of safety program elements, various experts (primarily associated with the petro-chemical and industrial sectors) in industry were contacted. This exercise revealed that experiences vary and that costs vary for specified safety program elements; some cost differences can be attributed to geographic influences while others relate to the nature of the local economy.

Substance Abuse Testing

One element of a safety program that has consistently been shown to be effective in reducing the incidence of injuries is drug testing. Drug testing is a common means of addressing safety, especially on large projects or in large construction firms. For large construction firms, especially those with annual construction volumes exceeding $50 million, almost all companies have a standard practice of conducting prescreening drug tests before hiring any workers. That is, every new employee must submit to a drug test and produce a negative test response as a condition to be considered for being hired by the company.

The failure rate of those workers given prescreening tests ranges from less than one percent to as high as 30%. The most typical failure rate is about 4%. While it is often reported that drug use among construction workers exceeds 10%, it must be recognized that drug users will often refuse to even apply for employment with a firm if a drug test must be passed. Drug users will tend to migrate to those firms that do no testing. For testing positive on a prescreening test, it is common for firms to not hire that individual unless that worker can submit to and pass a subsequent test.

Drug testing is regarded as helping construction firms in promoting safety. This benefit is not achieved without considerable expense, as the costs of conducting drug tests on a project can be considerable. The costs of drug tests can vary by geographic region, the types of substances tested for, and possibly the number of tests to be conducted. The costs of drug tests reportedly range from $12 to $42, with the most often cited cost being about $28 per test conducted.

Prescreening tests give employers some assurance that the workers who are hired are drug-free. Unfortunately, these prescreening tests do not give any assurances that the workers will all remain drug free. This is where subsequent drug testing plays a very valuable role. Because drug tests can be costly when considered in aggregate, these subsequent drug tests tend to be more in the vein of sampling. Construction companies that conduct prescreening tests for all new hires tend to conduct tests on some of the workers each month. It is common for the number actually being sampled to range from about 1% to a maximum of 15% of the company employees. The most typical number of individuals tested is about 10% of the workforce. The failure rate of the workers taking these monthly drug tests ranges from less than 1% to a high of 7%, with 2% being the most typical.

The testing for drugs is a primary cost, but other costs may also arise in the area of substance abuse. One such cost relates to the education of the workforce about the ills of substance abuse. This cost is generally borne by the other programs supported by the safety program, namely through the safety meetings held on site and the literature distributed by the firm.

Staffing

In order to promote safety on the site, many firms have begun to recognize the value of committing resources to this effort. One of the most valuable resources that can be committed to this cause is personnel that have safety as their primary charge. While the nature of this type of staffing will vary by project size, some level of commitment of personnel is imperative to aggressively promote project safety.

It is common to employ safety representatives that assist in the promotion of safety on the job site. Safety representatives are not regarded as assuming the safety responsibilities otherwise held by the project superintendent and the project manager, as their safety responsibilities cannot be delegated. The safety representative is to assist the superintendent and the project manager in promoting project safety. On smaller projects, the safety representative will be expected to allocate the field time between the various company projects. The safety representative may even be shared between several small construction firms.

As projects get larger, the company may very well decide to employ a full-time safety representative on each project. The size at which the decision is made to employ a full-time safety representative will vary but it is generally related to the number of company employees on site or the total number of workers on the site. The range of the number of company employees that relate to the assignment of a full-time safety representative is between as few as 25 workers to as many as 250 workers, but the most typical number is about 50. Note that when a general contractor employs 50 workers on a site, the total number of workers, including the employees of the subcontractors, will readily be in the hundreds or even thousands of workers.

A full-time safety representative can be a tremendous asset on a project. His or her mission is clear-cut and the focus should constantly be on the safety practices and physical conditions existent on the project. The primary cost of a full-time safety representative lies in the salary. The salary of a safety representative will vary by region and with the level of expertise of the individual, but can generally be expected to range from $3,000 to $4,800 per month, with the most typical salary being about $3,500 per month. If the safety representative must allocate time between projects, it is common to have a company vehicle provided or to reimburse the individual for mileage accumulated on a private vehicle.

As the size of the job site increases, it may be necessary to have other safety personnel employed to assist the safety representative, often referred to as the safety director. This will vary by job size and the level of commitment that others on the project have made to the safety effort. In some instances, the owner of the project may dictate the minimum number of safety personnel to be employed on site.

Depending on job size and possibly the project location, the company may decide to establish a safety and health station that is supported by a nurse or emergency medical technician (EMT). Such nurse/medic stations are not common, but can be found on many large projects. The smallest size of project that might have a nurse/medic station will employ about 150 workers. Naturally, a project near to medical services may elect to utilize the services that are readily available. The decision to employ a nurse or EMT must be made based on the job conditions. The cost of employing a nurse will typically be about $3,000 per month with the salary of an EMT being slightly less, perhaps about $2,600 per month.

The medic station will consist of more than a commitment to the salary of the individuals assigned to the station. Such stations can only function with proper supplies, some of which may have a limited shelf life. The supplies may include educational materials that the nurse or EMT will distribute in some manner. The cost of maintaining a medic station is not trivial. Common estimates of the monthly cost of maintaining a medic station range from $150 to $600, with the most typical amount being about $500.

Training

The OSHA regulations (CFR 1926.21 (a)) also mandate that employers must "establish and supervise programs for the education and training of employers and employees in the recognition, avoidance and prevention of unsafe conditions in employment covered by the act." There is a general understanding in the construction industry that workers, to perform work safely, must be knowledgeable about the work they are to perform. Thus, experienced workers are generally regarded as being the least likely to be involved in accidents. Nonetheless, it is common for companies to provide some minimum level of training to all workers, regardless of their reported level of competency in the trades. This initial training is in the form of an orientation session that is to acquaint all workers with the firm, the project, the key personnel, major safety issues on the project, and the necessary personal safety and health knowledge. This training is often provided to all workers regardless of their experience or tenure with the firm.

The nature of the orientation of workers varies by company. Some companies conduct the orientation in a period of one to two hours while others may commit the entire first day of employment of a worker to orientation. Thus, the cost of orientation may be as little as $15 or as much as $500. It is difficult to state a typical cost of orientation because of the varying nature of these sessions. The cost will likely be between $50 and $250, depending on the level of training included in the session.

The orientation sessions are conducted for all workers employed on the project. While this does place a heavy burden on project personnel when the project labor needs escalate, the sessions are needed throughout the project. As the project phases change, different trades are brought to the site and this will necessitate orientation sessions.

An unfortunate reality on construction sites is that turnover is often high, especially during economic boom periods. Large firms report turnover rates ranging from 10% to 33% per month, with 15% being most typical. This entails a large number of new hires and this is associated with the need for orientation sessions. The turnover rates must be considered when budgeting for these training costs. Obviously, there will be periods on some projects where most of the orientation sessions are conducted for workers that are hired simply to maintain the workforce level on site.

The safety training will extend beyond the orientation session. The training must be ongoing and consistent. One common means of maintaining the level of safety education at the project level is through weekly safety toolbox meetings. These meetings are generally held at a predetermined time each week and cause a virtual shutdown of the project operations. While some companies report dedicating more than an hour to such meetings each week, it is more typical to conduct such meetings for about 15 to 20 minutes. It must be recognized that a 20-minute meeting will probably have the impact of essentially shutting down the project for about 30 minutes. This is because workers must leave their work areas to attend the meetings and they must then return to the work areas after the meetings. On projects that cover a large area, or that entail a great deal of travel via ladders, the actual time lost will be considerably higher than on simple, small projects.

It is a simple matter to estimate the cost of safety toolbox meetings because most of the cost is in the wages of the workers. Thus, the cost of a toolbox meeting will be directly related to the wages paid. If a weekly 20-minute toolbox meeting is estimated to consume 30 minutes of downtime, the monthly cost of the meetings will be the equivalent of the wages of all workers for a period of two hours each.

The training needs of a project will not be limited to the workers. The foremen on the project also will need some training. This training is generally provided on a monthly basis, and it is also generally provided on site. The cost of this training has been reported to vary from $50 per month per foreman to $1,000 per month, but the most typical estimate is about $100 per month.

Some companies extend the training to an annual safety dinner. While training is generally not a major component of these dinners, recognition of those individuals who have performed particularly well in the area of safety is frequently a highlight. Companies vary the practice of holding safety dinners. Perhaps about half of the larger construction firms hold such dinners. Of these, some will limit the dinners to the supervisory and managerial personnel. Still others will invite all workers as a means of publicly demonstrating the firm's commitment to safety to all workers and their families. The dinners tend to be special events as evidenced by the range in cost, which is from $20 to $50 per attendee, with $40 being most typical.

Personal Protective Equipment

It is important that workers begin work with the proper tools and protective/safety gear. Providing the personal protective equipment, commonly referred to as PPE, is an obligation that falls on the employer. The protective gear will certainly vary by the type of work performed, but includes such items as hard hats, gloves, safety goggles, safety shields, safety harnesses, respirators, hearing preservation devices, etc. The nature of the work and the conditions on site will obviously dictate the specific needs.

The cost to outfit workers with the appropriate PPE may vary considerably, with estimates as low as $15 per worker to as high as $400 per worker. The basic gear to be provided to each worker will probably cost about $25. It must be recognized that the maintenance costs of PPE can be significant. An allowance of $15 per month for the maintenance of equipping the workers would appear appropriate for most types of work. This assumes that gloves and safety glasses will be replaced regularly as use deteriorates their safety value. The costs will be considerably higher if, for example, respirators must be worn. The initial respirator cost will be accompanied by the regular replacement of the filters.

Safety Committees

One means of ensuring that the physical conditions on the site are safe is through a safety committee. This committee will generally consist of workers from different trades. The committee will be given the task of taking a designated amount of time each week to tour the site to identify unsafe conditions and to point out any unsafe acts that are observed. Again, safety committees are more commonly utilized on larger projects and can be a valuable resource to assist in the safety mission of the company.

Safety committees require the commitment of resources. First of all, the committees generally consist of about seven or eight workers, but committees as small as five have been noted. The committee is then expected to convene once a week to inspect the project conditions to identify safety concerns. The size of the project will dictate the duration of each inspection, but a commitment of two hours is quite typical. It should be apparent that the cost of the safety committee can appear high, e.g., a committee of eight meeting two hours per week will consume 64 worker hours in the span of four weeks. It should also be noted that while only workers make up the safety committee, there is often a considerable investment in clerical time to support the work of the safety committee.

Investigations

The adage of "learning by our mistakes" is well known in safety circles. Many companies aggressively examine and study their failings in order that they do not experience a repetition of the event. Perhaps the most common practice in the construction industry in this regard is to investigate injury accidents. Some level of investigation is mandated by OSHA and, in most cases, by workers' compensation insurance carriers. It then becomes a natural outgrowth of these institutional inspections to try to directly benefit from the knowledge gained from these inspections. In recent years, these inspections have been broadened to include the inspection of near misses. Many firms have reported favorable results with this practice.

Inspections, whether for near misses or injury accidents, require the commitment of resources. The level of detail extracted through these investigations will obviously impact the costs incurred. The investigations of near misses reportedly range in cost from $50 to $2,000, with the most typical cost estimate being about $200. Likewise, the investigations of injury accidents range in cost from $100 to $2,000, with the most typical cost estimate being about $500. Coupled with the investigations are the reporting functions (as mandated by OSHA and the workers' compensation carrier) that take place whenever an injury occurs. This cost of maintaining records will vary with the number of incidents incurred. It is estimated that on the large projects this maintenance cost ranges from $150 per month to $3,000 per month, with the most typical estimated amount being about $200.

Safety Program

It has been said, "well begun is half done," inferring that planning is an integral component of success in the area of safety. The safety program for a construction project forms the basis for project safety—it functions as the safety blueprint for the entire project. All of the strategies and tasks to be performed to achieve safety success on the project will be included in the safety program.

Safety programs are to be project specific; however, there are safety programs that are commercially available. The unfortunate aspect of the "shelf" programs is that they are generic in nature and do not have any specific focus on any specific project. Thus, some additional effort must be expended to customize such safety programs. The ideal is to develop a unique safety program that addresses the specific conditions that are anticipated on the project in question. The cost of a safety program will vary considerably with the range in costs being from $200 to $10,000. Job size, job complexity and the nature of the hazards will dictate the actual cost to prepare a project specific safety program.

Part of the safety program will be the need to conduct a hazard analysis on the project. This information will be valuable in helping to finalize the safety program. This will require an evaluation of the various anticipated work phases and careful insight into the nature of the hazards that will be presented during the construction process. This hazard analysis will also be conducted at a cost. Again, depending on project size and characteristics, the cost of conducting the hazard analysis can range from $150 to $2,000, with the most typical cost being about $500.

The hazards communication (haz com) program must be maintained on the project. The conditions on the project may very well change and the haz com program must reflect those changes. Maintaining this program will depend on project specifics, but the cost can be expected to range from $20 to $500, with the most likely cost being in the vicinity of about $100 per month.

The safety program, to be effective, must stay "alive" in the eyes of the workers. This means that the elements of the safety program must be communicated to the workers in some way. This communication can take place through such means as posters, individual mailings, safety brochures, job signs, and a variety of related means. This too, will entail the expenditure of funds. Job size will probably influence the cost a great deal. Cost estimates of providing such communication on site range from $25 to $500, with the most typical estimate being about $75.

One way to ensure compliance with the safety program is to conduct regular safety inspections on site. The superintendent, safety personnel from the home office, or a host of other individuals that have been identified by the company might conduct such inspections. The level of detail that can be examined in a safety inspection will vary with the time committed to the effort, generally about a day. It is reported that the job inspections range from $150 to $350, with the most typical cost estimate of the inspections being $200 per inspection.

Safety Incentives

One technique that many companies employ to capture the interest of workers in the safety agenda is to provide safety incentives. Safety incentives can be structured in a variety of ways, but it is common for workers who receive no injuries in a given time period or who work in crews in which no injuries are incurred to receive a reward of some type. The reward may be cash, if for example $0.25 is set aside for each hour that a worker remains accident free. Some firms provide a variety of gifts that are considered to be valued by the workers. In some cases, the workers accumulate points which can be used to select gifts from the "company catalog" in which the number of points will dictate the gifts that can be selected. The gifts may consist of baseball caps, pocket knives, windbreakers, coffee mugs, household appliances, ice chests, and a host of other items. The cost of maintaining a safety incentive program may range from to $2 per month to $150 per month, but the most typical amount is about $20 per month per worker.

While safety incentives for workers are widely publicized, safety incentives for supervisors are also quite common. These may be based on overall project performance. The cost of maintaining such an incentive program ranges from $5 per month to $300 per month with the most typical being about $40 per month per supervisor.

Along with the incentives noted, there are also some companies that link bonuses with safety performance. These are perhaps encountered in only some (probably less than half) of the large firms, but their value should be considered. Bonuses tend to be larger in value than are typical incentives. The bonuses tend to range from $400 per year to $50,000 per year. With the wide variability of values noted, it is understandably difficult to derive a "typical" amount, but a typical amount might be estimated at about $2,500 per year.

EXAMPLE OF INVESTING IN SAFETY ON A SMALL PROJECT

The investment in safety will be demonstrated by applying the safety commitment to two projects. The first project will be a small project and the second will be a large one. On the small nine-month project the general contractor employed 30 workers and paid them a wage of $10.00 per hour. This contractor prepared a simple safety program for $500, conducted a hazard analysis for $200, maintained the haz com program at a cost of $50 per month, and spent $30 per month on posters, letters, etc. These costs are summarized as follows:

Safety Program	$500
Hazard Analysis	$200
Maintained HazCom Program (9 mo. x $50/mo.)	$450
Cost of posters, letters, etc. (9 mo. x $30/mo.)	$270
Total Project Safety Program Costs	*$1,420*

To assist in the effort of maintaining the overall safety program, a portion of the company safety representative's time was committed to the project. This cost was set at $1,000 per month.

Cost of Staffing with Part Time Safety Rep	(9 mo. x $1,000/mo.)	$9,000

Although the firm employed an average of 30 workers on the project, there was a monthly turnover rate of 10% (3 workers) each month. Thus, in the 9-month duration of the project, a total of 57 workers were hired. Each new hire received an orientation training that cost the contractor $30 per worker. In addition, each newly hired worker received personal protective equipment (PPE) at an average cost $10 per worker. Maintaining the PPE cost an average of $5 each month for each worker. The orientation and PPE costs are summarized as follows:

Orientation of each newly-hired worker (57 workers x $30/workers)	$1,710
Initial PPE cost: 57 workers x $25	$1,425
Maintaining PPE (9 mo. x $10/mo. x 30 workers)	$2,700
Total Project Orientation and PPE costs	*$5,835*

Training took place on a weekly basis in the form of toolbox safety meetings. Each meeting took about 30 minutes when allowances were made for workers to walk from the work areas to the meeting location and then to return to work. Thus, the safety meetings consumed about 2 hours of each worker's time each month or 60 worker hours (2 hours times 30 workers on site) each month. The supervisors (6 foremen on the site) also received training that was estimated to cost about $30 per foreman or about $180 per month. The training costs are tabulated as follows:

Toolbox Safety Meetings (60 hours x $10/hr. X 9 mo.)	$5,400
Supervisory Training ($180/mo. x 9 mo.)	$1,620
Total Project Training Costs	*$7,020*

The contractor estimated the cost of conducting accident investigations at $50 each. There were a total of three injury accidents and each of these was investigated. An additional cost incurred by the contractor was an incentive program that was implemented at a cost of $10 per month per worker. Thus, the incentive costs on the project added up to $300 each month. These costs are represented as follows:

Cost of investigations (3 @ $50/injury accident)	$150
Cost of incentives ($300/mo. x 9 mo.)	$2,700
Total Project Cost of Investigations and Incentives	*$2,850*

For this contractor, the investment in safety for this project totaled $26,125. This represents an investment of $870.83 per worker for the duration of the project or $96.76 per worker each month.

EXAMPLE OF INVESTING IN SAFETY ON A LARGE PROJECT

The general contractor on the large project maintained a regular level of employment of 300 workers per month for the 15-month project. The average wage was $12 per hour. The safety program for the project was prepared at a cost of $5,000; the hazard analysis was conducted for a cost of $1,000; the haz com program was maintained at a cost of $500 per month; and other incidental costs (posters, brochures, signs, billboards, letters) cost $100 each month. The basic safety program costs are summarized as follows:

Safety Program	$5,000
Hazard Analysis	$1,000
Maintained Haz Com Program (15 mo. x $500/mo.)	$7,500
Cost of posters, letters, etc. (15 mo. x $100/mo.)	$1,500
Total Project Safety Program Costs	*$15,000*

To assist in the effort of maintaining the overall safety program, a full-time safety representative (earning $4,500 per month) was assigned to the project. An assistant safety representative was also hired for the project at a salary of $2,500 per month. An EMT, earning $3,000 per month, was also assigned to the project. It was estimated that the medic station was maintained at a cost of $500 per month. The staffing costs are summarized as follows:

Full-time Safety Rep. (15 mo. x $4,500/mo.)	$67,500
Assist. Safety Rep. (15 mo. x $2,500/mo.)	$37,500
EMT (15 mo. x $3,000/mo.)	$45,000
Medic Station (15 mo. x $500)	$7,500
Total Project Safety Staffing	*$157,500*

The project employed 300 workers and the monthly turnover rate was 10% (30 workers). During the 15 months of the project, a total of 750 workers were hired. Each new hire received an orientation training that cost the contractor $100 per worker. The personal protective equipment (PPE) provided to each new worker cost an average of $20 per worker. The PPE was maintained at an average cost of $5 each month for each worker. The orientation and PPE costs are summarized as follows:

Orientation of each newly-hired worker (750 workers x $100/workers)	$75,000
Initial PPE cost: 750 workers x $40	$30,000
Maintaining PPE (15 mo. x $5/mo. x 300 workers)	$67,500
Total Project Orientation and PPE costs	*$172,500*

Toolbox safety meetings were conducted each week on this project. Each meeting took about 30 minutes when allowances were made for lost productivity resulting from the meetings. The safety meetings then required about 2 hours of each worker's time each month or 600 worker hours each month. The supervisors (40 foremen on the site) also received training that was estimated to cost about $100 per foreman or about $4,000 per month. The training costs are computed as follows:

Toolbox Safety Meetings (600 hours x $12/hr. x 15 mo.)	$108,000
Supervisory Training ($4,000/mo. x 15 mo.)	$60,000
Total Project Training Costs	*$168,000*

To emphasize the safety commitment of the company, the contractor held an annual safety dinner for the workers (one was held for the project). The 40 foremen, 20 selected workers, and their spouses were invited to this dinner. This dinner was deemed so special to the company that it committed $80 per person for the event. These dinners were budgeted as follows:

Safety dinners (120 persons x $80 per person)	$9,600

To ensure safety conditions on site during construction, a safety committee was maintained. This committee consisted of eight workers, representing different crafts, who were asked to commit two hours each week to conduct safety tours (inspections) and compile their findings. Thus, the committee consumed about 68 worker hours each month (4 weeks per month x 2 hours per week x 8 workers). In addition, administrative time was entailed to assist the safety committee in its efforts that totaled about $150 each month. The safety committee costs were as follows:

Safety committee (68 hours/month x 15 mo. x $12/hr.)	$11,520
Administrative Cost ($150/mo. x 15 mo.)	$2,250
Total Project Safety Committee Costs	*$13,770*

The estimated cost of conducting accident investigations was $150 each. There were a total of 25 injury accidents and each of these was investigated. An additional cost incurred by the contractor was an incentive program that was implemented at a cost of $25 per month per worker. Thus, the incentive costs on the project added up to $7,500 each month. A safety incentive program was also implemented for the foremen. The supervisory incentives cost $40 per month per foreman. An added feature of the safety emphasis of the firm was a safety bonus (valued at $10,000) that was dedicated to the foremen. These costs are represented as follows:

Cost of investigations (25 x $150/injury accident)	$3,750
Cost of worker incentives ($7,500/mo. x 15 mo.)	$112,500
Cost of foremen incentives ($1,600/mo. x 15 mo.)	$24,000
Bonuses	$10,000
Total Project Cost of Investigations and Incentives	*$150,250*

Drug testing was also a special program on this project. A drug test was conducted on each new hire at a cost of $28 per test. The company also had a practice of testing, on a random basis, 10% of the workers each month. The drug-testing program was estimated to cost the following amount:

Prescreening test for each new hire ($28/test x 750 hires)	$21,000
Random tests ($28/test x 30 workers x 15 mo.)	$12,600
Total Project Drug Testing Cost	*$33,600*

For this contractor, the investment in safety for this project totaled $725,420. This represents an investment of $2,418.07 per worker for the duration of the project or $161.20 per worker each month. Note that while the emphasis on safety is seemingly much greater on the larger project, the cost per worker each month is only slightly more than 60% more per worker each month.

THE BOTTOM LINE ON INVESTING IN SAFETY

The small and large project just described demonstrated a certain level of commitment to safety. These projects will now be compared to comparably sized projects where the commitment was not particularly strong. The small projects will be compared first. It is assumed that the projects are similar in every way, except for the emphasis placed on safety. This was exemplified in the experience modification ratings (EMRs) of these firms. The EMR for the company with the commitment to safety was .80 while its competitor's EMR was 1.0. Both companies employed 30 workers at a pay rate of $10 per hour and the manual rate on their workers' compensation was $28 per $100 of worker payroll. The resultant costs of these firms are compared in Table 2–1.

Note that the firm that committed $26,125 (4.6% of the total cost of labor and workers' compensation) to the safety program recovered its investment through the reduction in the overall labor cost and accounted for a 21.5% return on the safety investment. While other costs were also most likely impacted by this safety commitment, these will not be discussed here. The same type of comparison can be made of the large project described earlier. Note that this project too will be compared to one that has not been committed to the safety effort. The large project will be compared to one that has not had a strong commitment to safety. Nonetheless,

TABLE 2–1
Comparison of two small projects.

Descriptor	Safety-Minded Company	Other Company
Number of workers	30	30
Wages per worker per hour	$10	$10
Hours worked each month	168	168
Labor cost per month	$50,400/mo.	$50,400/mo.
W. Comp. Manual Rate	$28 per $100 payroll	$28 per $100 payroll
Unadjusted W. Comp. Cost	$14,112/mo.	$14,112/mo.
EMR	0.75	1.00
Adjusted W. Comp. Cost	$10,584/mo.	$14,112/mo.
Wages & W. Comp. per mo.	$60,984	$64,512/mo.
Duration of project	9 months	9 months
Project Wages & W. Comp.	$548,856	$580,608
Safety Investment	$26,125	0
Total Labor Cost	$574,981	$580,608
Savings from safety	**$5,627**	

TABLE 2–2
Comparison of two large projects.

Descriptor	Safety-Minded Company	Other Company
Number of workers	300	300
Wages per worker per hour	$12	$12
Hours worked each month	168	168
Labor cost per month	$604,800/mo.	$604,800/mo.
W. Comp. Manual Rate	$28 per $100 payroll	$28 per $100 payroll
Unadjusted W. Comp. Cost	$169,344	$169,344
EMR	0.65	0.95
Adjusted W. Comp. Cost	$110,073.60/mo.	$160,876.80/mo.
Wages & W. Comp. per mo.	$714,873.60	$765,676.80
Duration of project	15 months	15 months
Project Wages & W. Comp.	$10,723,104	$11,485,152
Safety Investment	$725,420	0
Total Labor Cost	$11,448,524	$11,485,152
Savings from safety	**$36,628**	

the two large projects are similar in every respect except for the differences in their commitments to safety and their EMRs. The results of the comparison are shown in Table 2–2.

The seemingly considerable investment of $655,420 (6.3% of the cost of labor and workers' compensation on the project) in the safety efforts of the company is warranted. Not only is that cost recovered, additional funds are generated. The added savings of $36,628 represent a rate of return of 5.0%, a viable investment.

FINAL COMMENTS ON INVESTMENT IN SAFETY

Some basic conclusions might be drawn from the examples related to investments in safety. First of all, it should be accepted that these are presumed to be reasonable numbers for the overall comparison. It is generally true that larger projects have greater investments in safety when measured in terms of the overall labor cost. The EMR values used in the comparisons are also quite realistic. It should be noted that smaller firms have greater limits placed on them in terms of how low the EMR can get or how high the EMR can realistically go. For example, a small firm with only five employees may have 0.80 as the lower bound of the EMR and an upper bound of 1.12. Conversely, a large firm may have the lower bound for the EMR being 0.20 and the upper bound being essentially unlimited. This sensitivity of the EMR to company size is known by many, but the actual extent of the range in EMR values is probably not fully understood. Conceptually, the intent of the EMR computations is to prevent a small firm from being adversely and severely impacted by a single costly injury case. While this certainly seems reasonable, what is not as clear is why a similar limit has been placed on how low the EMR value can be for a smaller firm. The unfortunate result of this phenomenon is that smaller firms with high values for the lower limit for the EMR have a smaller incentive or motivation to be safe. The large firms have the added motivation that the return on a safety investment will generally be greater in a large firm than in a small one.

While the commitment of funds to safety on a smaller project may well be disproportionately smaller than on a large project, no implication is being made that safety is not to be aggressively pursued. As shown in the examples, the investment "turned a profit" in both scenarios. In other words, the financial commitment in safety makes good business sense. Remember also that this needs to be weighed against the added costs imposed by injuries. Even if the investment in safety simply recovers the investment amount, the dedication of these funds will have been worth it.

CONCLUSION

Quantifying the costs of injuries and the investment being made in safety is not a simple or easy task. Injuries consist of the direct costs, which can be determined with accuracy after a workers' compensation injury claim is closed, and the indirect costs, which are rarely even estimated by construction firms. The direct costs have a time lag that provides an accurate cost, but often after a considerable time period has passed. The indirect costs consist of many costs that are incurred due to injuries that relate to lost productivity, damaged materials/equipment, and the commitment of administrative time. These indirect costs are rarely estimated despite the fact that these costs are often quite substantial.

The quantification of the investment in safety can be determined with some accuracy. The unknown that is associated with the investment in safety is the eventual influence that these efforts will have on injury occurrence. The most encouraging aspect of the positive influence that the investment in safety has on injury occurrence is that many of the elements of a safety program place greater demands on managerial commitments than on financial commitments. If a close look is taken at the different costs, whether it be related to injuries or the efforts to prevent injuries, it is readily apparent why such slogans as "Safety Pays" and "It Pays To Be Safe" become part of the culture of firms that truly are committed to the well being of their employees.

REFERENCES

Accident Facts, National Safety Council, 1998.

Blake, R. *Industrial Safety,* Second Ed., Prentice-Hall, New York, NY, 1946.

Brown, Derek. *A Historical Examination of Accidents Within the U.S. Army Corps of Engineers*, Master of Science Research Report, University of Washington, Seattle, 1988.

Chaney, P. *The Hidden Costs of Jobsite Accidents, Constructor,* Vol. 73, No. 4, 1991.

Heinrich, H. *Industrial Accident Prevention*, McGraw-Hill, New York, 1941.

Hinze, Jimmie. "The Full Implications of Injuries," *The National Utility Contractor*, Vol. 14, No. 6, June 1990.

Hinze, Jimmie. "A New Study of Construction Injury Costs," *EXCEL, A Quarterly Newsletter*, Center for Excellence in Construction Safety, Vol. 4, No. 1, Fall, 1990.

Hinze, Jimmie. "The Painful Cost of Construction Injuries," *Builder and Contractor*, Vol. 39, No. 4, April 1991.

Hinze, Jimmie. "The High Cost of Construction Injuries," *Concrete Construction*, April 1992.

Hinze, J., and Appelgate, L. "Costs of Construction Injuries," *Journal of Construction Engineering and Management*, Vol. 117, No. 3, September 1991.

Improving Construction Safety Performance, Report A-3, The Business Roundtable, January 1982.

Leopold, E., and Leonard, S. "Costs of Construction Accidents to Employers," *Journal of Occupational Accidents*, 1987.

Levitt, R., and Samelson, N. *Construction Safety Management*, Second Edition, John Wiley & Sons, Inc., New York, NY, 1993.

Naquin, A. J. "The Hidden Costs of Accidents," *Professional Safety*, Vol. 20, No. 12, 1975.

Robinson, Michal Roger. "Accident Cost Accounting as a Means of Improving Construction Safety," Technical Report No. 242, The Construction Institute, Stanford University, August 1979.

"Safety: A Profitable Priority," *Builder and Contractor*, Vol. 31, No. 10, 1983.

Sheriff, R. "Loss Control Comes of Age," Professional Safety, September 1980.

Simpson, C. A. "Safety Pays on Contractors," *Construction Equipment*, Vol. 82, No. 2, 1990.

CHAPTER 3

SCHEDULING FOR CONSTRUCTION SAFETY

Richard J. Coble, Ph.D.
University of Florida, Gainesville, Florida, U.S.A.
Brent R. Elliott, MSBC
University of Florida, Gainesville, Florida, U.S.A.

ABSTRACT

Integrating safety into every aspect of the construction process is something that must first start with the schedule. Construction safety is achievable, but only through planning and accountability. Scheduling for safety is a process that starts with the job activity schedule. Safety action items are then identified and correlated with the identified work activities. This chapter presents examples of how safety can be integrated into the scheduling process. It provides examples of how safety needs can be analyzed and developed into a schedule that addresses these needs.

This chapter also discusses the use of visual flags in a CPM network or bar chart diagram, which can provide electronic links to relevant mitigation and training information. Training is a crucial part of ensuring worker safety, and proper integration of safety and scheduling techniques will yield the highest level of training efficiency. The status of the work at any given time dictates the safety concerns at that particular stage of work. Safety-schedule integration enables management to maintain control in the dynamic job site environment.

The focus of this chapter is on the use of safety software to identify safety needs, integrate safety data bases into the schedule, and provide field access to this information. Developments in related software which apply to safety and scheduling are reviewed as to their potential for training and other uses in an integrated system. These developments include the use of icons and recorded dialogue in training software aimed at a semiliterate or multilingual work force.

KEYWORDS

scheduling, safety-schedule integration, safety training, software

INTRODUCTION

Time is most often the key factor in successful construction safety management. When a hazard is identified, time becomes an essential factor. Special equipment or materials may need to be ordered well in advance of performing the hazardous task. A worker who was trained two years ago will not be adequately prepared to avoid hazards. Obviously, one should not train too far in advance or train after the work is done.

Time sensitivity includes management, supervision and the workforce. The involvement of these participants cannot be separated. The workforce must be trained in their work. To accomplish this, supervision must train the trainers and management must make a commitment to safety. Scheduling is the primary tool to manage time, and includes planning, time considerations, relationships of activities, and priority of work. Safety plays a role in each of these components.

Construction safety has three primary aspects: (1) hazard awareness, (2) hazard avoidance or elimination, and (3) accountability.

Hazard awareness, for example, would include properly addressing concerns regarding carbon monoxide, a hazard which is common on job sites with enclosed spaces and small engines. Often, such hazards are not obvious to workers, so they need to be educated by means of hazard training. It is important not to assume that safe performance of an activity is common sense. Common sense in one culture may not be common in another.

Regardless of the culture, however, construction safety involves hazard avoidance or elimination. Hazard avoidance might include clearing an area and providing controlled access while unloading bricks or blocks from scaffolding. Elimination may include erecting portions of the structure on the ground and hoisting the work into place rather than working at a height.

Finally, safety includes accountability. Safety will not work without accountability. Each person must be accountable, including workers, management, and supervision, in some way. Construction is so demanding that without accountability, safety may be overlooked as a priority.

Each of the three components of construction safety (hazard awareness, hazard avoidance or elimination, and accountability) needs to be integrated into scheduling.

DETERMINING SAFETY NEEDS

Safety action items needs should be determined by more than one person, including someone from the workforce. This team concept is essential to allow construction safety to become a reality. Often a safety consultant is appropriate to add to the team.

Requirements of the Project

The project requirements may include compliance with government regulations. In the United States, such regulations are often issued by the Occupational Safety and Health Administration (OSHA). Specific project requirements may also include other regulations. For example, tripping hazards are not covered by OSHA. However, any ground level difference greater than one-quarter inch should be leveled or ramped. Manufacturing requirements may also play a role. For example, all machinery except for side booms requires rollover protection. Finally, industry standards may apply. Industry standards are simply the way the industry does the work. The industry standard should be used as a minimum.

Many projects have similar repeat requirements, such as hard hats and personal protective equipment (PPE). Therefore, a checklist should be used to keep track of job-specific requirements, such as those concerning carbon monoxide, confined spaces, or fall protection.

ASSESSING WHEN HAZARD EXPOSURE WILL OCCUR

Hazard exposure may occur at the beginning, middle, or end of a job. It is imperative to have training in place before exposure occurs. Well before exposure, management must prepare a plan to deal with the exposure.

Training should be done the first time there is an exposure regardless of the cost of work or the degree of difficulty. Often companies are reluctant to train before a minor activity. However, this is the ideal time. It is beneficial, for example, to get people involved in trench safety early, while in shallow trenches, rather than waiting for work in a deep trench. Such training can be easily accomplished using videos or interactive CD-ROMs.

The job team (project manager, estimator, superintendent, and workforce employee representative) should jointly decide what hazards need identification on the schedule, with minimum standards set by management and government as required.

Identification of Work Tasks

An important consideration in safety planning is the level of detail of the safety information to be provided within the schedule. Common safety concerns are applicable to many tasks. Training, hazard recognition, and personal protective equipment, for example, would be appropriate safety concerns for many activities. In order to be useful for field supervisors, however, information must be provided that is specific to individual work tasks.

Such information is currently available in a computer program called Construction Inspection Guide (Gambatese and Hinze 1996). This program incorporates OSHA's Safety and Health Regulations for the Construction Industry into a format designed for performing customized job site safety inspections. It embodies essentially all the construction safety regulations in a logically organized manner, and is ideal for providing the activity-specific safety information necessary to develop an integrated safety/scheduling system that is practical for use in the construction industry.

The Construction Inspection Guide uses four basic categories which help identify the OSHA safety regulations that will apply to a given work situation: General Requirements, Work Phases, Temporary Structures, and Construction Materials. The Work Phases category is the category most appropriate to integrate with the work activities in a schedule. The user selects phases of work being performed in order to proceed to more detailed screens, which then enable the selection of specific safety requirements for inclusion in the final customized checklist (see Figure 3–1).

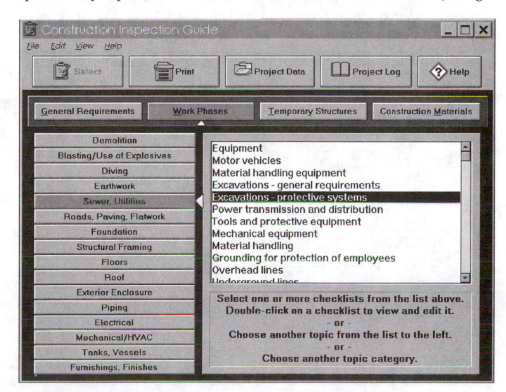

FIGURE 3–1
Construction inspection guide.

Source: Gambatese and Hinze.

Flagging Safety Exposure on the Construction Activity Schedule

Once hazard exposures have been assessed, management can begin to integrate safety with the schedule. This begins by flagging hazardous activities and activities which require safety training or safety equipment before work begins.

The flag indicates a need for training prior to work. This training may include a lecture, videos, or interactive CD-ROMs. Training videos are available from both Associated Builders and Contractors (ABC) and Associated General Contractors (AGC).

For example, a schedule may include the task "Exterior Wall Scaffolding" (see Figure 3–2). A flag graphic on this task indicates that safety concerns exist for this activity and that necessary preparations should be performed before the work activity. Clicking on the flag would then provide an electronic link to training and detailed information on scaffold erection, including design specifications, as shown in Figure 3–3.

As a company makes a long-term commitment to scheduling for safety, they should consider using Internet-based information. Many job sites have Internet connections. A project-specific web site could provide access to the current schedule, with flagged hazard exposures. These flags could provide links to appropriate training material. Another alternative is a CD-ROM. The CD-ROM could provide video on the proper use of equipment and then test the user on the proper use. Once set up, these CD-ROMS could be used on multiple jobs.

Requiring Safety Training Before the Work Activity Starts

As stated earlier, safety training requires a commitment from management, supervision, and workers. Management must demonstrate full commitment to the safety requirements and provide their endorsement that the job site be a safe work place.

Supervision is responsible first for training of the trainer. A flagged activity should therefore indicate a need to train the trainer, then a need to train employees. Often the trainer will be a foreman. Supervision must gear training toward the needs of the foreman. Material presented at safety meetings should be well prepared. The person conducting the meeting should

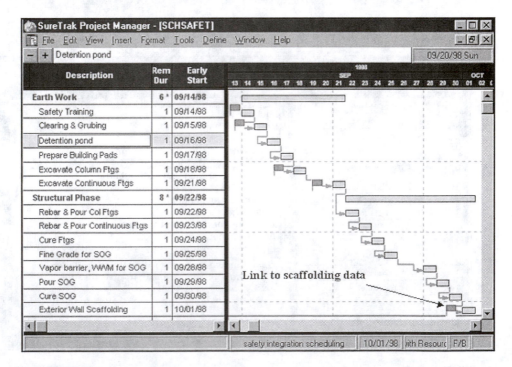

FIGURE 3–2
Safety flags on schedule.

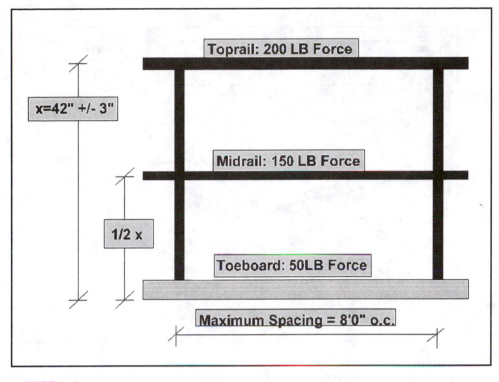

FIGURE 3–3
Training and detailed information.

Source: CEC, Inc. 1996

be able to deliver the information in his or her own words, consider using props, and give quizzes. In the best safety programs, safety is integrated into any group discussion. Additional assistance may be required to provide a better understanding of the subject. Supervision then must see that the workers are trained by certified trainers. OSHA requires that trainers be certified by the contractor or the manufacturer.

Finally, workers are responsible for not working until they are trained and tested. This testing should be conducted on a regular basis at appropriate intervals. Again, safety is time sensitive, and training must not occur too long before exposure to hazards.

Workers unions must take a strong stand, and not allow actions that would put workers in jeopardy. Obviously, exposing workers to hazards for which they were not properly trained should be considered a form of putting the workers in jeopardy. In addition to the union, management needs to make a statement to the workers that they also will not tolerate exposing workers to hazards for which they were not trained.

LINKING INTERACTIVELY BETWEEN
ACTIVITY SCHEDULE AND SAFETY TRAINING

Integrating safety and scheduling requires a commitment from management, supervision, and the workforce. These layers of management and workers need to work together to produce effective results in the form of safe job sites (see Figure 3–4). Top management must show their personal commitment. Supervision must make sure the trainer is trained. Often the foreman will be the trainer. The foreman wants to appear highly competent in front of his crew, and will resent being responsible to train workers without first being properly trained. Finally, supervision should provide video or interactive material to train the workers. The workers must be

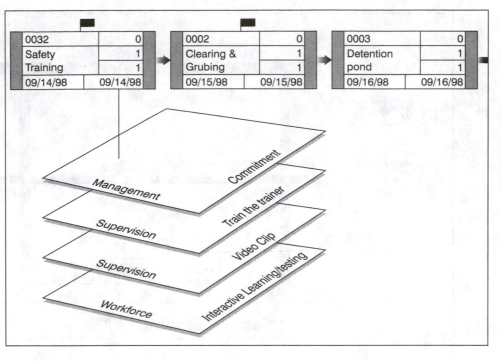

FIGURE 3–4
Scheduling for safety requires collaborative effort.

interactively involved with the training in order to derive the highest benefit from it. Interactive CD-ROM technology is an ideal method of training.

Training should be specific to worker needs, eliminating or minimizing nonessentials. Training should be very simple. For example, training for shallow excavation work should not cover boring, tunneling, or deep excavation. To avoid training material that is too broad or irrelevant, specific training modules could be developed.

Training must not be too complicated, because overcomplicated material will discourage workers. Once workers have become alienated by inappropriate training material, it may be difficult to regain their confidence. Trainers should strive to use verbal and visual media, avoiding written documents if at all possible. In some situations, the work force may be semiliterate or illiterate. An interactive approach works best, utilizing such means as video clips, sound, and voice.

Automated Links

Research has successfully demonstrated that computer technology can be used to integrate safety information into a CPM schedule electronically. Computerized integration of safety data bases and scheduling software was performed in research funded by the Center to Protect Workers' Rights (CPWR) through a contract with the University of Maryland (Kartam 1995). The program is designed to electronically integrate safety information with computerized CPM schedules, linking individual work activities with relevant safety information. The Safety CPM/NET Works program currently works with Primavera Project Planner, and will also be compatible with Microsoft Project, Symantec Timeline, and Primavera SureTrak (see Figure 3–5). While the shell of the program is functional, the safety suggestions and OSHA regulations are only included to a limited extent.

Safety CPM/NET Works uses a data base consisting of safety records and links. Safety records are linked to work activities via three types of links: CSI codes, keywords, and OSHA codes (Kartam 1995). These links enable the program to integrate specific safety and health recommendations into the appropriate work activities in the schedule.

FIGURE 3–5
Integrator module of safety CPM/NET Works

Source: Center to Protect Workers' Rights, 1996

Combining Safety CPM/NET Works and Other Data bases

Although the Safety CPM/NET Works program performs an extremely useful function by serving as the vehicle for integrating safety data bases with scheduling software, the safety information in the current version of the program is only partially developed. The Construction Inspection Guide program, however, has a comprehensive database of safety regulations and good safety practices which have been specifically organized to effectively guide the safe operation of a wide range of construction work activities. It has the ability to reflect changes in safety regulations, customize individual checklists, and improve management control of safety inspection records. Ideally, the two programs could be combined to create a very strong system. The synthesis of these programs could provide a complete application for integration of safety and scheduling.

Linked Material

Linked material should be verbal and visual wherever possible, to better serve the needs of the construction workforce. Written material alone is insufficient.

An example of the use of verbal and visual information is HAZCOM Interactive, a CD-ROM developed by Conceptual Arts, which derives material from the International Chemical Safety Cards (ICSC) series, and presents it in multimedia format, utilizing interactive video, audio, and icons (see Figure 3–6).

Once training has been completed, training comprehension must be tested. However, this testing must be done on a uniform basis and in a manner that is nondiscriminatory. One person must be tested in the same manner as another. In this respect, CD-ROMs are ideal, provid-

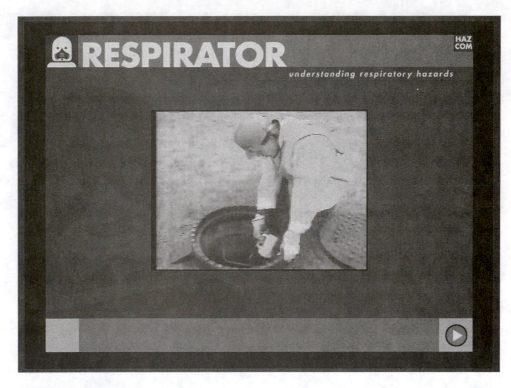

FIGURE 3–6
HAZCOM Interactive training.

Source: Conceptual Arts, Inc., 1998

ing a consistent testing environment. For example, HAZCOM Interactive provides games to test training comprehension (see Figure 3–7). These games are entertaining and easy to use, while reinforcing the training at the same time.

Finally, participant accountability must be verified. Participants—including project managers, supervisors, and workers—must verify in written form that they have fulfilled their roles in the training process and can be held accountable.

Figure 3–8 shows another view of the CPM schedule which could be used to access such interactive training materials for the flagged activities. The flags provide the initial electronic link to the data base of training and related information.

THE FUTURE OF SCHEDULING FOR CONSTRUCTION SAFETY

Internet Incorporation

The integration of construction software lends itself to Internet-based data bases. Companies could maintain job-specific web sites, which would contain an updated, current version of the schedule, complete with flagged tasks that provide links to databases of safety information.

An Internet-based system would allow for access to training materials and detailed information from the field via wireless devices. Field supervisors could obtain the information they need to address current needs, and any modifications to the material could be easily updated for all users.

Because many organizations have a stake in safety training, companies could jointly develop training modules. The projected $5,000 cost of a training module could be shared by ten companies, and the material could be put on the Internet for all to use.

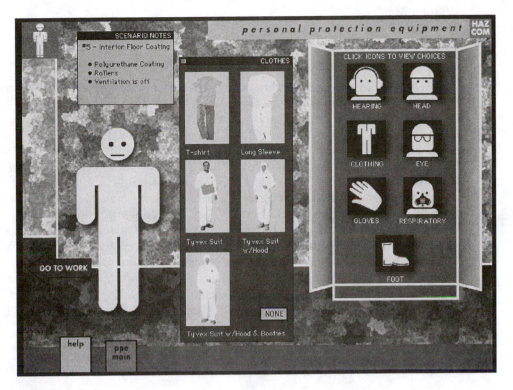

FIGURE 3–7
HAZCOM Interactive training.

Source: Conceptual Arts, Inc., 1998

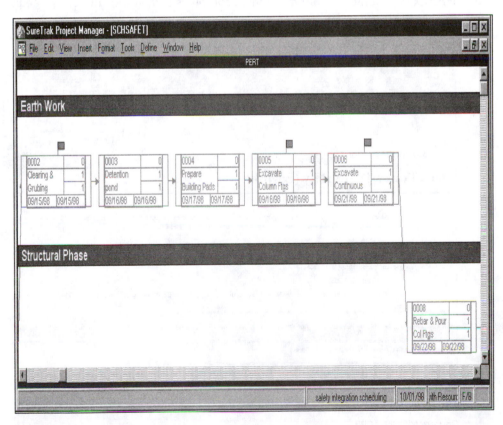

FIGURE 3–8
Accessing interactive training materials with safety flag links.

CD-ROMs

CD-ROMs could be used to augment the safety data bases of an Internet-based system. Multiple organizations produce CD-ROMs with detailed safety information. The challenge is to find information that is appropriate to the specific job.

As opposed to the Internet, CD-ROMs lend themselves to company-specific training. It is advisable to try to avoid using generic training data. Ideally, an interactive safety training CD-ROM should show the company's worker, using the company's equipment, doing work the company would normally do. However, some tasks are common to most projects and most companies. The vast majority of general contractors, for example, do formwork and excavation. In such cases, more than one activity may be included per training module.

The National Agriculture Safety Database (NASD), developed by Conceptual Arts in conjunction with NIOSH and CDC, utilizes WebCD technology. The WebCD Viewer works with Microsoft Internet Explorer or Netscape Navigator browsers. It contains over 2,500 agricultural health and safety publications from 32 states, 4 federal agencies, and 5 national organizations. It includes OSHA and Environmental Protection Agency (EPA) standards, a data base of abstracts and ordering information for over 1,500 agricultural safety-related videos (see Figure 3–9). It also includes training programs and posters.

Icon Access to Databases

Construction foremen have different needs than management. In addition, construction foremen usually have different education levels than management. Obviously, this requires training software to be needs sensitive. As a result, software may need to be designed for some semiliterate or illiterate users. In addition, it must be enjoyable. One key element in such a design is the use of icons. Icons can be animated and supplemented with voices, as in the aforementioned HAZCOM interactive software, which combines text, voice, and icons (see Figure 3–10).

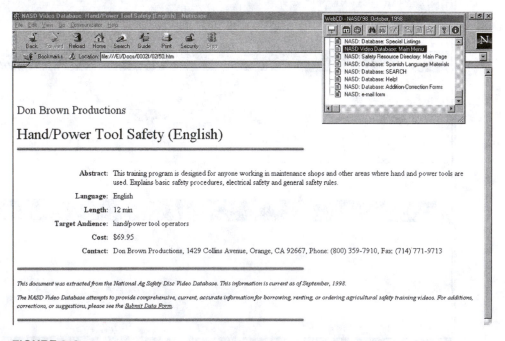

FIGURE 3–9
The National Agriculture Safety Database (NASD).

Source: NIOSH, 1998

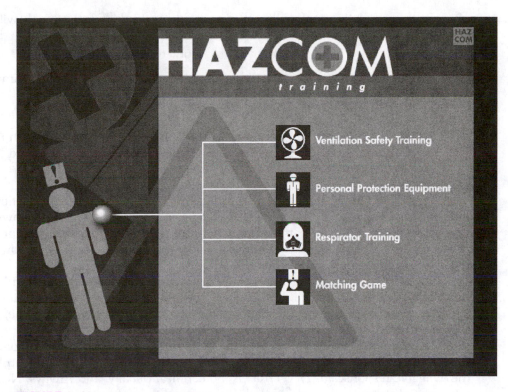

FIGURE 3–10
HAZCOM Interactive training.

Source: Conceptual Arts, Inc., 1998

Overlay Schedule Updating

With the use of photogrammetry software, stereo digital images can produce a three-dimensional object that can be overlaid on a computer assisted design (CAD) plan. This can be used to determine the amount of work completed by comparing the current status of completion in the image to the planned work in the CAD file, update the project schedule, and forecast the appropriate safety needs. For example, if masonry work is currently at the stage of scaffolding erection, proper training information will be triggered.

HUMAN FACTORS INVOLVED IN SCHEDULING FOR SAFETY

The attitudes and beliefs of each level of management regarding the relationship between scheduling and safety should be understood in order to effectively integrate scheduling and safety. Field supervision, for example, is an important level of management to consider because of the key role that these individuals play in the actual implementation of corporate procedures and systems.

Research has been performed to investigate the attitudes of construction foremen regarding the relationship between safety and scheduling (Elliott, 1999). Foremen on large commercial construction projects were asked a number of questions during job site interviews, including the following:

1. How does following safety rules affect production?
   A. slows down production
   B. does not affect production
   C. speeds up production

2. Do the completion goals of the schedule make it difficult to deal properly with safety issues?

1	2	3	4	5
never	rarely	sometimes	usually	always

3. Do you think you can make good job progress and be safe at the same time?

1	2	3	4	5
strongly disagree	disagree	no opinion	agree	strongly agree

4. Do you think that having safety activities in the written schedule which relate to upcoming work activities would help you to know what safety issues should be dealt with at each stage of the job?

Regarding Question #1 (How does following safety rules affect production?), Figure 3–11 indicates that the majority of foremen (57%) believe following safety rules slows down production, 22% believe it does not affect production, and 17% believe it speeds up production. Other responses (4%) described a more complex relationship, such as short term slow-downs leading to long term increases in production (Elliott 1999).

It is important to note that the foremen who believed following safety rules slowed down production did not have a negative attitude toward following safety rules due to its perceived effect on production. Rather, they indicated that although it takes more time, it is well worth the time to ensure the safety of their crews (Elliott 1999).

As shown in Figure 3–12, answers by foremen to Question #2 (Do the completion goals of the schedule make it difficult to deal properly with safety issues?) were distributed across all the available responses of Never, Rarely, Sometimes, Usually, and Always. Nearly all foremen interviewed strongly emphasized their commitment to safety, and it should be pointed out that those foremen who indicated that the completion goals of the schedule *do* make it difficult to deal properly with safety issues also expressed that safety is their first priority, regardless of the effect on the schedule (Elliott, 1999). Foremen place the safety of their men at a higher priority than meeting the goals of the schedule.

In a related interview outside of the foreman sample discussed herein, a superintendent for a general contractor stated that safety "drives the entire schedule," and if a contractor does not put safety ahead of the schedule, that contractor will soon be out of business. He also emphasized that this perspective is a major change of attitude in the construction industry that has only developed within the last five to ten years (Elliott 1999).

Responses to Question #3 (Do you think you can make good job progress and be safe at the same time?), as shown in Figure 3–13, are interesting when compared to the responses to Question #1 and Question #2 above. Although 57% of foremen believe following safety rules

Question #1: How does following safety rules affect production?

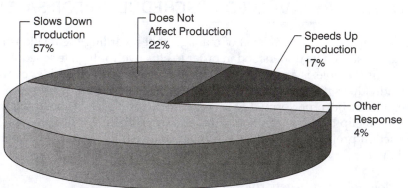

FIGURE 3–11

Foreman attitudes: effect of safety rules on production.

Source: Elliott 1999

Question #2: Do the completion goals of the schedule make it difficult to deal properly with safety issues?

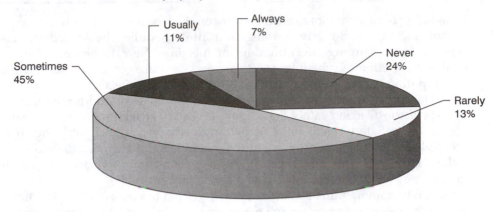

FIGURE 3–12

Foreman attitudes: dealing with safety and completion goals

Source: Elliott 1999

Question #3: Do you think you can make good job progress and be safe at the same time?

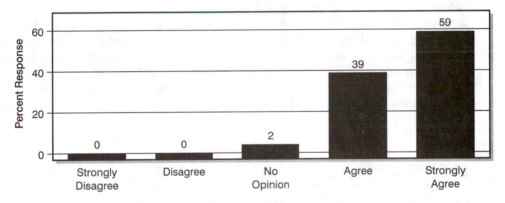

FIGURE 3–13

Foreman attitudes: Making good job progress while working safely.

Source: Elliott 1999

slows down production (Question #1), and 63% of foremen believe the completion goals of the schedule make it difficult (sometimes, usually, or always) to deal properly with safety issues (Question #2), 98% of foremen still believe they can make good job progress and be safe at the same time (Question #3) (Elliott 1999).

Regarding Question #4 (Do you think that having safety activities in the written schedule which relate to upcoming work activities would help you to know what safety issues should be dealt with at each stage of the job?), preliminary analysis of responses indicates that approximately one-half of the 89 foremen interviewed to date gave a favorable response to incorporating safety activities into the written schedule (Elliott 1999).

Integrating scheduling and safety is an important step toward recognizing that these two entities are not independent of each other, but rather that safety and scheduling actually have a close relationship. All levels of management can benefit by using a system which ties the two together and provides controls for managing this integration throughout an entire project or group of projects.

CONCLUSION

Scheduling is an ideal tool to ensure safety on the job site, as it involves time, relationships, and priorities. Safety can easily be integrated into scheduling by identifying tasks, flagging the schedule, and planning safety training and meetings. New developments in computer software enable integration of scheduling software and databases of safety training material. Advances in computing hardware allow remote access to the schedule and attached safety information.

Hazard awareness, hazard avoidance or elimination, and accountability are three main aspects of construction safety. Scheduling for safety facilitates successful management in these critical areas. Safety needs must be determined in accordance with the current status of the schedule. Safety flags on activities in the schedule provide notice to field supervisors that special attention is warranted, and electronic links enable supervisors to access the detailed information they need to deal properly with safety concerns.

Safety training must conform to job needs and be cost-effective. The training must be relative to the tasks being performed; a generic solution may be counterproductive. Custom training modules may need to be developed. Current technology can be utilized to raise the effectiveness of safety management to a new level. The integration of scheduling software and safety data bases provides a tremendous resource for both safety managers and field supervisors.

Training must meet owner requirements and government regulations, such as OSHA, Corps of Engineers, and Water Management District. Safety information should be drawn from data bases including government regulations, such as OSHA. Finally, training must be accepted by its users (management, supervision, and workforce). Interactive training software, including icons and voices, can make software accessible to the workforce. Such software should be easily accessible from the field. Workers won't pay attention to outdated, boring, or irrelevant material. The workers know their job and will lose interest in training information that they know does not apply.

Integration of safety and scheduling must have management commitment. Safety must be seen as an integral part of a schedule that cannot be sacrificed. The cost of prevention is much less than the cost of accidents. Upper management commitment is critical for the success of any safety program, and this commitment must extend to an integrated safety-scheduling management program.

REFERENCES

CEC, Inc. *OSHA Training: Subparts M and L*, Gainesville, FL, 1996.

Center to Protect Workers' Rights (CPWR). Safety CPM/NET Works: Beta Version 1. 7 for Windows?. CPWR, Washington, DC, 1996.

Coble, Richard J., and Blatter, Robert. "Concerns with Safety in the Design/Build Process," American Society of Civil Engineers (ASCE) *Journal of Architectural Engineering*, June, 1999.

Coble, Richard J., Alexander, John F., Qu, Tan, and Sun, Wei. "The Use of Mobile GIS by Construction Foremen," American Institute of Constructors (AIC), *The American Professional Constructor*, Vol. 22, No. 2, December, 1998, pp. 19–23.

Coble, Richard J., Elliott, Brent R., and Coble, Brennon J. "Automation of Construction Site Supervision," International Council for Building Research Studies and Documentation (CIB), Proceedings of Construction Modernization and Education International Conference, Beijing, China, October 21–24, 1996, pp. 202–207.

Conceptual Arts, Inc. *HAZCOM Interactive*, Gainesville, FL, 1998.

Elliott, Brent R. Unpublished Ph.D. Dissertation, University of Florida, 1999.

Gambatese, John, and Hinze, Jimmie. "A Guide for Safety Inspections." Proceedings of Implementation of Safety and Health on Construction Sites International Conference, International Council for Building Research Studies and Documentation (CIB), Lisbon, Portugal, September 4–7, 1996, pp. 553–563.

Hinze, Jimmie, Coble, Richard J., and Elliott, Brent R. "CPM Scheduling as a Tool for Construction Safety Planning," International Council for Building Research Studies and Documentation (CIB), Proceedings of 2nd South African Construction Health and Safety Conference: Health and Safety in Construction: Accident Free Construction, Capetown, South Africa, November, 1998, pp. 76–81.

Hinze, Jimmie, Coble, Richard J. and Elliott, Brent R. "Integrating Safety Planning with CPM Scheduling," Eighth Rinker International Conference, M.E. Rinker, Sr., School of Building Construction, University of Florida, February, 1998.

Kartam, Nabil. "Integrating Construction Safety and Health Performance into CPM." Construction Congress: Proceedings of the 1995 Conference, American Society of Civil Engineers (ASCE), San Diego, CA, Oct. 22–26, 1995, pp. 456–462.

Mselle, P. C. "Management of Construction Safety: The Cost Implication of Safety." In *Health & Safety in Construction*, T. Haupt/Rwelamila, editors.

NIOSH. National Agriculture Safety Database, 1998.

United States Department of Labor. Code of Federal Regulations, Title 29-Labor, Part 1926: Safety and Health Regulations for the Construction Industry, Washington, DC, 1998.

4

HUMAN FACTORS IN CONSTRUCTION SAFETY—MANAGEMENT ISSUES

Steve Rowlinson, Ph.D.

Department of Real Estate & Construction,

The University of Hong Kong, Hong Kong, China

ABSTRACT

This chapter discusses the roles of the men and women who manage the construction company, who manage the construction project and, to begin with, those at the sharp end of the industry who are exposed to the risk, currently one in three in Hong Kong, of injury on a construction site. The nature of the workers and their preparedness for work are discussed. The issue of training is addressed, along with issues such as induction courses and safety culture. The role of management is then focused upon, along with the tools and techniques which managers and supervisors might use.

KEYWORDS

safety culture, safety management systems, behavior modification, accident causation, safety initiatives

INTRODUCTION

This chapter deals with safety management, particularly focusing on human factors and using the Hong Kong construction industry as an example. The following sections provide some background information to the situation in Hong Kong.

BACKGROUND ON HONG KONG

Crafts and Trades

Many different skills are required on site to undertake construction site works; an important point to bear in mind when considering the nature of the construction site worker is his or her education level and training. Construction is a hard job, undertaken outdoors in Hong Kong in a hot and humid climate. The work is often dangerous and difficult and requires a degree of independence on the part of the worker. Hence, to many the job of a construction worker is unattractive, and some of those entering the industry do so because they have few other alternatives.

Until very recently virtually anyone could walk off the street onto a construction site and start work. With the introduction, on government sites, of the Green Card induction training system, a new worker at least receives a basic orientation in construction site safety. This is not an ideal situation, especially as the construction environment is far less controlled than a factory setting, but it is a step in the right direction.

In many southeast Asian countries construction workers are drawn from the ranks of farm workers who migrate to large cities outside of the harvest period to earn hard cash on construction sites. This is not the case in Hong Kong as Hong Kong does not have this hinterland to draw upon. However, many of the site workers are recent immigrants from the People's Republic of China who do not have skills or trades and so move into construction as the easiest industry in which to be employed. One can reasonably assume that direct entrants into the industry, i.e., those who have no training, have a comparably low level of formal education. Hence, training this group of workers to work safely is a formidable task.

Apprenticeships

As is the case in many countries around the world, apprenticeships are increasingly uncommon in the Hong Kong construction industry. One reason for this is a structural problem facing the industry—the high levels of subcontracting. Due to these high levels of subcontracting, many firms in the industry are very small, often comprising a proprietor and a few daily paid staff. Such firms have neither the resources nor the desire to provide apprenticeships, and so a downward spiral in terms of training provision ensues. For those fortunate enough to be taken on as apprentices, the standard of training and instruction can vary tremendously.

The author has personal knowledge of two instances where recent graduates of the Construction Industry Training Authority (CITA) were being trained and were left to fend for themselves in dangerous situations which they had not encountered before. In the first instance a trainee had been erecting hangers for suspended ceilings; his past work had involved office buildings where ceilings are typically three meters above floor level. In this instance he was asked to work in an exhibition space with ceilings around 10 meters high and, while trying to get access to an area where another trainee needed assistance, he fell and was seriously injured. No senior worker or master was present at the time. In a similar way a scaffolding apprentice fell from a scaffold erected outside of a building when a piece of weak scaffold, which he had erected, broke. Again, no senior worker was on hand to supervise the apprentice.

The fast track nature of Hong Kong construction, skilled labor shortage, and very tight margins of contractors have led to a situation in Hong Kong in which training of new entrants has been neglected. This neglect is sadly evident in the accident statistics.

Certification and Trade Testing

Government policy requires operators of construction plants to be certified and CITA runs a Certification Course (with Certification Tests) for Temporary Suspended Working Platforms (Gondolas) to meet the requirements of Section 17 of the Factories and Industrial Undertakings (Suspended Working Platforms) Regulation. Two other Courses with Certification Tests, for

Operators of Builder's Lifts and Tower Working Platforms, are also run to meet the requirements of the Builders' Lifts and Tower Working Platforms (Safety) Ordinance.

During 1994 the authority's trade testing scheme for construction workers was expanded to cover all 15 principal trades in the industry. The committee on trade testing initiated a series of promotional activities for the scheme which included press conferences, posters distributed to construction sites, dinner receptions for subcontractors, awards presented to outstanding candidates, and early bird discounts.

Certification of crane operators met up with serious problems in 1995 when over 50% of applicants for the crane operator's certification test failed the course. This is symptomatic of a problem which affects all trades; currently, normal practice on Hong Kong sites is just not good enough. However, as it is current practice it is accepted and so accidents are inevitable. Only when proper certification is introduced at all levels on construction sites can it be hoped that the current situation will improve. This calls for a change of attitude by employer and employee alike.

Recruitment

The majority of Hong Kong's construction site workers are recruited on a daily or weekly basis. Very few workers are employed directly by the main contractor; there is an extensive system of subcontracting in Hong Kong with typically three or four layers of sub-contracting taking place. Workers will often gather in a tea house in the early morning and wait to be approached by agents who will arrange construction work for them. Many of the subcontracting organizations are little more than one man bands where the tradesman sets himself up as a subcontractor and then employs his colleagues on a job by job basis.

This subcontracting system is basically a structural problem which afflicts the industry. Its consequences are the lack of apprenticeships, the difficulty in arranging regular and directed training courses, and the general lack of control which exists on construction sites. The subcontracting system does not provide any career prospects nor continuity of workload for the average construction site worker. Hence, the levels of commitment shown by workers to their companies, and even to their colleagues, is very low (see Lingard 1995).

Induction Courses

In an ideal world all site personnel should receive a safety induction course; many of the government developers have made this a mandatory requirement (see Rowlinson 1997, Chapter 7). As a minimum this course should cover the topics listed below:

- Site introduction
- General duties and responsibilities
- Site safety procedures
- Personal protective equipment
- Working at height
- Lifting gear and appliances
- Electricity
- Accident reporting procedures

The site introduction should include topics such as site layout, the type of works being carried out, location of key points (such as first aid boxes and fire extinguishers), the main hazards present on the site, and company safety policy. The introduction to duties and responsibilities should include employee responsibilities such as personal safety and the safety of others, the wearing of personal protective equipment, and compliance with safety rules. The employer's responsibilities, which the new employee should be aware of, include safe systems of work, plant maintenance and inspection, and training and supervision requirements.

An introduction to site safety procedures should include site emergency procedures, special procedures laid down for certain tasks, and the penalties for non-compliance. Personal protective equipment induction training should address issues such as eye protection (including the different types of eye protectors), foot protection and the provision of safety boots, and the provision and maintenance of all items of personal protective equipment.

Working at height is always a dangerous activity and an induction course should include coverage of the safe use of working platforms and ladders, safe means of access and egress, the use of safety belts and provision of suitable anchorage points, and the proper use of handrails and toeboards. The types of lifting gear used on site and the maintenance and inspection of chains and shackles which go with them should be included in an induction course. Particular emphasis should be placed on overhead hazards, such as electrical cables, and signaling requirements and procedures. Electrical hazards and the correct use of power tools and repair of the same is another very important induction issue.

A brief introduction to the types and causes of accidents, how accidents and incidents should be reported, and the responsibility of all site staff for reporting potential hazards should be emphasized. The induction course should be a key element of any safety management system and should emphasise the responsibility that all workers have for their own and others' safety.

Safety Culture

The concept of a safety culture has been promoted during the late 1990s. Hong Kong construction site workers adopt a very *macho* attitude to site safety. This is apparent in their disregard for many safety procedures such as the wearing of personal protective equipment. One can regularly see Hong Kong workers climbing at high levels without any safety belt being worn and often wearing only canvas shoes rather than proper site safety boots. Risk taking is readily accepted in the Hong Kong construction industry. The aim has been to modify this attitude to one of carefulness rather than carelessness. In order for a culture change to take place, employers must be committed whole-heartedly to such a change.

A culture change cannot affect the whole industry without a government commitment and sense of direction being made apparent. This requires the profile of both the Labour Department and the factory inspectorate to be raised significantly. Thus, changes are needed in both the structure and management of the Labour Department. If a culture which accepts only zero fatalities on construction sites and low accident rates is to be engendered then attitudes and culture must change all round.

This culture change will take some time to come about. The government initiative toward self-regulation cannot succeed if this culture change does not take place. Hence promotion and support for a safety culture from the major public and private clients is essential. Only then will responsible contractors feel that by emphasising safety and safety culture they are participating in a match played on a level playing field.

Communicating this message of a safety culture to the construction site worker is no easy task. It will certainly not be completed in a short space of time, but if it is apparent to the worker that the employers are serious about this change in attitude, the process will be much easier. Techniques such as behavioral safety management (BSM), reported in Rowlinson, 1997, Chapter 7, can help in this regard, but it must be borne in mind that such techniques are not a panacea for the industry. In fact, the nature of the construction industry, with its organic organization structures and decentralization of decision making and emphasis on self-reliance, makes the implementation of BSM very difficult compared with other industries. See also Lingard and Rowlinson (1997 & 1998) for a discussion of this issue.

Imported Labor

Traditionally, many of Hong Kong's construction site workers have been immigrants from southern China. However, when the Airport Core Programme began construction, site workers were imported from many other countries such as the Philippines, Eastern Europe, and the

United Kingdom. There has been for many centuries a precedent for the movement of skilled labor from East to West, but the importation of unskilled labor from the United Kingdom was an unusual phenomenon.

Given that these imported workers were working in a new environment and were often supervised by Cantonese speaking staff, one might have expected a higher accident rate amongst these workers. However, this was found not to be the case. Figures show that the accident rate for imported labor on the airport platform was less than that for local labor (Rowlinson, 1997:109). This difference was rationalized as being due to differences in both training levels and safety culture and in safety awareness.

THE COST OF LACK OF SAFETY

Putting together a safety program costs money but the absence of safety costs more in the long run.

Accident Costs on a Construction Site

The United Kingdom Health and Safety Executive conducted an 18 week study on a United Kingdom construction site. During the course of this study the costs of all accidents were recorded; accidents were deemed to include cases of property damage where no person suffered injury. The total direct financial losses were calculated to be in the region of US$120,000. Indirect costs were calculated as opportunity costs, in this case mainly payment of wages during periods of low production. The total of indirect losses came to a further US$240,000. It was calculated that if accidents occurred at the same rates during the course of the project then the total losses would be around US$360,000 which was in fact equal to around 8.5% of the tender price.

If this situation was replicated in Hong Kong, contractors might be quite surprised to find that their losses from dangerous incidents, accidents which involve injury or no injury, were greater than the margin mark-up they put in on the tender bid. This surely brings home the importance of site safety management systems being properly implemented. If the costs of accidents exceeds the expected profit margin on a project, then the construction industry must sit up and take notice. The authors of the report drew two conclusions from this analysis. These conclusions referred to previous research which had used the analogies of the cost iceberg and the accident triangle.

The Cost Iceberg

The cost iceberg was used by Heinrich, *et al.* (1980) to investigate how the real costs of accidents can be measured and controlled. In the U.K. study of a construction contract, it was determined that the ratio of uninsured costs to insured costs was 11 to 1. In the U.S., Hinze (1997:59) calculates a lower ratio, around 2 to 1, but he points out that this ratio is influenced by the costs of medical care which vary from place to place. Uninsured costs were categorized by Heinrich as property damage costs and miscellaneous costs. These can be seen as including property damage costs, being items such as product damage, plant damage, equipment damage, and building damage. The miscellaneous costs include items such as emergency supplies, legal costs, production delays, clerical work, fines, and, somewhat more intangibly, loss of expertise and experience.

The Accident Triangle

The accident triangle deals with accident ratios. In this particular study there was only one accident which required a worker to stay away from work for over three days. There were over 50 minor injuries which required first aid treatment only and there were over 3,600 non-injury incidents which could, without good luck, have turned to minor or major injuries. The study reported that the ratio of non-injury accidents to injury accidents was far greater in the construction industry than in the other four industries which were studied. The conclusion drawn from this was that there is massive potential for costs savings by reducing accidental loss from accidents in the construction industry.

The ratio reported in the U.K. study is very little different from that reported many years ago by Heinrich and Bird and other researchers in this area. It seems that time has passed, but things have not changed, particularly in the construction industry. The potential for savings due to proper safety measures and accident prevention techniques is still huge. It was the view of the U.K. researchers that if proprietors can be convinced of the cost saving potential of safety management systems then self-regulation has a chance to succeed.

Insurance

In 1993, the cost of insurance became a key issue for Hong Kong's contractors. As reported by Ball in the South China *Morning Post* of November 20th, 1993:

> A huge increase in construction site accidents and subsequent claims for damages is threatening to put some firms out of business. Insurers forecast yesterday that premiums would rise dramatically and said some construction companies were finding it almost impossible to get cover. The prediction came as the Hong Kong Construction Association (HKCA) warned members they could be finished if they did not make their building site safe.
>
> Adrian King, chairman of the Hong Kong Confederation of Insurance Brokers, said: "Without these safety measures, insurance is just going to become impossible." And the president of the Accident and Insurance Association of Hong Kong, Peter Dunn, said: "Some contractors with particularly poor records are finding the cost of insurance prohibitive. This is already happening." Mr. Chan, secretary-general of the HKCA, said premiums were now a major part of any contractor's bill. "A few years ago they were less than one per cent of the price of a contract. Now people are talking about eight per cent."

Insurance coverage is a major cost to the construction contractor. However, the system of employees compensation (EC) insurance in Hong Kong is different from that in the U. S. A. and Australia. Poorly performing contractors have not been punished in the past with markedly higher premiums, the corollary to this being that good contractors with good safety performance were not rewarded for this. Because insurance is included in a contractor's bid, there has been little incentive in construction contract terms for contractors to improve safety performance. This situation is now changing but the change could be brought about more quickly by bringing the employees compensation insurance system into line with that of other countries, wherein contractors with good safety records pay less. Also, claimants in Hong Kong are at liberty to institute a civil law claim even though they have already received compensation through EC, markedly pushing up costs compared with the U.S. and Australian systems.

Subcontracting

The extensive use of subcontracting in the Hong Kong construction industry has been identified as a key source of problems in site safety management, quality assurance, and productivity. However, the very existence of this extensive, multi-layered subcontracting system is a pointer to the economic conditions that exist in Hong Kong's construction industry. This is undoubtedly a structural problem which the industry as a whole must face. Hence, the issue must be addressed by government bodies and government clients as a social and economic issue if change is to take place. This was recognized by Hillebrandt and Cannon (1989), who wrote:

> It is possible that subcontracting may generate negative externalities, thus raising social costs, and these may be industry costs or national costs. One area where this is particularly likely is safety. The system of subcontracting clouds the division of responsibilities over aspects of health and safety. This is of some significance in the U.K. where reliance is placed on a self-regulating system. In the

U.S.A., it has been estimated that the total cost (the sum of social and private costs) of an accident is five times the private cost . . .

It is found that the special characteristics of construction—notably fluctuations and uncertainty—mean that, unlike the situation in manufacturing industry, subcontracting offers a low cost mode of organizing work in the construction industry, and this is borne out by the discussions with contractors reported in the companion volume. The weaknesses of subcontracting in manufacturing in terms of product flow and incentives are attenuated in the construction industry, and there are great advantages in the assignment of individuals to tasks.

The issue in the balance is social costs versus private costs. If it is true that subcontracting offers substantial economic advantages to the contractor then it is very unlikely that this system will be abandoned without some form of compensation or guarantee that all will abandon this system. But, if the social costs associated with the inability to manage safety in a subcontract environment are too great for society to bear then change must come. No matter how persuasive the argument is that a well devised and constructed safety management system will reduce the costs of accidents in the long term, it is impossible to expect such a system to be effectively implemented until the structural problem of subcontracting is addressed.

SAFETY AS AN INTEGRAL PART OF THE PROJECT

In order for safety management to be truly effective, safety has to be seen to be an integral part of the management process. This implies that safety needs to be on the agenda at all project meetings and should be considered at the inception phase of a project

Unfortunately, such a holistic approach is rarely found in Hong Kong. As Rheo Lam, a safety officer at Hong Kong University, pointed out in his submission to the Hong Kong Institute of Engineers (HKIE) working party on construction site safety:

For most projects safety is not taken to be part and parcel of the project. Many of the safety matters are left in the hands of the safety officer who is a "lonely boy" of the project team. With this lack of recognition and loss of identity the main function of the safety officer is seen to be dealing with the Factory Inspectors when they come along. (This is done) to comply with the requirements of the law because the law said the site requires a safety officer, to handle queries after an accident.

Such an attitude is obviously detrimental to good safety management and at the same time is demotivating to the safety officer. As Mr. Lam went on to explain, with many contractors few if any of the safety officers are involved, or invited to be involved, at the design and planning stage of a project. They are not asked to contribute their safety knowledge to the project management team so that the hazards associated with the project can be identified in advance, thereby allowing ample time and resources to eliminate or overcome the hazards and safety problems. The safety officer is cast into a reactive role, tidying up the mess afterwards, rather than taking a proactive stance in project discussions.

Self-Regulation

In its White Paper of July, 1995, the Hong Kong Government proposed a move toward self-regulation and the adoption by contractors of safety management systems. This was described as follows:

The Government's view on industrial safety is that the primary responsibility for safety and health at work rest with those who create the risks and those who work with such risks, i.e., the proprietors and the workers. The ultimate goal is self-regulation by the proprietor and his workforce. The Government should provide a framework with legislative and administrative components within which self-regulation is to be achieved through a company system of safety management. This should be backed by enhanced enforcement focused on establishments where self-regulation is not working (Hong Kong Government, July 1995).

ACCIDENT CAUSATION

One of the first theories of accident causation was developed by Heinrich (Heinrich *et al.*, 1980) in the 1920s. Heinrich developed his "axioms of industrial safety." These axioms dealt with areas such as accident causation, the interface between worker and machine, the relationship between accident frequency and accident severity, the underlying reasons for unsafe acts, the relationship between management functions and accident control, organizational responsibility and authority, the costs of accidents, and the relationship between efficiency and safety.

Heinrich's axioms are summarised below:

1. Injuries result from a sequence of factors, the last of which is the accident itself.
2. Unsafe acts of persons cause the majority of accidents.
3. Three hundred narrow escapes from serious accidents will have occurred before a person suffers injury caused by an unsafe act.
4. The severity of injury incurred is largely a matter of chance.
5. Accident prevention methods are similar to those methods used for cost control, quality control, and production management. Management is in the best position to initiate accident revention strategies.
6. The art of supervision is the most important influence on successful accident prevention.
7. The humanist view of accident prevention can be usefully enhanced by a consideration of economic forces.

Bird (1974) extended the scope of Heinrich's work by drawing on other work done in the field of management in order to produce a model known as the domino sequence (see Figure 4-1). The analogy of the domino sequence works like a line of dominos whereby when the first domino falls the next is knocked onto another domino and the whole line of dominos falls to the ground. Bird's contention was that if the first domino is stabilized then the whole line is safe. The relationship he described is as follows.

Lack of management control leads to a lowering of performance standards; these standards may be training, communication, program, etc. According to classical management theorists such as Henri Fayol (1949), management's functions are to plan, organize, command, coordinate and control, and all managers are expected to fulfill these functions.

The consequences of this lack of control allows the existence of other factors which contribute to the accident and are considered basic causes of the accident. These factors might be:

- Personal factors such as lack of training, knowledge, or aptitude for the task at hand.
- Work factors such as inadequate work standards, poor design of work processes, inadequate maintenance, or lack of supervision.

The symptoms of the accident, those issues that are often picked up wrongly as the root cause of the accident, are the unsafe acts and unsafe conditions which are observed such as:

- Using defective equipment, using the wrong item of equipment, failing to secure loads, driving too quickly or disabling safety devices.
- Poor housekeeping and general untidiness, fitting of inadequate or ineffective guards, using broken or defective tools.

Bird's contention was that these unsafe conditions were symptoms of management oversight and mismanagement. If management was doing its job properly such conditions could not exist. One might argue that workers are capable of putting themselves at risk by not following rules or management's instructions, but Bird would have countered this argument by pointing to the first domino in his sequence, that is, management control involves responsibilities for selection of workers, training of workers, and their supervision. Hence Bird places the responsibility firmly back in the employers' or managers' court.

The fourth domino in the sequence is the unplanned and undesired event, the accident itself. Now, this accident, or incident, may not result in loss of any kind; the outcome of the accident is difficult to predict but if contact with an energy source is involved then damage is likely to occur. The outcome of the accident may be property damage, injury, or death. These are the chance outcomes of the incident. Hence, Bird's contention is that the only chance involved in an accident is whether loss or damage actually occurs. The sequence of events is logical and can be predicted.

Lingard (1995) reports on how Adams (1976) elaborated the concept of managerial error and built this into a domino sequence. Adams renamed the immediate causes of an accident as tactical errors. Errors in employee behavior and work conditions arise from operational errors made by managers and supervisors. Such errors have their root cause in the organizational structure of the company. Adams' version of the domino theory is comprised of the following elements:

Management structures consist of the organization's objectives such as its goals, standards of performance and appraisal systems. The organization is defined by concepts such as chain of command, span of control, and decentralization of decision making. The final element of the management structure is the operational systems such as plant layout, provision of equipment, working procedures and the working environment.

The second domino in the sequence is operational areas. These include both management behavior and supervisor behavior. Under the heading of management behavior, the following areas are covered. Policy is a reflection of management's commitment to safety management. Typical examples of operational policy errors which may take place are unclear goal setting, failure to exercise authority and evasion of decision-making, the overlapping of jurisdictions, and inadequacies in job descriptions which may well lead to goal conflicts. Other errors relate to accountability such as the failure to appraise and measure results and an over-emphasis on short term outcomes. The final managerial error identified is inappropriate delegation to subordinates, which can mean either too little or too much responsibility being delegated.

Under the heading of supervisor behavior, administrative errors and omissions are identified. A key issue for supervisors is their conduct, the ability to set a good example. Technical errors include not accepting responsibility, failing to exercise authority, failing to give clear instructions, making decisions beyond one's authority, failure to make and publicize rules, and inadequate enforcement of such rules. Fairness is a key issue here in terms of enforcement of rules and procedures and use of disciplinary measures. A further important area of supervisory responsibility is coaching of subordinates. The supervisor should explain why things have to be done in a particular manner and also listen to subordinates' comments on work methods. Omissions and bad practices should be corrected and new or unusual situations identified for the novice worker. A supervisor should also deal with morale issues and needs to keep a close eye on operations; placing people in appropriate jobs, ensuring good housekeeping, maintaining realistic work flows and pace of work are all issues which need to be addressed if errors are not to be avoided.

The final three dominos in Adams' sequence are very similar to those proposed by Heinrich and Bird. These dominos are tactical errors, such as unsafe acts or conditions, the accident itself, and the resulting injury or damage.

Another approach that adds to the previously presented causal models is the concept of multi-causality. Peterson (1971) queried the basis of the domino theories. He asked the question, when an act or condition that caused an accident is identified, how many other causes are overlooked? Hence, his view is that many causes may come together to cause an accident. Peterson used the example of a man falling from a defective step ladder to illustrate his point. Under the domino theory one act or condition would be identified as the underlying cause of the accident:

The unsafe act is climbing a defective ladder;

The unsafe condition is the defective ladder;

The corrective action is to remove the defective ladder from use.

However, if one was to view the accident from a multiple causality viewpoint then the contributing factors to the accident could be probed by asking questions such as:

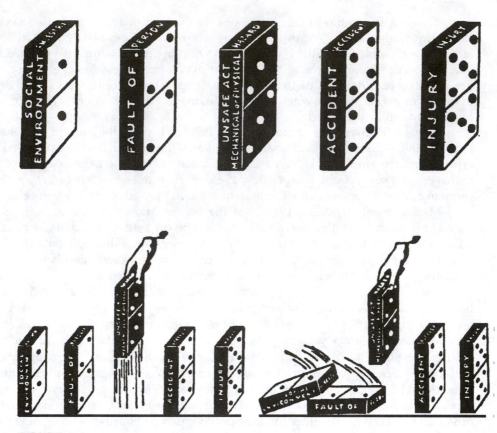

FIGURE 4–1
A theory of accident causation from Heinrich and Bird's work.

Source: Petersen (1984)

Why was the defective ladder not identified during inspections?

Why did the supervisor allow the ladder to be used?

Why did the employee use the ladder when he should have known that it was defective?

Had the employee been properly trained?

Did anybody consider the safety infrastructure required when assigning this task?

Answering the questions above might lead to the following actions:

Improvements in inspection procedures;

Improved training courses;

A review of supervisors' responsibilities and roles.

The underlying principles which can gleaned from this brief review of accident causation models is that most accidents occur due to a sequence of events and the underlying root causes of accidents may well be multiple. Hence, one must identify these root causes during accident investigation, not just the unsafe acts or conditions which are the symptoms of a problem. Such a philosophy has led to the adoption of an epidemiological approach to accident analysis (see Lingard 1992).

TRENDS IN ACCIDENT CAUSATION—AN EXAMPLE

The following section reports on an ongoing study of accident causation undertaken for the housing authority in Hong Kong (Rowlinson *et al.*, 1996). The lessons learned from this have some general applicability, particularly for construction in densely populated urban environments.

Occupation

Using frequency of accident occurrence as a measure, the following trades were found to be the most accident prone:

Trade	% of total
Carpenter/formworker	19%
Laborer	19%
Steel bender/fixer	17%
Painter/plasterer	8%
Caisson worker	6%
Drain layer	5%
Scaffolding worker	4%

When analyzing these results and taking into account the types of accidents it was apparent that painters, plasterers, and scaffolding workers were, as one might expect, particularly susceptible to falls from height. Caisson workers, those who dig by hand piles of diameter 600 millimeters and more, and drain layers were particularly likely to slip and trip on objects at the same level. Only 17% of accidents to all trades were classified as struck against stationary objects but 36% of accidents to drain layers were of this nature. It is important to be aware of these trends and communicate them to workers so that safety improvement measures can be targetted effectively.

Figs. 4–2, 4–3, and 4–4 show the type of accidents which occur to carpenters, steel fixers, and general laborers. Carpenters and steelfixers—ironworkers—suffer a high portion of accidents involving slipping or tripping at the same level. These workers tend to work on wooden boards or metal plates which are covered with both release agents and steel bars so this is not surprising. Tripping in such circumstances is inevitable. One might then consider why these workers are forced to work in such a manner. It is, of course, possible to prefabricate steel reinforcing cages and drop them into position. Such an approach may help considerably in reducing the number of tripping accidents. Carpenters and the laborers are also susceptible to being struck by falling objects; this is one of the most dangerous accident types. Laborers and carpenters also suffer from hand tool injuries and striking against fixed object accidents. The former probably reflects a lack of a proper training in the use of tools and the latter is probably due to the state of housekeeping in the work area. Machinery operation accidents account for 13% of steel fixer accidents, research by Lingard and Rowlinson has indicated that the nature of the bar bending machines used is a particular hazard on Hong Kong construction sites.

In discussing manual handling accidents Lingard (in Lingard & Rowlinson 1994) states:

Both steelbenders and caisson workers suffered a disproportionate number of injuries to the spine. Only 9% of injuries to all occupational groupings were spinal but 20% of injuries to caisson workers

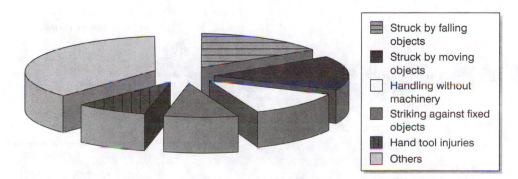

Struck by falling objects

Struck by moving objects

Handling without machinery

Striking against fixed objects

Hand tool injuries

Others

FIGURE 4–2
General laborers—accident types

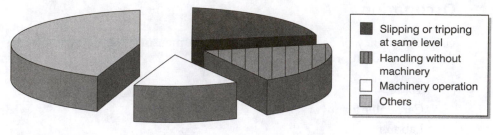

FIGURE 4–3
Carpenters—accident types

and 29% of injuries to steelbenders/fixers were to the spine. Both caisson workers and steelfixers have to lift and manipulate heavy loads in confined spaces and are rarely provided with mechanical help in these operations. 20% of injuries to caisson workers were to the head while only 12% of injuries to all occupational groupings were head injuries. This is probably a function of the very confined space at the bottom of the hole in which caisson workers work. Scaffolding workers are particularly susceptible to trunk injuries, 27% as compared with 12% for all occupational groupings. The fact that they have to balance precariously and lift long lengths of bamboo pole probably causes this. Interestingly, scaffolding workers also suffer a disproportionate number of hand injuries, 55% as compared to 22% for all occupations, again associated with the lifting and manoeuvring of heavy poles. 29% of injuries to painters/plasterers were to the leg while only 15% of injuries to all occupational groupings were leg injuries. Drainlayers were commonly affected by foot injuries, 28% as compared with 14% for all occupational groupings; this is almost certainly due to heavy pipes falling on their feet and the wearing of inappropriate footwear.

Time of Day

There is a pronounced peak in accident occurrence between the hours of 10 A.M. and 11 A.M. During this time 24% of all accidents occur. Later in the day two smaller peaks occur between 2 P.M. and 3 P.M. and between 4 P.M. and 5 P.M. Hinze (1997:32) confirms this and indicates that these peaks are likely to represents the times at which peak work load is being undertaken. Hinze is of the opinion that these peaks are not to do with fatigue but with workload being undertaken.

Agent Involved

The agents most commonly involved in construction injuries are shown in Figure 4–5. The majority of accidents involving unpowered hand tools were to the hands (62%). Forty-six percent of accidents involving portable power-driven hand-tools were also to the hands but it is worth noting that another 17% of these accidents were also to the feet. Stored materials mainly damaged the legs (29%), the feet (26%), and the trunk (21%). The high incidence of foot and leg injuries associated with stored materials suggests that the problem here is walking into materi-

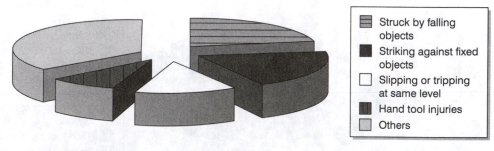

FIGURE 4–4
Steelfixers (ironworkers)—accident types

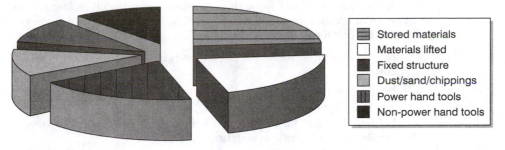

FIGURE 4–5
Agent involved in accident.

als and that better housekeeping may help to solve the problem. Not surprisingly, injuries involving dust/sand/chippings most commonly affected the eye (29%), reflecting lack of use of PPE, and injuries involving materials being lifted most commonly affected the spine (36%), reflecting inappropriate manual handling procedures. Carpenters and formworkers also suffered the largest proportion (71%) of accidents involving unpowered hand tools. Accidents involving portable power-driven hand tools affected a number of different trades.

These were as follows:

Caisson workers	26%
Steelbenders/fixers	21%
Carpenters/formworkers	26%
Laborers	21%

Stored materials accidents most commonly occurred to steelbenders/fixers, carpenters/formworkers and laborers (27% each). Laborers were found to suffer most of the accidents involving dust, sand, and chippings (33%). Thirty-three percent of accidents involving materials being lifted occurred to steelbenders/fixers.

The following observations on manual handling accidents and hand tool injuries were made at the Rinker School in 1994 by Lingard (in Lingard & Rowlinson 1994) and bear repetition here.

Manual Handling Accidents

Sixteen percent of all accidents reported were of the manual lifting type. In 80% of these cases it was reported that the victim had undergone no training. Stubbs and Nicholson (1979) found that manual handling accidents, back injuries and back injures attributed to manual handling accidents all occurred more frequently to younger workers. Analysis of data in the Housing Authority sample showed that few workers younger than 30 suffered manual lifting accidents and the age group most commonly affected by manual lifting accidents is 45-50 as opposed to 40-45 for all accidents. This suggests, contrary to the finding of Stubbs and Nicholson, that older workers may tend to be more susceptible to manual lifting accidents. Owing to the small sample size, the effect of age on manual lifting accidents cannot be determined with any degree of certainty. It is probably likely that manual lifting accidents have less to do with age than with other factors such as the use of incorrect lifting methods or poor work design. These are the factors on which management should focus since these factors could be controlled more easily and effectively.

Steelbenders/fixers suffer a disproportionately high number of manual lifting accidents. A subsequent analysis showed that most of these manual lifting accidents resulted in sprains or strains (82%) and that a large proportion of resulting injuries were to the spine (59%). These high proportions are reflected in the general manual handling statistics presented by the U.K.'s Health and Safety Executive in their booklet entitled Manual Handling (H.S.E. 1992) H.S.E. figures show that 65% of manual handling accidents resulted in sprains or strains and 45% of the manual handling injuries reported were to the back. As would be expected, many of the accidents to steelbenders/fixers occurred at the steelbending yard but the majority (53%) occurred at other locations on site.

It has been noted in Europe that those performing steelbending and fixing jobs place a great deal of strain on their backs (Wickstrom *et al.*, 1985) and are more susceptible to sciatic back pain than, say, are painters. They describe the tasks required of a steel reinforcement worker as follows:

cutting (the disentanglement of steel rods from stacks, pulling rods to cutting machines and cutting);

bending (bending the rods with electrical or manual machines, tying bent rods up in bundles, carrying the rods to intermediary storage);

binding (bringing the cut and bent rods from intermediary storage, putting the rods in places, binding the rods together with iron thread).

They directly observed the requirements of steel reinforcement work and painting work in terms of posture, lifting of loads, and carrying of loads. The results showed that a double bent posture was much more common in reinforcement workers than painters. Likewise, reinforcement workers subjected their back muscles to a static load much more often than painters. Reinforcement workers were found to do a great deal more lifting than painters. Weights over 20 kg were lifted five times an hour by the reinforcement workers compared with less than once every two hours by painters. In reinforcement work many lifts were made from hip to hip level (43%) but 39% were from toe to hip level. In painting 76% of lifts were from hip to hip level and only 10% were from toe to hip level. Lifting and carrying was much more common for reinforcement workers than painters and reinforcement workers were much more likely to work on a poor work surface than were painters. In terms of the occurrence of both minor injuries and registered occupational accidents, reinforcement workers were found to suffer more back problems than painters.

The Manual Handling Operations Regulations came into force in the U.K. in January 1993. These regulations emphasize an ergonomic approach to manual handling and a hierarchy of measures is laid down as follows:

(a)   avoid hazardous manual lifting operations so far as is reasonably practicable—this may be done by redesigning the task to avoid moving the load or by automating or mechanizing the process;

(b)   make a suitable and sufficient assessment of any hazardous manual handling operations that cannot be avoided; and

(c)   reduce the risk of injury from those operations so far as is reasonably practicable—particular consideration should be given to the provision of mechanical assistance but where this is not reasonably practicable then other improvements to the task, the load and the working environment should be explored. (H.S.E. 1992)

Although the regulations do not apply in Hong Kong, it would be prudent to heed the advice given by the H.S.E. and conduct a thorough assessment of the risks posed by manual handling to steelbenders/fixers working in Hong Kong's construction industry. This should include a detailed assessment of the risks associated with loads lifted or carried by steelbenders/fixers and a consideration of the working environment and job layout. Potential for mechanization and off-site prefabrication should be considered.

Hand Tool Injuries

Most non-power-driven hand tool accidents and portable power-driven hand tool accidents result in abrasions (87% and 75% respectively). An overwhelming proportion of non-power-driven hand tools injuries occur to carpenters/formworkers (70%). Carpenters and formworkers also suffer 26% of all accidents involving portable power-driven hand tools. It does not appear that a lack of experience was associated with either type of hand tool injuries. The largest proportion of non-power-driven hand tool accidents occurred to workers with between seven and twelve years of experience in their occupation. These figures indicate that bad habits, irrespective of experience, may be a factor associated with these accidents. It was reported that 68% of workers injured using non power-driven hand tools were untrained and 81% of those injured using portable power-driven hand tools were untrained.

Accidents involving hand tools are not unique to Hong Kong. A Swedish study of construction accidents found that 18% of accidents involved hand-held machines or tools (Axelsson & Fang, 1985 (in Swedish) reported in Helander, 1991). The same study found that knives and hammers were the tools most commonly involved in accidents. Furthermore the majority of accidents involving knives and hammers were handling accidents implying that the worker was cut or hit. Myers and Trent (1988) found that construction was the industry with the second highest number of non-power-driven hand tool accidents (the first was agriculture) and construction accounted for more power-driven hand tool accidents than any other industry. Olsen and Gerberich (1986) reported the construction industry as having a higher rate of finger amputations than other industries.

Preventive measures to combat hand-tool accidents could include better training for those who use these tools. Training for carpenters/formworkers is of particular relevance since they are most commonly affected by hand-tool injuries. The use of personal protective equipment such as gloves may, in certain circumstances, prevent hand-tool injuries. Again, an ergonomic approach could be adopted to ensure that hand-held tools are designed with safety and comfort in mind.

Training and Accident Recurrence

Figures 4–6 and 4–7 are the most negative of all the statistics displayed here. Figure 4–6 indicates that only 50% of workers involved in accidents had received training of any sort whatsoever; this figure has increased from less than 20% in the past two years due to the introduction of the Green Card system on government and Housing Authority sites. Figure 4–7 indicates that there was almost a 50:50 chance of an accident recurring. This figure comes from the opinions of the persons responsible for reporting the accidents. If this figure is a reasonably true estimate of this probability then the situation in Hong Kong is very serious; it appears that an attitude of carelessness does prevail. Attention should be paid to training. A figure of only 50% of site staff who have been involved in an accident having received training is not acceptable. It is also unacceptable to allow a situation where there is an even chance of an accident recurring in the same manner. Both of these responses show that whatever safety management systems are in place are either inadequate or are not working and that there appear to be no champions in many companies who are pushing for safety improvements.

CHANGING ATTITUDES

It is not good enough to analyze accidents and report on the most commonly occurring accidents without doing something to improve the situation. In order to do this one has to change the attitudes of those involved in the industry; that means the attitudes of management, supervisory staff, and the site workers. It appears from the analysis above that many of the accidents occur because the workers, supervisors, and managers are unaware of the dangers that exist in particular work processes and certain areas of the site. Additionally, many workers appear to be inadequately trained. The combination of these two factors has led to a situation where careless actions and hazardous situations are allowed to exist unchecked. It is necessary to develop an attitude of carefulness among all levels of staff so that each understands that it is their responsibility to spot and remove hazards in the workplace. Safety has to become the responsibility of everyone on the construction site. This may well lead to conflicts—much construction work in Hong Kong is constructed under heavy time pressure. This is an issue that must be addressed by the clients of the industry who set the agenda for each project; they can no longer sit back and ignore their role in the safety management system—clients and consultants in Europe are now under strict obligations to manage safety from the very inception of a project.

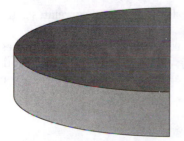
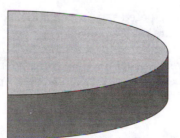

Yes
No

FIGURE 4–6
Training received by workers.

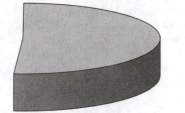

■ Unlikely
■ Fair chance
■ Likely

FIGURE 4–7
Chance of accident recurrence.

Behavioral Safety Management (BSM)

There are a number of methods that can be used to improve site safety. As far as the individual site is concerned, techniques aimed at behavior modification have been found to be effective. In 1993 the University of Hong Kong commenced a series of site based experiments into behavior modification. These were described by Lingard and Rowlinson (1995) as follows:

> Behavioral safety management comprises a range of techniques which seek to improve safety performance by setting goals, measuring performance, and providing performance feedback. It generally follows the pattern below:
>
>> behaviors or conditions which are critical to safety management are identified (e.g., access to heights)
>>
>> these behaviors are defined (in terms of good practice); performance in these specific items is audited (to identify a current baseline)
>>
>> behaviorally based performance goals in these items are then set (by workers, management or others)
>>
>> performance is again assessed (on a continuous basis)
>>
>> regular and continuing feedback is given to the subjects

If the techniques are successful, performance should improve (all things being equal). Goal setting as a motivational technique is based upon the premise that performance is closely related to goals which individuals set for themselves or accept from others. Goal setting theorists propose that an individual's goal or intention vis-à-vis a given task is the most immediate motivational determinant of an individual's choices and level of effort. Goals or intentions are defined as objectives which the individual has made a conscious decision to pursue. Locke, *et al.* (1970) suggest that an individual will be satisfied or dissatisfied with performance to the extent that performance matches the goals accepted by that individual. If performance does not meet a goal, dissatisfaction will occur and the individual will try to reduce his/her dissatisfaction by setting a further goal to improve performance by the necessary amount.

A review of goal setting research has shown that:

■ Anticipated satisfaction attached to a performance goal correlates significantly with future performance.
■ Percent of field experiments, lab experiments, and correlational studies supported the premise that the harder the goal (so long as it is accepted), the better the performance.
■ Specific, hard goals yield better performance results than easy, "do your best" goals of the general type.

Feedback

In addition to specific hard goals, individuals need feedback or knowledge of results to perform at a high level (see, for example, Locke, *et al.*, 1981). Feedback enables individuals to assess how much extra effort is required to attain a goal. Feedback may also serve to reinforce behaviors. If feedback shows an improvement in performance, an individual may find this improvement satisfying. The awareness that this improvement is being monitored and recognized by management may enhance this satisfaction and the performance feedback may act as a reward which elicits further improvement (Fellner & Sulzer, 1984)

Measurement

A key element of behavioral safety management is the provision of feedback on current performance. This demands the use of a reliable and accurate measurement system which can identify small deviations in performance as feedback.

Lingard & Rowlinson (1995) report on a system used in studies on Hong Kong Housing Authority sites, the proportional rating scheme (PRS) developed by Phillips (1992). This method is not a binary system; it does not use an all or nothing scoring system, such as the Hong Kong Housing Authority (HKHA, 1990) Performance Assessment Scoring System (PASS), which rates items as 100% safe or 100% unsafe. Rather, this system rates each item, or group of items, on a scale of 0-100%. Such a scheme counts the number of items observed in a category, e.g., working platforms, and then counts the number of complying and non-complying instances, e.g., working platforms with and without toe boards. Thus, under a PRS, if 20 working platforms were observed and 6 had no toe boards then this item within the access to heights category would score as 30% unsafe. All items in a category would be summed and the average level of safety recorded.

This system is very simple but easy to operate and has been found to produce good results as long as relevant items are chosen to make up each category. The advantage of this method is that it is sensitive to changes in each category, it is objective, and it is easy to implement in the construction environment which is regularly changing and has no set basis against which to assess performance.

The disadvantages of all or nothing performance assessment systems are:

- They are not sensitive to small or even medium size changes in performance.
- They are subject to large degrees of variance (and subjective judgment) which can lead to ceiling effects and a tendency to group scores as all very high or all very low.

Both of these effects lead to a shortage of data for use as constructive feedback.

In order to determine which categories of safety performance to assess, use was made of research undertaken by the Department of Surveying, HKU for the HKHA. The reason for this was three-fold:

1. The data supplied by the Labor Department was not detailed enough to be of use in identifying dangerous safety categories.
2. The standard housing blocks produced by HKHA gave the opportunity to develop a detailed, focused research base which pinpointed specific problem areas in construction safety.
3. The research could be conducted in a homogeneous, controlled environment.

An observer with safety training was employed to assess each site. The observer was instructed to investigate as much of the site as possible on each visit, including external areas and at least six floors above ground. Two visits per week were undertaken and site staff were not forewarned as to when a visit was due.

Goal Setting

Site goal setting meetings were conducted in the site offices and were attended by site safety officers, a number of workers, and, in some cases, members of the site management team. During the meetings, workers and site staff were shown slides depicting good and bad practices relating to the category of performance in which a goal was to be set. Those present were then introduced to the feedback chart on which the site's performance, in the category under discussion, for the eight weeks prior to the meeting was marked. Feedback charts measured 90 by 120 centimeters and were made from Perspex. Each chart was marked with a title in English and Chinese and had two axes. The y axis represented performance in percentage terms and the x axis represented 16 weeks.

Workers and site staff were then asked to suggest a realistic (i.e., attainable) goal to aim for in Housekeeping performance. Typically a discussion between workers and management ensued and eventually agreement as to a suitable goal was reached. Goal setting was intended to be participative since Cooper (1992) found that participative goal setting is more effective in bringing about improved safety performance. In the goal setting meetings, despite the fact that workers discussed the goal with management, the final decision was almost always made by the site project manager or senior management present.

Once the goal was set, it was explained that the goal would be marked on the chart in red and that at the end of each week, the observer would update the chart to show the site's weekly performance in relation to this goal. Actual performance was marked in black. After eight weeks of measurement and updating of the charts, the charts were removed from all sites.

Results

It was found that goal setting with feedback can be an effective tool for bringing about improved performance safety on Hong Kong sites, but only in certain circumstances. The success of the techniques when applied to the Housekeeping category was impressive but was in marked contrast to the mixed and disappointing results obtained in the Access to Heights and Bamboo Scaffolding categories. The reasons for this varied performance are explained below.

PREREQUISITES FOR BSM AND OTHER INITIATIVES TO BE EFFECTIVE

Management Commitment

Management commitment has been found to have a considerable impact on the effectiveness of behavioral safety management. It is possible that because site managers were not present at all goal setting meetings, workers did respond to goals set. They did not perceive that management were committed to the task. This is a central issue. If management is seen to be committed to improving safety performance, from the top down, then the message strikes home to workers and is acted upon at site level.

A Champion

In this context it is important that a champion within the company be identified. This person must be someone who has the respect of the management and workers and who has the the authority to push forward safety initiatives. This person must adopt a high profile in relation to safety, and probably other company issues as well. Such a champion serves to promote safety internally and to represent the organization and its achievements externally, thus bringing credibility to all within the organization in terms of safety performance. The role of the champion should not be neglected—it is one of the prerequisites for successful safety management.

Goal Difficulty

Housekeeping is a very different aspect of site safety than Access to Heights or Bamboo Scaffolding. Housekeeping is a highly visible aspect of safety to which everyone on site can make some contribution. Improvements can be made without the use of additional materials or equipment. On the other hand, Access to Heights and Bamboo Scaffolding items included in the measure would relate to only a few trades such as painters, plasterers, external finishing workers, and scaffolders. Workers in these trades would typically work for a subcontractor rather than for the main contractor, and improvements in these categories very often require that additional materials and equipment be deployed. Consequently, goal attainment in these categories is subject to constraints which are not in the power of individual workers to control. Thus the goal becomes too difficult for the worker to attain and so, following Vroom's expectancy theory of motivation (1964), workers will not be motivated to strive for improvement.

Bamboo scaffolding is typically erected by a specialist subcontractor and the extent to which this subcontractor will incorporate working platforms, guard rails, or toe boards into the scaffold will depend upon the specifications and cost agreed between the main contractor and the scaffolding subcontractor. Unlike Housekeeping, improvements in Bamboo Scaffolding cannot be made by every person on the site. Furthermore, the extent to which a safe scaffold is provided for use is pre-determined by an agreement, often verbal, between the main contractor and scaffolding firm. Under these circumstances, it is not within the control of the majority of operatives on site to make improvements in this area (Lingard & Rowlinson 1997). The lack of a safety infrastructure, both at the hard—equipment—level and the soft—management—level was an obvious impediment to the success of BSM in this setting.

Safety Infrastructure

Under these circumstances behavioral safety techniques could not be expected to effectively bring about improved performance. Behavioral safety techniques are effective as a result of their ability to motivate workers to make changes to the way in which they carry out their work. However, in order for workers to be in a position to behave safely, they must first be provided with adequate resources, ample time to carry out work in a safe manner, training, a safe working environment, and a safe system of work. These prerequisites require an appropriate safety infrastructure to be in place within an organization before the techniques are introduced. In the absence of such an infrastructure, it is likely that motivational techniques such as behavioral safety management will not succeed.

Goal Setting and Expectancy Theory

Housekeeping represents an area of safety performance in which improvements can be made relatively easily. The expectancy that increased effort will lead to improved performance and a specified outcome, i.e., goal attainment, is high. The value associated with goal attainment must also be reasonably high and, under Vroom's expectancy theory of motivation (1964), the goal would be accepted and workers would be sufficiently motivated to attain the goal.

On the other hand, organizational constraints, such as inadequate resourcing, time pressure, and reward systems, may impose upon workers an inability to perform work safely in the areas of access to heights or bamboo scaffolding. Hence, workers perceive that it is not in their power to improve their performance through increased effort and goal attainment would therefore not be achieved if they did try harder. This perception may lead workers to reject the goal. Enhanced commitment to work safely would not occur.

Organizational Structures

The construction industry can be described as an industry exhibiting an organic organizational form. By this it is implied that the nature of relationships on the project site vary from time to time and as circumstances dictate and that decision-making is decentralized. In such situations workers are expected to rely on their own initiative in constantly changing circumstances. Behavioral safety management techniques have been found to be effective in organizations which are mechanistic in nature; that is they are heavily structured and ordered and the nature of the tasks being undertaken is clearly defined and the roles and responsibilities of workers change little. In such circumstances it is not surprising that BSM techniques have not per-formed well on the construction sites in Hong Kong.

Reward Structures

How workers and supervisors are rewarded is also an important variable when considering the use of BSM techniques. Commonly, construction workers are paid on a piece rate basis. Often, workers are rewarded for completing work as quickly as possible, and this tends to focus atten-tion on speed and productivity rather than safety issues. In the absence of adequate supervi-sion, discussed briefly later, and an appropriate reward system for safe working, it is highly likely that the monetary reward factor will outweigh any initiatives brought into play by BSM techniques.

Hazard Perception and Recognition

A major problem with improving site safety is the degree to which workers perceive that haz-ards exist and recognize the need to avoid them. A safety management system cannot be suc-cessful if workers continually ignore hazards. This "ignoring" may come about not through a deliberate act but through the lack of perception that a situation is risky. This easily occurs in construction where bad practices have been perpetuated through lack of formal training and informal apprenticeships. This is an issue which Lingard (1995) discusses in some detail.

Consistency

It is important that a degree of consistency exist in relation to safety management. This consis-tency must take place at two levels.

Policy
At the policy level it must be ensured that policies are maintained throughout an extended period of time with emphasis on continual improvement, akin to what happens in quality management systems. Hence, a well-defined safety policy must be rapidly established and be seen to be implemented.

Staffing
This policy cannot be properly implemented without the cooperation of management and workers. Hence, it is essential that key safety personnel are kept on staff and are visible on the construction site over a long period of time. If workers recognize that particular individuals have responsibility for safety, and these individuals ensure that safety standards are main-tained, then the workers will get into the habit of performing safely. Hence, the consistency in terms of policy implementation and in terms of those who are seen to implement policy rein-forces the safety management systems in place.

Usefulness of Behavioral Techniques

Lingard and Rowlinson, 1997, report that:

> Behavioral safety management techniques were found not to be universally effective when applied to the Hong Kong building construction industry and their role in the overall management of health & safety in the construction industry should not be over-emphasised. Employers' responsi-bilities for providing adequate resources to ensure that construction work can be carried out with-out risk to health or safety of operatives must be stressed. Unless construction employers accept this responsibility and, in tendering for work, realistically account for the costs associated with ensuring that the workplace and systems of work adopted are safe do not present a hazard then motivational techniques such as the behavioral approach to safety management will not be highly effective.

ASSURING SAFE PERFORMANCE

Safety Assurance, like quality assurance and environmental management, is an issue that each contractor and worker must address for themselves. Safety systems can be put in place, safety training can be provided, tool box talks can be conducted, and safety manuals produced, but none of these can be effective unless they are implemented properly and wholeheartedly by all levels of site staff. Safety can only be assured by committed leadership on site and at the head office in parallel with an adequate safety management infrastructure.

Supervision

The role of the supervisors is extremely important in ensuring safe construction. The supervisor is the link between site worker and management and the supervisor is fully aware of site conditions as they change from day to day. The supervisor is also aware of the strengths and weaknesses of each individual worker and is thus in the best position to both spot hazards and to coach workers. Therefore, it is vitally important that supervisory level staff are thoroughly trained in all safety issues if they are to fulfill their role of assuring safety.

Research undertaken by Rowlinson and Lam (1999) came up with the following findings from a survey. Sixty-nine supervisors from 13 construction companies were invited to answer a questionnaire designed to investigate supervisors' opinions regarding 27 safety supervisory tasks in six categories, including handling new workers, training, safety, discipline, coordinating, and motivating, in the construction industry in Hong Kong. The survey showed that while only 67% of supervisors claimed that they had the responsibility to perform these tasks only 53% of supervisors said that they had the authority to perform these tasks. It was concluded that supervisors play a key role in ensuring safety management systems operate effectively but it appears from the results of this study that this role is not being performed adequately in Hong Kong. One of the reasons for this appeared to be that supervisors' performance in accomplishing safety tasks was not monitored by management. This implied a lack of leadership in safety management and the inability to develop a safety culture throughout the company.

Responsibility for Safety

The responsibility for safety is a key area that has been addressed by governments around the world over the past decade. The European Union has taken the lead in this issue by making safety the responsibility of all involved in the construction process, from inception to realization. Clients, designers and contractors (and subcontractors) all have responsibility for construction site safety. This holistic approach to the issue of site safety forces all involved in the construction process to make themselves aware of the risks involved in construction and to prepare plans of action in order to mitigate the effects of these risks.

The European system places the following legal duties on clients:

- A safety planning coordinator must be appointed as soon as the decision to proceed with a project is taken.
- A competent principal contractor must be appointed as soon as possible.
- Pre-tender and construction phase safety plans must be required.
- Competent designers must be appointed who will take into account safety in not only the construction process but also the repair and maintenance of the finished structure.
- The client must ensure that those appointed allocate sufficient resources to undertake their tasks.
- The client may refuse payment in the event of safety plans not being followed.
- The client must give all necessary safety information to its contractors and consultants.
- A project safety and health file must be prepared and this must remain in existence throughout the life of the structure, no matter who the future owner may be.

The designers, which include surveyors, engineers, architects, planners, etc., also have a series of responsibilities under the European regulations:

- Consideration must be given to the construction methods, maintenance, and repair of any structure being designed.
- Clients must be advised of their duties under the regulations.
- The safety planning coordinator must be assisted in his role of complying with the regulations and he must be provided with all necessary information.

Those contractors on site which are not the principal contractor also have a series of defined responsibilities:

- They must cooperate with the principal contractor.
- They must comply with the principal contractor's directions on safety.
- They thus provide all necessary reports concerning site safety to the principal contractor.
- They must ensure proper safety management of their own employees.
- They must comply with and allocate adequate resources to the project safety plan.

Such an approach to safety management is all encompassing and shares the responsibility for construction site safety among all those involved in the construction process, not just placing it on the principal contractor. One of the advantages of such a system is that it draws subcontractors into the sphere of responsibility for safety plan implementation. The nature of the industry could be changed for the better by the contractor being able to exercise much greater influence over how the subcontractors employed on its site approach safety issues.

This approach been may well prove successful if applied in an atmosphere of self-regulation, that is where all those involved in the construction process voluntarily take an interest in developing a culture of safety throughout the whole of the development process. This obviously requires a change in attitude among all of those involved in construction projects, but by bringing safety to the forefront at the outset of a project, it is more likely that safety will be properly and carefully considered. However, small subcontractors do face problems in developing and implementing safety management systems. In such circumstances, partnering may well prove effective.

Partnering and Safety Management

Partnering has proved successful in a commercial context. Can it assist in applying safety legislation, rules, and management systems to a construction project? Partnering advocates an open and trusting relationship between all parties—can this philosophy be used to assist the management of site safety?

Implementing the partnering concept in the construction project environment provides an opportunity for the continuous improvement of safety performance. Drawing from an example of partnering in the United Kingdom, Matthews and Rowlinson (1999) identify a number of characteristics of partnering agreements which can assist in promoting safety. These characteristics are continuous evaluation, the project charter, mutual objectives, and team building.

The global trend to move away from prescriptive legislation toward performance-based legislation in the regulation of safety provides an ideal opportunity to adopt partnering as a methodology for safety improvement. Such an approach may help restructure the current subcontractor/main contractor relationship that is in part responsible for poor quality and low safety levels on construction sites. The partnering approach provides the opportunity for the smaller subcontractors with inadequate resources to develop their own safety management systems, to engage in organizational learning from main contractors with the goal of implementing their own safety management systems.

An example of successful partnering, at the industry rather than company level, is the Hong Kong Government Works Bureau Pay for Safety Scheme—discussed later. In 1996 the

Hong Kong Government conducted discussions with the Hong Kong Construction Association that eventually resulted in the implementation of a pay for safety scheme for Hong Kong Government Works Bureau projects. The aim of this scheme was to remove site safety from the pressure of competitive bidding and to attempt to reward those contractors that comply with safety requirements while punishing those which do not.

INDUSTRY LEVEL ISSUES

The following issues are broad-ranging factors that affect the industry as a whole and need to be dealt with at an industry level if a general improvement in safety performance is to be seen.

The Competitive Tendering System

The competitive tendering system has always posed problems for the construction industry; on the one hand it ensures value for money to the client, but on the other hand it is the enemy of good quality construction and safe construction. It is essential that criteria other than cost are used in the assessment of contractors if the vicious cycle of the lowest price competitive tendering system is to be broken. This requires a move on the part of clients to consider their selection processes carefully and incorporate factors into them such as past safety performance, safety management system adequacy, and commitment to partnering with smaller contractors.

Hong Kong Government Works Branch "Pay for Safety" Scheme

In 1996 the Hong Kong Government implemented a pay for safety scheme, with the collaboration of the Construction Association, for Hong Kong Government Works Branch projects. The aim of this scheme was to remove site safety from the pressure of competitive bidding and to attempt to reward those contractors that complied with safety requirements while punishing those that do not. Again, as Berry stated at an October 1996 meeting of the Lighthouse Club:

> Hong Kong Construction Association gave its support to the removal of site safety from competitive tendering by means of paying for safety properly carried out, based on an agreed schedule of items and prices. Their view was underlined by a report they had commissioned from Hong Kong University which had noted "research has shown that where safety costs are included in a tender and are accepted by the client the frequency rate of time-lost accidents for major construction projects is decreased considerably."

This was done by including a fixed sum in the bill of quantities for safety-related elements such as personal protective equipment, temporary works, site meetings, and safety committees. These items would then be paid for in interim valuations when these items had been audited. The aim was to set a fixed sum aside in every contract payment for the provision of a minimum level of site safety infrastructure on each Works Branch project. This scheme was piloted successfully in 1994 and, as a means of regulating the scheme, the Occupational Safety and Health Council introduced an Independent Safety Audit Scheme.

Induction Systems—The "Green Card" Scheme

A recent initiative in Hong Kong, an example of industry level partnering, has seen the introduction of a green card system whereby workers new to a site must be able to produce a green card certifying that they have been on a safety induction course. If a worker is unable to produce a green card, he or she will be unable to work on a construction site. The first green card system in Hong Kong was set up as a Hong Kong Construction Association initiative in partnership with the Hong Kong Housing Authority and the Government Works Bureau. Having identified that recent arrivals on site were more likely to be involved in accidents (Rowlinson &

Lingard 1995), an induction scheme was formulated that aimed at building a basic safety awareness in workers before they actually set foot on site. The course was specified by the Hong Kong Housing Authority and lasted for one half day, at which point the worker received his green card. While supportive of the initiative, both the Hong Kong Housing Authority and Works Bureau felt that the induction course was too short and needed to be extended to cover all the basics of site safety. So, together with the Construction Industry Training Authority (CITA), a more extensive course was devised, lasting two days, in which workers were taught by the independent CITA and were expected to prove that they had learned from the course before being issued a green card. This card would be a mandatory prerequisite for entry to and work on any Hong Kong Housing Authority and Works Bureau site.

Education and Training

A key problem faced by the industry in Hong Kong is the emphasis on monetary reward to the neglect of proper safety and work attitudes. The culture of safety does not exist naturally on Hong Kong construction sites, and this is an aspect that must be nurtured if safety is to improve. Rowlinson & Lam's study (1999), has highlighted the need for better training and education at all levels within the industry.

EFFECTIVENESS IN SAFETY MANAGEMENT

Safety management systems are a combination of all of the subsystems of multi-organizations and as such are complex managerial problems. The model below (Figure 4–8) attempts to draw together some of the key management and interpersonal system variables in a way that illustrates their strong interdependence. The core of the model is leadership, motivation, and commitment. However, all of these variables are affected by the organization's structure, the organization culture, the prevailing national cultures, and the environment of the project. Hence, what is being presented here is a complex conceptual model of the way that a safety management system works; at the project and the company level the systems are very similar. This model is a simple conceptual model and is capable of being expanded at a number of levels for any of the variables shown in it. The essence of the model is that safety management systems are complex organizational issues and past attempts to model safety management systems by simple sequential management processes have been too impatient of the system complexity. There is no simple solution to the design of safety management systems, but there are a whole series of key variables which need to be addressed.

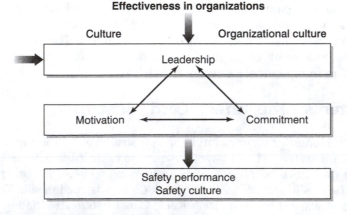

FIGURE 4–8
Effectiveness in safety management.

Thus any safety performance factors that have been identified need also to be reviewed in the light of environmental circumstances within which the system operates. The framework within which this review should take place is the classical systems theory framework of political environment, economic environment, environmental issues, socio-technical system (including culture), organizational system, and structural system.

If the key issues of leadership, motivation, and commitment are properly dealt with, then, given an appropriate organizational culture, a culture of carefulness and safety, and if the cultural traits of the workers are sympathetically dealt with, then the basis exists for a well thought out safety mangement system to work successfully. Hence, the safety management system provides the essential safety infrastructure within which organizational effectiveness can be achieved.

CONCLUSION

For safety initiatives to be successful there are a number of prerequisites required at both the company level and the industry level. At the industry level certain leading clients must take the initiative in demanding safe construction sites. Traditionally, this responsibility has fallen on the public sector. However, examples do exist of good performance being demanded by private sector clients, China Light and Power being only one example of this. Over the past decade the Hong Kong Housing Authority has led the way in demanding safe construction in the public sector. The initiative has been taken up by Works Branch and the Airport Core Program.

At the company level, site safety needs a champion; in many instances this champion is the managing director of the construction company. If top level management commitment does not exist, then a proper safety management system stands no chance of being implemented. On the contrary, it is likely that a piecemeal approach to site safety will meet with no success whatsoever.

The current direction given by government in Hong Kong is to move in the direction of self-regulation for site safety. If self-regulation is to work, then it is necessary to provide incentives for the employing organizations. The Hong Kong government Works Branch have made some progress in this direction by linking tendering opportunities to site safety performance. This approach can only work if a level playing field is provided. In order to do this, techniques such as site safety auditing by independent organizations must be introduced as part of the contract package. A note of caution is necessary; however, self-regulation is much more easily implemented in mechanistic organizations than organic organizations, as often evidenced in construction projects.

In the past, site safety has been dealt with in a piecemeal fashion, and the results of such an approach are clear to see in the site accident statistics. Only when a rational, comprehensive site safety system is implemented by both contractors and clients alike will a significant improvement in site safety performance be seen.

In essence, there are a number of issues that need to be addressed, which I have termed "The Seven S's."

- Safety Culture
- Source of Labor (importation)
- Skill and Perceptions
- Supervision
- Safety Infrastructure
- Subcontracting
- Self-Regulation

ACKNOWLEDGMENTS

The author acknowledges the financial support of the Research Grants Committee of the Hong Kong University Grants Council and the Occupational Safety and Health Council for parts of the research reported here. Also, the Hong Kong Housing Authority for allowing publication of the results of their Site Safety Studies. Specifically, Dr. Helen Lingard for her work in the realization of many of the studies reported here and her permission to cite her work in this chapter.

REFERENCES

Adams, E. 1976. "Accident Causation and the Management System," *Professional Safety*.

Bird, F. 1974. *Management Guide to Loss Control*, Institute Press, Atlanta.

Cooper, M. D. 1992. "An Examination of Assigned and Participative Goal Setting in Relation to the Improvement of Safety on Construction Sites," Ph.D. Thesis, School of Management, U.M.I.S.T., U.K.

Fayol, H. 1949. *General and Industrial Management*, Pitman, London (translated from the original Administration Industrielle et Generale, 1916, by Constance Storrs).

Fellner, J. and Sulzer-Azaroff, B. 1984. "A Behavioral Analysis of Goal Setting," *Journal of Organizational Behavior Management*, pp. 33–51.

Heinrich, H. W., Peterson, D., and Roos, N. 1980. *Industrial Accident Prevention*, McGraw-Hill Book Company, New York.

Helander, M. G. 1991. "Safety Hazards and Motivation for Safe Work in the Construction Industry," *International Journal of Industrial Ergonomics*, Vol. 8, pp. 205–223.

Hillebrandt, P., and Cannon, J. 1989. *The Modern Construction Firm*, Macmillan, London, pp. 121 & 124.

Hinze, J. W. 1997. *Construction Safety*, Prentice-Hall, New Jersey.

Hong Kong Government, Education and Manpower Branch, July 1995, *Consultation Paper on the Review of Industrial Safety in Hong Kong*, Hong Kong.

Hong Kong Housing Authority. 1990. *Performance Assessment Scoring System Manual*, Hong Kong Housing Authority, Hong Kong.

Health and Safety Executive. 1992. *Manual Handling, Guidance on Manual Handling Operations Regulations*, HMSO, London.

Hong Kong Occupational Safety and Health Association. Nov/Dec, Vol. 12, No. 6, pp. 1–2.

Lam, Rheo. 1993. Written Submission to HKIE Working Group on Site Safety.

Lingard, H. C., and Rowlinson, S. 1994. "The Hong Kong Housing Authority Accident Information System: The First Sixteen Months," *Proceedings of Rinker Conference on Construction Site Safety*, University of Florida, Gainesville, November, pp. 79–87.

Lingard, H. C., and Rowlinson, S. 1998. "Behavior-based Safety Management in Hong Kong's Construction Industry: The Results of a Field Study," *Construction Management & Economics*, E&FN Spon, London, 16, p. 4.

Lingard, H. C., and Rowlinson, S. 1997. "Behavior-based Safety Management in Hong Kong's Construction Industry," *Journal of Safety Research*, Elsevier, 28, 4, pp. 243–256.

Lingard, H. C., and Rowlinson, S. 1995. "Behavior Modification: A New Approach to Improving Site Safety in Hong Kong," *Asia Pacific Building and Construction Management Journal*, Vol. 1, pp. 25–34.

Lingard, H. C. 1995. *Safety in Hong Kong's Construction Industry: Changing Worker Behavior*, Ph.D. Thesis, Department Of Surveying, The University of Hong Kong.

Lingard, H. C. 1992. "The Epidemiology of Accidents: The Hong Kong Housing Authority Approach," *Proceedings of ARCOM Conference*, Isle of Mann, September.

Locke, E. A., Cartledge N., and Knerr, C. S. 1970. "Studies of the Relationships Between Satisfaction, Goal Setting and Performance," *Organizational Behavior and Human Performance*, No. 5, pp. l35–158.

Locke, E. A., Shaw, K. N., Saan, L. M., and Latham, G. P. 1981. "Goal-setting and Task Performance: 1969-1980," *Psychological Bulletin*, No. 90, pp. 125–152.

Matthews, J., and Rowlinson S. 1999. "Partnering: Incorporating Safety Management," accepted by *Engineering, Construction and Architectural Management*, Blackwell Science: Oxford, U.K.

Myers, J. R., and Trent, R. B. 1988. "Hand Tool Injuries at Work: A Surveillance Perspective," *Journal of Safety Research*, No. 19, pp. 165–176.

Olsen, D. K., and Gerberich, S. G. 1986. "Traumatic Amputations in the Workplace," *Journal of Occupational Medicine*, No. 28, pp. 480–485.

Petersen, D. 1971. *Techniques of Safety Management*, McGraw-Hill, New York.

Phillips, R. A. 1992. *The Development of a Safety Performance Measure for the Construction Industry*, M.Sc. Thesis, Department of Building Engineering, University of Manchester Institute of Science and Technology, U.K.

Rowlinson, S., and Lam, S. W. 1999. "Hong Kong Construction Foremen's Opinions on their Safety Responsibilities," *Journal of IOSH*, London.

Rowlinson, S., and Lingard, H. C. 1995. *Hong Kong Housing Authority Report No. 9*, Department of Surveying, The University of Hong Kong.

Rowlinson, S., Reece, J., and Yeung, R. 1996. *Hong Kong Housing Authority Report No. 15*, Department of Surveying, The University of Hong Kong.

Rowlinson, S. *Hong Kong Construction—Site Safety Management*, Sweet & Maxwell, Hong Kong, August 1997, pp. 245 + xvii.

Stubbs, D. A., and Nicholson, A. S. 1979. "Manual Handling and Back Injuries in the Construction Industry: An Investigation," *Journal of Occupational Accidents*, No. 2, pp. 179–190.

Vroom, V. H. 1964. *Work and Motivation*, Wiley, New York.

Wickstrom, G., Niskanen, T., and Riihimaki, H. 1985. "Strain on the Back in Concrete Reinforcement Work," *British Journal of Industrial Medicine*, Vol. 42, pp. 233–239.

C H A P T E R

5

INNOVATIVE FALL PROTECTION FOR CONSTRUCTION WORKERS ON LOW-RISE ROOFS

Dr. Amarjit Singh, P.Eng., C.Eng.
Department of Civil Engineering
University of Hawaii at Manoa, Honolulu, Hawaii

ABSTRACT

This chapter presents results of two research studies sponsored by the Hawaii Occupational Safety and Health Division (HIOSH), and undertaken in the Hawaiian Islands. Falls are a major cause of accidents and injuries, with private, single-home dwellings being their primary source. The research methodology encompassed interviews, job site visits, and questionnaires circulated to construction managers and roofing workers. The level of compliance with HIOSH regulations was reported as being poor. There were also some major differences of viewpoints reported between workers and construction managers, such as with the prevalent fall protection devices used on sites, and the necessity of fall protection in general. The two groups also reported different needs for protection systems during truss installation and roof sheathing. Correlation analysis was undertaken to identify factors associated with the differences. The lack of communication and shared vision between workers and construction managers is a cause of considerable concern.

This research purported to determine the most suitable fall protection system, given the current state of the art and technology. It was decided that the variables of feasibility, simplicity, economy, flexibility, passivity, and protection need to be optimized. Eight fall protection systems were analyzed for optimization. The Multiple Attribute Decision-Making (MADM) method was used for the evaluation. Weights were assigned to the variables after consultation with workers, construction managers, and enforcement officials. The highest weights were given to simplicity, feasibility, and economy. The results revealed that no single method can be everything to everybody at all times, but prefabrication is the most promising method, followed closely by the Personal Fall Arrest System (PFAS) and its variants. Prefabrication systems are highly feasible, protective, and simple.

KEYWORDS

accidents, economy, HIOSH, injuries, PFAS, prefabrication, roofing, safety, work pressure

INTRODUCTION

Falls are currently the highest cause of injuries in the construction industry of Hawaii, and a large majority of these accidents occur during the construction of residential buildings. It is generally realized in Hawaii that large projects have skilled construction crews employed by large, well-experienced contractors. Small projects, such as residential construction, suffer from a general lack of supervision, with construction often being undertaken by the small sole proprietor who does not utilize adequate safety practices.

    The problem of implementing proper safety practice in Hawaii is compounded by a general difficulty in using Personal Fall Arrest Systems (PFAS), an inclination to avoid usage if enforcement is lax, the insufficiency of any particular fall protection method, and a general lack of education. Correspondingly, it is understood among enforcement officials, such as the Hawaii Occupational Safety and Health Division (HIOSH), that the current construction practices regarding safety can be greatly improved. Consequently, HIOSH commissioned a research team to investigate the issues surrounding the problem and to recommend possible solutions for simplifying the management of fall protection.

OBJECTIVES OF STUDY

The information presented here relates to a research report by Johnson and Singh (1997) submitted to HIOSH. The objectives of the research were as follows:

1. To determine the state of safety compliance and the standards of practice regarding safety.
2. To determine the opinions of construction personnel on various fall protection topics.
3. To identify suitable fall protection systems for use on residential construction sites.

FALL STATISTICS

National Construction Industry Statistics

Falls are the leading cause of accidents in the construction industry. In 1994 and 1995, falls accounted for one-third of the fatal injuries to construction workers. Over 300 workers fall to their death every year. One-fifth of these falls occur from roofs, and most of these are incurred by roofers and framers ("National" 1995; "National" 1996). In 1993, 42,000 disabling falls were reported in the construction industry, amounting to 1% of all construction workers that year. Each of those falls required an average of 14 days recuperation. This is more than twice the recuperation time for falls sustained in other industries ("New" 1996).

National Residential Construction Fall Statistics

Thirty-three percent (33%) of all occupational fatalities in the nationwide residential building industry occur as a result of falls. In 1994, 27 workers died from falls. Falls are the leading cause of death for both carpenters and roofers, accounting for 52% and 72% of the fatalities, respectively (Toscano *et al.*, 1996).

Hawaii Residential Construction Fall Statistics

Of the 41 falls reported in 1995 for residential construction alone, there was one death and 24 falls involving temporary total disability. The total lost time was 1,597 days, an average of 67 days per fall, compared to the 1994 national construction industry average of 14 days per fall ("Custom" 1997a).

Maui Statistics

On the island of Maui alone, there were a *total* of 1,477 fall cases processed in 1996 and 1,584 cases in 1995, for all industry segments. It is generally believed that the culture and devices used for fall protection on residential building roofs are the same as used for other projects, such as steel erection and high-rise building construction. Generally, it is the same workers, and often the same contractors, who move from project to project but neglect to use proper fall protection no matter which type of project they work on. In the 1990s there were three fatalities reported in Maui ("Workers'" 1990-96; Baker and Singh 1998).

HIOSH statistics

HIOSH records indicate that 20 residential inspections resulted in fall protection citations for the two year period, 1995-97 ("Custom" 1997b). An unknown number of cases were contested by contractors and not prosecuted for unknown reasons. A majority of the relevant cases cited were assessed for "walking the top plate" unprotected during truss installation. (The "top plate" is the 50 mm x 100 mm flat member on top of the frame wall, on which the roof truss is erected. The conventional method of installing the trusses is for workers to balance themselves on this top plate while moving the trusses into place for bracing. This practice offers no protection to workers and is of significant concern to HIOSH.)

Economic Impacts

The total cost of all lost-time falls in Hawaii in 1995 was $341,395 ("Custom" 1997a). The total fines issued in FY96 totaled $50,752. These figures do not include the additional millions of dollars associated with increased Workers' Compensation premiums.

BACKGROUND AND LITERATURE REVIEW

Safety in low-rise building construction is a concern in every country. Injuries also are of the same nature whether a worker falls off during construction of a grass-thatched roof or a more solid clay tile roof. Safety precautions during building work of some countries, such as Hong Kong, are very poor (Rowlinson, 1996). In the experience of the author, accident prevention planning is missing from most developing countries, such as on the Indian subcontinent, and, where used, is often incomplete. Coble *et al.* (1997) have outlined methods to use in mitigating fall protection, such as use of slide guards, guardrails, scaffoldings, and good housekeeping. However, it is observed that injury statistics for falls are at an unacceptable level even in the United States, where considerable emphasis is placed on zero accidents ("Injuries," 1984; "New," 1996; "Improving," 1987; "Zero," 1993). For instance, in 1990, The National Institute for Occupational Safety and Health (NIOSH) issued an "Alert," asking for assistance in preventing worker falls through roof openings. In response, Bobick *et al.* (1994) prepared an injury reduction matrix, which delineates responsibility for controlling fall hazards to various construction parties.

NIOSH also conducted a study on the particular hazards found in the roofing industry. The investigators found that roofers took needless risks on the job sites observed, such as failing to cover roof openings. Roofers felt that the key to improving safety would be to eliminate the conflict between productivity and safety ("Behavioral" 1975).

Duncan and Bennett (1991) reviewed the performance of various fall protection systems. They compared the performance of active versus passive protection systems, where an active system is defined as one which actively prevents workers from falling off roofs, while passive systems "catch" the worker after the fall. The authors present several interesting variations of fall protection systems found in other countries. Finally, they conclude that active and passive systems both have a role to play in fall protection.

Vargas *et al.* (1996a and 1996b) performed studies involving the development of an expert system for construction falls. The project involved the use of fault-tree models for analyzing the cause of falls. The authors propose in that there are two main types of fall accidents—basic causes, which are "primary faults or failures which [can] lead to the occurrence of a fall," and conditioning causes, which are "problems or conditions in the system that, if combined with primary causes, enable the occurrence of a fall accident."

Vargas *et al.* (1996b) suggest that guardrails, safety nets, and PFAS can all be inadequate due to faulty erection. They also felt that the passive measures of warning line systems and controlled access zones (CAZ) could be similarly inadequate. Thus, immense quality control in safety management is indicated for fall prevention systems to succeed.

Dangers during frame construction were considered the most hazardous part of the residential framing industry in the United States (Hanna *et al.*, 1996). (This idea can possibly be extended to other parts of the western world and Japan where light gauge steel construction is becoming popular.) Falls were the third most frequent cause of accidents behind foreign body penetration and struck by object. In order to reduce injuries, Hanna *et al.* suggest that OSHA regulations be followed more strictly and that mechanical equipment such as lift trucks be used wherever possible.

In summary, there have been several studies and investigations related to fall protection on low rise roofs, especially in the residential construction industry. Some studies have evaluated the advantages/disadvantages of various fall protection devices. The study presented in this article, however, goes a little beyond by evaluating the effectiveness of various active and passive fall protection systems using objective decision analysis schemes. Also, whereas some studies have highlighted the role of management and appropriate safety cultures for reduced injuries, comparisons are made here between worker and manager attitudes, serving to illustrate and specify the many site problems that are due to a poor match of concepts, ideas, and priorities between the two groups.

RESEARCH METHODOLOGY

The HIOSH-funded research was conducted during 1997. Multiple strategies and instruments were employed to get the optimal information for decision analysis, as follows:

1. Surveys were sent out to carpenters and roofers to solicit their views on fall protection. The questionnaire included questions on accident history, knowledge of various fall protection systems, and opinions on fall protection systems and approaches.

2. Interviews were conducted with company construction managers, residential home builders, union representatives, fall protection equipment suppliers, roofing contractors, safety officers, and HIOSH personnel. The construction managers included representatives of roofers, contractors, owners, and framers. The interviews with workers included members of Carpenters Local 745 and Roofers Local 221. Suppliers provided information on fall protection devices available on the market. Safety officers of construction companies were able to provide information on the implementation of statutory regulations. Enforcement officials of HIOSH were interviewed on their perspective on the applicability and completeness of regulations, specifically with reference to OSHA regulations 29 CFR § 1926.500 to §1926.503, collectively called Subpart M. The questions asked of construction managers are given in Figure 5–1.

3. Construction sites were visited and inspected for their state of compliance with fall protection standards. These were conducted in conjunction with interviews of project managers. These job sites included large developments, military projects, and single homes. The inspections afforded an opportunity to discover, first hand, the presence and absence of fall protection precautions. This information was compared to opinion responses received from workers and construction managers. A check-off sheet, Figure 5–2, was used to guide the researcher during each site inspection.

ANALYSIS APPROACH

The following approach was followed in the analysis of data:

1. The data received was analyzed qualitatively and quantitatively using graphical and statistical analysis.

1. How compelled do you currently feel to comply with the existing fall protection regulations?

2. What methods of fall protection have you used and how? Which method do you feel is most appropriate for each stage of roof construction?

3. At what roof slope do you feel positive fall protection is needed?

4. How frequently do you encounter problems that make it difficult for you to comply with the existing regulations? How would you characterize these problems?

5. How would you regard your workers' level of compliance? Your supervisors'—including subcontractors'—level of enforcement?

6. Why do your workers use positive fall protection? Why don't they?

7. What could be done to increase worker protection while reducing current compliance problems?

FIGURE 5–1
Questions asked of construction managers.

2. Alternative proposals involving different fall protection methods/systems were prepared, based on the ideas suggested by participants in the study.

3. The alternatives were analyzed to meet suitable parameters for implementation and to fulfill the requirements of contractors, workers, and enforcement officials.

4. Recommendations were developed for regulatory agencies.

Response Rates and Validity

The breakdown of responses for the different instruments used are as follows:

1. Twenty-one (21) interviews were conducted of construction managers.

2. Sixteen (16) job sites were visited in various stages of construction.

3. Twenty-three (23) worker surveys were returned to the researchers, which included 13 carpenters and 10 roofers.

4. Forty (40) contractors from the island of Maui returned surveys. These were 32 building contractors and 9 roofing contractors.

Validity of Sample Sizes

Job sites of every major builder in the city and county of Honolulu were visited. The construction managers at those job sites were interviewed. The sample job sites were stratified. The stratified job sites were either systematic or clustered. Consequently, the samples are probability samples, in contrast to being judgmental samples.

Similarly, the workers were stratified among carpenters and roofers for the survey that was distributed. Consequently, the carpenters and roofers responding to the surveys are considered to be a systematic sample, since they work on all sorts of residential building projects.

Therefore, probability sampling can be undertaken, if desired, for all data provided here (Freund and Williams 1972).

Findings

Various questions asked of construction managers and workers were recorded and compared. These findings are presented below, along with inferences and commentary. The workers and construction managers were asked questions in different ways, so the responses are distinct, yet answer the same basic questions.

JOB SITE INSPECTION SHEET

Date of inspection: _____ Location: _____

Ownership: PRIVATE   PUBLIC

Type of construction: NEW   RENOVATION   REROOFING

Number of units: ONE   MULTIPLE

Type of units: SINGLE-FAMILY HOME   TOWNHOME   CONDOMINIUM
COMMERCIAL BUILDING/RESIDENTIAL ROOF

Stage of roof construction: FRAMING   SHEATHING   ROOFING   COMPLETE

Type of roof:

    Slope: ____:12

    Material: ASPHALT   CEDAR   TILE   METAL   OTHER

    Shape: GABLE   HIP

Overall Compliance:

	Not Observed	Never	Seldom	Somewhat	Mostly	Always
Supervisory enforcement level						
Worker compliance level						

Methods Used:

PFAS: _____

_____

Guardrails: _____

_____

Scaffolds: _____

_____

Fall protection plans: _____

_____

Other: _____

_____

Photographs: _____

_____

FIGURE 5–2
Template of the job site inspection sheet.

STATE OF COMPLIANCE

Response of Workers

The two unions surveyed, Carpenters Local 745 and Roofers Local 221, felt that the state of compliance was poor. Unlike the contractors, unions felt that the issue was related to poor management, not worker behavior. The contractors' push for production was cited as the primary reason for non-compliance. Union workers reported several ways in which contractors push for production at the expense of safety, as follows (Johnson and Singh 1997):

1. Contractors may not assign enough workers to the job, nor assign enough time for the task to be done safely. When insufficient time is allocated, pre-task planning is not done.

2. Contractors may not provide the appropriate safety equipment or may pay at a piece-meal rate. Both of these are against collective bargaining agreements with unions, but non-union contractors often pay wages according to production, encouraging workers to cut corners as far as safety is concerned. Often, contractors expect workers to bring their own safety equipment as they do their own tools.

3. Contractors do not provide sufficient training and may not be knowledgeable themselves. Training programs, when given, may include only rudimentary instructions, and nothing more. When the training is incomplete, workers desist from using safety equipment.

Response of Construction Managers

Fifty-seven percent (n=12) of construction managers feel compelled to comply, but 43% feel otherwise. The responses are recorded in Figure 5–3. The main reason for not complying was competitive advantage and push for production. Apparently, a long vision of the competitive advantage of promoting safety is missing. The main reason for compliance was given as enforcement by HIOSH.

Frequency of Non-Compliance

Workers and CMs were asked how frequently they encountered problems that made it difficult to comply with regulations. Their answers are given in Figure 5-4. Many of the CMs think that problems are frequent, suggesting that something should be done about the regulations. The workers think that compliance problems are less frequent. Correlation between the two groups is only moderate, $r=0.52$, which is significant at ?=2%. This partial mismatch can influence how the two groups work together to attack safety problems.

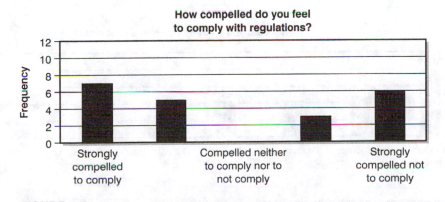

FIGURE 5–3
Construction managers' views on current regulatory state.

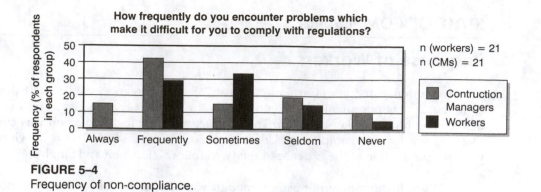

FIGURE 5–4
Frequency of non-compliance.

Sources of Non-Compliance

The workers and CMs gave widely differing reasons for non-compliance. Workers felt that production issues were the main reason for non-compliance, while CMs thought that worker behavior was the prime reason. It is interesting that the two groups both blamed each other for lapses in implementation. This can hardly improve teamwork. The data is presented in Figures 5–5 and 5–6.

Level of Worker Compliance

Three-fourths of all workers felt that they generally complied with regulations, whereas CMs stated that workers complied only some of the time. On a scale of 5 (5=high compliance, 1=low compliance) the mean score of workers' compliance as reported by workers was 2.12, while the managers rated their workers at 3.21. Table 5–1 illustrates the responses.

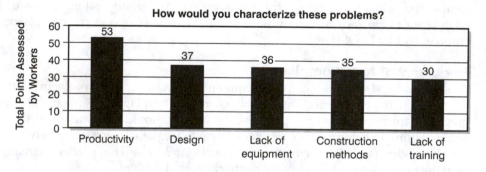

FIGURE 5–5
Sources of non-compliance, as reported by workers.

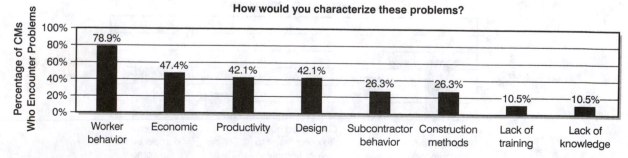

FIGURE 5–6
Sources of non-compliance, as rated by construction managers.

TABLE 5–1
Perceived and actual average compliance and enforcement levels.

Sample (population)	Worker compliance (mean of responses & correlation with inspection results)	Supervisory enforcement (mean of responses & correlation with inspection results)
Construction managers' interviews (n=21)	3.21 $r = 0.62$	2.89 $r = -0.32$
Workers' surveys (n=23)	2.12 $r = 0.87$	2.47 $r = 0.34$
Job site inspections (n=16)	3.69	3.44
5= high compliance; 1=low compliance		r = correlation at α=10%

Level of Supervisory Enforcement

Workers were asked how much their supervisors enforced the safety regulations. Workers were more considerate of their supervisors than supervisors were of workers. Workers stated that their supervisors enforced regulations, most of the time, score = 2.47. The supervisors rated themselves at 2.89. This indicates that workers are not quite as critical of their supervisors as supervisors are of their workers. The information is also presented in Table 5–1.

Reasons for Worker Compliance and Non-Compliance

Since supervisors claimed that worker behavior was the primary source of non-compliance, it was decided to ask why workers comply. The CMs reported that compliance was due mainly to it being a requirement of employment "or else." The workers reported that the main reason was really their own personal concern for safety. This data is reported in Table 5-2. Again, each group claims that safety is because of them, as if the other group was a non-participant altogether.

However, workers and supervisors were agreed considerably on why they don't comply. They didn't blame each other. The top two reasons given by both groups were:

1. Fall protection systems slow them down.
2. They feel uncomfortable with any type of fall protection system.

TABLE 5–2
Reasons for worker compliance and non-compliance.

Reasons for Worker Compliance		Reasons for Worker Non-Compliance	
Workers' responses (points assessed)[1]	Managers' responses (% of respondents)[2]	Workers' responses (points assessed)[1]	Managers' responses (% of respondents)[2]
Personal concern for safety (52)	Requirement of employment (32%)	Slows them down (54)	Slows them down (68%)
Requirement of employment (50)	Supervisory enforcement (32%)	Uncomfortable (46)	Uncomfortable (53%)
Supervisory enforcement (47)	Personal concern for safety (16%)	Not a requirement of employment (26)	Believe they won't fall (53%)
Peer pressure (31)	Peer pressure (11%)	Supervisor doesn't enforce (25)	Peer pressure (32%)
		Believe they won't fall (23)	Supervisor doesn't enforce (16%)
		Peer pressure (22)	Not a requirement of employment (5%)

[1]Points were assessed from rankings provided by workers.
[2]Percentages were assessed from responses received during interviews.

The reasons for non-compliance are reported in Table 5-2. It is realized that both these reasons are against safety philosophy (Baker and Singh, 1998), since safety implementation must be willing to accept hardship, if necessary, to be successful.

Compliance in Public Sector versus Private Sector

Compliance on public sector projects and large private projects is higher than in single home-owner projects. The reason is presumably that public sector projects are more in the public eye and are inspected frequently by enforcement officials. Large private projects are typically under-taken by large contractors who have dedicated safety officers and an established safety division, so errors and accidents are minimized as a result. Single homeowner developments, however, are less visible and also are generally not inspected by enforcement officials. The scores for com-pliance by industry sector are given in Table 5–3, as found during site inspections.

RELATIVE DANGER OF ROOFING SURFACES

There are a wide variety of roofing surfaces that are used in construction. Workers were asked to rank seven common roofing surfaces according to their relative dangers. Each worker ranked the surfaces from 0 to 6, with 0 being the least dangerous surface, and 6 being the most dangerous surface. As Figure 5–7 shows, the truss system, or bare rafters, were considered the most dangerous. This is where workers often "walk the top plate." Metal and clay tile roofs had the next highest ranks. It might be surmised that safety precautions should be proportional to the inherent danger.

USE OF DIFFERENT FALL PROTECTION SYSTEMS

Responses of Workers

In our study on Oahu, workers ($n=21$) reported they do not particularly like to use restraining devices, such as PFAS, since they felt it slowed them down (Johnson and Singh 1997). They would much rather use passive systems, such as guardrails and scaffolds. Workers did not express a good opinion of fall protection plans, because plans do not consider intimately the safety of workers. (Fall protection plans are a formal method of the contractor submitting a written "plan" of safety to enforcement authorities; under OSHA conditions recently promul-

TABLE 5–3
Average compliance and enforcement levels by sector.

Industry sector (sample population)	Worker compliance[1] (mean)	Supervisory enforcement[2] (mean)
Public sector ($n=5$)	2.80	2.80
Private developer ($n=7$)	3.57	3.00
Single homeowner ($n=4$)	5.00	5.00
Overall industry ($n=16$)	3.69	3.44

[1]For worker compliance, 5=never comply; 4=seldom comply; 3=sometimes comply; 2=comply most of the time; 1=always comply.

[2]For supervisory enforcement, 5= never enforce; 4=seldom enforce; 3=sometimes enforce; 2=enforce most of the time; 1=always enforce.

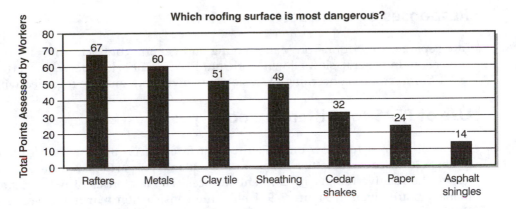

FIGURE 5–7
Relative danger of various working surfaces, as rated by workers.

gated, contractors may submit a plan and be in compliance.) However, workers suggested that contractors should work systematically at eliminating the hazards altogether, such as to erect work platforms and scaffolds (also refer to Ellis 1993).

Nevertheless, 75% of the workers used PFAS, with 55% having used the protection plan ($n=20$). This information is summarized in Figure 5–8.

Responses of Construction Managers

Construction managers report that PFAS are the most prevalent system used, with protection plans coming in second ($n=21$). The information is presented in Figure 5–8. Two construction managers, 9% of the population, had never used any fall protection system. They were involved mostly in renovation work of privately owned homes. This may indicate why private home roof work is possibly the most dangerous. The correlation between workers and construction managers, from Figure 5–8, is $r=0.96$, which implies that the reporting had a high degree of agreement.

The correlation between actual use as observed on sites during job inspections and the reports of the construction managers indicated a high correlation, $r=0.90$. (Therefore, actual observations are not reported in Figure 5–8.)

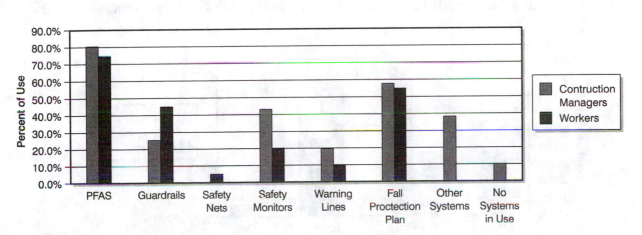

FIGURE 5–8
Fall protection systems in use in Hawaii's residential construction industry.

Responses of Contractors on Maui

In a separate study done on Maui, roofing and general contractors ($n=12$) reported that fall protection, in general, slows down work, but PFAS do not slow down work (Baker and Singh, 1998). So, assertions concerning PFAS slowing down work must be regarded with skepticism.

Use of PFAS for Different Roof Types

It was of interest to know on which roof surfaces PFASs are used most often. This was an attempt to discover whether PFAS are not suitable on particular surfaces, and thereby also gauge the relative danger of different surfaces. The responses of workers and construction managers are given in Figure 5–9. Unlike the construction managers, workers reported that PFAS are used most during roof sheathing. There is a very poor correlation of 0.09 between the workers' observations and those of the construction managers. This difference is hard to explain—either one or both groups were misreporting. This shows there is a wide gap in the perceptions of workers and construction managers. This wide gap represents a gap in communication, in understanding of priorities, and in the use of safety devices. Frequently, accidents are due to failures in communication between workers and construction managers. The correlation between CMs and actual job site inspections is $r=0.97$. Since the correlation of workers with CM perceptions is low ($r=0.09$, mentioned above), the relationships indicate that workers have virtually no clue to what is used in reality.

Use of Fall Protection Plan for Different Roof Types

Figure 5–10 shows the roofing surfaces on which the fall protection plan is used. The correlation between perceptions of worker and CMs is higher, $r=0.65$. The job site inspections also reveal a high correlation, $r=0.87$, between the CMs and job site inspections. Again, this goes to show that workers do not have as good an estimate of reality as the CMs.

Use of Fall Protection During Truss Installation

Figure 5–11 shows the type of fall protection devices most appropriate during truss installation. Construction managers think that the fall protection plan is most suited, whereas workers think that PFAS are most suited. Correlation between the two groups is very low, $r=0.15$, again showing that the understanding between the two groups is poor.

Some construction managers find that it is difficult to install an anchor point in the building structure that can resist a minimum standard force of 5,000 lbs. of mass. Consequently, they

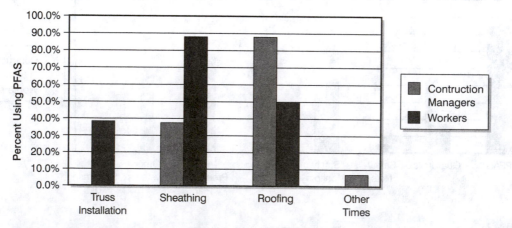

FIGURE 5–9
Use of personal fall arrest systems.

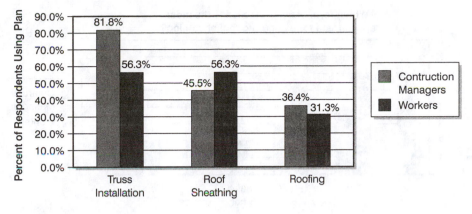

FIGURE 5–10
Use of fall protection plans.

believe that the plan is most suited. However, the workers believe that PFAS is still the best solution. Obviously something creative needs to be introduced that can satisfy both groups.

Use of Fall Protection During Sheathing

Figure 5–12 shows the type of fall protection device most appropriate during roof sheathing. When considering some of the earlier correlations between CMs and workers, the correlation between them is better, though moderate, at $r=0.66$. Workers think that the plan is most suited, while CMs think that the PFAS is most suited. (We also observed in Figure 5–8 that PFAS is the most used method of fall protection.)

SLOPE CONSIDERATIONS IN FALL PROTECTION METHODS

Slopes at Which Fall Protection Is Required

It is often felt that flat or low slope roofs do not require fall protection. The experience of HIOSH has been that workers fall off flat roofs as well. HIOSH regulations state that some fall

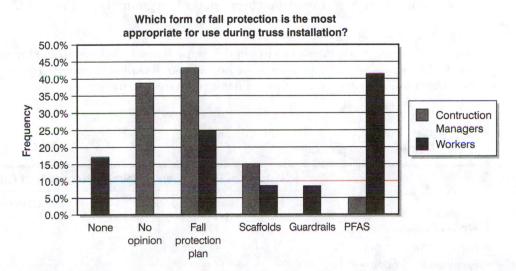

FIGURE 5–11
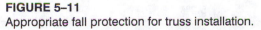
Appropriate fall protection for truss installation.

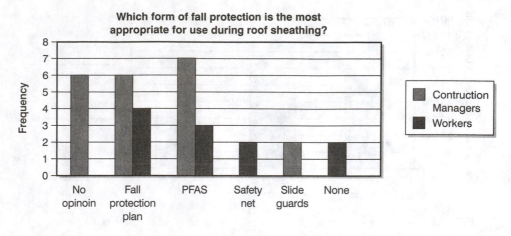

FIGURE 5–12
Appropriate fall protection for roof sheathing.

protection method must be in place for every roof whenever the elevation is more than 6 ft. (1.8 m). The workers and CMs were asked at which slope fall protection is necessary. Their responses are given in Table 5–4.

It is apparent that most respondents (>50%) in both groups suggest fall protection for slopes greater than 4:12 (since many state that fall protection is always needed). More workers find the necessity of fall protection in contrast to CMs. Perhaps this is because it is their lives on the line. However, the correlation between the two groups is very poor (non-existent), with $r=-0.037$. A large number of CMs (25%), claimed that fall protection was never required. Again, this represents a major difference of vision and opinion in how fall protection should be organized. It was noted that the opinion of the workers is more in line with the enforcement agency, HIOSH, but enforcement is impeded because the CMs—construction managers—have a lax opinion.

The Maui study (Baker and Singh 1998) discovered that the most prevalent roof slope was 4:12, followed by 5:12. A total of 78% of the contractors reported slope prevalence at 5:12 or less.

Slope < 4:12

Workers and CMs were asked which type of fall protection is best suited for different slopes. For slopes less than 4:12, most CMs had no opinion, whereas workers favored guardrails and fall protection plans. The CMs had a wider range of devices to use than workers. The data is presented in Figure 5–13. Correlation between the two groups is poor at $r=0.27$.

4:12 < Slope < 8:12

Workers reported more devices to use in this slope range compared to the lower slope ranges. The PFAS increases as the preferred method of use. Results are reported in Figure 5–14. The increase in use of PFAS is rational, since it is a very effective device.

TABLE 5–4
Necessity of positive fall protection.

	Percent of Respondents Claiming Necessity of Fall Protection	
	% of Workers Responding	% of CMs responding
Always Required	37%	33.5%
Required for Slopes > 4:12	42%	19%
Required for Slopes > 8:12	15.8%	19%
Never Required	5.2%	28.5%

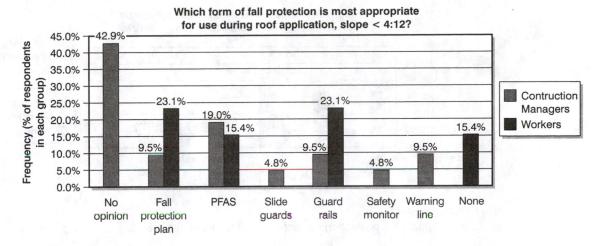

FIGURE 5–13
Appropriate fall protection for roofing application, slope < 4:12.

Slope > 8:12

Figure 5–15 shows the responses for roofs with slopes above 8:12. The PFAS becomes *the primary* method among workers and CMs alike. They probably realize that in those high slopes, an active fall protection device is necessary. The PFAS is perhaps the only certain fall protection device, besides safety nets (which are often impossible to use in residential construction). The correlation between workers and CMs increases to $r=0.72$.

WORK PRESSURE

Does work pressure affect safety? It is realized that a highly pressured person can become absent-minded and walk into an accident. The highly pressured person can become depressed and subconsciously neglect to use safety precautions, expressing a death wish. However, work pressure itself cannot be removed entirely. A minimum to reasonable amount of pressure is necessary to motivate the employees and make them work. Nevertheless, unnecessary work pressure must be avoided. This requires trained workers, motivated in doing a good job, and

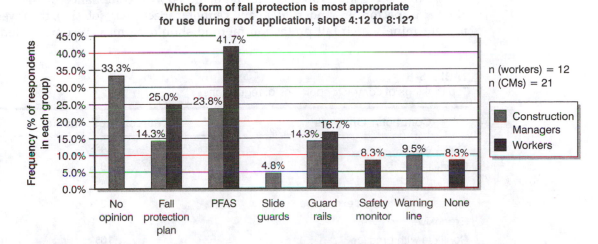

FIGURE 5–14
Appropriate fall protection for roofing application, slope 4:12 to 8:12.

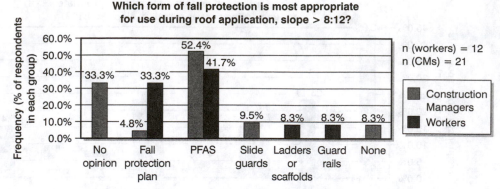

FIGURE 5–15
Appropriate fall protection for roofing application, slope > 8:12.

supervisors who can plan ahead with them. Contractors must desist from making a worker work to exhaustion or in humiliating the employee.

Maui contractors were sent a survey. Forty responses were received, representing an overall return rate of 32%. Half the respondents answered that work pressure reduces safety, while the other half felt work pressure had no effect on safety. Those that think that work pressure has no effect on safety, either genuinely feel that way, or else are insensitive to the adverse long-term effects of high pressure, seeing only that short-term pressures do not reduce safety.

PROBLEM WITH REGULATIONS

The Maui contractors were asked what they thought was wrong with regulations. Both roofing contractors and building contractors claimed that regulations slowed down the work, were expensive, complicated, and overkill when greater responsibility could be left with contractors. The data received is given in Table 5–5. However, given the visible neglect by many contractors, many of these reasons can be viewed as excuses.

ACTIONS TO INCREASE WORKER PROTECTION

Seeing that there are problems with regulations, with compliance, with enforcement (since HIOSH inspectors are understaffed and cannot inspect every job site), the investigators sought to determine which fall protection method should be most recommended or developed.

TABLE 5–5
Top rankings of contractor opinions of regulations.

Contractor Opinions	Percent Responding
Slows work	24%
Overkill	18%
Complicated	14%
Makes fall protection expensive	13%
Expensive	13%
Conflicts with practice	10%
Other	21%

TABLE 5–6
Actions to increase worker protection.

	Contractors	Workers	Enforcement
Change safety culture	X	—	—
Increase enforcement	X	X	—
Subsidize costs of equipment	X	X	—
Increase cooperation with HIOSH	X	X	—
Increase worker training	X	X	—
Develop innovative protection methods	X	X	X

Enforcement officials, union officials, and construction managers were asked for their ideas on how the state of compliance could be improved. These various solutions are shown in Table 5–6. Each party emphasized the need to develop innovative solutions. No other idea was shared by all groups. Enforcement was particularly and positively sensitive to the idea of developing innovative methodologies. In their experience, only a new technology can help, since they claimed they had tried everything else.

Hierarchy of Fall Protection

In attempting to discover which method might be most suitable, it is relevant to mention that Ellis (1993) wrote to introduce construction safety managers to concepts involved in reducing employee falls. He presented useful interesting findings, such as

- "Falls are the major cause of losses [from occupational injuries]."
- "Construction projects can benefit from an average of 35% bare labor savings [both time lost and productivity lost] when a 100% fall policy is adopted and applied."

This motivates interest in developing fall protection schemes. More importantly, however, Ellis presented a hierarchy of fall protection approaches, explaining that protection is a four-step process of:

i. Elimination of Fall Hazard
ii. Prevention of Fall hazard
iii. Restraint of Fall Hazard
iv. Warning of Fall Hazard

This means that the first priority should be to completely eliminate the fall hazard, such as by doing *something else* altogether. If elimination is not possible, the hazard should be prevented, such as through heavy-duty guardrails. If prevention is not possible, then restraint (arrest) devices should be used, such as PFAS. If arrest is not possible, then, at the very least, warning systems should be used.

Active systems of fall restraint, such as PFAS, reportedly offer better protection than passive systems, such as a sidewalk bridge, even though both active and passive types offer tangible protection (Duncan and Bennett 1991). Both passive and active systems are analyzed next, covering the various hierarchies of Ellis.

Systems Analyzed

Several protection methods—both innovative and conventional—were evaluated for their overall applicability of implementation. Among these were:

1. Fall Protection Plans
2. Guardrail Systems
3. Roof Jack (or Slide Guard) system proposed by HIOSH
4. Combination warning line/lifeline system
5. PFAS using a roof truss anchor system
6. PFAS using the Safe-T-Strap system
7. Scaffolds and/or work platforms
8. Prefabrication of roof systems on ground, followed by lifting into place.

Criteria for Analysis

How should the different fall protection methods be analyzed? What should be the evaluation criteria for them? The different parties to safety—contractors, workers, and enforcement officials—all have valid concerns that must be addressed and fulfilled. They expressed certain criteria that should be fulfilled. Though they could not quantify their criteria, they expressed the belief that fall protection methods should be feasible, simple, passive, economic, flexible, and should be capable of being significantly protective. Their contribution to these criteria is given in Table 5–7.

The definitions of the criteria are provided as follows:

Feasibility   This is the degree to which the system is practical to implement and does not require unusual equipment, expensive materials, or specialized equipment to implement.

Simplicity   This is the degree to which the system does not require any specialized skill or technique to implement. Thus, it should be easy for the workers to implement with their existing knowledge.

Passivity   Passive protection is preferable because it does not impinge upon the mobility of the worker. These do not foster the objections that are common with active systems—that are cumbersome, inconvenient, and impractical.

Economy   There is no doubt that the costs of the system should be low. Definitely, the benefits should outweigh the costs. Ideally, the system should not affect productivity.

Flexibility   The system should be capable of being used on different sites, under varying conditions. The system should be capable of being applied to different types of residential roofs—with differing slopes, shapes, and materials.

Protectiveness   Finally, and indisputably, the system must positively protect the worker. Strangely, contractors did not think this was an important criterion (Table 5–7).

To ensure a systematic and consistent approach for the analysis of the different systems, a system analysis form was developed, Figure 5–16. Whereas the analysis is partially subjective, partially objective, the degree of subjectivity was minimized through uniform scoring undertaken after objectively consulting various individuals. Evaluations were only made after con-

TABLE 5–7
Criteria parameters proposed by different groups.

	Contractors	Workers	Enforcement
Feasibility	X	X	X
Simplicity	X	X	X
Passivity	X	X	X
Economy	X	X	X
Flexibility	X	X	—
Protective	—	X	X

RESOURCES REQUIRED TO IMPLEMENT						APPLICABILITY					
Labor					Materials		NOT AT ALL APPLICABLE	APPLICABLE IF MODIFIED	SOMEWHAT APPLICABLE	MOSTLY APPLICABLE	HIGHLY APPLICABLE
Equipment						Truss Installation	-2	-1	0	1	2
						Sheathing	-2	-1	0	1	2
						Roofing, slope <4:12	-2	-1	0	1	2
	HIGHLY INFEASIBLE	SOMEWHAT INFEASIBLE	SLIGHTLY INFEASIBLE	SOMEWHAT INFEASIBLE	HIGHLY INFEASIBLE	Roofing, slope 4:12 to 8:12	-2	-1	0	1	2
						Roofing, slope >8:12	-2	-1	0	1	2
Degree of Feasibility:	-2	-1	0	1	2	Roofing, hip	-2	-1	0	1	2
						Roofing, gable	-2	-1	0	1	2
						Roofing, asphalt	-2	-1	0	1	2
	HIGHLY COMPLEX	SOMEWHAT COMPLEX	SLIGHTLY COMPLEX	SOMEWHAT SIMPLE	VERY SIMPLE	Roofing, cedar	-2	-1	0	1	2
						Roofing, clay	-2	-1	0	1	2
						Roofing, metal	-2	-1	0	1	2
Degree of Simplicity:	-2	-1	0	1	2	Finish work	-2	-1	0	1	2
						Degree of Flexibility: _____ (Mean)					

WORKER INVOLVEMENT						WORKER PROTECTION					
	REQUIRES EXTENSIVE WORKER INVOLVEMENT	REQUIRES FREQUENT INVOLVEMENT	REQUIRES SOME INVOLVEMENT	REQUIRES LOW INVOLVEMENT	REQUIRES NO INVOLVEMENT		VERY LOW PROTECTION	SUBSTANDARD PROTECTION	STANDARD PROTECTION	ABOVE SUBSTANDARD PROTECTION	VERY HIGH PROTECTION
Degree of Passivity:	-2	-1	0	1	2	Degree of Protection:	-2	-1	0	1	2

FIGURE 5–16
Fall protection system analysis form.

sulting construction managers and equipment suppliers, and their different viewpoints were synthesized in the evaluations. Therefore, the evaluations are normalized and representative.

MADM Evaluation of the Analysis

Table 5–8 shows the criteria scores for each of the systems described. No single system meets every criterion. Those coming closest, however, are prefabrication and the PFAS variants. Recall that many workers and CMs describe PFAS as uncomfortable, even though they find it an important life saving device.

The systems were then compared using Multiple Attribute Decision-Making (MADM). The weights of each criterion were assessed based on the importance of the system to the three parties—

TABLE 5–8
Comparison of discovered fall protection systems.

	Degree of feasibility	Degree of simplicity	Degree of economy	Degree of flexibility	Degree of passivity	Degree of protection
Guardrail system	1	2	−1	0.92	1	−1
PFAS: roof truss anchor variant	2	1	1	1.25	−1	2
PFAS: Safe-T-Strap TM variant	2	1	1	1.25	−1	2
Combination warning line/lifeline system	1	1	0	−0.50	0	0
Fall protection plan	2	−2	−1	2.00	n/a	n/a
Roof jack system, condition 1 (roof jacks alone)	2	0	1	0.64	1	−1
Roof jack system, condition 2 (roof jacks and positioning device system)	0	0	−2	1.00	2	2
Roof jack system, condition 3 (PFAS)	2	0	0	0.91	−1	2
Scaffolds and work platforms	−1	−1	−1	−0.83	2	2
Prefabrication	0	2	1	0.50	2	2

enforcement, labor, and contractors. The weights were evaluated on a three-point Likert Scale—0, 1, 2: if a party expressed great importance, the weight assigned had a value of two; some degree of importance had a value of one; and not important had no value at all. The total importance factor was then found by summing the three parties' weights. These importance factors are given in Table 5–9. Thus, the weights reflect the needs and preferences of the construction safety groups and people involved. It represents the most of what will be found acceptable, minimizing objections and rejection, the net result being to increase compliance through acceptability of the method. The parameters of feasibility, simplicity, and economy have a weight of four each. Passivity and Protectiveness have a weight of three each, while flexibility is least important at a weight of two.

Results of MADM Evaluation

Each of the systems criterion scores is multiplied by its weight to produce a weighted criterion score. Thus, the values in Table 5–8 were multiplied by the overall weights in Table 5–9. These weighted criterion were summed for each system to produce an overall score between the

TABLE 5–9
Relative importance of the selection criteria to each party.

	Degree of feasibility	Degree of simplicity	Degree of economy	Degree of flexibility	Degree of passivity	Degree of protection
Contractors	2	1	2	1	1	0
Labor	1	2	1	1	2	1
Enforcement	1	1	1	0	0	2
Total importance factor	4	4	4	2	3	3

range of -40 and +40. The final results of this evaluation are presented in Figure 5–17. Though no method has all the desirable characteristics, it is clear that prefabrication is the most acceptable and suitable method. This is followed closely by the PFAS variants.

Prefabricated systems have high weighted scores in simplicity, passivity, and protection. Thus, they offer the best promise. Scaffolds and platforms actually have an overall negative score. Scaffolds have high negative scores in feasibility, simplicity, and economy.

TYPICAL ROOF CONSTRUCTION SCHEDULE

A typical roof construction schedule for a two-story, single family dwelling unit is shown in Figure 5-18. This construction sequence is utilized by 70% of the construction managers interviewed. Under the approach, the framing contractor will first construct the 2nd story interiors and exterior frame walls to support the roof system. Next, trusses are "rolled" into place by two framers. This is where workers perform the infamous "walking of the top plate." Each framer climbs to the top plate of the exterior wall on his or her side of the roof. The framers bend down, pick up the truss, and choreograph their movements while walking forward to the final coordinates of the truss. Once in position, the trusses are braced by spacers placed between the trusses. The process is repeated for other trusses on the roof.

Once trusses are in place, the roof sheathing, consisting of plywood sheets, is installed. Typically, the framers will begin roof sheathing at the lower end of the roof, working their way to the peak. During sheathing, workers will frequently use the PFAS for fall protection.

Following roof sheathing, the fascia is installed at the eaves. The framer will typically balance from the edge of the roof sheathing and bend over to install the fascia.

Next roofers will nail down a waterproofing paper over the sheathing, followed by the roofing tiles — asphalt shingles, cedar shakes, clay tiles, etc. This roofing process can be finished in a day for one home. A typical construction cycle for a conventional home is 13 days requiring a total of 26 worker days (Figure 5–18).

ROOF CONSTRUCTION SCHEDULE FOR PREFABRICATION

In the prefabrication schedule shown in Figure 5–19, the trusses are made on the ground and lifted into place. There is no need for workers to walk the top plate, thereby eliminating a serious fall hazard. A few activities can occur simultaneously, such as truss installation and 2nd story framing. Activities such as bracing are done on the ground. Fascia and roof installation are done, as usual, on the rooftop after trusses are installed.

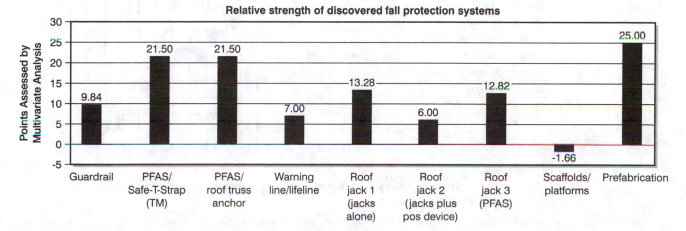

FIGURE 5–17
Results of multiple attribute decision-making.

Activity	Manpower Required	Days												
		1	2	3	4	5	6	7	8	9	10	11	12	13
Frame 2nd story exterior walls[a]	2	■	■											
Frame 2nd story interior walls	2			■	■									
Load trusses	2					■								
Set & brace trusses	2						■	■						
Roof sheathing	2								■	■				
Fascia installation	1										■			
Roof loading	1											■		
Roof installation	2													■

FIGURE 5–18
Typical construction schedule for building the roof system of a new home.

[a] Denotes 2nd story walls, which are separate from the 1st story exterior wall system. There are places on a typical single family home where the exterior walls extend from the foundation to the roof system. Those walls are framed in with the 1st story exterior walls.

The major change or improvement here is that the trusses are prefabricated on the ground. It is perceived that a time reduction in erection schedule takes place, with the total cycle now taking 10 days instead of the earlier 13 days. The entire effort takes 28 man-days instead of the 26 man-days earlier, implying that roof erection will cost 7.7% more per roof, approximately $640 more. However, since roof construction is frequently—if not invariably—on the critical path of a home construction, the builder is likely to save two days of overhead costs, which will probably balance out the added cost. Is the immediate added cost worth it? The author thinks it is, since lives and injuries are drastically reduced, and since the final increased cost is partially, if not entirely, balanced by the savings.

ILLUSTRATION OF PREFAB SYSTEMS FOR RESIDENTIAL ROOFS

Photographs of the prefab system are provided, Figures 5–20 to 5–23. Prefabrication requires that the builder make a yard on site, and designate a crane for lifting purposes. Asking for a

Activity	Manpower Required	Days									
		1	2	3	4	5	6	7	8	9	10
Frame 2nd story exterior walls[a]	2	■									
Frame 2nd story interior walls	2			■	■						
Frame "top plate" system on ground	1		■								
Load trusses onto "top plate" system	2				■						
Set & brace trusses on "top plate" system	2					■					
Lift truss system onto walls	3						■				
Roof sheathing	2							■			
Fascia installation	1								■		
Roof loading	1									■	
Roof installation	2										■

FIGURE 5–19
Modified construction schedule for building the roof system of a new home when using prefabrication for truss installation.

[a] Denotes 2nd story walls, which are separate from the 1st story exterior wall system. There are places on a typical single family home where the exterior walls extend from the foundation to the roof system. Those walls are framed in with the 1st story exterior walls.

FIGURE 5–20
Prefabricated roof system.

crane is not far-fetched, since developers generally have cranes on site, especially for the construction of multiple dwelling unit projects.

Prefabrication affords the ease of quality control on the ground, and speedier manufacture and assembly. For large projects, the schedule of construction can be expected to become lower, because the framing of the top plate on ground can be accomplished at a fast, continuous rate.

SUMMARY

Falls are one of the major causes of accidents and injuries on construction sites and residential buildings. The frequency of compliance is not adequate. The main reason for non-compliance was cited as the push for production. A systematic approach should be taken to tackle this

FIGURE 5–21
Prefabricated roof system.

FIGURE 5–22
Prefabricated floor joist system, ready for lifting.

FIGURE 5–23
Prefabrication; lifting and placing the prefabricated floor joist system.

issue. The established approach (Ellis 1993) is to first try to eliminate the hazard, else prevent the hazard. If going to the root of the matter does not succeed, then the fall hazard should be restrained; at the very least, there should be adequate warning provided of dangers. A common complaint voiced in this research was that fall protection systems slow down work and are cumbersome, bothersome, and uncomfortable. Truss installation was mentioned as being the most dangerous roof activity. The maximum citations by Hawaii Occupational Safety and Health (HIOSH) are for "walking the top plate," which is a truss installation activity.

Private sector construction, especially the construction of single homes, is the most dangerous sector for falls from roofs. While HIOSH regulations note that fall protection should always be used when working at elevations above 6 ft., only 37% of workers and 33.5% of construction managers, think that fall protection is always required. Only half of all workers and contractors think that work pressure reduces safety, even though they realize that the main source of non-compliance is the production issue.

Correlation Exercises

Workers and construction managers frequently have opposing views of how things are—and should be—done. A listing of the correlation of viewpoints is provided in Table 5–10.

For quite a few questions asked, the workers and CMs have diametrically opposite views. For quite a few other questions, the correlation is moderate to low. This does not bode well for site communication and good teamwork. Clearly, workers and CMs must discuss the matter of fall protection to greater extent.

Prefabrication

The workers, construction managers, and enforcement officials all desire innovative ways of fall protection. There was little emphasis placed on other fall protection improvements such as

TABLE 5–10
Correlation results for various questions asked.

Question Asked	R_1	R_2	Comment
Frequency of non-compliance	+0.52	—	CMs think problems are frequent; workers think problems are occasional.
Prevalence of system used	+0.96	+0.90	Both groups report that PFAS is most prevalent, followed by Plans.
Use of PFAS for roof types	+0.09	+0.97	Workers: PFAS used most in roof sheathing; CMs: PFAS used most in truss installation. Corr. Between CMs and actual is *very high*.
Use of plan for different roof surfaces	+0.65	+0.87	CMs have a more correct view of reality than workers.
Use of appropriate system during truss installation	+0.15	—	CMs think Plan is most suited; Workers think PFAS is most suited.
Use of appropriate system during roof sheathing	+0.66	—	CMs think PFAS is most suited; Workers think Plan is most suited.
Necessity of fall protection	−0.037	—	Many CMs think protection is never required, in contrast to workers.
System reqd. for slope < 4:12	+0.27	—	Workers favor guardrails and Plan; CMs have no opinion.
System reqd. for slope > 8:12	+0.72	—	PFAS is the primary choice.

R_1 = Correlation between workers and CMs.

R_2 = Correlation between CMs and actual site observations.

improving safety culture and offering training. Consequently, the groups were asked what features they would like to see in innovative products. The answer was that they wanted the product to be feasible, simple, flexible, passive, economic, and protective. If these variables could be maximized, their satisfaction would be maximized too.

Correspondingly, criteria were set up to evaluate eight promising fall protection systems—guardrails, warning lines, slide guards, prefabrication methods, PFAS (and its variants), the fall protection plan, and scaffolds and work platforms. The classic Multiple Attribute Decision-Making Method (MADM) was used for analysis. Scores were assigned from –2 to +2 for each.

Next, weights were assigned to the variables after discussions with the groups. For instance, degree of feasibility, simplicity, and economy received the highest weights; flexibility received the lowest weight, while passivity and protection were in between.

The weights were multiplied by the scores obtained. The resulting scores ranged from –40 to +40. Only scaffolds scored negatively, implying that they are not an attractive alternative for site personnel and contractors. No single system is wholly adequate, complete, or sufficient in itself. Prefabrication received the highest scores, implying that it offers the greatest attraction and promise. Prefabrication would be most acceptable to all parties. Prefabricated systems have high scores in simplicity, passivity, and protection. It is quite certain that prefab systems will be instrumental in bringing down the frequency and intensity of accidents.

Prefabricated roofs take less time to construct, but require more worker-days. However, the cost of extra worker-days would be offset by lower overhead over the duration of the contract, since the project is likely to finish earlier.

CONCLUSION

Based on the conclusions and findings during the investigation, the following recommendations are proposed:

1. Provide incentives for compliance to contracting companies. Many studies have already been done earlier on improving incentives to workers. However, to companies who bear the brunt of insurance premiums and are wholly responsible to OSHA for safety on the job site, state governments could do more by way of providing subsidies or granting tax credits for purchase of safety equipment. Since contractors are often inadequately motivated to spend money on fall protection devices, and are sometimes hesitant to enforce fall protection systems on their workers and subcontractors, tax credits and subsidies will greatly assist in improving site safety and community health as a result.

2. Reduce compliance inspections. If the contractor exhibits a commitment to working safely, compliance inspections can be reduced, thereby allowing the contractor time to devote to consciously improving their safety performance. OSHA has two such programs in effect: the Voluntary Protection Program (VPP) and the Safety and Health Achievement Program (SHARP). If contractors meet OSHA's safety levels, contractors can be exempted from OSHA inspections for one year. Under VPP, specifically, OSHA removes the site from routine inspections. The site is reassessed every 1-3 years.

3. Increase external supervision of the single homeowner sector. Since the single homeowner residential construction of rooftops has the worst safety record, it is absolutely necessary that supervision, if not enforcement, should increase dramatically in this sector. Special permits can be required of homeowners before they commence renovations and home repair. Currently, no permits are required for roof renewal, for instance. If permits are required, then safety can be emphasized and an inspector can be sent to check on the safety of workers. If this will not help 100% to reduce accidents, it will surely go a long way.

4. Improve manager-worker communication. We have seen through our findings that workers and managers frequently have opposing perceptions of safety matters, and they many times have significantly different perceptions. Among the many ways in management science to improve communication between parties in the same organization, the method of safety cir-

cles is highly recommended. When management and workers get together, essentially to discuss safety, they begin to understand each others' differences, priorities, and needs. This ends up helping the safety effort. For roof safety on low-rise roofs, safety circles are considered the answer to manager-worker communication problems.

5. Improve training. Specific training needs to be provided to roof workers on the different safety hazards and prevention devices. The training can be an 8-hour formal review of materials and videos, in addition to presentations by trained specialists. Workers would be required to show certification at having completed the roof safety orientation course. This same concept can later be extended to any specialty worker working in different areas of construction.

6. Improve the regulations. The fall protection regulation of OSHA, 1926.501(k), does not require a thorough analysis from contractors who use it. Additionally, the current regulations do not provide for the adequate protection of workers under a fall protection plan. Most plans do not address the fall hazards or provide a detailed hazard analysis. Contractors assume that the hazards cannot be eliminated, and therefore conclude that fall protection measures are not feasible. In most instances, the fall hazards could be eliminated or reduced, as called for by the hierarchy of fall protection (Ellis 1993).

7. Finally, prefabricated methods of protecting workers must be developed. Prefabricated systems are the most effective compared to all other methods evaluated, and therefore hold the greatest promise of reducing the incidences of accidents from roofs.

ACKNOWLEDGMENTS

Acknowledgments are extended to Hawaii Occupational Safety and Health Division (HIOSH), Hawaii Department of Labor and Industrial Relations, for sponsoring this research project.

REFERENCES

Baker, E., and Singh, A. (1998). "A Survey of Fall Protection on Maui for Roof Construction Works." A research report submitted to Hawaii Occupational Safety and Health Division, Department of Labor and Industrial Relations, Honolulu.

"Behavioral Analysis of Workers and Job Hazards in the Roofing Industry," (1975). NIOSH, HEW Publication #75-16, Cincinnati, OH, United States Department of Health, Education, and Welfare.

Bobick, T., Stanevich, R., Pizatella, T., Keane, P., and Smith, D. (1994). "Preventing Falls through Skylights and Roof Openings." *Professional Safety*, September, pp. 33–37.

"Custom Profile of Workmen's Compensation Data for Falls in Residential Construction in 1995," (1997a). Department of Labor and Industrial Relations, Honolulu.

"Custom Report of Fall Protection Citations for Residential Construction," (1997b). Hawaii Occupational Safety and Health Division, Department of Labor and Industrial Relations, Honolulu.

Duncan C. W., and Bennett III, R. (1991). "Fall Protection and Debris Containment During Construction." *Preparing for Construction in the 21st Century*. Proceedings of the ASCE Construction Congress, New York.

Ellis, J. Nigel (1993). "Introduction to Fall Protection," 2nd ed. American Society of Safety Engineers, Des Plaines, IL.

Freund, J. E., and Williams, F. J. (1972). *Elementary Business Statistics*, Prentice Hall, Englewood Cliffs, NJ.

Hanna, A., Isidore, L., and Kammel, D. (1996). "Safety Evaluation for Frame Building Contractors." In Alves Dias, L. and Coble R. (eds.), *Proc.of the 1st International Conference, CIB W99, Implementation of Safety and Health on Construction Sites*, Lisbon, Portugal, Sept. 4–7, 1996. Balkema Publishers, Rotterdam, Netherlands.

"Improving Construction Safety Performance," (1987). *A Construction Industry Cost Effectiveness Report*, The Business Roundtable, New York.

"Injuries Resulting from Falls from Elevations," (1984). Bulletin 2195, United States Department of Labor, Washington, DC.

Johnson, H. M., and Singh, A. (1997). "Residential Roof Construction Fall Protection Analysis and Recommendations." Research Report UHM/CE/97-06, University of Hawaii, Honolulu.

"National Census of Fatal Occupational Injuries, 1994," (1995). News Release 95-288, Bureau of Labor Statistics, August 3.

"National Census of Fatal Occupational Injuries, 1995," (1996). News Release 96-315, Bureau of Labor Statistics, August 8.

"New Data Highlight Gravity of Construction Falls," (1996). *Issues in Labor Statistics*, Bureau of Labor Statistics, Summary 96-1, January.

Toscano, G., Windau, J., and Drudi, D. (1996). "Using the Bureau of Labor Statistics Occupational Injury and Illness Classification System as a Safety and Health Management Tool." *Fatal Workplace Injuries in 1994: A Collection of Data and Analysis*. Report #908, Washington D.C., U. S. Department of Labor, Bureau of Labor Statistics.

Vargas, C., Hadipriono, F., and Larew, R. (1996a). "A Fault Tree Model for Falls from a Form Scaffolding." In Alves Dias, L. and Coble R. (eds.), *Proc.of the 1st International Conference, CIB W99, Implementation of Safety and Health on Construction Sites*, Lisbon, Portugal, Sept. 4–7, 1996. Balkema Publishers, Rotterdam, Netherlands.

Vargas, C., Hadipriono, F., and Larew, R. (1996b). "Causes of Falls from Floor Openings and Edges." In Alves Dias, L. and Coble R. (eds.), *Proc.of the 1st International Conference, CIB W99, Implementation of Safety and Health on Construction Sites*, Lisbon, Portugal, Sept. 4–7, 1996. Balkema Publishers, Rotterdam, Netherlands.

Workers' Compensation Data Book. (1990–96). State of Hawaii, Department of Labor and Industrial Relations, Research and Statistics Office, Honolulu.

"Zero Injury Techniques," (1993). Construction Industry Institute, Publication 32-1, Austin, TX.

SAFETY AND HEALTH TEAM BUILDING

John Smallwood, M. Sc., MSAIB
Department of Construction Management
University of Port Elizabeth, South Africa
Theo C. Haupt, M.Phil., MSAIB, MASI
Department of Construction Management and Quantity Surveying
Peninsula Technikow, South Africa

ABSTRACT

Although often incorrectly described as being inherently dangerous, the construction industry is unique in that it is characterized by features that include separation of the design from the actual construction; reliance on the consistency of natural phenomena such as weather conditions; the lack of continuity in management, supervision, and work teams; dispersed activities; poorly skilled workforce; and divergent stakeholder goals, expertise, and skills. Additionally, interdependence is required between many stakeholders such as clients, designers, construction managers, and workers, which contributes to the construction process. Given the unique nature of the industry and the interdependence of the large number of stakeholders, teamwork is crucial to achieve safety and health on construction projects. Teamwork has been described as the ability to work together toward a common vision and the ability to direct individual accomplishment toward organizational objectives. It is the fuel that allows common people to attain uncommon results. Since safety is everybody's business, requiring the commitment and involvement of every stakeholder in achieving this common vision, team building can effectively ensure that everyone can and will work together. The process of team building also requires the facilitation of certain strategies, systems, and processes. Included among these is constructability management, design-build, partnering, quality management systems, and safe work procedures. This chapter discusses how team building and the development of a teamwork ethic can contribute to the achievement of zero accidents and incidents on construction projects. In particular the roles and contributions of stakeholders, as well as several strategies, systems, and processes are investigated. The results of interviews conducted with stakeholders are used to demonstrate the effectiveness of team building, team-based structures, and teamwork in achieving adequate safety and health performance on construction projects.

KEYWORDS

stakeholders, team building, teamwork, strategies, systems, processes

INTRODUCTION

In the industrialized nations of the world, accidents now cause more deaths than all infectious diseases and more than any single illness except those related to heart disease and cancer (Britannica Online 1998). The construction industry, which has often been incorrectly described as being an inherently dangerous industry, has earned this reputation as a result of the disproportionately high incidence of accidents and fatalities which continue to occur on construction sites around the globe. The term "inherent" has been defined as "existing as an essential element or feature: intrinsic" (Websters 1984) and also "existing in something especially as a permanent or characteristic attribute" (Allen 1992). Accidents and fatalities are most certainly not an essential, permanent, or intrinsic part of construction. This notion would imply that since this is so, absolutely nothing can be done to change this characteristic attribute of the industry. Rather than being inherently dangerous the construction industry is a highly hazardous one in which the hazards may be identified, reduced, or eliminated. According to Joyce (1995) the construction industry has always had the highest incident rate with respect to fatal accidents and serious injuries of all industries. The number of fatalities in the industry are only the tip of the iceberg, with thousands of major injuries and even more minor ones resulting in lost time.

The construction industry worldwide is a significant employer of labor. This fact is not surprising when it is recognized that large proportions of its activities and operations have labor intensive characteristics. A study conducted by Turin (1969) has shown that regular construction employment contributes between four and eight workers per 1,000 workers at the lower end and between 30 and 40 workers per 1,000 workers at the upper end of the range.

The construction industry in the United States of America, for example, employs about 5% of the entire industrial workforce (Hinze 1997). However, the construction sector has generally accounted for nearly 20% of all industrial worker deaths (Hinze 1997, Center to Protect Workers Rights 1995). In Europe the situation is more serious with the construction industry employing 7.5% of the industrial workforce, accounting for 15% of all accidents and injuries and responsible for 30% of all fatalities (Berger 1998). Moreover construction has for many years consistently been among those industries with the highest injury and fatality rates. Even though the incidence of injuries and fatalities has decreased by more than 50% during the last 30 years, the number of accidents, injuries, and deaths remains unacceptably high. In the United States accidents in the construction industry alone cost over $17 billion annually (Levitt and Samelson 1993).

The statistics in Table 6–1 indicate the severity of fatalities in the construction industries of several countries. Construction sites have been described as crawling with hazards, which affect the health of construction workers (Marsicano 1995). Some of these include:

TABLE 6–1
Fatality rates in the construction industries of selected countries.

Country/State	Fatality Rate / 100,000 workers
Germany	14.0
Japan	19.0
New South Wales	11.0
Ontario	7.4
South Africa[+]	53.5
Sweden	6.0
The Netherlands	3.3
USA	18.6

[+]1990 being the latest year for which statistics are available.
Source: Center to Protect Workers' Rights 1995 and Compensation Commissioner 1995.

- noise and particulates associated with the operation of heavy equipment
- dust produced during drywall operations
- metal fumes associated with welding and cutting

For this dismal scenario to continue unabated is untenable.

The advancement of technology, the development of sophisticated plants, new construction techniques, the increased size and complexity of construction works, and the improvements in the recognition of risks and hazards suggest that there is still scope for improvement in the safety record of the construction industry (Joyce 1995).

The success of any construction project is usually measured in terms of the universally acceptable project parameters of time, cost, and quality. Safety performance on projects should be just as much a measure of the success of that project as are project completion within the desired time frame, within the budget, and to satisfactory quality performance standards (Hinze 1997). It is inconceivable to regard a project as "successful" when limbs and lives have been lost through accidents which could have been prevented had achieving adequate safety performance on the project been regarded as just as important as the other parameters.

However in order to achieve the goals of zero accidents and zero incidents a concerted and coordinated effort will of necessity be required on the part of all the participants in the construction process. Statements such as "None of us is as smart as all of us" and "Safety is everyone's job" made by senior staff within Boeing and Universal Studios respectively suggest that achieving improved safety and health performance involves teamwork. This observation is not surprising in the context of the construction industry, which is a complex one with critical relationships between so many key players. In fact, the monumental task which faces the construction industry is to indoctrinate every person engaged in the design, management, and execution of construction projects to give health and safety issues the priority which has been lacking—especially among clients and designers.

This chapter discusses how team building and the development of a teamwork ethic can contribute to the achievement of zero accidents and incidents on construction projects. In particular the roles and contributions of stakeholders as well as several strategies, systems, and processes are investigated. The concept of "Total Safety Culture" is discussed and considered as a strategy for improving safety performance.

The results of interviews conducted with stakeholders are used to demonstrate the effectiveness of team building, team-based structures, and teamwork in achieving adequate safety and health performance on construction projects.

THE NATURE OF THE CONSTRUCTION INDUSTRY

The construction industry is characteristically one in which most of its products are unique with respect to form, size, and purpose (Berger 1998). Whereas they are not unique, work operations, which are similar and repetitive are often executed in work environments which change from hour to hour due to several factors such as weather conditions, location, and height. Construction workers are constantly expected, therefore, to familiarize themselves with new situations that may be potentially hazardous. Construction sites are subject to local conditions (Berger 1998). Moreover, each building site represents in effect the creation of a production site where new workplaces are set up. The term "mobile factories" could be used to describe this phenomenon.

Additionally, the composition of construction project teams—involving the design, project management, and execution teams—varies from project to project, resulting in a lack of continuity and consistency. Traditionally, design is separated from the actual construction process with resultant problems in communication, coordination, and interpretation. This separation is the ideal breeding ground for disputes. This situation is further exacerbated by the divergent objectives of the major contracting parties, namely the client and contractor, with respect to the project parameters of time, cost, and quality. Clients desire their buildings to be constructed within the shortest possible time, at the lowest cost, and to the highest quality standards. The contracting fraternity would prefer to construct buildings within a reasonable time, at the lowest cost and maximum margins, and to reasonable quality standards. This tension between the parties contributes to the climate of disputes. Safety is one of the first areas to be sacrificed in the effort to bring about equilibrium in these divergent objectives.

The construction industry is subject to economic cycles and dependent on changing governmental priorities and policies producing "stop-go" approaches in the sector. Construction, furthermore, is often severely affected by natural phenomena such as changing weather and climatic conditions. The physical working environment is not constant and varies between work done below natural ground level, at ground level, at elevated heights, and sometimes even over water. This changing working environment produces several hazardous situations.

A further characteristic of the industry is the unfavorably high supervisor-worker ratio, which according to Hinze (1997) should be of the order of 2.7 workers to one supervisor. Supervisors who have a more personal and positive relationship with their workers have more favorable safety performance records (Hinze 1997, Levitt and Samelson 1993). This relationship is harder to develop if the ratio is too high—which it generally is.

The construction industry has often been described as an industry characterized by fragmentation. This description has arisen due to the number of stakeholders and participants in the construction process from project inception through to final project completion and beyond—each with divergent roles, goals, expertise, and skills.

Fragmentation, for example, results in:

- increased costs
- low productivity
- poor communication
- increased and often unnecessary documentation
- ineffective and inefficient project management
- unnecessary delays
- unsatisfactory quality performance
- rework
- poor safety performance
- costly and lengthy disputes

The construction industry has further been described as one with a poor health and safety culture. Efforts to improve health and safety performance will not be effective until the health and safety culture is improved (Dester and Blockley 1995). Put another way, there is the need for a major paradigm shift with respect to attitudes toward safety and health on construction sites.

TOTAL SAFETY CULTURE (TSC)

A safety culture is something that develops over time. From the Total Safety Culture (TSC) conceptual perspective, every person involved in the construction process has a personal, individual responsibility on a daily basis to maintain worker safety and health on construction sites regardless of size, form, or location. The TSC perspective according to Blair (1996) requires movement toward a philosophy that embraces total involvement, true empowerment, viewing safety as an intrinsic value rather than merely a priority, and improved and recurrent training methods. This approach promotes safe work practices which are supported via people who actively care about safety on a continuous basis (Geller 1994). If only management within construction firms were trying to bring this about, only 3% of the available workforce would be actively engaged while the remaining 97% would be uninvolved (Muller 1997). It is imperative, therefore, that clients, designers, contractors, manufacturers, suppliers, and all other participants in the construction process become involved in the processes of acculturation and assimilation in order to bring about this Total Safety Culture.

Acculturation is the process of change resulting from contact between different cultures whereby new cultural elements are incorporated into the existing culture. Assimilation, on the other hand, occurs when one culture is completely replaced by another. Both of these processes are necessary to arrive at a universal Total Safety Culture since each of the participants in construction are at different stages of development with respect to a culture of safety.

Two studies were undertaken in the United States to determine the main causes of accidents (HPT 1998). The National Safety Council study produced the following results with respect to the root causes of industrial accidents:

- 10% due to unsafe conditions
- 88% due to unsafe behaviors
- 2% due to unknown causes

The DuPont Company study produced similar results, namely:

- 96% due to unsafe behaviors
- 4% due to unsafe conditions

However, unsafe behavior is only one of a number of contributing factors and very often the final trigger event. Conditions such as poor management and lack of knowledge incubate into disaster and consequently are hazards. These hazards may then incubate other hazards which may incubate yet more hazards until a precipitating event triggers an incident. If one accepts this view, health and safety culture, management systems, technical difficulties, social factors, and behavior may consequently in certain circumstances be hazards. Focusing accident prevention at trigger hazard events implies that workers are at fault. However, work practices are influenced by the requirements, demands, and expectations of clients, designers, and managers. It is also likely that the beliefs, attitudes, and behavior of construction managers, clients, designers, educationalists, and researchers are reflected in the beliefs, attitudes, and behavior of workers. It is also reasonable to suggest that management practices, inter alia, lack of commitment, leadership and action are management manifestations of unsafe behavior.

If one accepts the results of the studies to imply that between 98% and 100% of industrial accidents are caused as a result of a combination of unsafe behaviors and unsafe conditions, it is plausible to deduce that both can be prevented by the implementation of reasonably practicable precautions, resulting in the avoidance of most accidents. However, to bring about this desired result will require the involvement and commitment of all participants in the construction process and calls for teamwork.

Human beings have a universal propensity for change rooted in the flexibility and adaptability of the human species, which has an enormous capacity for learning, symbolizing, and creating. It is this potential which is going to draw and fuse previously marginalized participants in the construction process into a tightly-knit and cohesive team committed to working together in search of a common goal—zero accidents, zero incidents on construction sites around the world.

There are ten basic principles on which to base the processes of people for achieving a Total Safety Culture (Griffiths 1995). When these principles are accepted on an industry-wide basis by all stakeholders and participants in the construction process, they can effectively contribute to the design and implementation of relevant safety and health action plans.

Principle 1: Culture and Not Legislation Should Drive the Occupational Safety and Health Process

Using existing legislation motivates people to avoid failure rather than achieve success. Put differently, legislation requires working to meet goals set by someone else as opposed to working to achieve outcomes for themselves such as injury-free workplaces.

Principle 2: Behavior-based and Person-based Approaches to Occupational Safety and Health Can Decrease Undesirable Behavior, Which is a Major Contributing Factor to the High Incidence of Accidents

Behavioral factors are observable activities, whereas personal factors are those feelings or attitudes that are unobservable such as knowledge, intentions, attitudes, expectancies, and moods.

Principle 3: Focus on Process, Not Outcomes

Too often organizations focus on outcome statistics such as reportable injuries, rather than the human processes (behavior and attitude), which give rise to these outcomes. This misdirected focus:

- diverts attention from processes designed to reduce injuries
- may induce non-reporting of injuries in an endeavor to maintain or achieve improved statistics such as Disabling Injury Incidence Rate (DIIR)
- may engender a perception among workers that injuries are rare and that "it's not going to happen to me"

When programs are refocused, people feel they personally control individual and team behavior rather than the DIIR, and that they can reduce injuries.

Principle 4: Behavior is Directed by Activators and Motivated by Consequences

The Activator-Behavior-Consequence (ABC) model represents the typical sequence of events and illustrates the nature of external influences. Activators are events that precede behavior and direct certain behavior. Consequences follow behavior and determine whether behavior will recur. Behavior followed by pleasant consequence (positive reinforcers) is more likely to be repeated than behavior followed by unpleasant consequences (negative reinforcers).

Certain natural features of a work setting imply either comfort, convenience, or faster job completion if certain unsafe work practices are followed, such as working without wearing a safety harness, for example. Activators such as policy, induction, memoranda, and signs are often introduced to prompt safe work practices at construction site level. Although these activators may announce potential unpleasant consequences for following unsafe behavior, without intermittent consequence to motivate safe behavior, unsafe behavior should be expected because natural consequences often motivate unsafe behavior.

When all stakeholders understand the ABC model they not only recognize why unsafe behavior is relatively common, they also acknowledge why activators and consequences are needed to initiate and maintain safe work practices and, more importantly, why they need to give each other reminders and feedback. This understanding promotes worker participation in the development and implementation of intervention strategies.

Principle 5: Focus on Achieving Success, and Not On Avoiding Failure

Productivity and quality goals receive more continuous proactive attention than health and safety goals as people are working to achieve success rather than to avoid failure. In this context safety and health are not included in what the industry accepts as being success. The construction industry needs to accept safety and health performance as a project parameter for success (Hinze 1997). Successful performance in this area is as important. However, the practice of measuring health and safety according to injury statistics limits evaluation to a reactive outcome-oriented perspective and creates a negative reinforcement motivational system. Preferably, a measurement system should continually track health and safety achievements and display them to the entire workforce.

Principle 6: Observation and Feedback Lead to Healthy and Safe Behavior

Given that workers change behavior in a desired direction when they know their behavior is being observed, then observing and displaying daily frequencies of certain work behavior is a key intervention for changing behavior. In the setting of construction sites workers need to observe the work practices of their fellow workers and offer supportive feedback for safe behavior and corrective feedback for unsafe behavior. This requires substantial employee training.

Increased observation by safety staff at Universal Studios, without any other additional changes, training, or action, resulted in a drastic reduction in the incidence of accidents and injuries on their Orlando, Florida site at a time when these were occurring at an alarmingly high rate (De Woody 1998).

Principle 7: Effective Feedback Occurs via Behavior and Person-based Coaching

The five letters of the acronym COACH are a reminder of key aspects of optimal safety coaching, namely,

- C = communication
- O = observation
- A = analysis
- C = change
- H = help

These aspects not only enable effective coaching, but they make people feel comfortable about giving or receiving coaching.

Feedback should:

- always be given in a one-on-one situation to avoid potential interference or embarrassment
- address alternative safe behavior
- discuss potential solutions for eliminating unsafe behavior

Principle 8: Observing and Coaching are Key Actively Caring Processes

Knowledge, ability, and skills alone are not sufficient for individuals to exceed the call of duty. To achieve a Total Safety Culture everyone must be willing and able to "actively care." Actively caring (AC) behaviors can be taught and motivated. Behavior focused AC attempts to influence the health and safety behavior of others by:

- rewarding or correcting feedback
- demonstrating or teaching desirable behavior
- conducting a behavioral audit for health and safety

Principle 9: Self-Esteem, Belonging, and Empowerment Increases AC for Health and Safety

People need to feel good about themselves (self-esteem) before they will act for the health and safety of others. Strategies to bring this self esteem about include:

- soliciting and following-up suggestions from workers
- facilitating peer monitoring and personal learning
- increasing management and peer attention on the occurrence of healthy and safe behaviors
- increasing recognition of personal competence and accomplishments

People who feel part of a cohesive team are more likely to actively care for those within and outside the team. Sense of belonging can be increased by:

- decreasing "top-down" directives and quick-fix programs
- team-building discussions
- group goal setting and feedback
- sponsoring celebrations for achievements
- self-managed (or self-directed) work teams

An attitude of empowerment increases motivation to make a difference. Some of the ways of enhancing empowerment include:

- breaking down of overwhelming tasks into more manageable smaller tasks
- setting and tracking short-term goals
- rewarding and correcting process activities rather than only outcomes

- allowing maximum participation in the setting of goals
- teaching how to define, observe, document, and monitor desired and undesired environments and behavior
- teaching basic behavioral change intervention strategies and providing the time necessary to do so
- training on how to graph daily records of baseline intervention and follow-up data

Principle 10: Shift Health and Safety from a Priority to a Value

Values remain constant, whereas priorities change relative to prevailing circumstances. Consequently health and safety should be a value which everyone integrates into every activity.

In order to optimize the effort to bring about a Total Safety Culture in construction it is necessary to weld every stakeholder in the construction process into a team committed to total safety on construction sites around the world.

TEAMWORK, TEAM BUILDING, AND VALUE SYSTEMS

The following words taken from a poster in the offices of Universal Studios Florida speak volumes:

> Teamwork is the ability to work together toward a common vision. The ability to direct individual accomplishment toward organizational objectives. It is the fuel that allows common people to attain uncommon results.

It is exactly this ability which is desired to achieve better safety and health performance in construction. Some of the characteristics of a successful team according to Carley (1996) are:

- *A clear focus on the task at hand.* On of the greatest problems is translating organizational visions into goals and objectives which are then integrated into action plans tied to the organizational business strategy. The "construction industry team" must be clearly focused on the task of the achievement of better safety performance on construction sites and the development of Total Safety Culture.

- *Firm deadlines with no excuses.* In order to realize this objective the team must be totally committed to achieving this goal within the shortest possible time, taking one project at a time. A commitment to this goal will require a lack of fear of tight deadlines. There should be no room for compromise.

- *Distinct and unique contributions.* It must be recognized that participants in the construction process have distinct and unique contributions to make based on their respective roles, expertise, and skills. An architect, for example, must not be doing what an engineer could best be doing. Similarly, the main contractor should not be doing what a specialized subcontractor could be doing better.

- *Mutual trust, reliance, and admiration.* Maximizing the distinct and unique contribution that each participant brings to the table requires delegation and mutual trust. A real team does not exist unless each team member has a unique contribution to make which is vital to the successful outcome of the project. Further, individual goals must be suppressed for the sake of team goals.

- *Well defined roles.* The role of each participant is well defined and clear with each ensuring that the contribution that they make is their best effort. No participant should covet the role of others. If the commitment of any single member of the team wavers or is in doubt, it will impact on the realization of the team vision and goal and could in fact jeopardize the entire effort. Each stakeholder in construction should be committed to the success of the others individually and collectively, if the teamwork approach is going to be successful in reducing accidents, injuries, and fatalities in the construction industry. It must be recognized that the task at hand cannot be accomplished alone and that each contribution is integral to the success of the project. Team cohesiveness is a factor that may impact on the success or failure of a team. Cohesion is, by definition, the total field of forces which act on members to remain in a group (Festinger, Schachter, and Black 1950). When members are cooperatively interdependent on each other instead of competitive the desire to remain in the group is greater (Gasparec 1984). Where the combined efforts of all members with specialized skills is required to achieve team goals, it has been found that this interdependence contributes to the ultimate successful performance of the team (Carron 1984, Bird 1977).

- *Frequent, sincere, positive feedback.* Sincere pride in the work of the other team members boosts their enthusiasm. Genuine, focused, positive feedback should be frequent.

- *Unambiguous and constructive criticism.* Criticism should be specific and targeted at improved performance rather than at other members of the team. Improvements should be suggested.

- *Maximum freedom of self-expression.* While boundaries must of necessity be set, each team member should be allowed to take credit for his or her contribution to the project. Direction should be given when this is necessary or requested. Each should realize their role and their creativity and energy will enhance their contribution to the project success.

- *Ability to solve problems directly.* Each participant should be encouraged to solve problems between themselves. Only if this fails should it become a problem for others to become involved with. Problems, and there will be many, should as far as possible remain localized. This approach fosters honesty and heightened respect and reduces distraction.

- *Flexible leadership.* While leadership is a necessary evil to maintain order and focus too much direction stifles the ability of others to solve problems. Every project should have a leader, and it is in precisely this area that there have been, and still are, problems. Traditional views about where leadership should vest should be abandoned in favor of a structure which will make the actualization of the goal of zero accidents, zero incidents on construction sites a reality. Leadership is necessary. It fosters friendship, mutual trust, heightened respect, and interpersonal warmth as well as establishes rules and regulations, channels of communication, procedural methods, and well-defined patterns of organization. These facilitate the achievement of the goals and objectives of the team—overall improvement in safety performance on construction sites.

- *Innovation and improvisation.* Once problems arise in a successful team, it becomes the responsibility of the entire team to fix them. On a good team everyone feels comfortable to be creative to constantly find ways to innovate.

- *Going above and beyond.* The team should have a passion to excel and be committed to work for the satisfaction of accomplishment and the respect of their peers.

- *Mutual respect.* While it is possible for team members to dislike each other intensely, each should have great respect for the abilities of the others.

- *Closure, reflection, and reformation.* A team needs to know when the task at hand is complete. Closure may be difficult to define in respect of the objective of improving safety performance in the construction industry. However, when each project is completed on time, within budget, to the required quality standards, and without accidents, injuries, and fatalities, the project has been successfully completed. During the course of pursuing this goal it will be essential to stop, assess the successes, and recommit to achieving new successes. Opportunity should be given for the assessment of the performance of team members and the redefinition of roles for future projects.

Some of the greatest persons in history, such as Martin Luther King, used team effort to create a better world. King inspired the support of millions of Americans for the equal rights of black Americans (Sanders 1997). Team members need to learn to cooperate. This is achieved by the adjusting of attitudes, dedication to a goal, and toleration for the differences of others. A good motto would be "Compete with yourself; co-operate with others" (Sanders 1997). And the power behind any team is vividly demonstrated in the saying "Together we stand, divided we fall" (Sanders 1997).

Together so much can be done. This is particularly true in the context of a team effort where the potential of each team member is tapped. There is so much to be done to bring about improved safety and health performance in construction with its accompanying benefits, and no contribution is regarded as being too small. Together significant differences can be brought about. However, it must be recognized that ends or goals of the actions of people and indeed the actions themselves are not randomly determined. There is an inherent consistency in them known as their value orientation or value system (Beal, Bohlen, and Raudebagh 1971). Members of the same culture and the same group, or team, tend to have similar value systems. The Oxford dictionary (Allen 1990) defines values as including codes of behavior, ethics, standards (morals), and principles. Smallwood (1995a) maintains that

> besides influencing vision, without values, there is unlikely to be any commitment and little, if any, effort and resources apportioned to the health and safety effort.

According to Mitchell (1978) goals, representing aspirations, serve as a common bond and as a standard of evaluation. In many cases organizational effectiveness is defined as the extent to which the goals have been attained. In fact, team productivity is greatest in those teams where techniques are used which simultaneously further the attainment of the team goals (Figure 6–1) and bring fulfilment of the wishes of individual members (Beal, Bohlen, and Raudebagh 1971).

Team building is a complex process by which an aggregate of people with a wide variety of individual goals (I), values and skills mold themselves into a productive team with common goals (G), and a common value system with their various skills directed at the achievement of the common goal (C). The relationship between I, G, and C is demonstrated in Figure 6–2.

The ideal is to increase the area of overlap (C) between the respective individual goals (I) and the common team goal (G) to the extent that (I) completely overlaps (G) so that the individual goals and the team goals become one and the same (Figure 6–3).

While it is recognized that injuries do occur, this recognition should never convey acceptance that injuries must occur (The Business Roundtable 1991). Zero accidents, zero incidents on construction sites is the only realistic goal since a lesser goal would represent compromise in that it leaves the subtle message that injuries will occur and that they are acceptable.

While it will not be able to change the entire construction industry overnight with respect to approaches to safety and health, if the team-building or teamwork approach is followed on a project for project basis, some measure of success will be attained toward achieving the industry-wide goal of zero accidents, zero incidents. According to Abraham Maslow two of the fun-

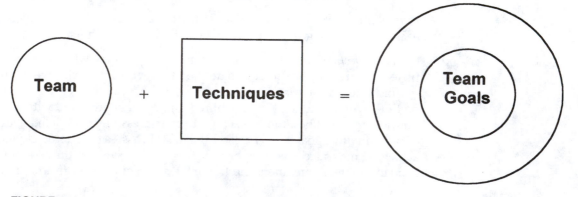

FIGURE 6–1
Team framework.

Source: Adapted from Beal, Bohlen, and Raudebagh 1971.

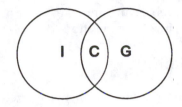

FIGURE 6–2
Relationship between individual and team goals.

Source: Adapted from Beal, Bohlen, and Raudebagh 1971.

damental needs of people are for belonging and self-fulfilment. Successful team members have both needs satisfied every time they complete a project or exceed a goal (Carley 1996). The construction industry is in need of so many more successful projects so that it becomes the industry norm that projects are completed within budget, on time, to the desired quality standards, and without accidents, injuries, and fatalities. It will however require the unique contributions and commitment of every participant in the construction process team to bring this to fruition.

The contribution to the construction safety and health effort of participants such as architects, engineers and designers, clients, construction managers, project managers, construction site workers, trade unions, suppliers, and subcontractors is significant. If each contribution were used to influence the construction process with accident prevention in mind, not only during the actual construction phase but throughout the life of the facility until its eventual demise with the demolition phase, a great contribution would have been made to the avoidance of accidents (Joyce 1995). However, each contribution becomes less significant if it is made merely on an individual basis.

PARTICIPANTS IN THE CONSTRUCTION PROCESS

Before considering the influence that participants in the construction process have and can potentially play in the effort to improve safety and health on construction sites, it is worth noting the results of a study concluded by the Health and Safety Executive in the United Kingdom (Joyce 1995) which found that the main causes of accidents were due to:

- A lack of supervision by the line managers in the industry; the increasing use of subcontractors and labor-only contractors led to problems of management and control in the context of new forms of contracting involving management remote from the site
- Failure to equip workers to identify hazards and take preventative measures to protect themselves
- A lack of coordination between members of the professional team at the pre-construction stage

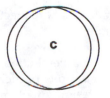

FIGURE 6–3
Relationship between individual and team goals—greater overlap.

Source: Adapted from Beal, Bohlen, and Raudebagh 1971.

This suggests that the problem of improving safety on construction sites has to be tackled at many levels at the same time, involving the efforts of every person involved in the construction process.

Designing for Safety

While there have been some improvements in safety performance, this improvement has taken place with the design profession not being an active participant (Gambatese 1998). Historically, the design profession has not addressed construction site safety in its scope of work. This lack of designer involvement has been attributed to their educational focus, which does typically not include safety and health as a topic, their limited practical experience in addressing construction site safety, restricted roles on the construction project team, and deliberate attempts to minimize liability exposure (Gambatese 1998). Current legislation and standards, such as the Uniform Building Code in the United States, typically target the safety of the end-users of buildings rather than the workers who construct them. According to MacCollum (1995), the primary and most effective method which should be used to reduce safety risks is designing to eliminate or minimize hazards, which suggests that designers are well placed to have significant impacts on construction site safety performance. They must be part of the team.

Designers influence construction health and safety both directly and indirectly. They have a direct influence through the selection of frame types, design, detail, and specifications. Indirectly they influence safety and health through the selection of procurement systems, preparation of contract documentation, and decisions about the duration of contracts (Smallwood 1996a).

In order to determine the influence of design on health and safety in the South African construction industry, a written survey was conducted among metropolitan area based general contractors (GCs) (Smallwood 1996a).

Seventy-one of the 252 metropolitan area based GCs surveyed responded, which constitutes a response rate of 28.2%. The salient findings include the following:

- 56.3% responded that health and safety is negatively affected by short project periods and 29.6% responded in the negative. Those GCs who responded in the affirmative identified general pressure (67.5%), less time per activity (65%), and more workers (57.5%) most frequently as ways in which health and safety are negatively affected by short project periods.
- 68.2% responded that health and safety is negatively affected by competitive tendering and 31.8% responded in the negative.
- 58.6% responded that there should be prequalification on health and safety and 31.4% responded in the negative.
- 59.2% responded that there should be a provisional sum for health and safety and 32.4% responded in the negative.
- GCs made use of a number of references when deliberating/pricing health and safety during tendering, but predominantly: site inspections (69%); drawings (59.2%); specification (46.5%), and geotechnical reports (26.8%).
- GCs identified a number of design related aspects/factors that can negatively affect health and safety, but predominantly: general design (50%); method of fixing (47.1%); content of material (38.6%); mass of material (38.6%); size of material (37.1%); and edge of material (35.7%).
- 87% or more responded that architects and engineers/designers should receive health and safety education.

Recently, there have been several attempts to redistribute the responsibility for safety of construction workers among various participants in the construction process. Of particular note are the Construction (Design and Management) Regulations in the United Kingdom which were enacted in 1994 with the objective of directing designers to address construction site safety as the design is being developed (CDM 1994). In terms of this legislation and the Council Directive of 25 June 1992 on the implementation of minimum safety and health requirements at temporary or mobile construction sites (92/57/EEC), designers have to be sufficiently competent to appreciate the impact on safety and health aspects of their designs. Hazards associated with construction activities have to be identified as the first step of risk assessment in terms of preventative design. The designer is required to weigh the risk to health and safety produced by a feature of a design against the cost of excluding that feature by:

- designing to avoid the risks to health and safety
- tackling the causes of risks at source; or if this is not possible, reducing and controlling the effects of risks by means aimed at protecting anyone at work who might be affected by the risks and so yielding the greatest benefit (Joyce 1995)

For example, many accidents due to falls during construction and cleaning work could be reduced by the pre-planning and design of cast-in eyebolts for the attachment of harnesses (Joyce 1995). Designers should in terms of these requirements set out very clearly the principles and assumptions involved in the design, and identify and describe any special requirements, which the contractor, for example, will need to know in considering the method of construction.

Teamwork and partnering will more and more often be a basic requirement for successful, complex design and construction projects of the future because of the shortage of capital and the need to maximize on investment in construction (Weingardt 1997).

Client Influence

Construction health and safety can be successfully influenced by clients (The Business Roundtable 1991, Hinze 1997). Clients have a legal and moral responsibility to, among other things,

- ensure that designers consider the impact on safety and health of workers during the construction phase in their designs
- ensure that safety plans taking into account all the potential hazards inherent in the final approved design are compiled and strictly adhered to
- warn contractors of any non-apparent hazards present on the site
- take reasonable care to prevent contractors from injuring others on the site
- make sure that contractors recognize their contractual responsibility to work in a healthy and safe manner

A further role identified for clients is that of optimal interaction with designers since they play a critical role in construction health and safety (Jeffrey and Douglas 1994). Health and safety is complementary to the client project requirements of completion on time, within budget, and in accordance with the specified quality standards. Successful projects also tend to be projects with optimal safety and health performance records. However, clients must know exactly what they require, and must, therefore, develop detailed comprehensive specifications for the project designers. This is probably the most crucial phase for the successful, healthy, and safe completion of any project. Deviations from the specifications at a later date could be the catalyst that triggers a series of events from designer through to the workers on the construction site which culminate in an avoidable accident, injury, or death.

Client pressure can negatively affect the construction safety and health effort as they may be under commercial pressure to complete a project as early as possible (O'Reilly *et al.* 1994). This may result in work being accelerated to the extent that it is becomes incompatible with normal safety standards. Acceleration of projects has been shown to be counterproductive as the resultant pressure to expedite work to meet deadlines can lead to accidents, injuries and fatalities (Hinze 1997).

The following actions, among others, may be taken by clients:

- become committed to safety and health
- support the safety and health efforts of contractors financially

- include safety and health performance track records as a criteria for pre-qualification
- schedule safety and health requirements prior to the bidding process
- structure documentation to ensure equitable provision for safety and health by contractors
- require a formal safety and health program
- the use of permit systems for potentially hazardous activities
- the designation of a contractor safety and health coordinator
- reporting and investigation of accidents
- conduct safety and health audits during construction
- adopt a partnering approach (The Business Roundtable 1991)

A study conducted by Stanford University determined that client involvement in contractor safety and health resulted in contractors achieving accident rates below the industry average. This was concluded from the study, which involved dividing the clients into groups according to contractor accident rates, either below or above the industry average. The findings of the study are summarized in Table 6–2.

The benefits of client involvement are:

- lower construction costs
- quality work
- improved productivity
- completion on schedule
- reduced exposure to bad publicity resulting from accidents
- minimal disruption of the employees and facilities of the client where work is in progress on existing premises (The Business Roundtable 1991)

In order to determine the influence of clients on contractor health and safety in South Africa a written survey was conducted among metropolitan area based GCs (Smallwood 1997b). The 71 responses constituted a response rate of 6.2%. The salient findings include the following:

- In terms of aspects negatively affecting health and safety competitive tendering was identified by 50% of respondents, shortened project periods by 69.7%, lack of contractor registration by 58.5%, and lack of health and safety prequalification by 63.6%.

TABLE 6–2

Nature of client involvement in contractor safety and health.

| | Frequency of client action (%) | |
| | Contractor accident rate | |
Client safety and health action	<Industry average	>Industry average
Require contractors to obtain work permits	100.0	0.0
Pre-qualified contractors	100.0	50.0
Conduct formal site inspections	100.0	0.0
Audit contractors	60.0	0.0
Use goal setting	100.0	15.0
Maintain contractor statistics	75.0	<40.0
Maintain a construction department	75.0	33.3
Stress safety and health during pre-bid activities and site visits	66.6	33.3
Train contractors' supervisors and workers	>50.0	10.0

Source: The Business Roundtable 1991.

- 47.8% responded that clients seldom influence their health and safety performance. The other frequencies were: always (4.4%); often (13%); regularly (14.5%); never (14.5%), and don't know (5.8%).
- Safe work procedures (SWPs) (44.9%), awareness (40.8%), require attendance at meetings (40.8%), required appointments (38.8%), contractor monitoring (34.7%), require health and safety plan (34.7%), reference to health and safety (32.7%), pre-qualification on health and safety (32.7%), and investigate accidents (32.7%) were ranked within the first 9 of 17 agencies of client influence on contractor health and safety.
- Of those GCs who responded that clients influence their health and safety, 76.6% responded that their health and safety performance had improved.
- Fewer accidents (72.7%) predominated among the nature of contractors' health and safety improvement; less rework was cited by 29.5%, increased productivity by 25%, reduced accident costs by 25%, and compensation insurance rebates by 22.7%.
- Based on the response to various frequencies quality is perceived by GCs to be clients' project priority. Quality was followed by cost, schedule, productivity, health and safety, and environment.
- Based upon an importance index computed for each occasion clients refer to health and safety, site meetings was ranked first, contractor pre-tender site inspections and client site inspection joint second, and site handover, site visits, and site discussions joint third.
- 53.8% responded that there should be prequalification on health and safety while 26.2% responded in the negative.
- 57.1% responded that there should be a provisional sum for health and safety while 3.8% responded in the negative.
- 67.7% responded that there should be project health and safety reporting while 15.4% responded in the negative.
- Contractor site inspection (50%), training (47.6%), education (45.2%), site handover (45.6%), and publicity (43.3%) predominated among aspects of health and safety which clients can influence or be linked to that require more attention.

Management Commitment

Management commitment has been identified as a prerequisite for effective health and safety performance (Levitt and Samelson 1993, Hinze 1997). General reasons given for this prerequisite are that management is responsible for:

- establishing objectives
- developing strategies to achieve the objectives
- all resources and their allocation
- the development and implementation of systems
- by virtue of its role, setting an example and assigning accountability (Meere 1990, International Labour Office 1995, Hinze 1997, and Jonas 1996)

Various health and safety practitioners and business authors emphasize the importance of management commitment, identifying it as a key element of a safety program (Hinze 1997, Levitt and Samelson 1993, Rozel 1992). The Associated General Contractors of America (AGC) (1990) maintain the best health and safety programs have commitment from all levels. They qualify this by saying that to establish commitment on all levels, top management must first be convinced that a health and safety program will be beneficial. When top management acknowledges the significance of a health and safety program a priority will be established which will filter down through middle management to all employees. At Universal Studios, management was convinced of the merits of prioritizing safety and health to the extent that they have become an essential part of their value system after the monetary value of the savings which would accrue due to this re-prioritization (De Woody 1998). The savings over a period of four years was of the order of $6 million.

Hinze (1997) maintains policy is one aspect, but that non-policy issues and actions represent the greatest opportunity for improvement in safety and health performance. Some of these non-policy issues and actions are:

- visits to site to discuss health and safety
- telephone contact with respect to health and safety
- personal attendance at health and safety meetings
- recognition of health and safety effort
- continual tangible and visible support
- accountability of all levels of management
- ensuring that health and safety training occurs
- injury analysis
- other general actions

In order to determine the nature, extent and benefits of management commitment 252 metropolitan area based GCs were surveyed during phase two of the study "The Influence of Management on the Occurrence of Loss Causative Incidents in the South African Construction Industry" (Smallwood 1995b). The 78 responses constituted a response rate of 31%. The following are the salient findings:

- Management focus (66.7%), experience (40%), enforcement of legislation (30%), and education (20%) predominated among agencies to which health and safety improvement is attributable.
- Reduced accident costs (41.4%), increased productivity (37.9%), and fewer complications (37.9%) predominated among the nature of health and safety improvement.
- Those GCs who had subscribed to the salient criteria relating to management commitment had shown greater improvement in health and safety performance than those who had not subscribed, health and safety rules excluded.
- A statistically significant relationship was determined to exist between cited health and safety improvement and the following criteria of management commitment: health and safety coordinator; health and safety meetings; health and safety competitions; star gradings; and computation of injury statistics.
- Although not statistically significant, the following criteria of management commitment appear to have an influence on cited health and safety improvement: health and safety policy; health and safety program; health and safety inspections; safe working procedures (SWPs); job/person matching; and following-up of incidents.
- A statistically significant relationship was determined to exist between cited health and safety improvement and construction management health and safety video viewing.

Project Manager Involvement

Project managers will be successful in their endeavors if they adopt a holistic approach, as health and safety, productivity, and quality are all inextricably intertwined (Oosthuizen 1994).

Project managers are in a unique position as they influence occupational health and safety indirectly in their capacity of project leaders and coordinators, and also through architects, engineers, and designers who design and detail, and specify materials and processes (Smallwood 1996b).

In order to determine the role of project managers in occupational health and safety a written survey was conducted among South African project management practitioners who are members of the Project Management Institute of South Africa (PMISA) (Smallwood 1996b). The 47 responses constituted a response rate of 21.2%. The salient findings include the following:

- 51.1% responded that health and safety is negatively affected by short project periods and 42.5% responded in the negative; general pressure (79.2%) predominated in terms of ways in which health and safety is negatively affected by short project period.

- 66% responded that health and safety is negatively affected by competitive tendering and 27.7% responded in the negative.
- 68.1% responded that there should be prequalification on health and safety and 23.4% responded in the negative.
- 46.8% responded that there should be a provisional sum for health and safety and 42.6% responded in the negative.
- Health and safety is considered most frequently when evaluating constructability and preparing project documentation; method of fixing (83.3%), design (80.5%), content of material (78.6%), and details (73.2%) predominated among aspects considered when deliberating constructability relative to health and safety when the always and often responses are consolidated.
- Site meetings (89.4%), site inspections (83%) and site discussions (83%) predominated among occasions health and safety is referred to when the always and often responses are consolidated.
- 89.4% responded that health and safety should be included in project management programs and courses.
- 95.8% responded that inadequate or the lack of health and safety increases project risk.

As a key participant in the construction process, project managers have a significant role to play in the team effort to improve safety and health on construction sites.

Optimum Worker Participation

Worker participation along with management support and supervisor accountability form the major pillars in a health and safety program, with the role of workers being to participate optimally in decision making and to share responsibility (Tyler 1992). Workers need to be empowered to participate in health and safety. This empowerment should constitute a mandatory condition of employment in terms of which workers have the responsibility to report any existing, new, or potential hazards in their workplaces. In this regard, workers should be trained to be able to identify and report hazards, serve on committees, and provide advice (Smallwood 1995b). Additionally, they should be made aware that they have the right to refuse to work in hazardous or potentially hazardous working environments.

The benefits of the Partners in Construction Cooperation (PICC) (Levitt and Samelson 1993) process, which entails 100% worker participation and cooperation between client, contractors, and unions, include a significant reduction in the lost time incident rate and rate of serious injuries. For example, on one project a lost time incidence rate less than one-third of the state rate was reported as well as no serious injuries or permanent disablements. Benefits cited on other projects include completion on schedule and overall cost savings. The PICC process entails among other things, 20-minute weekly or bi-weekly toolbox discussion groups that enable workers to suggest, recommend, inquire, or criticize without fear of victimization or reprisal.

In South Africa, 88 construction workers in the employ of three regional entities of national general contractors were consulted during a pilot study to determine, among other things, the nature, extent, and benefits of worker participation in health and safety (Smallwood 1997a). The salient findings include the following:

- Workers who were exposed to certain worker participation criteria felt more involved with health and safety than those who were not exposed thereto.
- A statistically significant relationship was determined to exist between feeling involved with health and safety and: reference to health and safety; knowledge of health and safety goals; being consulted about health and safety; reporting unsafe conditions to health and safety representatives, and receiving health and safety feedback.
- Workers who were exposed to certain worker participation criteria more readily reported unsafe conditions to their health and safety representative than those who were not similarly exposed.

- A statistically significant relationship was determined to exist between reporting unsafe conditions more readily to the health and safety representative and knowledge of health and safety goals; being consulted about health and safety; and receiving health and safety feedback.
- Workers who were exposed to various sources of health and safety knowledge were injured less frequently than those who had not been similarly exposed.
- A statistically significant relationship was determined to exist between frequency of injury and induction and acquiring health and safety knowledge from health and safety representative.
- Workers who were exposed to certain worker participation criteria were injured less frequently than those who had not been similarly exposed.
- A statistically significant relationship was determined to exist between frequency of injury and knowledge of health and safety policy and being consulted about health and safety.

In the metropolitan area, 114 GCs responded to a written survey to determine the nature, extent, and benefits of worker participation in health and safety as perceived by management (Smallwood 1997a). This constituted a response rate of 9.9%. The salient findings include the following:

- Problem solving (57.3%) and suggestion schemes (54.5%) predominated among the nature of worker participation.
- Approximately 60% consulted workers and approximately one-third presented toolbox talks of varying frequencies on a daily to monthly basis.
- 60.2% maintained that there should be more training.
- 66.4% maintained that there should be worker participation.
- Of those who responded to the question, 92.9% responded that workers should have the right to refuse dangerous work; this is likely to be attributable to 57.5% of GCs responding that health and safety is very important and 34.5% that it is important.

Many of the findings of the worker participation studies reinforce the ten basic principles of a TSC. The principle number is recorded between parentheses after the various findings: being consulted about health and safety (1); knowledge of health and safety goals (2); frequency of reporting unsafe conditions to health and safety representatives (3); knowledge of health and safety policy, induction, and acquiring knowledge from health and safety representative (4); knowledge of health and safety goals (5); receiving health and safety feedback (6); acquiring knowledge from health and safety representative (7 & 8); worker participation criteria statistically significantly related to feeling involved with health and safety (9); and reference to health and safety (10).

Knowledge, information and consequently education and training play a pivotal role in worker participation and a TSC. The study "The Influence of Management on the Occurrence of Loss Causative Incidents in the South African Construction Industry" (Smallwood 1995b) investigated the nature and extent of health and safety education and training and the relationship between it and health and safety performance. The salient findings include the following:

- Percentage wise, the GCs who had subscribed to the salient criteria relating to education and training had shown greater improvement in cited health and safety performance than those who had not subscribed.
- A statistically significant relationship was determined to exist between cited health and safety improvement and the following criteria of health and safety education and training: health and safety circles; instruction upon employment; and toolbox talks presented.
- Although not statistically significant, production worker health and safety training and video viewing appear to have an influence on cited health and safety improvement.
- 82.4% responded that there should be more health and safety education and 75.4% that there should be more health and safety training.

Contribution of Unions

Since workers are the constituency of trade or workers unions, the unions can play a pivotal role in promoting health and safety practices on construction sites where the workers whom they represent are employed. As such they are an essential participant in the effort to improve safety and health in construction.

The role of unions commences during the planning stage when health and safety is included in pre-project discussions and project agreements, the latter laying the groundwork for a cooperative approach to project health and safety. However, more and more contractors are adopting a partnering approach as opposed to relying on a clause pertaining to health and safety in the project agreement (Levitt and Samelson 1993).

Levitt and Samelson (1993) cite the Partners in Construction Cooperation (PICC) industry-wide labor management cooperative committee which is open to those stakeholders using unionized construction. The PICC process involves 100% worker participation and job-site cooperation among client, contractors and workers unions and is a means to:

- communicate direct information from the client and contractors to the whole workforce
- hear and respond quickly to the concerns, questions and suggestions of all members of the workforce

Unions should therefore become an integral member of the construction industry team in pursuit of zero accidents, zero incidents.

Role of Suppliers

Suppliers influence health and safety as they supply materials and services to contractors, including hazardous chemical substances (HCSs). In the terms of the Hazardous Chemical Regulations (1995) of the OHS Act (1993) suppliers are required to provide material safety data sheets (MSDs) in respect of HCSs. MSDSs detail, among other things, the composition of the material, labeling and highlighting the potential hazard, correct handling procedures, recommended storage requirements, and emergency measures.

Suppliers form an important link between the designers or specifiers and the workforce who will work with the hazardous materials and make use of the services provided. As such they should be co-opted onto the construction industry team and be more integrally involved with the safety of workers on construction sites which they supply with their materials and services.

Subcontractors

It is universally acknowledged that subcontractors undertake the greater percentage of work in the construction industry although in the civil engineering sector the portion subcontracted out by general contractors is usually less. Although clients generally have the contractual right to exercise final approval of non-nominated (designated) subcontractors, the first choice of general contractors is invariably approved.

During research conducted among metropolitan area based GCs in South Africa (Smallwood & Rwelamila 1996) 40.7% of GCs cited level of subcontracting as an aspect negatively affecting health and safety, while 28.4% responded in the negative and 30.9% didn't know.

According to Hinze (1997) subcontractor health and safety has its beginning in the selection of subcontractors. Health and safety should therefore be a definite criterion for subcontractor selection. Some suggested criteria that can be used to evaluate past health and safety performance of a subcontractor include:

- the experience modification rate
- compensation insurance claims ratio
- the injury frequency rate

The subcontractor agreement itself may address health and safety to some extent. Although standard subcontract agreements generally (certainly in South Africa!) require subcontractors to comply with the appropriate health and safety legislation and incumbent regulations, the requirement does little more than emphasize that health and safety regulations exist. In South Africa many general contractors enter into mandatory agreements with subcontractors where the agreement expressly states that the subcontractor is responsible for health and safety. This is to prevent possible liability in the South African context of the general contractor for subcontractor injuries in terms of Section 37 of the OHS Act.

Research conducted by Hinze and Figgone (Hinze 1997) to determine the influence of general contractors on subcontractor health and safety on medium-sized projects in California determined health and safety to most influenced by five broad categories:

- project pressures
- project coordination
- emphasis on health and safety
- concern for workers
- compliance with health and safety regulations

However, project pressures and project coordination are by far the most important.

Project pressure in turn was found to have the greatest impact. The health and safety performance of subcontractors:

- was inversely related to the degree of pressure experienced by superintendents of general contractors
- was linked to project subcontractor schedule performance; the relative injury frequency of subcontractors was commensurately less on projects ahead of subcontractor schedule than projects on subcontractor schedule and behind subcontractor schedule
- was better when managers of general contractors emphasized profits along with other goals as opposed to only profits
- was better when health and safety and quality were included as priorities as opposed to only cost and subcontractor schedule
- was better when subcontracts were negotiated as opposed to competitively bid

Project coordination by the general contractor was found to be directly related to subcontractor health and safety performance. Subcontractor health and safety performance was:

- better when general contractors were assessed as having good coordination skills
- better on the smaller projects as opposed to on the larger projects due to effectiveness of coordination being influenced by size and complexity of project
- inversely related to the number of subcontractors working on a project
- better when general contractors worked with familiar subcontractors

The emphasis on health and safety by general contractors is important to subcontractor health and safety. Two emphasis-related actions by general contractors were found to positively influence subcontractor health and safety performance: affording health and safety status equal to that of cost, subcontractor schedule, and quality; and daily communication pertaining to health and safety.

General contractors who express concern for workers were also found to have healthier and safer subcontractors. Concern was expressed by caring about the individual needs of workers and by inducting all workers (including the workers of subcontractors).

Compliance with health and safety regulations by general contractors was directly associated with better general contractors health and safety performance, namely:

- specific monitoring of handrails, floor openings, and overhead power lines
- frequent job-site inspections
- job-site inspections of subcontractor work

A second study on subcontractor health and safety by Hinze and Talley (Hinze 1997) entailed the analysis of large projects being constructed throughout the United States. The health and safety record of subcontractors was compared with the practices of general contractors to determine which practices had the greatest influence. Subcontractor health and safety on large projects was found to be mostly influenced by the strong emphasis of general contractors on health and safety and effective project coordination, the former having the greatest influence.

The following practices were found to be directly related to subcontractor health and safety performance:

- requirement that subcontractors hold their own toolbox talks
- induction of all subcontractors' workers
- review of subcontractor health and safety programs
- submission of health and safety reports by subcontractors to general contractors
- investigation of subcontractor accidents by project managers
- health and safety specific site inspections by the general contractor's project managers
- inspection of subcontractor work in terms of health and safety

The project coordination factors that benefited subcontractor health and safety included:

- the tasks of all trades and all subcontractors are carefully planned
- the coordination skills of the general contractor are highly rated by the subcontractor
- the projects are smaller
- subcontractor schedules are continually updated
- short-interval (look-ahead) subcontractor schedules are used in planning

All the large projects made use of the following practices, and consequently it could not be determined how the practices influenced subcontractor health and safety:

- a full-time project health and safety director is assigned
- all workers attend toolbox talks
- health and safety is discussed during coordination meetings
- health and safety is discussed at pre-job conference
- supervisory health and safety performance is monitored (accountability)
- top management discusses health and safety on job visits
- supervisors attend health and safety meetings
- bonuses are linked to health safety performance
- compliance with health and safety regulations is monitored

However, the most notable finding, in fact the bottom line of the study, was that general contractors have a stronger influence on discussed health and safety performance than the subcontractors themselves, i.e., the general contractor's role is pivotal in determining the success of health and safety on construction sites.

STRATEGIES, SYSTEMS, AND PROCESSES

Partnering

Sadly, the construction industry is no longer as renowned for its construction quality as it is for its confrontation, claims, and litigation. The time-honored attributes of honor, integrity, and pride in workmanship no longer characterize relationships within the industry. Partnering is a concept that focuses on returning to these same basic values which have been fundamental to honorable societies for centuries (Warne 1993). It is about getting along with the people you work with and it is about getting the job done in an honorable, dignified, efficient, and profitable way (McIntyre 1995).

Partnering takes cognizance of the fact that construction projects are a compilation of many processes and the efforts of numerous "customers" and "suppliers." It further recognizes that construction projects involve many stakeholders who have a vested interest in the successful completion of those projects. Partnering attempts to develop relationships among the parties or stakeholders through a mutually developed, formal strategy of commitment and communication. Partnering brings together the various stakeholders involved in a project—the client, designers, the general contractor, and subcontractors—to develop mutually acceptable goals for a project (Levitt and Samelson 1993).

Traditionally, however, there are considerable inequalities that bedevil the relationships between the stakeholders in the construction process such as access to the client, access to information, ability to understand risk, and position to negotiate fees (Roberts 1997). However, to achieve the common goal of improved safety performance in construction these inequalities must of necessity be overlooked.

According to Levitt and Samelson (1993) there are two reasons for expecting partnering to reduce accidents:

- the improvement in all-round relations on the job, which in turn according to research, results in reduced accidents
- the performance objectives contained in the partnering charter which usually includes specific reference to safety and health; "zero accidents, zero incidents on construction sites" could well be such a performance objective

Each stakeholder has a role in the construction process of any given project. Additionally, stakeholders have specific definitions of success that are unique to their role or perspective on the project. While these definitions may be unique they are not mutually exclusive. The partnering process recognizes that all stakeholders can be successful simultaneously in terms of their own perception of what that success is.

Fundamental to the success of any effort to improve safety and health performance on construction sites is the commitment of all stakeholders to safety for both their own workers but also those who will come into contact with the hazards presented by the work (De Woody 1998).

In the partnering process the organizational goals of all stakeholders are compared with those of other team members to identify common goals that can be shared by all participants. These would almost inevitably be the universally acceptable project parameters of time, cost, and quality. Safety performance on projects should be just as much a measure of the success of that project (Hinze 1997). The partnering team can and should be committed to working toward the realization of these common goals.

However, one of the key elements of any successful partnering arrangement is the creation of a "high-trust" culture (Warne 1993) which is characterized by the lack of the deceit, distrust, innuendo, and hidden agendas which are typical of the traditional construction process. Partnering teams concentrate all their energies to the development of a more productive and open relationship of honesty, trust and synergy (Warne 1993). It attempts to create an environment where trust and teamwork prevent disputes, foster a cooperative bond to the benefit of all in order to facilitate a successful project. Team members are encouraged to come forward and share in the resolution of problems while accepting the mistakes and errors of others in an effort to find solutions mutually acceptable to all the team members. Synergy is the working together of individuals and the expending of their energies in a team effort rather than their many individual efforts, and is a natural outcome of partnering, contributing to the overall success of the project as a whole.

The key elements of partnering as applied to the safety improvement effort should, therefore, be:

- commitment by all stakeholders or team members
- equity in relationships between team members
- trust as the team members develop relationships of understanding and communication leading to a synergistic relationship

- development of mutual goals and objectives, which in this case would include zero accidents and zero incidents on construction projects with which they are involved
- implementation on a project-by-project basis
- continuous evaluation as part of TSC
- timely responsiveness in respect of communication and decision making (McIntyre 1995)

The Construction Industry Institute (CII) in the United States reported that 196 projects using long-term partnering saved an average 15% of total installed cost. With respect to project-specific partnering an average of 7% savings was recorded on five very large projects. The CII maintains that partnering offers the most impressive savings in terms of health and safety, constructability and Total Quality Management (McGeorge and Palmer 1997).

The potential of the partnering process must be harnessed and included as one of the necessary strategies in the effort of achieving zero accidents and zero incidents on construction sites around the world. A benefit of partnering is a good or improved safety record (McIntyre 1995).

Based upon recommendations contained in the "Final Report on Initiatives to Promote Health and Safety, Productivity and Quality in South African Construction" (Smallwood and Rwelamila 1996) the Department of Public Works (DPW) (1997) proposes to implement partnering incrementally on public sector contracts. The DPW maintains that partnering will complement health and safety and overall performance.

Ultimately a partnering approach incorporating all the project stakeholders will complement Total Quality Management and the construction process (Levitt and Samelson 1993).

Total Quality Management (TQM)

Total Quality Management (TQM) has as its main thrust continuous improvement in customer satisfaction, employee satisfaction, health and safety, quality, and productivity. The TQM mission in construction is to construct a quality product—an error-free one—for the customer by preventing errors in the construction process. TQM is the linkage of the processes which deal with health and safety, productivity, quality, and satisfaction with the real benefit being the synergy between them (Levitt and Samelson 1993). However, to achieve TQM requires the commitment to the process of continuous improvement by every stakeholder in the construction process. The area of worker safety on construction sites is no exception.

There are three key principles on which TQM is based (AGC, 1992).

Customer Focus
Every participant in construction has both internal and external customers (clients) whose requirements need to be identified and met first time and every time. As all work is a process, internal customer satisfaction at each step is a prerequisite for external customer satisfaction, which affects, among other things, profit.

Process Improvement
Continuous improvement of the steps necessary to execute work will reduce the variability of the output, and ultimately result in zero defect, as well as zero accidents and zero incidents on construction sites.

Total Involvement
In the quest to improve safety performance the strategy of total involvement of all participants should be borrowed from TQM whereby they continuously engage in the process of improving their outputs by identifying and solving problems, improving processes, and consequently satisfying internal and external customers.

For example, a TQM process implemented by Texas Instruments in the U.S. (AGC 1992) to enhance contractor performance and realize overall savings realized the following:

- rework was reduced from a level in excess of 11% to a level less than 1% of project value
- improved health and safety
- reduced workers' compensation insurance
- completion on schedule

Dreger (1996) maintains that the application of the principles of TQM have the potential of realizing a quality project in all respects and giving beneficial results to all stakeholders.

Lack of improvement processes achieved a ranking of fifth out of 16 aspects negatively affecting health and safety during research conducted among metropolitan area based GCs in South Africa (Smallwood & Rwelamila 1996).

During the second survey of the current study "The Relationship Between Occupational Health and Safety, Labor Productivity and Quality in the South African Construction Industry" 71.3% of metropolitan area based GCs identified worker participation as an intervention which results in or can contribute to an improvement in health and safety performance. This resulted in a ranking of third out of 20.

Constructability Management

An additional strategy that could be influential in addressing safety and health on construction sites in the context of team building is constructability management.

Constructability management is a system for achieving optimum integration of construction knowledge and experience in planning, engineering, procurement, and site operations, and the balancing of various project and environmental constraints to achieve overall project objectives. Improved health and safety certainly should be one of these objectives.

The benefits of applying constructability management on the Toyota Car Manufacturing Facility at Altona, Australia included completion ahead of schedule and below budget; and to quality and health and safety standards (McGeorge and Palmer 1997).

The importance of constructability management was reinforced by the research conducted among project management pratitioners in South Africa (Smallwood 1996b). Of six possible occasions during design, health and safety was considered most frequently when evaluating constructability.

Standard Operating Procedures (SOPs)/Safe Work Procedures (SWPs)

According to Hood (1994) problems related to productivity, quality, and health and safety can frequently be traced to substandard, inconsistently applied, or non-existent operating procedures and practices. SOPs and procedures in general are the core component of quality management and health and safety management systems as they guarantee uniformity of operation throughout an organization. They effectively ensure that each time a task is performed it is done consistently, correctly and safely. SWPs should be available for all processes. Examples include support work check lists, slinging procedures, and crane operating signals.

During the second survey of the current study, SWPs were identified by 84.1% of metropolitan area based GCs and ranked as the most important intervention which results in or can contribute to an improvement in health and safety performance.

The features of SOPs and SWPs can be effectively incorporated into a teamwork approach toward safety and health on construction sites.

Quality Management System (QMS)

Both external customers (clients) and internal customers (workers) need assurance that projects will be completed according to requirements of clients and without workers being injured. Given that many clients prequalify contractors on health and safety performance records, and workers require preceding work to conform to requirements, a management system is required to assure quality.

Such a management system would not constitute any form of guarantee. Rather it would instill a sense of confidence. This confidence would, in turn, be a consequence of consistency. Since people are not similar in terms of personality traits, personal goals, philosophy, and culture, they require a system or systems to enable them to be consistent and achieve goals first time every time. It has been demonstrated that consistency results from a documented QMS which effectively integrates quality assurance (QA), quality control (QC), and quality improvement (QI) (Smallwood 1997b).

During research conducted among metropolitan area based GCs in South Africa (Smallwood and Rwelamila 1996) lack of QMS (65.4%) and lack of improvement processes (58%) were effectively ranked fourth and fifth out of 16 aspects negatively affecting health and safety by GCs.

It is therefore essential that all participants in the construction process commit themselves to the implementation of QMS in the effort to improve construction worker safety and health performance.

Impact of Legislation on Team Building

According to Jeffrey and Douglas (1994) the promulgation of the Construction (Design and Management) (CDM) Regulations 1994 in the United Kingdom is attributable to two aspects namely,

- the need for a radical improvement in health and safety resulting from a cultural change, and adoption of a health and safety culture by all stakeholders in the industry: clients; designers, and contractors, from inception through to execution
- the Temporary or Mobile Construction Sites Directive (TMCSD) in terms of which the contractor no longer takes sole responsibility for site health and safety as there is now a statutory link between clients and designers, site health and safety, fatalities and injury

These regulations (CDM) bring health and safety management, on an obligatory, yet not prescriptive, basis into the planning and design of construction work, on all but the smallest projects. No longer is the contractor left with the sole responsibility for health and safety during construction as has been the case in the past, for under the regulations, it is shared with other parties to a project. The participants are bound together by a health and safety plan to improve the exchange and communication of matters affecting health and safety. The health and safety plan is a dynamic document which is subject to continuous review and amendment, fulfilling its role as a coordinating and team-building mechanism, as construction progresses.

It has been acknowledged that there will be a significant cost in improving health and safety management, particularly in those entities that do not already have a well-developed approach. It has been suggested that the total cost to the UK construction industry in implementing the regulations would be in the region of $800 million, based on an industry output of $55,000 million for 1991 (Joyce 1995). This equates approximately to 1.5 % of total output. The main areas of additional cost were associated with the duties upon designers and the duty upon the planning supervisor and principal contractor to produce a health and safety plan. This cost would be of the order of $700 million per year (Joyce 1995).

The reduction of the frequency of accidents would be the principle quantifiable benefit. The reduction on small to medium-sized sites would be 33%, whereas on large sites, where safety management is usually better developed, a 20% reduction in accidents could be expected. The estimated benefit to the UK industry would be $330 million per year (Joyce 1995).

Based upon recommendations contained in the "Final Report on Initiatives to Promote Health and Safety, Productivity and Quality in South African Construction" (Smallwood & Rwelamila 1996) the Department of Public Works (DPW) (1997) proposes that similar legislation to the CDM Regulations be considered for South Africa.

The DPW in South Africa also proposes to make OHS Act requirements the minimum performance standard on all public sector projects to institute additional mechanisms to promote health and safety, including participative management linked to suitable procurement mechanisms; monitoring of performance requirements; and the requirement of certified health and safety training of workers.

The future will increasingly see legislation of a similar nature being introduced in order to place construction worker safety and health on the agenda of all stakeholders in construction.

Procurement Systems

Procurement systems have the potential to play a pivotal role in building the relationships between construction process participants in the effort to reduce accidents, injuries and fatalities on construction sites. According to Dreger (1996) the form of construction delivery affects contractual relationships and the development of mutual goals. Within the context of health and safety and sustainability the Design-Build contract form, which establishes one entity to provide both design and construction, has the greatest potential for success as it creates common project goals. However, generally procurement systems are such that contractors frequently find themselves in the iniquitous position, that should they make the requisite allowances for health and safety, they run the risk of losing a tender or negotiations to a less committed competitor (Smallwood 1996a).

Contract documentation and procedures need to become more conducive to creating the enabling environment necessary for the sharing of the responsibility for worker safety among all the stakeholders and players in the construction process from project inception through to final project completion and beyond.

While generally prequalification is applied to contractors it should be broadened to include other participants as well, especially with regard to their worker safety performance whether it be, for example, in respect of design, construction method, material specification and supply, financial provision for safety programs, training and education, or physical construction task execution.

A final consideration is that of determining the project duration, which if too compressed, invariably results in an increase in

- the number of workers
- the number of hours worked per worker, or even a combination of the two
- the amount of plant and equipment
- the number of subcontractors simultaneously undertaking work per period of time; the intensification increases the possibility of incidents (Smallwood 1996a)

Involving all stakeholders who are aware of these consequences will contribute to arriving at project duration periods which are conducive to the construction worker safety effort.

During research conducted among metropolitan area based GCs in South Africa (Smallwood & Rwelamila 1996) a number of important indicators arise from the GCs' stated frequency of exposure to various procurement system characteristics:

- Design is not complete before selecting a contractor.
- Prime costs, which do not constitute finality, are frequently made use of in contract documentation.
- Architects are not always able to coordinate and supervise the design team.
- Contractors are selected predominantly on price.
- Design is separated from construction.
- Contractors' expertise is not included in design.

The aforementioned findings indicate that currently procurement systems are not complementary to health and safety. To this end the DPW (1997) proposes to implement certain procurement and related reforms and actions:

- the requirement of GCs in terms of conditions of contract to furnish information on the identification and measurement of key contract performance indicators, including health and safety, productivity, and quality

TABLE 6–3
Aspects negatively affected by inadequate health and safety.

| | Response (%) | | | |
Aspect	Yes	No	Don't know	Total
Cost	72.3	19.2	8.5	100.0
Environment	66.0	23.4	10.6	100.0
Productivity	87.2	10.6	2.2	100.0
Quality	80.8	17.0	2.2	100.0
Schedule	57.4	29.8	12.8	100.0
Client perception	68.1	19.1	12.8	100.0

- the adoption of Design-Build and Design-Build-Operate-Transfer delivery models to foster unity of design and construction
- the introduction of participative management practices and partnering
- the engendering of the revision of existing education and training curricula for those involved in design and construction to ensure that issues of health and safety are adequately covered

Synergy

During the survey conducted among project management practitioners (PMPs) in South Africa, productivity and quality were the aspects identified most frequently as being negatively affected by inadequate health and safety (Table 6–3).

Health and safety is a prerequisite for productivity and quality as, housekeeping, among other factors, complements access and ergonomics. Productivity and quality (conformance to requirements) in turn complement the achievement of schedule requirements. Accidents result in increased cost and damage to the environment, and can substantially retard progress thereby compromising schedule. Clients' requirements include not only completion on time, to quality standards, and within budget, but also without fatalities and injuries which can have a negative effect not only on a client's perception of a contractor, but on the contractor's and client's image as well. There is clearly synergy between health and safety and the traditional project parameters, cost, quality, and schedule, and the non-traditional parameter, environment. The role of health and safety as the catalyst for the synergy between health and safety and the other project parameters is quantified by the 95.8% of PMPs who maintained that inadequate or the lack of health and safety increased project risk (accidents and disease result in variability of resource which in turn increases project risk).

CONCLUSION

The construction industry incurs a disproportionate number of fatalities and other classes of injury worldwide and in South Africa. However, the construction industry is unique in that design and production (construction) are separated and a large number of contributors (subcontractors) contribute to a once-off product in a single workplace. The aforementioned along with other unique characteristics amplify the need for a team approach to construction health and safety. Traditionally the construction health and safety effort has been spearheaded by the GC and then primarily by management and supervision, workers contributing to a marginal extent.

Descriptive research conducted in South Africa amplifies and reinforces the need for a team approach: clients, designers, and project managers positively influence health and safety both directly and indirectly; management commitment and worker participation positively influence health and safety performance; and subcontracting negatively affects health and safety performance. The descriptive research also quantifies the positive influence of various techniques which when collectively used or contributed to can influence health and safety performance: partnering; TQM; constructability management; SWPs; and QMSs. The importance of the aforementioned stakeholders and techniques quantifies the team framework equation (team + techniques = team goals) depicted in Figure 6–1. However, the development of mutual goals is a prerequisite and complementary requirement for team building, and consequently the achievement of team goals. "Zero injuries" is the most logical goal that will unite all stakeholders and ensure that individual and group goals completely overlap and become one and the same goals. Descriptive research quantifies the synergy between health and safety and cost, environment, productivity, quality, and schedule. This constitutes the motivation to all stakeholders to make health and safety a value as opposed to a priority and to evolve "zero injuries" as a mutual project goal.

The descriptive research conducted in South Africa also quantified the need for the development of a TSC as a result of the finding that health and safety performance is positively influenced by criteria of worker participation and education and training, which criteria are recognized as being integral principles to achieve a TSC.

In conclusion, although the findings of literature and descriptive surveys indicate and motivate the need for multi-stakeholder contributions to health and safety facilitated by various processes, systems, and procedures, an enabling environment needs to exist. Such an enabling environment needs to be created through "enabling environment" legislation similar to the CDM Regulations promulgated in the United Kingdom and the evolution of procurement systems which are complementary to multi-stakeholder contributions to health and safety.

First build the team . . . then build the project!

REFERENCES

Allen, R. E. (1990). *The Concise Oxford Dictionary of Current English,* 8th edition. Oxford University Press Inc., New York.

Beal, George M., Bohlen, Joe M., and Raudebagh, J. Neil. (1971). *Leadership and Dynamic Group Action.* Iowa, The Iowa State University Press.

Berger, Joachim. (1998). "The Health and Safety Protection Plan and the File containing Features of the Building according to EEC Directive (92/57)." Public Lecture, M. E. Rinker Lecture Series on Safety and Health in Construction, University of Florida, USA, 20 October 1998.

Bird, A. M. (1977). "Team structure and success as related to cohesiveness and leadership." *Journal of Social Psychology vol* 103, pp. 217–223.

Britannica Online. (1998). "Safety." *Britannica Online* http://www.eb.com/cgi-bin/g?DocF=micro/516/60.html.

The Business Roundtable. (1991). *Improving Construction Safety Performance.* The Business Roundtable, New York.

Carley, Mark S. (1996). "Teambuilding: Lessons from the Theatre." *Training and Development* vol 50 no 8, pp. 41–43.

Carron, A. V. (1984). "Cohesiveness in Sports Groups: Interpretations and Considerations." *Journal of Sport Psychology* vol 4, pp. 123–138.

CDM. (1994). *Construction (Design and Management) Regulations.* SI 1994/3140 HMSO.

Center to Protect Workers' Rights. (1995). *Program, 2nd National Conference on Ergonomics, Safety and Health in Construction.* Center to Protect Workers' Rights, Washington, D.C.

Department of Public Works. (1997). *Creating an Enabling Environment for Reconstruction, Growth and Development in the Construction Industry.* Department of Public Works, Pretoria.

Dester, W. S., and Blockley, D. I. (1995). "Safety-Behaviour and Culture in Construction." *Engineering, Construction and Architectural Management,* vol 2 (1), pp. 17–26.

De Woody, Barbara. (1998). Interviews conducted May and October 1998 with Barbara De Woody, Director of Safety at Universal Studios Florida, Orlando, Florida.

Dreger, G. T. (1996). *Sustainable Development in Construction: Management Strategies for Success.* Proceedings of the 1996 CIB W89 Beijing International Conference—Construction Modernization and Education, Beijing, October, CD-file://D1/papers/160-169/p163. Html.

Festinger, L., Shachter, S., and Black, K. (1950). *Social Pressures in Informal Groups: A Study of a Housing Project.* New York, Harper.

Gambatese, John. (1998). "Designing for Safety." Public Lecture, M. E. Rinker Lecture Series on Safety and Health in Construction, University of Florida, 21 September 1998.

Gasparec, S. B. (1984). *Team Cohesiveness and its Relationship to Performance Success in Women's Intercollegiate Softball.* Eugene, University of Oregon Publications.

Geller, Scott E. (1994). "Ten Principles for Achieving a Total Safety Culture." *Professional Safety, Journal of American Society of Safety Engineers,* vol 39.

Griffiths, B. (1995). "Ten principles for Achieving a Total Safety Culture." *National Safety,* July/August, pp. 7–9.

Griffiths, B. (1995). "Ten Principles for Achieving a Total Safety Culture." *National Safety,* September/October, p. 18.

Griffiths, B. (1995). "Ten Principles for Achieving a Total Safety Culture." *National Safety,* May/June, p. 19.

Hatush, Z., and Skitmore, M. (1997). "Criteria for Contractor Selection." *Construction Management and Economics* vol 15, no 1, pp. 19–38.

Hinze, Jimmie W. (1997). *Construction Safety.* New Jersey, Prentice-Hall, Inc.

Hood, S. (1994). "Developing Operating Procedures: 9 Steps to Success." *Accident Prevention,* May/June, pp. 18–21.

Human Performance Technologies. (1998). "Start a Behavioral Safety Program—Performance-based Safety Programs." http://www.qhpt.com/behavioral_safety.html.

International Labor Office (ILO). (1995). *Safety, Health and Welfare on Construction Sites.* International Labor Office, Geneva.

Jeffrey, J., and Douglas, I. (1994). *Safety Performance of the UK Construction Industry.* Proceedings of the 5th Annual M. E. Rinker International Conference Focusing on Construction Safety and Loss Control. University of Florida, Gainesville, Florida, pp. 233–253.

Jonas, P. (1996). "The Missing Letter in TQM." *Occupational Health and Safety,* March, pp. 18–19.

Joyce, Raymond. (1995). *The Construction (Design and Management) Regulations 1994 Explained.* London, Thomas Telford Publications.

Levitt, Raymond E., and Samelson, Nancy M. (1993). *Construction Safety Management.* New York, John Wiley and Sons, Inc.

MacCollum, D. V. (1995). *Construction Safety Planning.* New York, Van Nostrand Reinhold.

Marsicano, L. (1995). "Getting Lost in the Rubble." *Synergist* vol 6 no 8: pp. 18–19.

McGeorge, D., and Palmer, A. (1997). *Construction Management New Directions.* Blackwell Science, Oxford.

McIntyre, Marla. (1995). *Partnering: Changing Attitudes in Construction.* Washington, The Associated General Contractors of America.

Meere, R. (1990). "Building Can Seriously Damage Your Health." *Chartered Builder,* December, pp. 8 and 9.

Mitchell, T. R. (1978). *People in Organizations: Understanding their Behavior.* McGraw-Hill, Tokyo.

Muller, Neil. (1997). "Opening Address." 1st South African Construction Health and Safety Conference, Cape Town, 8 October 1997.

O'Reilly, M. G., Olomolaiye, P. O., Tyler, A. H., and Orr, T. (1994). "Issues of Health and Safety in the Irish Construction Industry." *Building Research and Information,* vol 22 no 5, pp. 247–251.

Roberts, Lois. (1997). "Partnering: Building a Stronger Design Team." *Journal of Architectural Engineering,* vol 3 no 3, p. 142.

Rozel, W. H. (1992). "Partnerships: Industry-driven, Government Supported OSH Programmes." *Professional Safety,* March, pp. 30–32.

Sanders, Lynn B. (1997). "Together We Can: How to be a Team Player."

Smallwood, J. J. (1995a). *Vision to Reality: The Role of Occupational Health and Safety.* Proceedings of the Australian Institute of Project Management 1995 National Conference, Adelaide, Australia, September, pp. 202–207.

Smallwood, J. J. (1995b). *The Influence of Management on the Occurrence of Loss Causative Incidents in the South African Construction Industry.* M.Sc. Dissertation, University of Port Elizabeth, Port Elizabeth.

Smallwood, J. J. (1996a). *The Influence of Designers on Occupational Health and Safety.* Proceedings of the 1st International Conference of CIB W99—Implementation of Safety and Health on Construction Sites, Lisbon, September, pp. 203–213.

Smallwood, J. J. (1996b). *The Role of Project Managers on Occupational Health and Safety.* Proceedings of the 1st International Conference of CIB W99—Implementation of Safety and Health on Construction Sites, Lisbon, September, pp. 203–213.

Smallwood, J. J. (1997a). "Worker Participation in South African Construction Health and Safety." In Haupt, Theo C., and Rwelamila, Pantaleo (eds), *Health and Safety in Construction: Current and Future Challenges.* Proceedings of the 1st South African Construction Health and Safety Conference, Cape Town, Pentech, October, pp. 95–104.

Smallwood, J. J. (1997b). "Client Influence on Contractor Health and Safety." In Haupt, Theo C., and Rwelamila, Pantaleo (eds), *Health and Safety in Construction: Current and Future Challenges.* Proceedings of the 1st South African Construction Health and Safety Conference, Cape Town, Pentech, October, pp. 95–104.

Smallwood, J. J., and Rwelamila, P. D. (1996). *Final Report on Initiatives to Promote Health and Safety, Productivity and Quality in the South African Construction Industry.*

The Associated General Contractors of America (AGC). (1990). *AGC Guide for a Basic Company Safety Program.* The Associated General Contractors of America, Washington, D.C.

The Associated General Contractors of America (AGC). (1992). *An Introduction to Total Quality Management.* The Associated General Contractors of America, Washington, D.C.

Turin, D. A. (1969). *The Construction Industry: Its Economic Significance and Its Role in Development.* London, Building Economic Research Unit, University College.

Tyler, W. W. (1992). "Total Involvement Safety." *Professional Safety,* March, pp. 26–29.

Warne, Thomas R. (1993). *Partnering for Success.* New York, ASCE Press.

Weingardt, Richard. (1997). "Partnering: Building a Stronger Design Team." Closure, *Journal of Architectural Engineering,* vol 3 no 3, p. 142.

IMPLICATIONS OF THE RELATIONSHIP BETWEEN CONSTRUCTION QUALITY AND SAFETY

Kent Davis, Ph.D.
Department of Construction Management
John Brown University
Siloam Springs, Arkansas, U.S.A.

ABSTRACT

An overview of construction quality and safety reveals many striking similarities including the scope, causes, and effects of associated problems. There are several contrasts including the typical failure scenario and the presence of a "third party" in safety. Programs that have been developed to improve quality and safety performance have many elements in common such as training, investigations, and record keeping. In some cases safety is considered a part of Total Quality Management (TQM). For both quality and safety it is difficult to optimize management efforts partly because it is difficult to determine the true cost of failures.

The close relationship between quality and safety implies that benefits would be derived by applying some or all of the following propositions: (1) Consolidate the safety and quality functions perhaps using a new name such as "Excellence Management"; (2) Apply cost of quality concepts to safety; (3) Optimize the costs of "Excellence Management"; and (4) Apply the results of safety research to quality.

A survey of 29 large construction firms shows general agreement that the idea of combining or better coordinating of the quality and safety management function has merit.

KEYWORDS

construction, safety, quality, management, costs

INTRODUCTION

Construction is the creation of physical entities in the face of powerful natural forces. Uncontrollable phenomena such as entropy, gravity, and adverse environmental conditions must be overcome. Human factors, including indifference and ignorance, are also challenging barriers.

Typically, construction must be done within the constraints of limited cost and time. However, constructors use energy, ingenuity, and persistence to build in spite of the obstacles. Beautiful and useful structures testify to the builders' art and science.

The difficulties cited above that inhibit construction in general also play a major role in the specific areas of construction safety and quality. The gravitational force that eventually brings a building down can bring a worker down immediately and catastrophically. The apparent randomness of the universe exhibited in the flooding of a city or a construction site today can be seen in the defective bolt of tomorrow. Bad weather is an obstacle to good construction. It is also an obstacle to safety and quality. Builders need to utilize the same level of determination and intelligence that creates a monument to be effective at the safety and quality subsystem level.

It is safe to assume that quality and safety issues have been a part of construction from the earliest time. The bible states that "There is risk in each stroke of your axe" (Ecclesiastes 10:9), a statement about safety. A well-known 18th century proverb states that "To err is human, to forgive divine," a comment on quality. Safety and quality issues are part of the fabric of existence. Systematic methods of dealing with safety and quality in construction are of more recent vintage.

While there has undoubtedly always been risk to construction employees, major improvements to guarantee the protection of all workers required acts of state legislatures and Congress. Among the most important pieces of legislation created are workers' compensation laws and OSHA regulations. These were written for industry in general and thereby include the construction industry. Workers' compensation legislation was passed at the state level during the early 1900s (Hammer 1985, p. 32). These laws require employers to purchase insurance to cover employees injured on the job. In exchange for this form of "no fault" insurance, the employer is supposed to be immune to employee suits related to injuries. The Williams-Steiger Occupational Safety and Health Act, federal legislation passed in 1970, created the now well-known OSHAdministration (Hammer 1985, p. 50). This far-reaching legislation placed the responsibility for employee safety on the employer and resulted in the creation of thousands of regulations. In spite of these and other legislative actions, it may be argued that the construction industry, with the exception of some of the more enlightened companies, has a poor safety record. There is evidence that the record on injuries, at least, improved somewhat in the last few years (*Engineering News Record* May 11, 1998, p. 11).

The interest in Construction Quality as an isolated component is very recent. The working definitions were not even published until 1987 (Burati & Farrington 1987). Their research showed that underachieved quality is a major component of the inefficiency of the American construction industry. There has been little published to indicate any great improvement since then, partly because many companies do not collect the necessary data (Hickman 1993, p. 14). In the past few years there has been an increase in the use of a concept known as Total Quality Management (TQM). The adoption of this approach has been seen as a necessity to remain competitive (Burati 1990).

Approaches to controlling construction quality and safety have developed on different but parallel tracks. The relationship between them has not been fully realized or exploited. To do so requires a basic understanding of both issues. The following pages provide a brief overview of construction quality and safety and a discussion of some of their major similarities, contrasts, and interrelationships. Based on these ideas, four propositions for improvement are advanced.

CONSTRUCTION QUALITY MANAGEMENT

Quality is defined as conformance to established requirements (not a degree of goodness) (Burati & Farrington 1987, p. 13). The requirements, which are objective, should be clearly communicated in the contract documents. This implies that the contract, specifications, and plans must be complete, accurate, and internally consistent. Furthermore, if changes are to be minimized, the requirements as communicated must be understood by all entities, including the owner. Failures to meet requirements are called deviations and include errors and omissions. One issue of interest is whether or not changes should be classified as deviations. By definition, a change is an alteration in the requirements rather than a failure to meet the requirements and is not, therefore, a real deviation. It may be argued, however, that an owner- or designer-initiated change usually represents a design deviation since it should have been anticipated. In any case, changes are so disruptive and expensive they were included as a type of deviation in the Burati and Farrington study (1987, p. 4).

Quality Management may be defined as the optimization of efforts to make sure that the requirements are met efficiently and on the first attempt. Things should be "done right" the first time and "rework" avoided. Optimization of effort implies that the most efficient level of effort is sought. This is done by minimizing the total costs of quality, a concept discussed later.

Quality does not happen automatically. Even if every participant in the construction effort has the best intentions, human factors such as haste and ignorance, management decisions such as sequencing and crew composition, and "uncontrollable" events such as vendor incompetence and adverse weather necessitate the creation of a system to make sure that tasks are accomplished correctly. This is the domain of quality control. Also, the owner, and sometimes the public, need assurance that the contracted product has been delivered. Providing this is often called quality assurance. The meanings of the terms "quality control" and "quality assurance" as used in the construction industry are sometimes blurred, but, however defined, they are both included in quality management.

To accomplish quality assurance and/or quality control generally requires designated personnel and equipment. The preparation of a quality program, a general document, and specific quality plans, as required by some contracts, constitute one level of quality effort. The implementation of the quality plan requires specific quality activities such as materials testing, submittal checking, equipment recalibration, and general inspection of work. Employee training may also be classified as a quality activity. It is obvious that there are many specific quality related expenditures.

In many cases there is no effort to distinguish a quality activity from ordinary work and in some cases it is difficult to judge the distinction. This was dramatically illustrated in an article in the periodical *Quality by Design* in which managers grossly overestimated the amount of time spent in quality management activities (Hayden 1992, p. 7). However, one way of distinguishing between "quality" activities and "ordinary" work activities is to answer the question, "Is this activity being done to *avoid, discover or fix a deviation*?" If the answer is "Yes," it is a quality activity. To put it another way, one can ask the question, "If there were no chance of a problem, would this activity be done?" If the answer is "No," it is a quality activity. Even with this guide, some situations are arguable. For example, teaching an employee how to use a new tool may or may not be classified as a quality activity. A major reason for distinguishing quality activities from ordinary work activities is to measure the effectiveness of a quality program which requires a cost breakdown by job category.

Quality programs are formal written systems for achieving quality. They typically include a policy statement, which states the support of top management. They also define quality-related responsibilities and include directions about such things as documentation, training, and general process control. The term "quality plan" usually refers to a job-specific application of the quality program. It will outline disciplined and detailed control and assurance activities such as vendor evaluation, plan checking, submittal reviewing, and materials testing. Some typical components of quality programs are listed in Table 7–1. In this case, the items indicated above as being in a quality plan would be under process control. Program performance refers to some method to determine if the program is successful or profitable. This might be done by measuring owner satisfaction or by financial results, as in the method described in the following section.

Cost of Quality Management

Construction quality management is not just about altruism; it is about cost efficiency. Given that quality is, by definition, required, the question is, "What is the most cost effective way to achieve it?" Certainly, some major expenses to be avoided are the costs of tear-out and rework and the costs of warranty work or "callbacks." The issue then becomes how much money

TABLE 7–1
Typical construction quality program components

Quality Program Components
Policy/mission statement
Organization structure and responsibilities
Document control
Training
Process control—specific procedures
Vendor selection
Deviation investigation and resolution
Record keeping
Field trials
Quality audit procedures
Program performance

Source: Davis 1987, pp. 39–43.

should be invested on quality management to avoid the deviations that lead to rework and callbacks, thus the need to know which activities provide quality. The tools needed to do this work are described by K. Davis and others (1989, pp. 385–400). In that work, total costs of quality (COQ) are defined as the sum of the cost of quality management (CQM) and the measurable costs associated with deviations (CD) as indicated in the equation below.

$$COQ = CQM + CD$$

The cost of quality management is relatively easy to capture with typical construction company cost coding. This includes the cost of personnel, equipment, and overhead involved in the quality management function. Estimates of these costs range from 1% to 5% of construction cost (Davis 1987, p. 69). Deviation costs are typically more difficult to separate. In Davis's research only the cost of labor, equipment, and materials involved in tear-out and rework were included. No attempt was made to include "impact costs" such as delay related costs and other difficult-to-measure costs such as the loss of efficiency or damage to company reputation.

A major function of tracking costs of quality is to provide management with adequate information so that the problem areas can be addressed. In addition to capturing the cost of deviations, the system provides other very valuable information. At a minimum, the deviation cost is described by task and "cause" (Ledbetter 1989, p. 5). In that research, "cause" referred to the source of the deviation (Design, Transportation or Construction) rather than the reason it occurred. This paper uses "origin" to refer to where the deviation originated and "cause" to refer to the reason it occurred. A more extensive set of descriptors was suggested by Davis as indicated in Figure 7–1. It is difficult, if not impossible, however, to code all of the information using normal construction cost coding systems. There are other practical difficulties about who does the coding and who makes the judgments, particularly about the cause. The person recording times (e.g., worker hours) may be using a card with a pre-recorded cost code and have neither the inclination, information, nor authority to re-code the work category. This probably necessitates that the quality management department code deviation costs to capture an adequate description. This cost tracking might be a companion to, rather than a replacement for, the routine cost coding. No matter how the coding is done, it represents an extra burden—but the benefits of doing it make it worthwhile. The accumulated information is the basis of addressing the real problems. Furthermore, the mere act of thoroughly monitoring and determining costs of deviations seems to have a salutary effect (Ledbetter 1998, pers. comm., April 14).

The total cost of quality is not trivial. It has been estimated to be as high as one-fourth of the total project cost (Ledbetter 1989, p. 1). This was verified in a study of mid-sized Michigan construction subcontractors by Mansour and Usmen (1993). The goal is to establish a level of quality management such that the total cost of quality is optimized. Davis's research and subse-

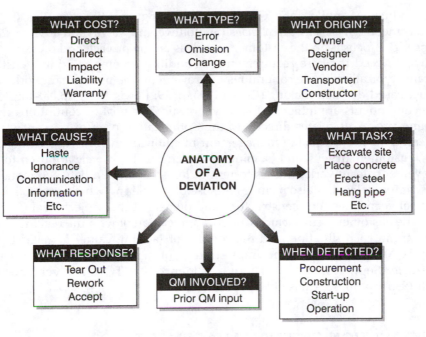

FIGURE 7–1

Anatomy of a deviation for cost coding

Source: Davis 1987, p. 106.

quent published and unpublished work by W. Ledbetter proves that sufficient costs of quality can be captured to suggest an optimum level of quality management (Ledbetter 1990, pp. 6–12). This concept is conveyed in Figure 7–2. The optimum level of quality management expense undoubtedly depends on the type of construction activity and the expertise of the workers.

Total Quality Management

Total Quality Management (TQM) is a broad management concept that includes, but transcends, the previously described quality management. QM deals with production techniques;

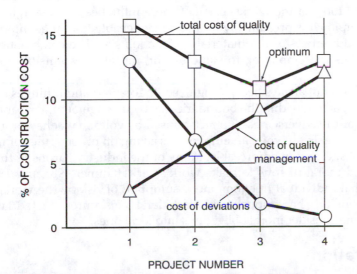

FIGURE 7–2

Optimization of costs of quality: COQ = CQM + CD.

TQM is a business philosophy. QM is about meeting *project requirements*; TQM is often said to be about meeting *customer expectations* (Shofoluwe and Varzavand 1993, p. 22). This is a major advance. The focus is on the customer as well as on the project, and on expectations which may very well exceed the bare requirements. In addition to emphasizing a customer focus, TQM programs typically include continuous improvement, the use of teamwork, strategic planning, and fact-based decision making (Chase 1993, p. 19; Lewis 1993, pp. 40-46; Bosshart 1992, p. 5). These components are integrated and synergistic. The goal of continuous improvement in all company processes relates directly to the optimization of efforts to ensure task accomplishment, an objective of quality management mentioned previously. Techniques such as quality circles, customer surveys, and Deming's act-plan-do-check cycle are used to aid in continuous improvement. Teamwork includes fostering close cooperation between management and labor at the company level. It also includes the use of partnering which creates cooperative arrangements between designers, constructors, and owners at the project level (*Constructor* Feb, 1996, p. 55). The customer focus includes a new appreciation of who the real internal or external customers are in each situation, and the concept of "adding value" at each stage of any process. Today, TQM is a part of the business strategy of many progressive construction companies (*Constructor* Sept, 1993, p. 12). There is evidence that TQM has very positive cost benefits (Burati 1990, pp. 14, 15; Chase 1993, pp. 226–264).

CONSTRUCTION SAFETY MANAGEMENT

Construction has a reputation of being an unsafe business, consistently ranking near the top in the number of injuries and fatalities per employee hours worked (*Concrete Construction* 1998, p. 345). There are at least four reasons for maintaining a safe construction site: the moral argument, the legal argument, the financial argument, and the public relations argument.

Moral Reasons

The moral principle that applies is the concept that a person bears the responsibility for prudence about the well being of others, particularly if the others' actions are directed to the benefit of the first person. Put negatively, the employer should not be the cause of harm to the employee. For strictly humanitarian reasons it is necessary for management to strive for a safe worksite. This acknowledges that management has a large measure of responsibility for the working conditions. Management establishes the time, tools, and techniques, as well as the rules and the general tone, of the worksite. All of these influence the health and safety of the workers. Also, the employer is presumably more knowledgeable than the employees about the potential chronic health effects of the materials on the job site. The combination of authority and knowledge makes the employer, to some extent, morally responsible for those in the employer's charge.

This obligation has not always been recognized or accepted and it hinges on the extent to which the employee is acting within the boundaries set by management. Probably few employers feel responsible for the adverse health effects caused by volitional behavior in contradiction of rules or common sense. Even when an employee is acting on orders, rules of morality can be subjective, individualistic, and unenforceable. Many of the industry barons of the 19th century United States resisted moral reasons to make work safer (Hammer 1985, pp. 18, 19). It seems that they believed that individual freedom and assumption of risk by the worker relieved the employer of responsibility. The various state and federal legislatures created laws to make at least part of what some consider moral obligations into legal ones.

Legal Considerations

The second major reason, then, for maintaining a safe construction site is the legal one: the laws demand it. In the Occupational Safety and Health Act of 1970 the declared purpose of Congress is " . . . to assure as far as possible every working man and women in the Nation safe and healthful working conditions" (Public Law 91-596, Section 2(b)). OSHA includes thousands of safety regulations pertaining to the construction industry. Many things are covered in great detail, others are included in the general safety and health provisions, which puts the largest measure of the responsibility of the safety of the employee on the employer (29CFR 1926.20,21). The regulations include requirements for, among other things, written documentation of a safety program, enforcement of the safety regulations, and record keeping of employee injuries.

OSHA is not a law to be ignored. The administration created by the act is empowered to enforce the regulations, and is currently staffed with about 2,500 compliance officers who have the authority to issue citations for violations (Talent 1998, p. 6). The fines may be as high as $7,000 per incident and up to $70,000 for flagrant violations. It was recently reported that one construction company was accessed a fine of $1.5 million (*Engineering News Record* Feb. 2, 1998, p. 12).

In spite of the above, OSHA regulations are not universally obeyed. The huge number of small construction companies, and the relatively small number of compliance officers, means that enforcement is sporadic at best. In some parts of the country, small residential contractors operate without regard to or knowledge of OSHA regulations. The National Association of Homebuilders (NAHB) has helped to address the misconception that small residential construction operations are immune to OSHA influences by jointly publishing a safety handbook with OSHA (OSHA news release USDL 97-16). However, many small contractors remain unaware of this handbook because many have no interaction with NAHB.

Another reason that OSHA regulations are disregarded is that it is sometimes thought that they are unreasonable (Peyton & Rubio 1991, p. 2). In recent years an effort has been made to establish a more cooperative relationship between OSHA and the construction industry (Talent 1998, p. 6; *Merit Shop Report* 1995). In spite of the shortcomings of OSHA, its influence alone is a compelling reason for maintaining a safe construction site.

While OSHA may be the most prominent legal reason for construction safety, there are other compelling legal issues to be considered. Workers' compensation laws will not always provide adequate protection for a contractor particularly if suit is brought against the general contractor by an employee of a subcontractor (Mol 1994, p. 21). There is also a legal duty to protect the safety of the public (Simon 1982, p. 2.5-1). Criminal negligence suits have also been filed in some states.

Financial Issues

The third reason for maintaining a safe construction site is financial. Numerous authorities have asserted that "safety pays" (Levitt & Samelson 1987, p. 3; Hinze 1997a, p. 68). Accidents have a serious effect on the cost of workers' compensation insurance, which is typically carried by the employer for the coverage of employees. The cost of premiums is a function of the experience modification rate (EMR) which is based on the frequency and severity of work related injuries (Hammer 1985, pp. 46, 47). An employer with an excellent safety record might have an EMR of 0.5, while one with a poor safety record might have an EMR of 1.5. If everything else is equal, the second pays three times as much for workers' compensation insurance premiums as the first. A simple example illustrates that this is a very significant amount of money. Assume the average workers' compensation (WC) rate is 15% and that the labor payroll is 30% of the construction cost. The WC cost to the first employer is $0.5 \times 0.15 \times 0.30 = 2.25\%$ of the construction cost; the WC cost to the second employer is $1.5 \times 0.15 \times 0.30 = 6.75\%$ of the construction cost. The difference of 4.5% could easily be the difference between a financial success and a financial failure. The difference may be thought of as a direct cost of the lack of safety. The cost of repair or replacement of equipment damaged in accidents is another direct cost, a cost not covered by workers' compensation.

In addition to the direct cost of accidents, there are numerous indirect costs. Among measurable indirect costs is the expense of the time involved in attending to an injured person and the time required for record keeping. An example of an indirect cost, which is more difficult to measure, is the productivity loss associated with an injury. Production is disrupted, and if the injured person must be replaced, a new worker may need training or at the least "breaking in" to the new situation. Estimates of indirect costs have varied widely, but, in every case, have been found to be significant—equaling or exceeding the direct costs (Hinze 1997a, p. 64; Levitt & Samelson 1987, pp. 18–23).

Public Relations

A fourth consideration concerns public relations (Geyer, 1991, cited in Liska, *et al.*, 1993, p. 3). Adverse publicity that can result from a bad accident or from apparent disregard for workers' safety will damage a company's reputation, which may affect its ability to obtain work. How public relations are to be handled, especially during a crisis, is something that the company must be prepared for (Peyton & Rubio 1991, p. 108).

There are clearly very compelling reasons to have a safe worksite. It is also clear from experience that the goal of a safe worksite must be aggressively pursued. The primary purpose of construction safety management is the preservation of life and health. This is done by attempting to prevent adverse events or "accidents." One approach is to have construction safety criteria considered during the design phase. While the safety of the finished building is perhaps the premier criterion of design, there has been little attention paid during design to protect the safety of the workers during construction. This issue has been addressed in a recent research report by the Construction Industry Institute (CII) (Hinze 1996). Therein specific suggestions are made for more safety-conscious design.

Proper design can help reduce hazards, but it is during construction that a strong safety program is needed. A safety program will typically incorporate the following features. It is customary to have a strong statement of support for safety from top management. Major elements of a typical program are hazard control, employee safety training, accident investigation procedures, and emergency procedures. There are also specific rules for various construction activities, a hazardous materials program (HazCom), and a substance abuse program. The program will list specific safety goals and may include an incentive program. The incentive program rewards employees who avoid accidents and may include substantial bonuses for those who supervise and manage the line workers. Record keeping is required by OSHA and is useful to management to indicate areas needing improvement as well as for determining who is deserving of rewards. A CII study identified five "high-impact zero injury safety techniques" that should be emphasized in safety programs. They are: (1) Safety Pre-project/Pre-task Planning; (2) Safety Orientation and Training; (3)Written Safety Incentive Program; (4) Alcohol and Substance Abuse Program; and (5) Accidents/Incidents Investigations (Nelson 1993). Typical components of a construction safety program are shown in Table 7–2.

TABLE 7–2
Typical construction safety program components

Safety Program Components

Policy/mission statement
Organization structure and responsibilities
Training
Work rules
Hazard identification and control
Hazardous communication program
Substance abuse prevention
Accident/incident investigation
Emergency procedures
Record keeping
Incentive program
Program performance

Source:Hinze 1997a, pp. 100–112; Peyton & Rubio
1991, pp.10-32.

OSHA regulations have a major influence on the safety program. Insurance companies also have an interest in making sure that construction firms create and follow safety programs. Model programs are published by contractors' associations such as the Associated General Contractors of America (AGC), the Associated Builders and Contractors (ABC) and the National Association of Home Builders (NAHB).

In addition to site specific safety plans, safety is enhanced by requiring that safety be "engineered into" the tools and systems that are used. For example, electrical and mechanical equipment and scaffolding are built and maintained in such a way that they are safe when used properly. Also, safety is "estimated into" the jobs by including enough money for the proper equipment and procedures to reduce the temptation for management to require dangerous shortcuts.

Another line of defense is to deal with human behavior. Selection and training of employees is of paramount importance. The idealized assumption is that if workers know how to do the job safely, and if the proper equipment is provided, they will work safely. This seems obvious in view of the fact that an accident may cause personal harm, but other factors such as haste or inattention may lead to injury-causing accidents. Also, distractions of many different kinds may lead to unsafe acts (Hinze 1997b, pp. 112–121).

The safety program requires an investment of resources for personnel and equipment. The reported cost of a safety program may range from 1% to 10% of project costs depending on what is included (Hinze 1997a, p. 66). An amount equal to 1% to 2.5% of direct labor costs has been suggested by Levitt and Samelson (1987, p. 24). The amount depends on the type of project, the nature of the program, and exactly what costs are included. It may be easily argued that a safety program will more than pay for itself in strictly financial terms. Given the many variables, however, it is difficult to establish the optimum level of expenditures to minimize the total cost of a safety program and losses due to accidents. To put it in the form of a question, "How much investment in safety management is needed to achieve the optimum results?" Of course, it may be thought that optimum results would be zero injuries, but the question remains about how much investment is needed to achieve that goal. The cost would undoubtedly depend on the particular type of construction project. This concept is discussed later.

SIMILARITIES BETWEEN CONSTRUCTION QUALITY AND SAFETY

It should be evident that the similarities between quality and safety issues in construction are striking. Among other things, they are similar in scope, in cause, in effect, and in challenge to management. Both quality and safety relate to the successful performance of the job and pervade the entire process from design to estimating to contract negotiation and throughout the construction process. Both quality and safety require constant vigilance and effort; everyone, including subcontractors, must participate in the effort. Yesterday's victories do not guarantee anything today. Some constructors consciously strive for perfection (zero defects in quality and zero injuries in safety) while others are apparently content to hope for the best and let nature take it course. A major failure in either safety or quality can have a devastating effect on a job. Conversely, a flawless performance has a positive effect on the profit margin. Another similarity in scope is that while many of the results are clear at the end of a project, both quality and safety have long term implications. Quality problems and chronic health problems may be discovered years after the project is completed.

Efforts to maintain quality and safety focus on a common objective: minimizing disruptions to the efficient process of completing a job. In both cases the disruptions are usually the result of human errors or adverse circumstances. In quality, the disruptions are called deviations; in safety they are called accidents. (In fact, an accident can be defined as a type of deviation. If the requirement of a zero injury job is established, an injury is a failure to meet the requirement and therefore, by definition, a deviation. This approach places the safety function within quality management.) "Doing it right the first time" can refer to the process (safety) as well as to the product (quality). To put it another way, both quality and safety efforts combat the seemingly universal principle known as Murphy's Law: if anything can go wrong, it will.

The real foe may be the laws of probability and an indifferent universe. If there are ten ways to do a task and two of them lead to the correct result but eight of them lead to the wrong result, it is probable that doing the task carelessly will lead to the bad result. There are many opportunities to fail. The element of chance tempts some to gamble with both quality and safety.

The nature of the disruptions caused by failures of quality and safety are often the same. They generate additional direct costs and indirect costs. They reduce productivity and hurt morale. To the disinterested observer, the immediate fallout from a newly discovered major quality problem and an injury causing accident looks the same. Work stops; management becomes involved; investigation is undertaken; blame is assigned; morale is eroded; and time and money are wasted. The results of a failure in either quality or safety may be immediately apparent; however, failures in either may not be apparent for some time. The latent quality failure may lead to warranty work; the hidden safety risk may lead to delayed chronic health problems. Either a poor safety record or a poor quality record can harm a company's reputation and may disqualify the company from bidding some jobs (ASCE 1990, p. 55).

Maintaining quality and safety represents a great challenge to managers because of the variety and complexity of the factors involved. Seemingly, problems are caused in both areas by many of the same factors. Some of the contributing factors are poor design, poor management practices, improper equipment, untrained personnel, adverse working conditions, and a host of human factors such as distractions, indifference, and substance abuse. Fortunately, many of these problems can be successfully addressed through a quality or safety program. A further challenge in connection with the program is measuring and verifying its monetary value. The question asked is, "How do you measure the savings of the accident (or deviation) that never happened?" And a corollary question is, "How much of a preventive program is enough?" The answer is that while a non-event cannot be measured, it is possible to gather enough statistical evidence to give adequate guidance for establishing an appropriate level of effort.

Some of the major similarities between quality and safety issues are indicated in Table 7–3.

In view of what is indicated above, it is not surprising that quality and safety programs have so much in common. The programs are compared in Table 7–4 using information from Tables 7–1 and 7–2. Even some of the items listed under "Safety" instead of "Both Quality and Safety" relate closely to quality. Substance abuse surely affects the ability of workers to "do it right," and an incentive program might be appropriate to quality. It is clear that quality and safety are very similar issues.

DIFFERENCES BETWEEN CONSTRUCTION QUALITY AND SAFETY

Although there are many similarities between quality and safety, there are several significant differences. There are differences in the areas of focus, moral and legal implications, the nature of failure scenarios, and in the actual product. In safety, the primary focus is on the employee;

TABLE 7–3
Similarities between construction quality and safety.

Similarities Between Quality and Safety

Scope—constant and pervasive
Criticality to success
Goal—no failures (deviations or injuries)
Obstacles—indifferent universe, probability, human nature
Problem causes—human, environment, equipment, etc.
Detection—immediate or delayed
Effect of failure—lost money, lost morale, lost reputation
Response—systematic program
Difficulty in optimizing the program

TABLE 7–4

Construction quality and safety program components comparison.

Quality	Both Quality and Safety	Safety
Document control	Policy/mission statement	Hazard identification and control
Vendor selection	Organization structure and responsibilities	Hazardous communication program (HazCom)
Field trials	Training	Substance abuse prevention
Quality audit procedures	Process control/work rules	Emergency procedures
	Investigations	Incentive program
	Record keeping	
	Program performance	

in quality, the primary focus is on the owner. In the language of TQM, the main customer is different in each case. This difference explains several of the components not characteristic of both programs as indicated in Table 7–4. All those components under "Safety" but not under "Quality" are employee related. This difference in emphasis can create a different outlook; the quality department could have a tendency to think of the employee as a tool rather than a responsibility. One interesting aspect of TQM, however, as advocated by some, is that the contractor's first responsibility is to the employee rather than to the owner (Rosenbluth & Peters 1992).

Another aspect of the difference in focus involves legal accountability. Because the government has a direct interest in day-to-day safety through OSHA, and the contractor must comply with those standards, a secondary customer is OSHA. This focus is apt to deal with compliance because legal accountability may be required at any time through an unannounced on-site visit or a visit if there is a serious accident. In contrast, the owner is usually more concerned with results than procedures and the main accountability to the owner is not until the time the project is delivered. Therefore, ordinary deviations that are discovered by the contractor can be corrected without penalties imposed by a "third party." Of course, this could lead to the attitude that it is better to proceed with work and correct mistakes if and when they are detected rather than avoid mistakes in the first place. This implies another difference. Work that has been done incorrectly can be removed and redone, but accidents that result in injuries or death are irreversible. Safety is personal; quality is institutional.

A third important customer in the safety realm is the workers' compensation insurance carrier. Since injuries affect how much is paid in claims, the insurance company has a legitimate interest in safety. Since it ultimately passes its costs onto the contractor, it provides a powerful incentive to the contractor for safety. Although it may be argued that bonding or liability insurance protect contractors from major losses that might be related to quality issues, there is nothing comparable to workers' compensation to provide coverage for quality losses. Workers' compensation, then, creates contrasts between safety and quality. It introduces a player into safety issues that does not typically exist in the United States on quality issues, and it provides insurance for safety losses that do not exist for quality losses. A further difference is that since injury payments are made directly to the employee there is an incentive for fraud (Hinze 1997a, pp. 66–68).

The moral implications of providing a safe work environment have been mentioned previously. Cain's biblical question, "Am I my brother's keeper?" must be answered in the affirmative. "Waste not, want not," a proverb that could be applied to quality, does not have the same weight. There is, then, a qualitative difference between the responsibility for human loss associated with the lack of safety and the loss of materials and time associated with the lack of quality. Surely a moral case can be made against the waste of time and material resources involved in many construction deviations, but it is not as compelling as the case against injuring persons. Up until now, appeals to morality seem more appropriate and effective in the safety arena than in the quality arena.

Another difference is how failures are likely to unfold. Many accidents tend to be sudden and often related to an unfortunate series of circumstances or events (Hinze 1997a, p. 21). One theory of accident prevention, then, is to remove or break at least one item in the chain of events. For example, a worker falls because of a combination of a slippery scaffold, a missing guardrail, and judgment impairment due to inebriation. If any of the three situations had been different the fall would not have occurred. In contrast to being sudden, many quality failures are created consciously and methodically. For example, a failure to install piping at the correct elevation may transpire over hours or days. Unlike the fall from elevation, there are numerous opportunities to catch and correct the problem in process before it becomes a major event. A more subtle contrast relates to the series of events analogy: in safety, removing one step *prevents the bad event*; in quality, removing one step *prevents the good event*. For example, the proper installation of the pipe requires that the plans be drawn correctly, that they be read correctly, that the instrument that is used be calibrated correctly, and that it be used correctly. One break in this chain of circumstances leads to a deviation. This contrast is illustrated in Figure 7–3. Based on this understanding it appears that it should be easier to achieve safety than it is to achieve quality.

The product of a successful safety program is most easily defined negatively: a job in which there are no injuries or other safety related losses. The status quo is maintained. The product of a successful quality program is most easily defined positively: a fulfilled contract, which is a project that meets the requirements. This difference may explain the apparently more common use of tangible incentives in safety programs. (See the survey results at the end of this chapter.)

Different theories of motivation apply to safety and quality. Safety is the next to the most important in Maslow's hierarchy of needs, second only to basic physiological needs (Hitt, Middlemist and Mathis 1983, p. 275). It appears that this is a good basis for encouraging workers to be careful. Motivation for quality seems to better fit achievement-oriented models. Perhaps the achievement of the building itself is a sufficient reward in the quality realm. This difference implies that different approaches to motivation may be warranted. Some of the contrasts between quality and safety are given in Table 7–5.

THE INTERACTION OF CONSTRUCTION QUALITY AND SAFETY

Although there are differences between quality and safety, as has been pointed out, they are not mutually exclusive nor contradictory. The fact that some sort of positive relationship exists between quality and safety is recognized in TQM programs. Safety is included as one of many elements of TQM in Associated General Contractors (AGC) publications on the subject (Chase 1993, p. 19). The cover of the October, 1993, *Constructor*, AGC's management periodical, proclaimed that safety is a key to TQM. Krause (1994 p. 51) lists eight TQM continuous improvement principles that he says apply directly to safety. In addition to the continuous improvement concept, the TQM concepts of teamwork and customer focus relate to safety. The

FIGURE 7–3
Series of circumstances contrast between quality and safety.

TABLE 7–5
Contrasts between construction quality and safety.

Contrast Area	Quality	Safety
The customer	Owner	Employee, OSHA, insurance
Legal accountability	Owner	Government
Loss liability	Contractor	Insurance company
Type of loss (morality)	Time and material	Human health
Typical failure scenario	Slow and recoverable	Sudden and unrecoverable
Circumstance chain	Break means failure	Break means success
Worker motivation	Achievement needs	Safety needs
Successful product	Fulfilled contract	No losses

employee is a vital part of the team as well as an important customer; therefore, worker well being and satisfaction are important. Quality management says "do it right the first time"; TQM adds new emphasis to the idea that "doing it right" includes doing it safely. *Thus, under TQM, safety is a quality issue.*

Even apart from TQM, quality management is important to safety. For example, materials testing, which is a function of quality management, may have a profound influence on safety. Concrete forms moved before the concrete was adequately cured led to the worst construction accident in American history resulting in 51 fatalities (Lew, Feb, 1980, pp. 62–67). Determining the maturity of concrete is the job of quality management. As another example, certain kinds of double connections for steel member assembly are unsafe (Zimmerman 1995, p. 31). These may be discovered and rejected by quality management while checking submittals. *Thus, quality leads to safety.*

In a very practical way, safety is also important to quality. A safe work environment which allows a worker to concentrate on the job surely increases the probability that the job will be done correctly; this is the definition of quality. At the very least, danger is an unnecessary distraction. *Thus, safety leads to quality.* It is difficult to think of a situation in which working safely could do anything but enhance quality. Putting it the other way, since quality is always desirable, the employee should have a safe environment to work in. It's difficult for a mason to lay brick in a straight line if one hand is needed to hang onto the scaffold.

There are other ways in which quality and safety intersect. Even if management thinks of employees as mere tools of production (which would be contrary to TQM theory), it is only good management to protect the means of production. It is becoming increasingly difficult to find qualified construction employees, especially in the crafts (Bennet 1997). Since quality requires well trained, well motivated workers, it is in the best interests of quality to support safety efforts merely to reduce losses of company quality assets. The interactive nature of quality and safety is illustrated in Figure 7–4.

Not only do quality and safety support each other, according to Krause, they can be synergistic, actually increasing their mutual effectiveness. "Process approaches to quality and safety are so complementary that, when they are both at work in a facility, they tend to reinforce each other" (Krause 1994, p. 51). If this is true, a good quality program by its mere presence should enhance the safety program and vice versa. A zero defects program should help with the zero accidents program.

In the international construction scene, the inclusion of both the traditional quality and safety efforts within a TQM system is advocated by Dias and Curado (1996). They suggest that the TQM emphasis on the customer will lead to protection of the employee who is a vital customer, as mentioned previously. They write that safety record keeping, particularly in Europe, would be improved and a needed "safety culture" comparable to the existing "quality culture" would result. They suggest that an international standard for safety measurement be developed comparable to the models for quality management such as the ISO 9000 series.

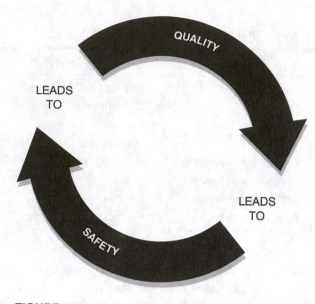

FIGURE 7–4
Interaction of quality and safety.

A research project done in collaboration with the European Construction Institute studied the state of integration of safety, quality, and environmental management (Ayoade & Gibb 1996). The finding was that the systems generally remain independent of each other in spite of probable benefits that would accrue from closer integration. Some of the reasons for the lack of integration are perceived difficulties due to project-specific requirements, legislative requirements, and a general lack of understanding and commitment.

A study of the Hong Kong construction industry concluded that mere legislation of safety requirements had been inadequate to protect the workers (Lo 1996). It is suggested that safety would be greatly improved by including it as part of the existing ISO 9000 quality management system. ISO 9000 accreditation is required for bidding on work for the Hong Kong Housing authority and this has been a major incentive to obtain accreditation. The author contends that having safety included in the quality standard would insure that it be treated more seriously. In Hong Kong, requiring company initiated and independently audited ISO 9000 has proved to be a more effective approach than detailed safety legislation.

It is clear that quality and safety are complementary issues. They are distinct but similar. The associated problems have common roots in the laws of probability, the indifferent universe and human nature. This is why the programs devised to manage these look so much alike. The value of including safety in TQM is recognized in the United States and in Europe. Given, then, that this close relationship exists, what are some possible implications? Each of the next four sections is a proposition based on the quality/safety relationship.

Proposition 1—Consolidate the Safety and Quality Functions

The similarity of the safety and quality functions and the fact that they operate simultaneously in the same environment leads to the conclusion that it might be beneficial to combine or at least closely coordinate the management activities. Some economies of operation might result; and making safety and quality a seamless whole in the employee's experience could have a positive effect. In a sense, this is done when safety is included as an element of a TQM program, but a greater emphasis on the nature and importance of safety and quality is warranted. One approach would be to combine the programs into a "Construction Excellence" or similarly named entity. The mission of this program would be to achieve the company construction goals in the most efficient and humane manner. This means that the goals would be achieved without any quality, safety, or efficiency related losses. The new name might reduce potential territorial disputes between quality and safety departments. Such a department could also encompass ethical and environmental concerns.

Table 7–4 suggests how things could be organized within the construction excellence group. Those elements in common would be combined and consolidated. Those elements unique to quality and safety would, of course, be retained. Table 7–6 lists major components of a program that combines quality and safety. Elements that are combined are followed by (c); safety elements are indicated by (s); quality elements by (q).

The following is a brief explanation of some components of Table 7–6. The mission statement states the goal of achieving excellence in construction by making the most efficient and careful use of human and material resources. This could encompass a goal of zero injuries, zero deviations, high efficiency, and zero conflicts.

One approach to management is to "walk around" and observe the work site. Alert managers look for both quality problems and safety problems. In other words, and with training if necessary, hazard identification can be combined with potential deviation identification. This is part of "Potential problem identification and resolution" as listed in Table 7–6. It is a short step from checking whether a scaffold is adequate from a safety standpoint to seeing if the mason is using the correct mortar. Both can be done at the same time.

Investigation techniques and record keeping already common for accidents, would, if applied to deviations, bring a salutary rigor and needed increased attention. This is called "Disruption investigation" because it applies to both deviations and accidents. Replacing the word "accident" might remove the connotation that safety mishaps are beyond human control.

A major item in both quality and safety is training. In this important area, both quality and safety training objectives can be achieved simultaneously. In fact this is already occurring in some situations. When an employee is instructed in the proper use of a piece of equipment, safety is a major issue, but not the only issue. A person being taught to rig a crane load or to use a paint sprayer can be taught safety and quality simultaneously. A person being taught to cut straight with a circular saw is taught to wear eye protection. The conscious combining of training for quality (making sure the job is done correctly) and safety offers an opportunity to improve the content, interest level, and usefulness of the training material. In view of the future labor force, companies may have to engage in more intensive training with the need to employ trained instructors as other industries have found necessary (Lagowski 1994). Capable instructors can teach quality and safety at the same time. The construction industry has much room for improvement in the area of training employees (McCollough & Benson 1993).

A similar argument applies to process control or work rules. The correct way to do a job includes safety. Concrete reinforcement is tied using certain tools and techniques and, not incidentally, protection is provided to prevent impalement on dowels. Proper techniques simply include safety. To treat it separately is to create an unnecessary dichotomy to the trainee.

As stated previously, functions such as HazCom and vendor selection that cannot be combined remain separate, but combining and consolidating the areas suggested previously should

TABLE 7–6

Components of a "construction excellence" program.

Construction Excellence Program Components	
Mission statement (c)	Substance abuse prevention (c)
Organization structure and responsibilities (c)	Incentive programs (c)
Documentation/record keeping (c)	Program audits (c)
Potential problem identification and resolution (c)	Performance measurements (c)
	Vendor selection (q)
Training (c)	Field trials (q)
Process control/work rules (c)	Emergency procedures (s)
Disruption investigation (c)	HazCom (s)

result in better efficiency. This was the hypothesis of Ayoade and Gibb (1996). Even the "new look" at quality by safety professionals and vice versa might produce useful insights.

There is another powerful argument for the creation of a consolidated approach to quality and safety. Companies with large, well-established and successful quality and safety programs might be reluctant to change, but what of the thousands of small construction companies who have neither safety nor quality programs? Rather than adopt either or both separately they would benefit from adopting a combined program. A well designed package called Construction Excellence, for example, might be attractive to some firms which could benefit from this new approach to management. It might also be a very useful approach to improving construction in less developed economies. A survey of the current degree of integration of the quality and safety functions of some major U.S. construction companies is discussed later in this chapter.

Proposition 2—Apply Cost of Quality Concepts to Costs of Safety

The concept of defining, collecting, and optimizing costs of quality was discussed previously. Some progress has been made in that area although more needs to be done. One obstacle to success was that there is no external agency monitoring the costs of deviations such as the insurance companies do for safety, so a system was devised to do that. It is proposed that some insights in the development of the cost of quality system might be useful for working with the cost of safety.

There is information available about some aspects of safety costs such as workers' compensation rates and OSHA fines, but apparently there is some confusion or disagreement about other safety related costs. Hinze (1997a) reported that there is lack of agreement about what to classify as legitimate safety costs. This is apparent from a study reported by Jaselskis, *et al.*, (1996). In that study, which covered fifty of the Engineering News-Record top 400 contractors, the subgroup of safer companies reported a ratio of money spent on safety to total billings of 0.000021. The less safe cohort reported a ratio of 0.0000089. What was included in safety expenditures was not reported, but there is clearly a problem. This works out to the safer companies spending an average of only $21 for each $1 million of billing. Even if the study intended to report $2,100 instead of $21 per $1 million, that amount still probably reflects a lack of uniformity about what is included as a safety cost.

In addition to defining what should be included as safety costs there is the issue of optimizing the safety system. An approach similar to that described for optimizing quality costs is proposed for consideration. The total cost of safety (COS) is the sum of the cost of the safety management program (CSM) and the cost of accidents (CA), broadly defined.

$$COS = CSM + CA$$

The CSM should include the cost of all safety and health personnel, equipment, and other costs incurred in running the safety program. (See Table 7–2 for program components.) Strictly speaking, everything from the time spent in safety meetings to seat belts on the backhoe are costs of safety management. A practical level of detail must be established. A decision rule is necessary to classify some costs as either a "safety cost" or an "ordinary cost." For example, is the cost of scaffolding a safety cost? The proposed method of deciding is to answer the question, "Is this device or technique used primarily to make the worker safe?" If the answer is "Yes", it is a safety cost. To put it another way, the question is, "If there were no chance of a health threatening accident would this be done?" If the answer is "No," it is a safety cost. Based on this, the cost of scaffolding is not a safety cost since it is presumably the logical way to do the job. (The cost of the scaffold railings is a safety cost, but, since railings are a part of the scaffold the cost is not separated. This is also true for safety features on vehicles.) The cost of shoring for a trench is more difficult to classify since it serves a dual purpose. A trench cave-in could cause an injury but it also would disrupt the efficient progress of the job and cause rework (a quality failure). By the decision rule, the judgment would concern the primary function of the shoring. That would depend on the soil condition and the type of work done in the trench. A final example is the cost of electrical safety requirements. A reasonable decision would be to consider OSHA requirements that exceed normal National Electrical Code rules to be safety costs.

Even with a decision rule, a cursory consideration of safety costs shows that there are difficult decisions about what to include. If there were an industry consensus, it would make it possible to collect and understand what it really costs to have a safe job.

Some may object to isolating safety costs because it can be difficult to do and because it de-emphasizes the concept that doing a job safely is really the only correct way to do it. But there are several benefits to knowing the total safety investment. The benefits given by Davis (1987, p. 60) for determining the costs of quality apply also to safety. These are given in Table 7–7. The only change from the original table is that the word "safety" has been substituted for the word "quality."

The other half of the equation is the cost of accidents and other costs associated with the lack of safety. This would include all direct costs including workers' compensation insurance, other accident insurance, and OSHA fines. It would also include indirect costs. As with quality failures there are impact costs associated with accidents that are very difficult to measure. A reliable technique to determine such costs would be useful for both safety and quality failures.

The safety system is optimized when the total cost of safety is minimized. This is shown in Figure 7–5. The data are illustrative only and do not represent any actual projects. A major weakness is that the system does not account for the value of human lives except in monetary terms as determined by OSHA, insurance, and liability costs.

Another approach to optimization of a safety system is to determine the level of safety management costs necessary to achieve zero injuries. This can be done by tracking the cost of safety of projects that achieve the zero accident goal. This is shown for projects 6 and 7 in Figure 7–5. Even when there are no accidents, safety costs continue because of workers' compensation and other insurance costs.

The cost of an accident is only one part of the required information. Many other items are needed if future occurrences are to be avoided. The same problem was faced in measuring quality failures, and the "Anatomy of a Deviation" (Figure 7–1) was developed. A similar device might be useful for analyzing accidents. Figure 7–6 is an adaptation appropriate for safety.

TABLE 7–7
Benefits of measuring costs of safety.

Benefits of Measuring the Costs of Safety

Short Term

Conveys high level of management concern about safety.

Heightens awareness of safety among workers.

Provides early detection of safety problem areas.

Demonstrates safety leadership to the industry and the public.

Intermediate Term

Provides a method for establishing and measuring safety goals.

Provides more precision in estimating costs.

Makes the safety function more profit oriented.

Provides the safety function hard cost data to use with management.

Indicates where serious safety problems are so they can be solved.

Long Term

Provides information to aid in optimizing safety management program, which should lead to greater competitiveness.

Reduces waste of human and material resources.

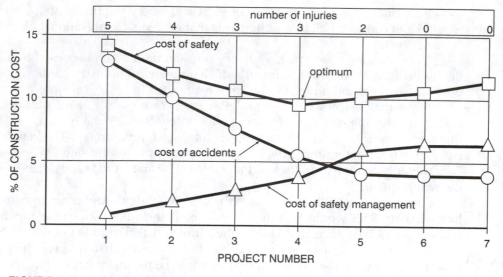

FIGURE 7–5
Optimization of costs of safety: COS = CSM + CA.

While there is little new information represented, it casts safety in the same style as quality and might encourage a common system of "disruption" cost coding.

Proposition 3—Optimize "Construction Excellence" Management

The idea of consolidating quality and safety into a "Construction Excellence" program was mentioned previously. Defining it negatively, the object of that program is to prevent quality and safety failures. Optimization of the program would use an analysis similar to that presented for quality and safety individually wherein the total cost of excellence (COE) is the sum of the cost of excellence management (CEM) and the cost of failures (CF).

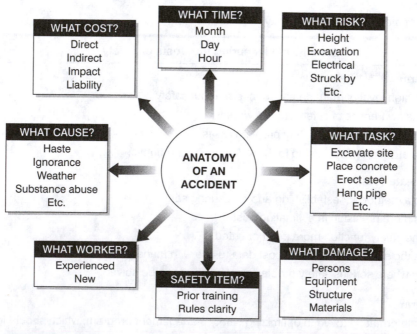

FIGURE 7–6
Anatomy of an accident.

COE = CEM + CF

The cost of excellence management combines the cost of quality and safety management and the cost of failures combines the cost of deviations and accidents. Using nomenclature previously defined:

COE = COQ + COS
CEM = CQM + CSM
CF = CD + CA

Combining the effects of failures in safety and quality should convey their business importance to management. Another advantage of combining information is that in a truly integrated approach to management it may be difficult to separate some aspects of safety and quality management. Finally, criteria such as that represented by Figure 7–7 would be ideal for use as one measurement for monitoring progress in continuous improvement.

Proposition 4—Apply Safety Research to Quality

In the final analysis the most important issue in both safety and quality failures is the cause. The object, after all, is to prevent recurrence; knowing why something happens is the first step in preventing it. Apparently, a major assumption has been that ignorance is a major factor in deviations and accidents. This is undoubtedly correct and explains why training is such a prominent element in both safety and quality programs. Training in both programs concerns knowledge about working the correct way. Published safety toolbox talks typically address safe techniques, that is, knowledge, not mental factors such as distractions or attitude. This is appropriate in view of the expertise of the trainer who is typically a constructor, not a psychologist. However, this leaves a serious deficiency in changing the human conditions that contribute to the problems.

Motivational theory teaches that knowing how to do something is only part of the formula; the worker must also want to do it. There is a desire to do it only if the worker is reasonably assured of an outcome that is sufficiently valued (Hitt, Middlemist, and Mathis 1983, pp. 285, 286). This is illustrated in Figure 7–8. In preventing accidents and deviations, on-site instruction tends to concentrate on the issue of "Can Do?" (Can the worker do it?) rather than on the "Want to Do?" (Does the worker want to do it?).

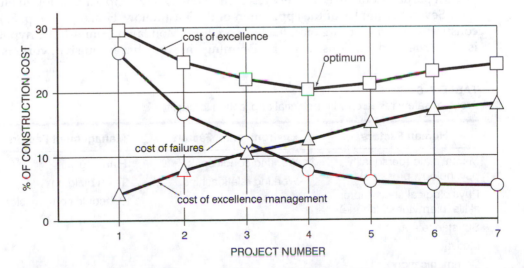

FIGURE 7–7
Optimization of cost of excellence COE: = CEM + CF.

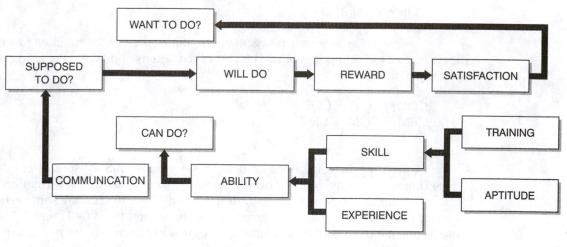

FIGURE 7–8
Motivation

Motivational research such as the expectancy theory referred to above applies generally. It was not developed for the construction industry but is a logical basis for incentive programs. It also relates to setting appropriate wage scales (Laufer & Jenkins 1982). It seems that motivation and other mental factors are the most challenging barriers to quality and safety and that they, as well as technique training, must be addressed for consistently good results.

One of the implications of the discussion above is that insights developed in other fields are very useful when applied to construction. Safety or quality research doesn't have to be developed with construction in mind to be valuable. Furthermore, it is argued herein that it is possible to apply knowledge gained by research in safety to improve quality.

In the United States, at least, there seems to be more information available about construction safety failures than about construction quality failures. Many insights have been developed in understanding the causes of accidents. This is true partly because of general interest in the subject of accidents that transcends construction. Construction quality research, being relatively young, has been occupied with trying to document and avoid failures without much work on determining root causes. Because of the similarities between quality and safety, it is suggested that, in many cases, the causes and conditions surrounding accidents also apply to deviations. This implies that some valuable research in safety also applies to quality. Table 7–8 is a partial list of areas of safety research that may have implications for quality.

Several examples of the application of this idea follow. Hinze (1997a, p. 33) reported that construction accidents are most likely to occur on Monday mornings. The hypothesis is that it is also true of deviations. Work by Denning showed that impulsive workers sustain more

TABLE 7–8
Areas of safety research with potential application to quality.

Human Factors	Environmental Factors	Management Factors
Mental state (personality, psychology, pressure)	Working conditions	Planning
	Working relationships	Team building
Physiological state (motor skills, biorhythms, fatigue)		Schedule compression
Substance abuse		
Motivation		
Communication		
Training		

injuries (1983, Cited in Hinze 1997a, p. 13). The hypothesis is that impulsive workers also create more deviations. If short interval schedules help subcontractor safety they might also help quality. Obviously, not all safety research is applicable to quality. For example, determination of the most hazardous activities may be of only tangential interest to quality. Whether incentives and disincentives that work for safety would work for quality is an open question. The point of the examples is that there is a wealth of safety knowledge already accumulated that can be applied, or at least tested, to help improve quality.

One further aspect of research bears consideration. In view of what has been said, it ought to be feasible to design research so as to directly obtain information about safety and quality simultaneously rather than trying to extrapolate from one to the other as demonstrated.

A SURVEY OF THE INTEGRATION OF QUALITY AND SAFETY

A survey was conducted during May and June, 1998, to determine the extent to which quality and safety are currently integrated by some large construction companies and to determine the extent of use of incentive programs. A copy of the survey instrument is included at the end of this chapter. Responses were received from 15 of the top 40 and 14 others of the top 400 construction companies as listed by the May 25, 1998, Engineering News-Record. Positive responses from the top 40 sample to the use of incentive programs were as follows:

Safety incentives for management	14 of 15
Safety incentives for field workers	13 of 15
Quality incentives for management	4 of 15
Quality incentives for field workers	4 of 15

Positive responses to the use of incentive programs from the other eleven construction companies were as follows:

Safety incentives for management	7 of 14
Safety incentives for field workers	10 of 14
Quality incentives for management	4 of 14
Quality incentives for field workers	3 of 14

This confirms the idea that safety incentives are more common than quality incentives. Based on this sample, safety incentives are very common in the largest construction companies and less common in others.

With respect to the question about coordination or integration, 9 of the 15 top 40 companies indicated that safety is considered a part of TQM. Of the other companies, 11 of 14 indicated that safety is considered a part of TQM.

The responses of the top 40 sample to the question that deals with the relationship between the quality and safety function in the company were as follows:

2 selected "A"—They operate independently with little or no interaction.

7 selected "B"—There is occasional interaction and some shared information and resources.

2 selected "C"—There is frequent interaction, coordinated efforts, and frequent sharing of information and resources.

4 selected "D"—They are very integrated.

The responses of the other eleven companies to the question that deals with the relationship between the quality and safety functions were as follows:

1 selected "A"—They operate independently with little or no interaction.

4 selected "B"—There is occasional interaction and some shared information and resources.

5 selected "C"—There is frequent interaction, coordinated efforts and frequent sharing of information and resources.

4 selected "D"—They are very integrated.

There is, then, a fair degree of interaction between quality and safety management with the "other" companies indicating greater integration. Of eighteen firms where safety is considered a part of TQM one selected "A," five selected "B," four selected "C," and eight selected "D." It appears that safety being considered part of TQM has little relationship to the degree of integration of quality and safety.

Question 4 about the value of combining or better coordinating quality and safety received an overall favorable response of the top 40 sample. Five think it is a "good idea," seven think it "has some potential," and three think it is a "bad idea." Of the other companies, eight think it is a "good idea," and six think it "has some potential." To summarize that part of the survey, there is opportunity and a fair amount of support for the better coordination of safety and quality management efforts.

CONCLUSION

Quality and safety are often thought of as separate issues, but there is sufficient reason to approach them as related. Treating safety as a subset of TQM is a step in the right direction, but doesn't take full advantage of the relationships that have been described. A new plateau of achievement with consequent benefits for competitiveness might be obtained by recognizing and acting on the relatedness and synergy of quality and safety. There are many possibilities for future studies in this connection. To name four:

1. How can the quality and safety functions best be integrated?
2. What is the true total cost of safety and quality failures?
3. What is the optimum level of "Construction Excellence" management?
4. Which safety research knowledge has direct bearing on quality?

Taken together, quality and safety losses represent a major unnecessary source of expenditure in construction. Treating them as related may give impetus to a more efficient use of limited resources. Furthermore, the application of existing safety research knowledge might be used to improve quality.

REFERENCES

Ayode, Aubrey I., and Gibb, Alistair, G. F. (1996). *Integration of Quality, Safety and Environmental Systems.* 1st International Conference, CIB: Working Commission W99—Safety and Health on Construction Sites, Lisbon, Portugal, pp. 11–19.

Bennet, D. J. (1997). *The Construction Labor Force in the 21st Century.* Proceedings of the Construction Congress V: Managing Engineered Construction in Expanding Global Markets, Minneapolis, Oct. 5, 1997, pp. 37–39.

Bosshart, Bob. (1992). "The Basics of Total Quality Management for Construction." Total Quality Management AIC Forum, Little Rock, Arkansas.

Burati, J. L., and Farrington, J. J. (1987). "Costs of Quality Deviations in Design and Construction" Construction Industry Institute, CII Source Document No. 29.

Burati, J. L. (1990). "Total Quality Management: The Competitive Edge." *Construction Industry Institute Publication 10-4,* August, 1990.

Chase, G. W. (1993). "Implementing TQM in a Construction Company" *The Associated General Contractors of America*, March, 1993.

Davis, Kent. (1987). *The Development of a Quality Performance Tracking System for Design and Construction*, August, 1987.

Davis, Kent *et al.* (1989) "Measuring Design and Construction Quality Costs." *Journal of Construction Engineering and Management*, September, 1989, pp. 385–400.

Dias, Luis M., and Curado, Miguel. (1996). *Integration of Quality and Safety in Construction Companies.* 1st International Conference, CIB: Working Commission W99—Safety and Health on Construction Sites, Lisbon, Portugal, pp. 21–28.

Hammer, Willie. (1985). *Occupational Safety Management and Engineering.* Prentice Hall.

Hayden, W. M., Jr. (1992). "Quality by Design." Total Quality Management AIC Forum, Little Rock, Arkansas.

Hickman, William D. (1993). "Contractors Getting Started in TQM." *Constructor,* September, 1993, pp.12–14.

Hinze, Jimmie W. (1997a). *Construction Safety.* Prentice Hall.

Hinze, Jimmie W. (1997b). "The Distraction Theory of Accident Causation." *CIB Publication 209,* October 10, 1997.

Hinze, Jimmie W. *et al.* (1996). "Design for Safety." *Construction Industry Institute Research Summary 101-1,* September 1996.

Hitt, Middlemist, and Mathis. (1983). *Management—Concepts and Effective Practice.* St. Paul, Minnesota, West Publishing Company.

Jaselskis, Edward J. *et al.* (1996). "Strategies for Achieving Excellence in Construction Safety Performance." *Journal of Construction Engineering and Management,* March, 1996, pp. 61–70.

Krause, Thomas R. (1994). "Safety and Quality: Two Sides of the Same Coin." *Quality Progress,* October, 1994, pp. 51–55.

Lagowski, J. J. (1994). "Education: An Industrial Imperative." *Journal of Chemical Education,* March, 1994, pp. 179, 180.

Laufer, A., and Jenkins, G. D. (1982). *Motivating Construction Workers.* American Society of Civil Engineers Proceedings, December, 1982, pp. 531–545.

Ledbetter, Bill *et al.* (1989). "Measuring the Cost of Quality in Design and Construction." *Construction Industry Institute Publication 10-2,* May, 1989.

Ledbetter, Bill *et al.* (1990). "The Quality Performance Management System: A Blueprint for Implementation." *Construction Industry Institute Publication 10-3 ,* February, 1990.

Levitt, Raymond E., and Samelson, Nancy M. (1987). *Construction Safety Management.* McGraw-Hill.

Lew, H. S. (1980). "America's Worst Construction Accident: Part One." *Civil Engineering-ASCE,* February, 1980, pp. 62–67.

Lewis, Gary F. (1993). *A Builder's Introduction to Total Quality Management.* NAHB Research Center, Inc., 1993, pp. 40–46.

Liska, Roger W. *et al.* (1993). "Construction Safety Self-Assessment Process." Construction Industry Institute, March, 1993.

Lo, Tommy Y. (1996) *An Element of Quality Management.* 1st International Conference, CIB: Working Commission W99—Safety and Health on Construction Sites, Lisbon, Portugal, pp. 195–200.

Mansour, F., and Usmen, M. (1993). *Analysis of Rework Costs in Construction and their Impact on Quality.* Proceedings of the Quality Concepts Conference, Warren, Michigan, October, 1993, pp. 97–121.

McCollough, M., and Benson, M. (1993). "Five Barriers to TQM in Construction." *Concrete Construction,* April 1993.

Mol, Hendrick, and Fox, Anthony. (1994). "Legal Aspects of Construction Safety." *The American Professional Constructor,* Vol. 18, No. 1, March, 1994, pp. 20–23.

Nelson, Emmitt J. *et al.* (1993). "Zero Injury Techniques." *Construction Industry Institute,* Publication 6-7, November 19, 1988.

Peyton, Robert X., and Rubio, Toni C. (1991). *Construction Safety Practices and Principles.* Van Nostrand Reinhold.

Rosenbluth, H., and Peters, D. M. (1992). *The Customer Comes Second: and Other Secrets of Exceptional Service.* New York, Morrow.

Shofoluwe, Musibau A., and Varzavand, Shahram. (1993). "The Need for Total Quality Management in Construction." *The American Professional Constructor,* September, 1993.

Simon, Michael S. (1982). *Construction Law Claims & Liability.* Arlyse Enterprises, Inc.

Talent, Jim. (1998). *Nation's Building News.* February 17, 1998, pp. 5, 6.

Zimmerman, William G. II. (1995). "Steel Erection Awareness: An Erector's View" *Modern Steel Construction,* May, 1995, pp. 30–33.

"Contractors Getting Started in TQM." *Constructor,* September, 1993, p. 345.

"Partnering: Changing Attitudes in Construction." *Constructor*, February, 1996.

"Safety: A Key to TQM." *Constructor*, October, 1993, cover.

"Workplace Injuries on the Decline." *Concrete Construction*, April, 1998, p. 345.

Engineering News Record, Vol. 240, No. 5, February 2, 1998, p. 12.

Engineering News Record, Vol. 240, No. 19, May 11, 1998, p. 11.

Engineering News Record, Vol. 240, No. 21, May 25, 1998, pp. 55–96.

Merit Shop Report, Vol. 22, No. 6, June, 1995, p. 1.

ASCE "Quality in the Constructed Project," 1990.

CFR: Code of Federal Regulations 29. Office of the Federal Register National Archives and Records Administration , Part 1926, Sections 20 and 21.

OSHA NEWS RELEASE USDL 97-16.

QUALITY-SAFETY RELATIONSHIP SURVEY

1. Company Name (OPTIONAL)_____.

   Respondent's Name (OPTIONAL) _____.

2. Select the description that best fits the relationship between the Quality and Safety functions as practiced in your company. (circle A, B, C, or D)

   A. They operate as entirely independent organizations with little or no interaction.

   B. There is occasional interaction, i.e., each department is aware of the other's activities, some information and possibly limited resources are occasionally shared.

   C. There is frequent interaction, i.e., efforts are coordinated; information and some resources are frequently shared.

   D. They are very integrated, i.e., one is a part of the other; staff works closely together, relevant information is routinely shared, quality and safety functions, such as inspections, are often combined.

   E. Other (please explain).

3. Safety is considered a part of TQM. (circle A or B)

   A. Yes

   B. No

   Comments:

4. Your reaction to combining and/or better coordinating the Quality and Safety functions. (circle A, B, or C)

   A. Good idea

   B. Has some potential

   C. Bad Idea

   Comments:

5. At your company is there an incentive program for Safety?

for management?	Yes	No
for field workers?	Yes	No

   Comments:

6. Is there an incentive program for Quality?

for management?	Yes	No
for field workers?	Yes	No

   Comment:

7. The information above is descriptive of all divisions of my company.

Yes	No	Not sure

If you would like the results of this survey or the paper, indicate below and include a mailing address.

Survey or Paper

C H A P T E R

8

DESIGNING FOR SAFETY

John A. Gambatese, Ph.D., P.E.
Department of Civil and Environmental Engineering
University of Nevada, Las Vegas, Nevada, U.S.A.

ABSTRACT

Improving worker safety continues to be a necessary goal in the construction industry. While significant improvements in safety performance have been made in the past few decades, in general the design profession has not been an active participant in this safety effort. The lack of designer involvement in worker safety has been attributed to their educational focus, limited experience in addressing construction site safety, restricted role on the project team, and a deliberate attempt to minimize liability exposure. Recent research studies have identified designers as parties who have a significant influence on construction safety. It is the design that dictates construction means and methods, and therefore affects the construction safety hazards that exist on a jobsite. Studies have led to the accumulation of design suggestions that can be implemented by a project design team with the intent of minimizing or eliminating construction site hazards. These design suggestions have been incorporated into a computer program that assists designers in recognizing project-specific safety hazards and incorporating the suggestions into the project design.

Design-for-safety knowledge and the design tool may potentially reduce a designer's liability exposure resulting from lawsuits initiated as a result of worker injuries. According to the current structure of the construction industry, on a typical design-bid-build project a designer crosses the boundary between design and construction when implementing design-for-safety knowledge. Based on past legal cases along with the concepts of standard of practice and professional duty, failure to employ the safety knowledge may lead to increased liability exposure for design professionals. As a result, the design community should consider adopting the philosophy that their scope of work includes designing for construction worker safety. Implementation of this knowledge represents a proactive effort to reduce worker injuries and fatalities and will ultimately create a safer construction workplace.

KEYWORDS

safety, construction, design, hazards, liability

INTRODUCTION

Safety on the construction site is a major issue of concern for the construction industry. The concern has been driven primarily by escalating costs of workers' compensation insurance, a rise in the number of third-party liability suits, and the intensification of safety regulations. In response to these influences, the construction industry has acted to control job site hazards, increase safety awareness, and improve construction worker safety in recent decades. As a result, there has been a slow, but steady, decline in the number of construction site injuries and fatalities (NSC 1952-1997). Despite the gains in safety awareness and performance, the safety record of the construction industry continues to lag behind all other industries, except for agriculture and mining (NSC 1997), and there still exists a mindset within the industry that construction work is inherently unsafe.

Current safety standards and legislation in the United States are "a result of a long history of change in the drive to reduce the number of worker injuries and fatalities" (Hinze and Gambatese 1994). Throughout the Industrial Revolution in the 19th century, common law assigned the employer the responsibility to maintain minimum safety measures on the job site. Common law also provided the employer with three important defenses: the Fellow Servant Rule, Contributory Negligence, and Assumption of Risk. These defenses effectively placed the responsibility for job site well-being and safety (and consequently worker injuries) on the workers themselves (Bonny 1973).

After the turn of the century, the responsibility for the care of worker injuries was transferred from the employee to the employer by various national and state workers' compensation laws. Some examples of these laws are the Federal Employers' Liability Act (1908), Longshore and Harbor Workers' Compensation Act (1927), Defense Base Act (1941), and Outer Continental Shelf Lands Act (1953). In the late 1960s, federal regulations broadened the employers' responsibility by charging them with overseeing worker well-being on the job site in addition to being responsible for caring for worker injuries. One example federal regulation is the Construction Safety Act (1969), which revised the Federal Contract Work Hours Standards Act of 1968.

The legislation enacted during the first half of the twentieth century was followed by several years of lobbying by public interest groups for a safer workplace. The intense lobbying efforts "proved to be the final punch in attaining safety legislation" (Haas *et al.* 1995). The result was the passage of the Williams-Steiger Act, commonly known as the Occupational Safety and Health Act of 1970 (hereinafter called OSH Act). This act created the Occupational Safety and Health Administration (OSHA), National Institute of Occupational Safety and Health (NIOSH), and Occupational Safety and Health Review Commission (OSHRC).

The OSH Act is particularly relevant to the construction industry where the need for safety awareness and improvement is perhaps greater than in most other industries. "Since its inception, OSHA regulations and inspections have been a driving force in improving construction jobsite safety" (Haas *et al.* 1995). It is particularly noteworthy that the OSH Act places the responsibility for employee safety on the employer. The Act's general duty clause given in Title 29, Section 654, of the United States Code imposes an obligation on employers by stating that:

> Each employer shall furnish to each of his employees employment and a place of employment which are free from recognized hazards that are causing or likely to cause death or serious physical harm to his employees.

EXPANDING THE RESPONSIBILITY FOR SAFETY

As a result of the passage of the OSH Act, construction site safety responsibility typically rests on the constructor's shoulders. This responsibility reflects the constructor's control of the worksite and the construction means and methods. Following the passage of the OSH Act, though, the responsibility for worker safety has frequently been extended to others involved in construction projects. Owners, designers, construction managers, suppliers, and lenders have been held responsible for worker safety in addition to the injured worker's employer. Courts have decided that although a party may not be a direct employer of an injured worker, that party's presence on the job site, involvement in the project design, or direction of the work sequence may justifiably transfer some of the responsibility for construction worker safety onto that party's shoulders. This broadening of responsibility, based on the extent of involvement in the construction effort, can be contractual or assumed. In *Duncan v. Pennington County Housing Authority* (283 N.W.2d 546, S.D. 1979), for example, the owner-architect contract required the architect to perform day-to-day supervision of the construction effort and to assure that all of the contractual documents, including the OSHA standards, were complied with throughout the construction period. This contractual agreement led the court to rule the architect partially responsible for injuries sustained by an ironworker in a fall due to inadequately designed temporary guardrails.

Similar expansion of the responsibility for safety resulted in response to the courts' views on contractual arrangements. In the late 1950s, courts judged that privity of contract did not isolate third parties from the responsibility for worker safety. Courts held that the responsibility for worker safety could be assumed, based on one's actions or duty. Assumed responsibility for worker safety by a third party is illustrated in *Phillips v. United Engineers & Constructors, Inc.* (500 N.E.2d 1265, Ind.App. 1 Dist. 1986). In that case, a construction manager was hired to provide engineering services for a project, coordinate the work among the contractors, and inspect materials and equipment to assure their conformance with the plans and specifications. During the course of construction, the construction manager also conducted safety meetings, toured the site, and noted safety violations and unsafe practices. Following the accidental death of a sheetmetal worker on site, the court placed responsibility for the worker's safety on the construction manager based on actions taken during construction regarding worker safety.

Efforts to expand the responsibility for safety continue to this date. A major effort to expand safety legislation resulted after twenty-eight workers died in the tragic collapse in Bridgeport, Connecticut of the L'Ambiance Plaza Building during its construction (Godfrey 1988). The accident became the driving force behind a bill introduced in Congress in 1988 to amend the OSH Act (Senate Bill 2518). A major component of this legislation was to:

> require all construction projects to be supervised by (i.e. controlled and directed by, with attendant duties, responsibilities and liabilities) a professional engineer-architect designated by the owner and registered in the state where the construction is to be performed (ASCE 1988).

This change was opposed by the American Society of Civil Engineers (ASCE), American Consulting Engineers Council (ACEC), and other professional societies, as well as construction contractors. The reasons for such widespread opposition include:

> the extension of the engineer's professional responsibilities to include activities for which he is not qualified, disruption of traditional working and contractual relationships, great increase in liability exposure for engineers, increase in cost for professional liability insurance, creation of a potential for an engineering manpower shortage, and increase in overall cost and time required for construction (ASCE 1988).

In its policy statement on construction site safety, ASCE responded to this bill by adding that it supported legislation that accomplishes a number of items including providing for:

> federal development of an overall approach to improving construction site safety which encourages cooperation among the parties to a construction project, rather than an approach which is chiefly punitive, administratively burdensome, and which tends to foster adversarial relationships (ASCE 1989).

Opposition to this bill from a large segment of the construction industry led to its failure, but further legislation was later proposed. In 1989, a subsequent bill presented before Congress (Senate Bill 930):

deleted the requirement that the owner retain an engineer for general oversight but would have required the contractor to employ a certified safety specialist (CSS) for the safety function with authority to stop work where there is imminent danger to workers (Sweet 1994).

Again, opposition from professional and trade associations based on similar arguments against the previous bill ultimately led to the failure of this subsequent bill.

The latest effort to enact safety legislation mandating more broad-based responsibility comes from OSHA's Steel Erection Negotiated Rulemaking Advisory Committee (SENRAC). This committee was commissioned by OSHA in 1994 to negotiate revisions to OSHA's construction safety regulations. The committee has proposed that the regulations be revised to state that accountability for worksite safety be assigned "among all employers who have responsibility for conception, design and execution of construction projects covered by part 1926 [of the OSHA regulations]" (OSHA 1994). The scope of the revisions includes requirements for the development of a site specific safety plan during the conception phase of the project, consideration of constructor safety performance in the bid phase, a pre-startup safety conference, and periodic monitoring of contractor safety performance. The proposed revisions are expected to be formally adopted by OSHA in 2000.

Legislation to formally distribute the responsibility for worker safety among the various parties involved in a project has been enacted outside the United States. The United Kingdom has recently enacted the Construction (Design and Management) Regulations (CDM 1994) which direct the designer to address construction site safety as the design is being developed. "The Regulations are not prescriptive; they avoid setting standards. Emphasis is placed on identifying hazards and the assessment of risk" (Joyce 1995). The CDM Regulations require designers to play a role in the identification and mitigation of safety hazards with limited guidance on how these efforts are to be accomplished. Reported impacts of this legislation on the United Kingdom's construction industry are still preliminary and include the following assessments:

> Many designers currently lack skills in designing to avoid or reduce health and safety risk and they feel uncomfortable and threatened by the [R]egulations (Jeffrey and Douglas 1994).

> The challenge facing designers is the ability to seek out and discover or develop other techniques or construction methods to produce the same or similar results than a more inherently high risk option (Joyce 1995).

> It is suggested then that the designer develops a methodical approach to recording the design considerations with reasoned outcomes (Joyce 1995).

While the requirements of this legislation will surely improve safety on the construction site, it appears that a major obstacle will be gaining acceptance and compliance from the entire construction community.

Legislation and legal case decisions appear to be pointing to an expansion of the responsibility for safety. Through these influences and the increased costs associated with worker injuries and fatalities, the role each party on a project team has with respect to safety is being evaluated. With construction site safety resting primarily with the constructor, current safety legislation primarily addresses the constructor's role. Similarly, the majority of past safety research has investigated how the constructor affects and can improve job site safety. Other parties on the project team have not traditionally been involved in the safety watch. Only recently have some owners become involved in ensuring safety on the job site. Increased owner involvement can be attributed to the rising costs associated with construction site injuries, which are ultimately reflected in higher costs of construction. Consequently, owners with sizable construction budgets have acted to improve safety by selecting constructors based on demonstrated safety performance, contractually addressing safety, and playing a more proactive role in safety.

One major party on the project team, the designer, has historically not been directly involved in construction site safety. Designers typically focus on safety of the "end-user" of the facility, and leave construction worker safety to be considered by others. The design profession is one area of construction that, while its involvement in safety is has been minimal or lacking, has a great influence on safety.

SAFETY AND THE DESIGNER

The typical design-bid-build project delivery system includes a design professional, or "designer," such as an architect, structural engineer, mechanical engineer, or electrical engineer. Historically, the design profession has not addressed construction site safety in its scope of work. Designers' lack of involvement can be attributed to their education and training, existing design tools and standards, their typical role on the project team, and their fear of liability exposure. Designer education and training typically focuses on safety of the end-user, such as the office worker, motorist, or equipment operator. Rarely do designers receive formal construction site safety education and training. "There appears to be a gap in knowledge and expertise regarding safety principles and practices" (Eck 1987). The problem can be compounded by the fact that "most engineering school faculty members who instruct students in safety matters have themselves been inadequately educated" (Hammer 1989).

Today's design standards reflect the designers' education and training. Design codes, such as the Uniform Building Code (ICBO 1994), typically provide standards that target the safety of the facility's end-user. User safety for the period of time between the start of construction and the transfer of the completed project to the owner is not specifically addressed. It is the mindset of the design code developers, who are typically city and county building officials, that construction site safety is covered by the OSHA regulations. As a result, no efforts have been undertaken or are currently underway to expand the scope of the design codes to include construction worker safety.

Designers have also based their lack of involvement in construction site safety on their typical role on the project team. The designers' role is typically limited to the preparation of the design documents for use by the constructor. In many cases the designer is also called on to verify that the completed work conforms to the requirements of the design documents. Although designers are usually given the authority to stop work that does not meet the design requirements, rarely are they given further control of the construction site. In fact, many owner-designer contracts, such as the American Institute of Architects (AIA) Document B163, Standard Form of Agreement Between Owner and Architect for Designated Services (AIA 1993), explicitly mandate that the designer

> shall not have control over or charge of and shall not be responsible for construction means, methods, techniques, sequences and procedures, or for safety precautions and programs in connection with the Work.

These on-site responsibilities are typically placed on the constructor, the party with primary responsibility for constructing the facility. AIA Document A201, General Conditions of the Contract for Construction (AIA 1997b) requires that the contractor

> shall be solely responsible for and have control over construction means, methods, techniques, sequences and procedures and for coordinating all portions of the Work under the Contract, unless Contract Documents give other specific instructions concerning these matters.

AIA Document A201, as with many contracts for construction, additionally places the responsibility for safety specifically on the constructor. Section 10.1.1 of Document A201 states that the contractor "shall be responsible for initiating, maintaining and supervising all safety precautions and programs in connection with the performance of the Contract."

Lastly, designers have minimized their involvement in construction site safety in order to limit their exposure to liability for worker injuries. Numerous court decisions extending the responsibility for safety to third parties (*Miller v. Dewitt*, 226 N.E.2d 630, Ill. 1967; *Welch v. Grant Development Co., Inc.*, 466 N.Y.S.2d 112; *Swarthout v. Beard*, 190 N.W.2d 373, Mich. App. 1971) reveal the courts' willingness and intention to compensate injured workers for their losses. Some may consider this theme as sympathetic towards the injured worker, who may be permanently disabled or out of work, at the expense of design firms and their insurance companies. Whether it is a "stab" at the "deep pockets" of large companies or a justified outcome based on one's contracted or assumed professional duty, mounting litigation regarding the safety of construction workers led to a liability crisis in the mid-1980s for third parties involved in the construction effort (Hinze and Lyneis 1988). As a result of this litigation and subsequent advice from their legal counsel, designers have deliberately excluded from their scope of work any involvement in construction worker safety.

Regardless of the aforementioned reasons why designers typically do not address construction worker safety, the construction industry has recently awakened to the need for designer involvement. It is becoming more evident that safety practices implemented solely by the constructor cannot eliminate all job site hazards. There is a growing opinion in the construction industry that "many site accidents are just waiting to happen, they are 'pre-programmed' due to a lack of planning and care by all parties concerned" (Jeffrey and Douglas 1994). Constructors and safety professionals have realized that the design is an underlying facet of construction site safety. "The selection of forming systems, cycle times, sequences, equipment, and design of temporary construction are significantly impacted by the performance capabilities and restraints of the permanent construction" (Stephan 1987). The industry has concluded that:

> the need for changes in attitude does not stop at educating erectors to work more safely. It has to go back to the architect and engineer who should not only ask themselves if it can be built, but can it be built safely (Baggs and Cunningham 1988).

The need to educate designers is reinforced by the "Order of Precedence" which ranks the methods used for reducing safety risks according to their priority and effectiveness (MacCollum 1995). These methods, listed in order of priority and effectiveness, are:

1. Design to eliminate or minimize the hazard
2. Guard the hazard
3. Give a warning
4. Provide special procedures and training
5. Provide personal protective equipment

The list clearly indicates that the designer is in the best position to affect construction site safety.

DESIGN-FOR-SAFETY RESEARCH: THE ROLE OF THE DESIGNER

Construction safety legislation and research have principally addressed the constructor's role in safety. This focus reflects the constructor's control of the job site and work practices. Though safety is thought of as primarily within the constructor's scope of work, research studies have exposed the significant role of design in providing a safe worksite. Design professionals dictate the configuration and components of a facility through the design documents. The nature of the design influences project construction means and methods, and therefore affects the safety hazards that exist on the job site. That is, the design causes the construction worker to be exposed to work-related safety hazards on the construction site.

The awareness of the designer's effect on worker safety has provided the stimulus for research regarding the designer's role in safety. A study based on a survey of design firms and firms conducting constructability reviews (Hinze and Wiegand 1992) found that "less than one-third of the design firms address construction worker safety in their designs, and less than one-half of the independent constructability reviews conducted address construction worker safety." Many designers commented that legal counsel specifically advised them not to address safety in order to avoid the assumption of any liability. The study revealed that the designers who addressed construction worker safety during the design phase tended to work in design-build firms. It is noteworthy that in these firms, the beneficiaries of the design effort include the construction entity of the same firm. With respect to increasing designer involvement, the authors recommend that designers be sensitized to the need for addressing worker safety and that a change must occur in the mindset of the design profession. To accomplish this important task, the authors recommend education of designers by existing construction industry groups and associations. It is proposed that "such an educational process could begin with a compilation of the various design approaches that have successfully addressed construction worker safety on past projects." Several examples of designs in which construction safety was addressed were received in the study. Finally, the authors also recommend that owners must communicate to the designers the need to address safety in the design phase. It was proposed that this could be accomplished by basing the selection of design firms, in part, on their willingness to address construction worker safety in the design.

Construction marketing studies conducted in 1993 and 1994 included a look at the designer's role in safety (Hinze 1991, 1994a,b). The studies involved surveying large owners in the United States, primarily those with large construction budgets. Although these studies had several different areas of focus, a few questions were asked about construction worker safety with regard to designers. Specifically, the owners were asked if the designers of their projects addressed construction worker safety in their designs. The results from the studies were similar and are represented in Figure 8–1.

It is readily apparent from Figure 8–1 that construction worker safety is not addressed by most designers. It is noteworthy, though, that 16% of the designers do see their role as encompassing the safety consideration of construction workers. While several designers (29%) were noted to occasionally address safety for specific items, these items were generally considered to be those related to both construction worker safety and safety of the end-user, e.g., a remodeling project where materials containing asbestos are encountered. It is interesting that a significant number of owners (10%) felt that designers would be addressing construction safety in their future designs. This indicates that a trend exists for greater future involvement of designers on construction worker safety issues.

DESIGN-FOR-SAFETY RESEARCH: CAPTURING AND RETRIEVING DESIGN-FOR-SAFETY IDEAS

A recent research project, funded by the Construction Industry Institute, expanded on this topic by investigating the extent to which a designer can influence construction worker safety (Gambatese *et al.* 1997). This multi-year, national research effort involved the development and accumulation of design suggestions, or "best design practices." A computer program was also

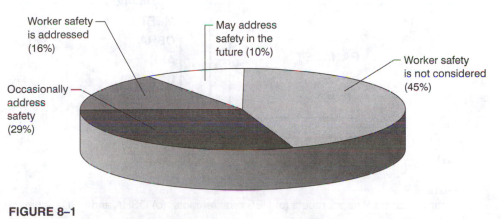

FIGURE 8–1
Designer role in addressing safety.

developed to assist designers in implementing the suggestions. The design suggestions and computer software will be described in further detail.

The initial thrust of the study focused on developing and accumulating ideas for a facility's design that minimize or eliminate safety hazards during construction. The design suggestions were generated from various sources including company design manuals, the Occupational Safety and Health Administration (OSHA) construction safety standards (U.S. 1995), interviews with construction industry personnel, and the experience of the researchers themselves. One design suggestion, for example, relates to the height of a parapet. The OSHA safety standards for construction require temporary guardrails to be 42 inches (1.07 meters) tall. The Uniform Building Code (UBC) standards (ICBO 1994) require parapets to be at least 30 inches (0.76 meters) tall. Figure 8–2a illustrates a 30 inch (0.76 meter) high parapet as modified with a temporary guardrail required to meet OSHA regulations. A design change that increases the parapet height to 42 inches (1.07 meters) would meet both the UBC and OSHA requirements as shown in Figure 8–2b.

Modifying the design of the parapet in this manner eliminates the need to construct guardrails during construction and future roof maintenance operations. The following is a sample of other design-for-safety suggestions that were recorded as part of the research project (Gambatese *et al.* 1997).

Suggestion: Design project components to facilitate pre-fabrication in the shop or on the ground so that they may be erected in place as complete assemblies.

Purpose: Reduce the amount of elevated work to minimize worker exposure to falls from elevation and being struck by falling objects.

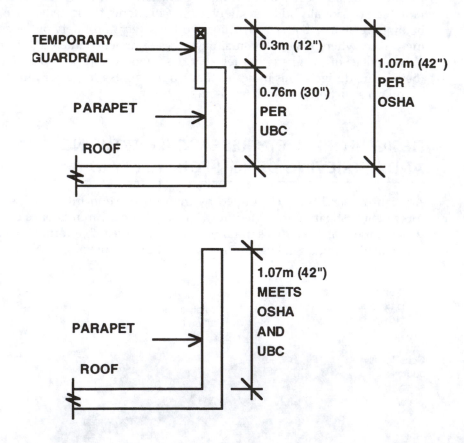

FIGURE 8–2
Parapet design: Parapet meets (a) UBC requirements, (b) OSHA and UBC requirements.

Suggestion: Design steel columns with holes in the web at 21 inches (0.53 meters) and 42 inches (1.07 meters) above the working level to provide support locations for guardrails.

Purpose: By eliminating the need to connect special guardrail connections, such fabrication details will facilitate worker safety immediately upon erection of the columns.

Suggestion: Design beam-to-column double-connections to have continual support for the beams during the connection process by adding a beam seat, extra bolt hole, or other redundant connection point.

Purpose: Continual support for beams during erection will eliminate falls due to unexpected vibrations, mis-alignment, and unexpected construction loads.

Suggestion: Minimize the number of offsets in a building plan. Make the offsets a consistent size and as large as possible.

Purpose: Prevent fall hazards by simplifying the work area for construction workers.

Suggestion: Design underground utilities to be placed using trenchless technologies.

Purpose: Eliminate the safety hazards associated with trenching, especially around roads and pedestrian traffic surfaces.

Suggestion: Design roadway edges and shoulders to support the weight of construction equipment.

Purpose: Prevent heavy construction equipment from crushing the edge of the roadway with an increased risk of overturning.

Suggestion: Position mechanical, piping, and electrical controls away from passageways and work areas but still within reach for easy operation.

Purpose: Controls that protrude into passageways and work areas, or are hard to operate, hidden, or inaccessible, create safety hazards for construction and maintenance workers.

Suggestion: Allow adequate clearance between the structure and overhead power lines. Bury, disconnect, or re-route existing power lines around the project before construction begins.

Purpose: Overhead power lines that are in service during construction create a hazard when operating cranes and other tall equipment.

Suggestion: Route piping lines that carry liquids below electrical cable trays.

Purpose: Prevent the chance of electrical shock due to leaking pipes.

Suggestion: Do not allow schedules with sustained overtime.

Purpose: Workers will not be alert if overtime is maintained over an extended period of time. Productivity and morale will also suffer.

In conjunction with the accumulation of design suggestions, the study included the development of a computer-based design tool titled "Design for Construction Safety ToolBox." Best practice manuals and checklists have been utilized by many large companies to facilitate the design and review process. These tools, traditionally in written document form, often fall short of successfully integrating safety into the design process. Additionally, a broad collection of safety-related design knowledge presented in written document form can become cumbersome and difficult to update. Incorporating such knowledge into a multimedia computer software design tool provides a number of advantages, including:

- more efficient utilization of the tool by a designer or design team
- the ability to frequently update the knowledge base
- easy management and control of the review process
- the ability to incorporate analytical functions, such as risk assessment and decision analysis

The main objective of the design tool is to provide a simple means by which a designer could be introduced to a variety of project-specific design suggestions that would improve safety during the construction phase of the project. To meet this objective, the software was designed to contain the following features and functions:

- a variety of approaches for reviewing a project
- identification of safety hazards
- presentation of suggestions to eliminate or reduce the likelihood of the occurrence of hazards
- documentation and generation of the results into reports in a usable format
- the ability for other design suggestions to be input and saved within the tool for future reference

Construction projects vary in many ways including size, features, function, job site safety hazards, and operating systems. In order to focus on the characteristics of a particular project, the design tool allows the user to select which topics to address. This feature enables the user to customize the review process to more efficiently perform a thorough and complete project review. After entering initial information about the project and the user's design discipline, the program allows the user to access the design suggestions by focusing on the project in one of three ways or "paths":

- Project Components
- Construction Site Hazards
- Project Systems

Regardless of the path taken, the user has complete access to all of the design suggestions. A review can be conducted by focusing on typical project components, such as the foundation, structural framing, roof, piping, tanks, and doors. If the designer wants to address specific safety hazards, the review can be conducted by focusing on construction site hazards, such as cave-ins, falls, fire, and electrical shock. Lastly, the program allows the designer to focus on project systems organized according to the Construction Specifications Institute (CSI) divisions, such as metals, finishes, mechanical, and electrical. For example, if a project includes the design of underground piping, the designer may select "Project Components" to specifically address piping issues. The program then presents a list of components typically found in construction projects, shown in Figure 8–3. When a particular component is selected, the review will focus on safety concerns and design suggestions related to that particular component. In this example, the designer would choose "Piping."

After selecting a component, the program presents a number of questions regarding the project features, as shown in Figure 8–4. Here, the program allows for further focus on the characteristics of a component that are relevant to the particular project. The answers to the questions will direct the program's search for applicable safety concerns and design suggestions. To address underground piping, the designer would answer "Yes" to question #2: "Does the project include the design of underground piping lines?"

Based on the responses to the questions, the program then presents safety concerns and design suggestions that address the selected component, as shown in Figure 8–5. Safety concerns are presented to educate designers of construction site hazards. The design suggestions provide a means of reducing or eliminating the identified safety concerns. The safety concerns can be reviewed and, if applicable to the project, one or more design suggestions can be recorded. For example, the designer could select suggestion #2: "When new piping lines are to be placed below existing concrete surfaces, roads, or other traffic areas, design the lines so that they may be placed

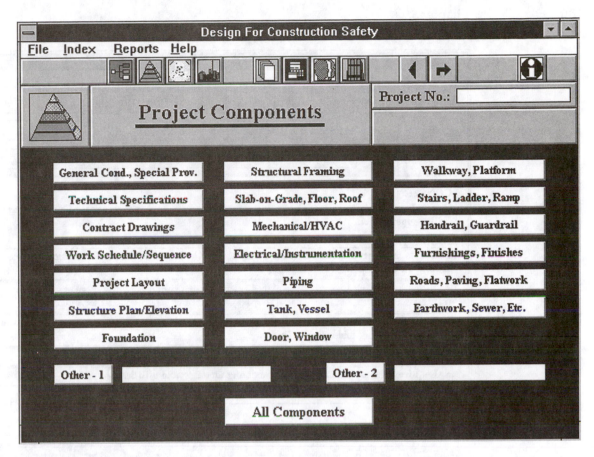

FIGURE 8–3
Project components.

Design For Construction Safety

File   Index   Reports   Help

Project Features   Project No.:

Piping

1. Does the project include the design of any of the following piping related items? (Select all that apply.)

○ Pipes   ○ Controls/Valves   ○ Piping Location   ○ Piping Supports   ○ Drains

2. Does the project include the design of underground piping lines?   ○ Yes   ○ No

3. Does the project include the design of new fire water systems, or working with existing fire water systems.   ○ Yes   ○ No

4. Does the project include the design of new piping systems which will carry hazardous materials?   ○ Yes   ○ No

5. Is the review of the piping erection and/or placement schedule or sequence included in the design effort?   ○ Yes   ○ No

6. Will testing of piping systems be required during the construction or initial startup phase?   ○ Yes   ○ No

7. Will new piping systems be tied in to existing systems?   ○ Yes   ○ No

FIGURE 8–4
Project features—piping.

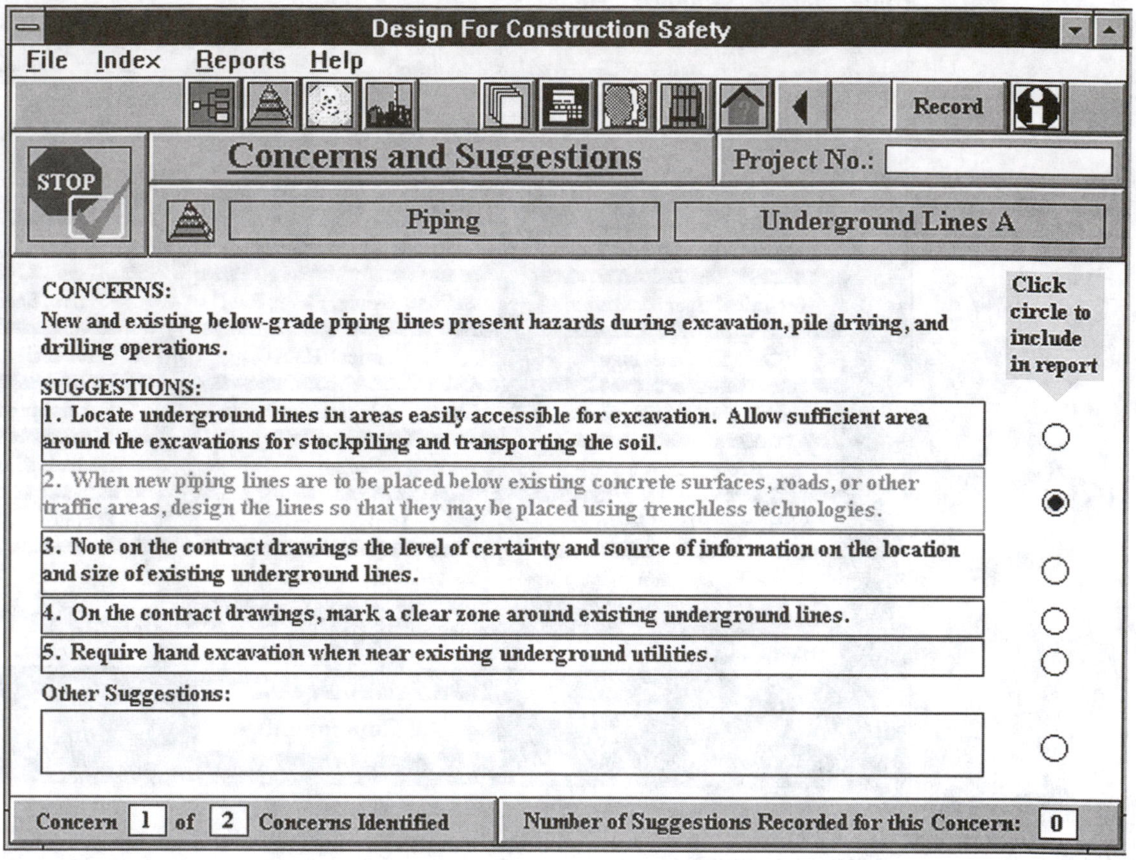

FIGURE 8–5
Concerns and suggestions—piping/underground lines.

using trenchless technologies." Other suggestions (unique ideas generated by the user) can also be input and recorded, and will be saved within the program for future reference.

The design suggestions presented are directed at a particular component. When the construction project is large and complex, the design suggestions may be applicable to more than one location in the design. Or, if more than one location exists for a particular concern, different design suggestions may be appropriate for different locations. Therefore, for each design suggestion recorded, the program allows the input of information relevant to that particular suggestion, such as the location within the project, task number, trade, worker, recommendations for implementation, and an action/status.

Rather than examining a particular project component, the designer could address specific job site hazards. For example, to address fall hazards due to the design of structural steel connections, the designer would select "Construction Site Hazards" rather than "Project Components" or "Project Systems." By selecting this path, the program presents a list of safety hazards construction workers typically experience on-site, shown in Figure 8–6. By selecting one or more hazards, the program will focus on safety concerns and design suggestions related to the particular hazard(s). In this example, the designer would choose "Falls."

The review of safety concerns and design suggestions related to specific project systems, such as steel, finishes, and mechanical, is performed in a manner similar to that for project components and construction site hazards. The project systems, shown in Figure 8–7, reflect the standard Construction Specifications Institute (CSI) format and numbering system.

Accurate and thorough record keeping on any construction project is essential for producing a quality product. All design calculations, sketches, notes, and computer results should be documented not only for future reference, but also for communication with other parties

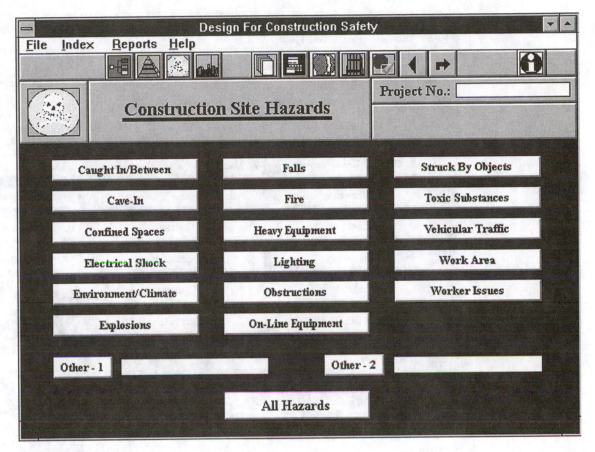

FIGURE 8–6
Construction site hazards.

involved in the project. The program offers a variety of printed reports to help record and communicate the results of a project design review.

The software provides two on-line sources for help and assistance in using the program. For each screen, help menus are provided which give information about the program's features and assistance in navigating through the program. For first-time users, an interactive tutorial consisting of a short guided tour of the program's features and functions is provided at the beginning of the program.

The Design for Construction Safety ToolBox can be obtained directly from the Construction Industry Institute (3208 Red River St., Austin, Texas, 78705-2650. Telephone: 512-471-4319).

DESIGNER LIABILITY

The design-for-safety knowledge and design tool allow designers to play a part in ensuring construction worker safety. The decision to implement the safety knowledge is made by the design professional. According to the current structure of the construction industry, on a traditional design-bid-build project a designer would cross the boundary between design and construction by addressing construction worker safety. Crossing the boundary attracts additional responsibility. The design tool does not make any decisions based on risk management practices. Thus, the designer must weigh the merits of implementation of the safety knowledge against not only the characteristics of each particular project, such as physical constraints, project funding, and schedule, but also the anticipated duties and ramifications regarding the assumed professional responsibility. The fear of many designers is that the assumed responsibility results in added liability.

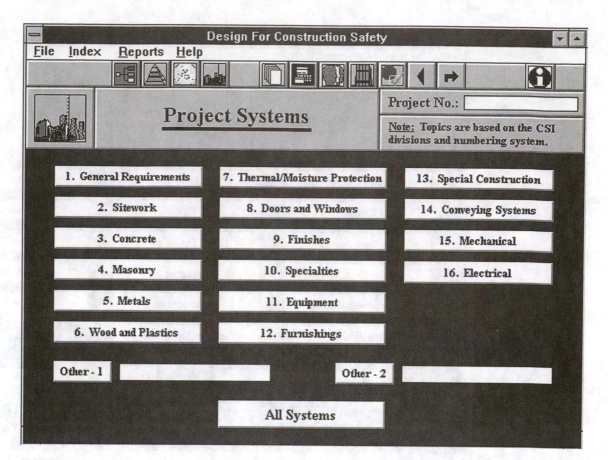

FIGURE 8–7
Project systems.

An investigation of designer liability associated with designing for safety starts with a look at the evolution of the construction industry. In past centuries, a construction project revolved around a "master builder." Through extensive training and education, the master builder provided the expertise and knowledge necessary for constructing many of the historic landmarks still in existence around the world. Under direct contract with the owner, the master builder developed a project from concept through construction, filling the shoes of the architect, engineer, general contractor, and construction manager as defined today. Laborers representing various trades performed the construction work under the master builder's direct supervision and employment. With this all-encompassing role, the master builder sat at the focal point of a project and ultimately shouldered the responsibility for a project's success or failure.

The evolution of the modern construction industry has resulted in the disintegration of the master builder system. The expertise and knowledge that was once solely provided by the master builder is now essentially divided between two distinct divisions within the industry: design and construction. Development of the divisions occurred primarily as a result of education. Architectural and engineering training began to emphasize theory and engineering principles through academic education, while the manual skills of artisans and craftworkers tended to be learned through hands-on job site training. Formally educated architects and engineers eventually recognized that "in order to achieve 'professional' status as viewed by society, and in order to be accepted as an academic discipline, they had to first separate themselves from the *manual* processes of construction" (Robson and Bashford 1997). Formalization of the divisions transpired with the establishment of The Royal Institute of British Architects in 1834, followed by the creation of other similar organizations in Europe and America in the mid-1800s (Mitchell 1977). The boundary between the divisions solidified with the passage of an amendment to The American Institute of Architects (AIA) By-Laws in 1900 that required new candidates to graduate from an approved school or pass an Institute examination (Kostof 1977). Shortly thereafter, professional licensing and registration laws enacted by most states secured the boundary between design and construction, and effectively replaced the master builder with a design professional and a constructor.

In conjunction with the creation of two distinct divisions, the construction industry experienced segmentation within each division. Within design, increased specialization resulted in a profession composed of consultants, each representing a specific design discipline such as architecture, civil engineering, and mechanical engineering. A similar fragmentation occurred in construction where master tradeworkers became specialty tradeworkers through increased concentration on specific skills (Robson and Bashford 1997). Specialty contractor talents focus on skilled crafts such as bricklaying, plumbing, and carpentry. Each consultant performs a unique design function and each specialty contractor constructs a specific product which, when integrated with that of the other consultants and specialty contractors, provide a complete project for the client (owner). All of the entities are bound contractually to work toward a common goal of completing the project in a timely and cost-effective manner.

Project Responsibility

Partitioning the fields of design and construction requires refining and ultimately defining the work of each design discipline and specialty contractor. For designers, professional organizations and state licensing and registration laws define each design discipline. The expertise provided by each discipline constitutes a unique subset of the entire knowledge required to design a project. By combining their knowledge, design consultants conceptualize, engineer, and prepare a complete design that is then given to a constructor to build. On the construction side, the work is organized by trade with labor skills and contractor licensing laws playing major roles in defining the skills each trade incorporates. Each trade's expertise is methodically applied to produce a completed product that reflects the intended design. By defining a realm of expertise and knowledge, design disciplines and construction trades place borders around their work. The borders both limit the work that the designers and specialty contractors are expected to perform, and surround the work to which they are entitled. The borders are fortified contractually and positioned by standards of practice.

Through industry segmentation, the responsibility for a project that once solely rested on the master builder is now spread across many entities. Distribution of the responsibility for project success or failure reflects the work input to the project, i.e., a mechanical engineer is responsible for the design of the mechanical system, while the mechanical subcontractor becomes accountable for the construction of the mechanical system. Consequently, the boundary between design and construction, and the borders around design disciplines and construction trades, not only outline scopes of work, but also delineate responsibility. Each design discipline and construction trade shoulders the responsibility of carrying out the work contained in its realm of knowledge within the established borders. Acceptance and dismissal of the responsibility for all or a portion of the work is outlined contractually prior to performing the work.

Challenging Industry Boundaries and Borders

The construction industry continues to be transformed by technological advancements, changing economic climates, and modified values and perceptions of design and construction. Elements stimulating the change often challenge both the boundary between design and construction and the borders around design disciplines and construction trades. One example of such a challenge is a jurisdictional dispute between labor unions. A labor union's jurisdiction signifies the extent of work controlled and performed by its members. Each craft is expected to honor the "ownership" rights of other crafts over such work (Hinze 1993). Disputes regarding the right to perform specific work can arise during hard economic times when work is slow. To keep its members employed, a union may attempt to "claim" the work of another union and, as a result, initiate a dispute. Disputes can also originate following the development of new technologies that sit on or near the border between union jurisdictions. Several unions may try to lay claim to the work associated with the new technology, giving rise to a jurisdictional dispute. The resolution of jurisdictional disputes may re-locate, weaken, or even dissolve the border between trade unions.

On the design side, negotiation between consultants may be required to determine the party responsible for or entitled to the design of a particular element or system. Structural and mechanical engineers, for example, may disagree about who is responsible for designing the support for a heating, ventilating, and air-conditioning (HVAC) system. Similarly, negotiation between the architect and structural engineer may be required to determine the party responsible for designing metal stud partition walls. Like the border between labor unions, the border between design disciplines is contested and sometimes modified.

While both design and construction sometimes appear fully entrenched in how each views its scope of work and role in the industry, the boundary that separates them has been modified to reflect changes in the construction industry. The most recent modification occurred when the Associated General Contractors (AGC) endorsed the revised version of the AIA's Document A201, General Conditions of the Contract for Construction (Ichniowski 1997). The revised document delegates a greater amount of the design responsibility to the constructor for certain design details. AIA instituted the change to reflect the customary practice of contractors and suppliers providing design details for particular systems. This practice occurs when the constructor sits in a better position to design the system than the design professional, e.g., the design of support structures for an HVAC system that will vary depending on the as-built configuration of the HVAC system. The change also reflects AIA's intent to better represent the associated risk distribution. While divided in its support for the document, AGC endorsement indicates an increased realization that the construction industry revolves around and relies on both design and construction working together rather than independently. The document revisions and endorsement resulted in a shift of the boundary between design and construction to formally expand the constructor's scope of work and responsibility.

Designing for construction worker safety is another area that is challenging the boundary between design and construction. Before design-for-safety information is implemented, though, designers must first accept the knowledge and be willing to use it. An understanding of how implementation of the knowledge will affect one's legal duty toward ensuring job site safety and liability assumed for worker injuries will greatly influence the willingness of designers to implement the knowledge. Within the design-bid-build project delivery system, how will incorporation, or non-incorporation, of the safety knowledge influence a designer's duty toward ensuring safety on the construction site? Will the designer's liability exposure to construction worker injuries increase by utilizing the knowledge? A substantial increase in liability may discourage designers from implementing the safety knowledge. Past legal cases, professional practice standards, and current safety legislation reveal the liability exposure associated with designing for construction worker safety.

A designer's liability exposure to construction worker injuries has been frequently addressed in past legal cases. Most of the arguments presented in the court cases relate to the depth of a designer's involvement in safety during construction and the designer's relationship, contractual or assumed, to the injured worker. Traditionally, unless explicitly written in the contract, a designer participating in a design-bid-build arrangement is not responsible for overseeing construction worker safety (*Krieger v. J.E. Greiner Co.*, 282 Md. 50, 382 A.2d 1069; *Amant v. Pacific Power & Light Co.*, 520 P.2d 181, 10 Wash.App. 785). The designer typically contracts with the owner to create a design and ensure that the facility is constructed according to the intent of the design. However, if the designer directs the construction means and methods to some extent, the designer assumes partial responsibility for the construction effort. Past litigation reveals that through this action the designer also assumes some responsibility for the safety of the workers who perform the work (*Phillips v. United Engineers & Constructors, Inc.*, 500 N.E.2d 1265, Ind.App. 1 Dist. 1986; *Clyde E. Williams and Associates, Inc. v. Boatman*, 375 N.E.2d 1138, 176 Ind.App. 1978; *Plan-Tec, Inc. v. Wiggins*, 443 N.E.2d 1212, Ind.App. 1983).

An architect or engineer using current design codes and standards designs for the safety of the end-user of the facility. Constructability, quality, economy of the design, and safety of the end-user are generally the designer's main concerns. When implementing the design-for-safety knowledge, however, the "user" of particular interest becomes the construction worker. That is, the designer is designing for the safety of the construction worker. Thus, by implementing the safety knowledge, an architect or engineer modifies the traditional relationship between the designer and the construction worker. The designer is placed in a position to affect worker safety. How is a design professional's liability exposure affected in this modified relationship? If a construction site injury or fatality occurs that can be linked to the designer's use or non-use of the safety knowledge, will the designer be held accountable? The answers to these questions depend on the standard of practice and whether the design knowledge was implemented.

A Professional's Duty

Design professionals typically have an obligation to protect the public in their work. This responsibility is outlined in the codes of ethics assumed by the professionals as part of licensure. For example, the first Fundamental Canon of the National Society of Professional Engineers Code of Ethics (NSPE 1996) requires that:

> Engineers, in the fulfillment of their professional duties, shall:
> 1. Hold paramount the safety, health, and welfare of the public.

Given such an all-inclusive statement, is it ethical, or even morally acceptable, to exclude construction workers from the general public when considering safety? Current practice of design professionals with regard to the safety of construction workers seems to contradict this first rule, especially when safety is to be held "paramount."

States have set similar standards of reasonable care for the performance of design professionals through legislation. Although the standards can be specifically modified by contract, they establish the states' underlying minimum expectations for the performance of professionals. In performing professional services, the states require the designer to use ordinary care and skill. Specifically, the designer is required to do what a reasonably prudent design professional would do in the same community and in the same time frame, given the same or similar facts and circumstances (Abramowitz 1988). As an example, the Revised Code of Washington (RCW 1992) declares:

> As used in this chapter, "misconduct or malpractice in the practice of engineering" shall include but not be limited to the following: . . .
> (11) Committing any other act, or failing to act, which act or failure are customarily regarded as being contrary to the accepted professional conduct or standard generally accepted of those practicing professional engineering or land surveying.

The designer's legal responsibilities are examined in light of what reasonable, prudent designers would have known and done at the time the services were performed (Abramowitz 1988). Past court cases have reflected this legislation by asserting, for example, "One who undertakes to render professional services is under a duty to the person for whom the service is to be performed to exercise such care, skill, and diligence as men in that profession ordinarily exercise under like circumstances" (*City of Eveleth v. Ruble*, 302 Minn. 249, 253, 225 N.W.2d 521, 524).

Historically, if a design professional failed to meet the standard of care while performing services on a project, the designer would potentially be liable to only the party with whom a contract had been entered. This protection afforded the designer is merited on the privity of contract. In recent court cases, though, the "privity rule" has been overlooked. It has been viewed that an architect and engineer's duty of care supersedes other duties established by contract. Breaches of these duties may give rise to actions against design professionals by third parties—such as injured workers—relying upon the professional's performance (Loulakis 1989). Litigation is triggered by a claim by or on behalf of an injured worker that seeks to transfer losses suffered to the design professional based upon a claim of negligence (Sweet 1994). This negligence claim usually asserts that the designer did not take reasonable steps to prevent workers from performing work in a way that unreasonably exposes the claimant to personal harm or property damage (Sweet 1994).

Implementation of Safety Knowledge

Just as variations in designs can be limitless, the circumstances leading to court cases vary significantly. Though the details of the cases may be different, arguments frequently common to cases involving design professionals concern standard of practice and reasonable care. Specifically, questions arise as to whether the designer acted with reasonable care and stayed within the boundary of the current practice standards of the particular design profession. Answering these questions can highlight the designer's liability exposure. In this light, when designing for construction worker safety, designer liability can be ascertained by evaluating the relationship between use of the design-for-safety knowledge and whether utilization of the knowledge constitutes a standard practice for the profession. This relationship is depicted in Figure 8–8 for the traditional design-bid-build system of project delivery. The figure illustrates a designer's liability exposure if a worker injury or fatality can be linked to the implementation or non-implementation of the safety knowledge based on the extent of use of the knowledge in the profession. A description of the basis for the liability associated with each scenario follows.

Implementing Safety Knowledge that is Not Standard Practice
Use of design-for-safety knowledge is not part of the current standard of practice for the design profession. A design for a multi-story, steel-framed building that, for example, includes holes in

Implementation / Standard Practice	Design-for-safety knowledge is implemented in the facility design	Design-for-safety knowledge is NOT implemented in the facility design
Industry standard practice does NOT incorporate design-for-safety knowledge	**Designer actions:** • Go beyond standard practice. • Fulfill his/her professional duty to take reasonable steps to prevent worker injuries. **Result:** Designer is NOT LIABLE for worker injuries related to the (safe) design as a result of acting with reasonable care.	**Designer actions:** • Are consistent with standard practice. • Do not fulfill his/her professional duty to take reasonable steps to prevent worker injuries. **Result:** Designer is LIABLE for worker injuries related to the design for not acting with reasonable care.
Industry standard practice does incorporate design-for-safety knowledge	**Designer actions:** • Are consistent with standard practice. • Fulfill his/her professional duty to take reasonable steps to prevent worker injuries. **Result:** Designer is NOT LIABLE for worker injuries related to the (safe) design by acting consistent with standard practice and with reasonable care.	**Designer actions:** • Contrary to standard practice. • Do not fulfill his/her professional duty to take reasonable steps to prevent worker injuries. **Result:** Designer is LIABLE for worker injuries related to the design for not acting consistent with standard practice and with reasonable care.

FIGURE 8–8
Designer liability associated with applying design-for-safety knowledge.

the column webs at 21 inches (0.53 meters) and 42 inches (1.07 meters) above the working levels to provide support locations for guardrails would not reflect the current standard practice of structural design. Consequently, by designing the columns with this feature, a designer crosses the boundary between design and construction. Suppose a worker falls from elevation and sustains an injury when such a guardrail support was used. If the incident can be linked to the use of the holes for a guardrail during construction, the protection afforded by the concept of standard of practice cannot be claimed in defense of the design.

When designing the columns to include the holes, though, the design professional aims to reduce or eliminate the construction site hazards associated with installing guardrails. By acknowledging the safety hazards and taking measures to mitigate the hazards, the designer places safety above all other project and professional objectives, as required by the professional code of ethics. In addition, the designer fulfills his or her professional duty by taking a reasonable step to prevent worker injuries and fatalities. Therefore, as illustrated in this example, implementing the safety knowledge when it has not become standard practice to do so should not increase a designer's liability exposure to injured workers. Past legal cases do not reveal any judgments addressing this scenario, reflecting perhaps the lack of use of specific design-for-safety knowledge in current industry design practice. Expanded implementation of the design-for-safety knowledge on future projects will provide more concrete guidance regarding designer liability.

Implementing Safety Knowledge that is Standard Practice

Continued and widespread implementation of the design-for-safety knowledge may eventually lead to it being considered part of standard design practice. Standard building construction may someday, for example, include 42 inch (1.07 meter) high rooftop parapets rather than the required building code minimum of 30 inches (0.76 meters) to provide guardrail protection for workers during construction. An injury or fatality resulting from the taller parapet design, while not likely, could perhaps still occur. In this scenario, by including taller parapets the designer acts according to standard practice as other reasonably prudent professionals would, but the outcome is neither as anticipated nor as desired.

Given these circumstances, past court cases have judged that in their work, designers guarantee to provide learned skills and abilities reasonably and without neglect, but that this does not imply or warrant a satisfactory result (*City of Mounds View v. Walijarvi*, 263 N.W.2d 420; *Coombs v. Beede*, 89 Me. 187, 188, 36 A. 104; *City of Eveleth v. Ruble*, 302 Minn. 249, 253, 225 N.W.2d 521, 524). In one particular case (*Kemper Architects v. McFall, Konkel & Kimball Consulting Engineers*, 843 P.2d 1178, 1186, Wyo. 1992), for example, it was declared that:

> Where a professional is retained to provide design services, the likely understanding between the client and the professional designer is not that a successful outcome will be achieved when professional services are purchased but that the professional will perform as would other professionals.

Therefore, when implementing design-for-safety knowledge as part of standard practice, as illustrated in the example above, an unsuccessful outcome would not increase a designer's liability exposure to injured workers.

Not Implementing Safety Knowledge that is Not Standard Practice

The design professional must make the ultimate decision to modify a design with the specific intent of improving construction worker safety. A situation may occur, for example, in the design of a steel-framed structure where the physical aspects of the design prevent the constructor from attaching a guardrail or other practical means of fall protection. If the structural engineer is knowledgeable about this fall hazard during the design phase, the engineer has the opportunity to implement design features that will help eliminate the hazard, such as designing the structural members with holes in the webs for guardrail or lifeline support. Based on current practice, the engineer must decide whether to implement a design feature that addresses construction worker safety but which is not standard design practice. Other project objectives that come into consideration for the engineer in making the decision might be cost, quality, or aesthetics. The engineer may feel that these other objectives outweigh the need to help eliminate the fall hazard, and thus forego implementing the design feature.

Common law has imposed a duty on design professionals to protect third parties whose lives may be endangered when the professional becomes aware of this risk. While use of the design-for-safety knowledge may not be considered standard practice, as a professional, an architect or engineer cannot stand idly by with actual knowledge of unsafe designs or construction practices and not take steps to address the hazards (*Hanna v. Huer, Johns, Neel, Rivers and Webb*, 233 Kan. 206, 662 P.2d 243). Those who support this duty feel that safety is everyone's business and the more people who are concerned, the less likely injuries will occur. Past court cases have justified this position (*Mallow v. Tucker, Sadler & Bennett, Architects & Engineers, Inc.*, 54 Cal.Rptr. 174; *Caldwell v. Bechtel, Inc.*, 631 F.2d 989, D.C.Cir. 1980). The decision in *Caldwell v. Bechtel*, for example, stated:

> The court pointed to . . . Bechtel's superior skills, and its ability to foresee the harm that might be expected to befall the worker. The court saw these as creating a duty in Bechtel to take reasonable steps to prevent harm to the worker.

Knowledge of a safety hazard and the actions that can mitigate the hazard (whether obtained through job site visits, past experience, the design-for-safety tool, or other means) affect a designer's duty toward ensuring worker safety. If reasonable care with regard to addressing the hazard is not provided, the designer may very well be considered negligent in the performance of professional duties and be held liable for resulting worker injuries.

Not Implementing Safety Knowledge that is Standard Practice

When implementation of the safety knowledge becomes standard practice, as hypothesized in the rooftop parapet example described above, a designer is expected to employ the knowledge when performing design services. In this case, if a designer is aware of ways to eliminate a construction safety hazard through design and chooses not to implement the safe design, the designer fails to act according to the standard of the profession. In addition, the designer fails to meet the ethical criteria of the design profession by not holding safety paramount and does not fulfill his or her professional duty by acting with reasonable care. For this scenario, the liability associated with the designer's actions is similar to that associated with not addressing safety of the end-user. The designer would be held liable for injuries to the construction worker (*George v. Morgan Construction Co.*, 389 F.Supp. 253, E.D.Pa. 1975; *Ins. Co. of North America v. G.M.R., Ltd.*, 499 A.2d 878, D.C.App. 1985).

CONCLUSIONS

The safety of construction workers is an issue of importance to the construction industry. The industry has recognized that it lags behind most other industries in providing a safe workplace for its employees. In an effort to improve its safety performance, construction research has been undertaken and legislation passed to address the issue of safety on the construction site. While these efforts have improved safety conditions, unwarranted injuries and fatalities still exist on the construction site. Further efforts must be taken to bring the industry closer to a zero accidents objective.

Except for those employed in design-build firms, design professionals historically are not involved in the safety watch. Design professionals typically distance themselves from the responsibility for safety of the construction workers. This position is based on a number of reasons including their lack of safety education and training, restricted role on the project team, and an attempt to limit their liability exposure. Today's design codes and standards reflect this attitude—worker safety typically rests solely on the constructors' shoulders.

Overlooking safety until the start of the construction phase ignores the effect that designers have on construction safety. The methods of assembly are often not recognized as being dictated by the designers. In reality, designers play a very real role in influencing construction worker safety. It is the design that dictates how a particular project or its components will be assembled and how construction tasks are undertaken. Unfortunately, most designers have not been cognizant of their influence and, as a profession, have not acknowledged the importance or relevance of their role in safety.

As the concern for construction worker safety continues to grow, it is expected that each member of the project team will be called on to contribute. While the constructor's role in safety is well established, the designer's participation must be increased. The current design-for-safety knowledge and tool alert designers of construction site hazards and allow for consideration of worker safety during the design phase of the project. The knowledge relates to the project design—the portion of the project over which the designer has control and responsibility. If designers are cognizant of and responsive to the safety consequences of their design decisions, the inherent safety of construction projects will be improved. Consideration of construction worker safety by designers can lead to a reduction in injuries and associated costs during the construction phase. Because of the close relationship between construction and maintenance, addressing safety in the design will often also lead to improved safety while performing maintenance during facility operation.

The emphasis on designer responsibility for safety stems from the fact that worker safety and unsafe site conditions are matters of great importance and that all influencing parties should be involved in establishing safe construction sites. The difficulty with this position is that it places responsibility on persons who are not trained for the job and who do not want to accept any more responsibility. The design tool confronts both of these problems. It provides a link between the design and construction phases with regard to construction worker safety. It educates the design community about ways to improve construction worker safety, and it places additional responsibility on the design professional's shoulders. Unfortunately, increased liability exposure is not a voluntary goal of the design community. Ultimately, use of the tool by designers may be difficult to achieve since many are reluctant to undertake any activity that might increase their liability exposure.

It should be recognized that construction workers are unique facility users. Their safety warrants the attention of designers in a manner similar to the consideration given the end-user. The design-for-safety knowledge and tool allow designers to fulfill this charge by focusing their designs on construction worker safety. The legal ramifications of this action are similar to those resulting when designing for the end-user. Past litigation involving safety of the end-user reveals that a design professional has a duty, assumed or negotiated, to act with reasonable care and in accordance with the standard of practice of the profession in the execution of the contracted design scope of work. The designer does not warrant a successful project outcome, but only guarantees that the design will be done with appropriate skill and ability reflecting reasonable care.

Utilization of the design knowledge signifies employing the "best design practices" for resolving safety hazards in the construction phase of a project. Within the design-bid-build project delivery system, it is not expected that a designer would be considered negligent in the performance of professional duties if an unsuccessful outcome, such as an injury accident, occurs that can be related to the implementation of the design-for-safety knowledge. On the other hand, whether standard practice or not, failure to incorporate the safety knowledge could signify negligence in performing professional duties if an injury occurs that can be related to non-implementation of the knowledge. Similar to hazards that affect the end-user, mere knowledge of a construction site hazard represents sufficient evidence for a designer to take action to mitigate the hazard. If prudent action is not taken to mitigate the hazard, the designer could be held liable for worker injuries.

Although a designer's effect on safety is understood, a gap exists between constructors and designers in their knowledge of and commitment to job site safety. Information about designing for construction worker safety must ultimately be drawn from the construction personnel and transferred to the designers. Designers must be educated on how to design for construction worker safety. Design for Construction Safety ToolBox is an ideal instrument to facilitate this educational process.

The design-for-safety knowledge and related design tool are currently available to the design profession. Research efforts continue to expand the knowledge to evaluate and refine the role of designers in addressing safety. Consequently, the related liability exposure is an issue of concern today. It is apparent that in order to minimize liability exposure, the design profession should contemplate enlarging its boundary to incorporate addressing construction worker safety in the design scope of work. While this change may not be well-received, it represents a proactive, morally-based position by the design profession to prevent worker injuries and fatalities. It is ultimately through the prevention of worker injuries and fatalities that the chances of being involved in a third-party lawsuit are reduced.

Accepting the responsibility to design for construction worker safety can be accomplished in various ways. The design community could voluntarily enlarge its scope of work to include addressing safety. Just as recent changes have been made to AIA Document A201, revisions that incorporate designing for safety could be made to AIA Document B141, Standard Form of Agreement Between Owner and Architect (AIA 1997a). This action would not only formally shift the boundary between design and construction, but also indicate a willingness by designers to improve the entire construction industry.

Reluctance to voluntarily accept the added responsibility will diminish when clients insist that designers address construction safety concerns. Currently, the costs associated with worker injuries and fatalities are passed on to the client as part of the cost of construction. Implementing safety measures through the design will prevent injuries and fatalities and, thus, reduce both the cost of construction and the possibility that clients will be involved in third-party lawsuits. Consequently, clients may provide the initial impetus by requesting, or requiring by contract terms, that designers consider construction worker safety in their designs.

Addressing safety may lead to higher design fees to cover added effort and responsibility. For many designers, this may very well be a welcome change. Shifting the design responsibility to other parties, whether formally through contract document revisions or informally through the submittal process, has played a part in the erosion of design fees. Added responsibility will help to counteract this effect. From the client's perspective, the higher fees would be acceptable compared to the injury and fatality-related costs of construction and third-party lawsuits. For the construction industry, the higher fees would be a small investment compared to the larger expected return of a safer place to work.

REFERENCES

Abramowitz, A. J. (1988). "The Legal Environment." *The Architect's Handbook of Professional Practice*, American Institute of Architects, 11th Edition, Ch. 1.6, p. 3.

AIA. (1993). "Standard Form of Agreement Between Owner and Architect for Designated Services." American Institute of Architects, Document B163, Sect. 3.3.6.3.

AIA. (1997a). "Standard Form of Agreement Between Owner and Architect." American Institute of Architects, Document B141.

AIA. (1997b). "General Conditions of the Contract for Construction." American Institute of Architects, Document A201.

ASCE. (1988). "Report of the Task Committee on Construction Site Safety." American Society of Civil Engineers, Reston, VA.

ASCE. (1989). "Construction Site Safety." American Society of Civil Engineers, Reston, VA, Policy Statement 350.

Baggs, R. E. and Cunningham, J. (1988). "Safety and Efficiency in Steel Construction—The Broadgate Experience." *Civil Engineering* (London), May 1988, p. 35.

Bonny, J. B. (1973). *Handbook of Construction Management and Organization.* Van Nostrand Reinhold, New York, NY.

CDM. (1994). *Construction (Design and Management) Regulations.* SI 1994/3140 HMSO.

CII. (1996a). "Addressing Construction Worker Safety in the Project Design." Construction Industry Institute, Austin, Texas, Research Report 101-11.

CII. (1996b). "Design for Construction Safety ToolBox User's Reference Manual." Construction Industry Institute, Austin, Texas, Implementation Resource 101-2.

CII. (1996c). "Design for Safety." Construction Industry Institute, Austin, Texas, Research Summary 101-1.

Construction Safety Act. (1969). Revisions to Federal Contract Work Hours Standards Act, 1968. Pub. L. 87-581, Title I, Sec. 107, as amended Pub. L. 91-54, Sec. 1, August 9, 1969, (83 Stat. 96), 40 U.S.C. 333.

Defense Base Act. (1941). Ch. 357, Sec. 1, (55 Stat. 622), 42 U.S.C. 1651 et seq.

Eck, R. W. (1987), "Center for Excellence in Construction Safety." *Journal of Performance of Constructed Facilities*, 1987, 1(3) pp. 122–131.

Federal Employers' Liability Act. (1908). Ch. 149, Sec. 1, (35 Stat. 65), 45 U.S.C. 51 et seq.

Gambatese, J. A. (1996). "Addressing Construction Worker Safety in the Project Design." A dissertation submitted to the University of Washington in partial fulfillment of the requirements for the degree of Doctor of Philosophy.

Gambatese, J. A. (1998). "Liability in Designing for Construction Worker Safety." *Journal of Architectural Engineering*, 1998, 4(3) pp. 107–112.

Gambatese, J. A. and Hinze, J. W. (1996). "Addressing Construction Worker Safety in the Design Phase." *International Symposium for the Organization and Management of Construction: Shaping Theory and Practice (Volume Two)*, E & FN Spon, London, U.K., 1996, pp. 871–880.

Gambatese, J. A., Hinze, J. W., and Haas, C. T. (1997). "A Tool to Design for Construction Worker Safety." *Journal of Architectural Engineering*, 1997, 3(1) pp. 32–41.

Godfrey, K. A. (1988). "After L'Ambiance Plaza." *Civil Engineering*, 1988, 58(1) pp. 36–39.

Haas, C., Burleson, R., and Goodrum, P. (1995). "A Multimedia Design Aid for Project Hazard Identification and Remediation." *The Construction Industry Institute Task Force (Source Document 107)*, The Construction Industry Institute, Austin, Texas.

Hammer, W. (1989). *Product Safety Management and Engineering*. Prentice-Hall, Englewood Cliffs, N.J.

Hinze, J. (1991). "A Study of the Construction Activity and Procurement Policies of Major Consumers of Construction Services." Associated Builders and Contractors, Inc., Rosslyn, VA.

Hinze, J. (1993). *Construction Contracts*. McGraw-Hill, Inc., New York, NY.

Hinze, J. (1994a). "A Study of the Construction Activity Projections for 1994." Associated Builders and Contractors, Inc., Rosslyn, VA.

Hinze, J. (1994b). "A Study of the Construction Activity Projections for 1995." Associated Builders and Contractors, Inc., Rosslyn, VA.

Hinze, J. (1997). "Safety Roles Expanding in Design." *Engineering Times*. National Society of Professional Engineers, 19(6).

Hinze, J. (1997). "Moral, Ethical Obligations an Issue for Safety in Design." *Engineering Times*. National Society of Professional Engineers, 19(8).

Hinze, J. (1997). "Some More Proven Ways to Design for Safety." *Engineering Times*. National Society of Professional Engineers, 19(10).

Hinze, J., and Gambatese, J. (1994). *Design Decisions that Impact Construction Worker Safety*. Proceedings of the Fifth Annual Rinker International Conference Focusing on Construction Safety and Loss Control, University of Florida, Gainesville, Florida, 1994, pp. 187–199.

Hinze, J., and Lyneis, P. (1988). "The Liability Crisis." *The National Utility Contractor*, National Utility Contractors Association, 12(8), pp. 24–27.

Hinze, J., and Wiegand, F. (1992). "Role of Designers in Construction Worker Safety." *Journal of Construction Engineering and Management*, 1992, 118(4) pp. 677–684.

Ichniowski, T. (1997). "Divided AGC Endorses AIA's New A201 Construction Contract." *Engineering News Record*, McGraw-Hill, Inc., New York, NY, 239(18) p. 14.

ICBO. (1994). *Uniform Building Code*. International Conference of Building Officials, Whittier, CA.

Jeffrey, J., and Douglas, I. (1994). *Safety Performance of the UK Construction Industry*. Proceedings of the Fifth Annual Rinker International Conference Focusing on Construction Safety and Loss Control, University of Florida, Gainesville, Florida, 1994, pp. 233–253.

Joyce, R. (1995). *The Construction (Design and Management) Regulations Explained*. Thomas Telford Publications, London.

Kostoff, S. (1977). *The Architect*. Oxford University Press, New York, NY.

Longshore and Harbor Workers' Compensation Act. (1927). Ch. 509, Sec. 1, (44 Stat. 1424), 33 U.S.C. 901 et seq.

Loulakis, M. C. (1989). "Limiting the Economic Loss Defense." *Civil Engineering*, 1989, 59(7) p. 33.

MacCollum, D. V. (1995). *Construction Safety Planning*. Van Nostrand Reinhold, New York, N.Y.

Mitchell, W. J. (1977). *Computer-Aided Architectural Design*. Mason/Charter Publishers, Inc., New York, NY.

NSC. (1952–1997): *Accident Facts*. National Safety Council, Itasca, IL.

NSC. (1997). *Accident Facts*. National Safety Council, Itasca, IL.

NSPE. (1996). *Code of Ethics for Engineers*. National Society of Professional Engineers, Pub. No. 1102.

Occupational Safety and Health Act. (1970). Pub. L. 91-596, Sec. 2, (84 Stat. 1590), 29 U.S.C. 651.

OSHA. (1994), "Proposal to Properly Allocate Accountability for Construction Worksite Safety." *Occupational Safety and Health Administration, Steel Erection Negotiated Rulemaking Advisory Committee 1994*. Occupational Safety and Health Administration, draft August 17, 1994.

Outer Continental Shelf Lands Act. (1953). Ch. 345, Sec. 2, (67 Stat. 462), 43 U.S.C. 1331 et seq.

RCW. (1992). "Title 18—Businesses and Professions."*Revised Code of Washington*, State of Wasington, Sec. 18.43.105.

Robson, K. F., and Bashford, H. H. (1997). "The Emergence of Construction as a Recognized Profession and as an Academic Discipline." *The American Professional Constructor*, 1997, 21(3) pp. 2–9.

Senate Bill 2518. (1988). U.S.A., 100th Congress, 2nd Session.

Senate Bill 930. (1989). U.S.A., 101st Congress, 1st Session. (House of Representatives Bill 2254).

Stephan, D. E. (1987). "Professional Responsibility—Instructor's Role." *Journal of Professional Issues in Engineering*, 1987, 113(4) pp. 311–316.

Sweet, J. (1994). *Legal Aspects of Architecture, Engineering and the Construction Process*. West Publishing Co., St. Paul, MN.

U.S. Department of Labor. (1995). *Safety and Health Regulations for Construction*. Department of Labor, Occupational Safety and Health Administration, Code of Federal Regulations, Part 1926.

C H A P T E R

9

AN OWNER LOOKS AT SAFETY

Ronald W. Sikes

Universal Studios, Orlando, Florida, U.S.A.

Tan Qu

College of Architecture

University of Florida, Gainesville, Florida, U.S.A.

Richard J. Coble

M.E. Rinker, Sr., School of Building Construction

Center for Construction Safety and Loss Control

University of Florida, Gainesville, Florida, U.S.A.

The lyrics to Jimmy Buffett's popular song "A Pirate Looks at Forty" include a lament that the pirate singing the song is "an over-forty victim of fate." In this chapter (and with apologies to Mr. Buffett), "An Owner Looks at Safety." In so doing, we ask, "Are we who are cast in the role of the owner in the construction process victims of fate, as well?" What are our responsibilities? What are our rights? What may we reasonably expect from our contractors and laborers and what may they expect from us?

INTRODUCTION

Let's step back for a moment and examine the overall concept of a construction project. Distilled to its simplest: an owner has property on which it wants to build something and, presumably, the cash or other funding to do it. The contractor has the equipment, experience, knowledge, and licenses necessary to build what the owner wants and to make a profit in the process. The personnel who will actually build what the owner wants under the direction of the contractor (or subcontractors) expect to get paid in return for lending their physical labor and expertise to the project.

The goal of this discussion is to look at the role of the owner with regard to job site safety. We will examine humanitarian considerations, legal consequences, and business considerations. Perhaps we will even challenge some of the prevailing practices and philosophies that seem to exist in commercial construction projects. And, in the process of this self-examination, maybe we'll even change some thoughts on a few of the "hows" and "whys" of construction safety.

In its publication entitled "Accident Investigation," the Occupational Safety & Health Administration (OSHA) defines an accident as "any unplanned event that results in personal injury or property damage." In observing that "[t]housands of accidents occur throughout the United States every day," OSHA has concluded that "[t]he failure of people, equipment, supplies, or surroundings to behave or react as expected causes most of the accidents." OSHA has determined that accident investigations typically reveal basic, indirect, and direct "cause levels." As indicated in Figure 9–1, OSHA views management policies and decision, personal factors, and environmental factors among the "Basic Causes" of occupational accidents.

In explaining these "cause levels," OSHA points out:

> Accidents are usually complex. An accident may have 10 or more events that can be causes. A detailed analysis of an accident will normally reveal three cause levels: basis, indirect, and direct. At the lowest level, an accident results only when a person or object receives an amount of energy or hazardous material that cannot be absorbed safely. This energy or hazardous material is the DIRECT CAUSE of the accident. The direct cause is usually the result of one or more unsafe acts or unsafe conditions, or both. Unsafe acts and conditions are the INDIRECT CAUSES or symptoms. In turn, indirect causes are usually traceable to poor management policies and decisions, or to personal or environmental factors. These are the BASIC CAUSES.

Trends detected from monitoring industrial accidents and illnesses ratios indicate that private industry is moving in the right direction with regard to reducing losses (Bureau of Labor Statistics Workplace Injury and Illness Summary, released 12/17/98). In its measurement of reported industrial injuries and illnesses from 1993 through 1997, the Bureau of Labor Statistics found a reduction in overall incidence rates from 8.5 incidents per 100 full-time workers in 1993 to 7.1 incidents per 100 in 1997.

Similarly, in the "Goods-producing" category (which includes the construction industry), while substantially higher than in the "Service-producing" category, the frequency of accidents and injuries dropped progressively over the past five years (11.9 in 1993; 11.9 in 1994; 11.2 in 1995; 10.2 in 1996; and 9.9 in 1997). Although the ratios for 1993 and 1994 were essentially flat, the hours worked overall increased three percent (3%). (See also U.S. Department of Labor, Bureau of Labor Statistics, Summary 95-3, January, 1995.

Nevertheless, eliminating, or at least reducing, accidents by providing a safe and healthy work environment for all employees is, at the very least, an ethical responsibility of all owners. Owners must take proactive measures in an effort to protect the safety and well being of all of their employees through implementation of total safety management.

From a total safety management perspective, *every person involved in the construction process has a personal, individual responsibility in maintaining worker safety and health on construction sites.* From a legal standpoint, the following tenets are well-entrenched:

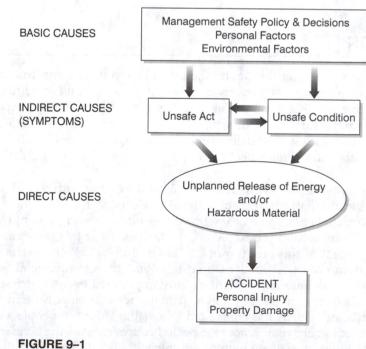

FIGURE 9–1
Accident cause levels (OSHA).

- Contractors and subcontractors, as the independent entities executing the work, have the inexorable direct responsibility for job site safety and health.
- Design professionals have a duty to consider safety and health factors throughout the design and construction phases as they consider the consequences of their design upon the execution of the work and its intended program.
- Owners, although they may contractually allocate certain legal responsibilities for protecting worker safety and health to others, retain non-delegable statutory duties as the job site title-holder.
- Individuals working on the project have the ultimate duty to protect their own safety and to perform their work in a manner which does not expose coworkers to an unreasonable risk.
- Governmental agencies with jurisdiction have a right (if not a responsibility) to take both proactive and reactive actions with regard to job site safety. (See, for example, 29 CFR Part 1926, Safety and Health Regulations for Construction.)

There is, however, a great deal more than legal considerations that play into job site safety and health from an owner's perspective. "Victims of fate?" Perhaps; but not necessarily so.

CURRENT ROLE OF OWNERS IN SAFETY AND HEALTH MANAGEMENT

Figure 9–2 depicts the inter-relationship between the different participants in a construction project regarding employee safety and health during the construction process. We have placed the owner in the center of the process because it is the one entity with "privity," or a direct contractual or legal relationship, with most of the other entities listed (and an indirect legal relationship with the others—subcontractors and workers). A further review of the respective responsibilities of the various players is essential.

Although the conception of a responsibility to design with *project* safety in mind has been recently promoted, widely used design contract provisions (understandably promoted by professional groups such as the American Institute of Architects and the National Society of Professional Engineers) work to eliminate (or, at least minimize) the designer's responsibility for job

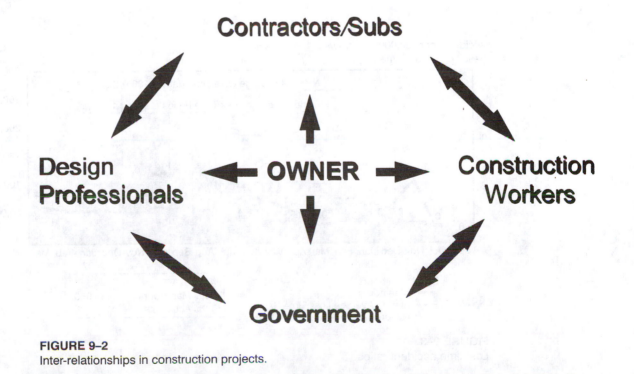

FIGURE 9–2
Inter-relationships in construction projects.

site safety. To suggest that the allocation to the contractor of responsibility of determining the "means, methods, and techniques" of performing the work absolves the design professionals from both legal and ethical responsibility belies the functional criticality of the designer's role in the project. Assignment of legal risk aside, the design team *must* consider the consequences of their creativity as the project "comes to life" in the field.

Owners, design professionals, and governmental regulatory personnel agree that contractors, especially the general contractors, are held responsible for job site safety. This concept has been codified in 29 CFR 1926.16(c), where it is stated that "[w]ith respect to subcontracted work, the prime contractor and any subcontractors shall be deemed to have joint responsibility" with regard to worker safety.

Since the major part of responsibility for job site safety is allocated to the contractors, owners have traditionally adopted a passive role in job site safety. While perhaps legally desirable and fiscally accepted through the contractual allocation of risk, this scenario may mask the true impact to an owner of being associated with an unsafe job site. As we will examine below, what appears to bring little adverse impact to an owner may, in fact, have a significant effect.

TAKING A PROACTIVE POSITION AS AN OWNER

Unlike the brutal realities of war, construction job site fatalities and serious injuries are *never* assumed or accepted as foregone conclusions. Of course, experience will demonstrate that on any given project a statistical probability exists suggesting that a certain number of fatalities is likely to occur or that we may expect "x" number of lost time injuries (i.e., an injury that requires the worker to miss work beyond a visit to the first aid provider for a bandage). In fact, detailed tracking of the number of *recordable, lost time,* and *fatal* accidents by man-hours and by payroll is regularly monitored on most major job sites by insurance interests. Figure 9–3 reflects an example of how actual lost-time accidents on a recent project compared against state and national averages.

If we canvassed one hundred business owners as to what their number one goal in business is, the candid ones would probably state, without exception, "to make a profit." If we narrowed our inquiry to their primary goal with regard to the execution of a construction project, the group would probably respond "to bring it in on time and on (or under) budget." But, if we

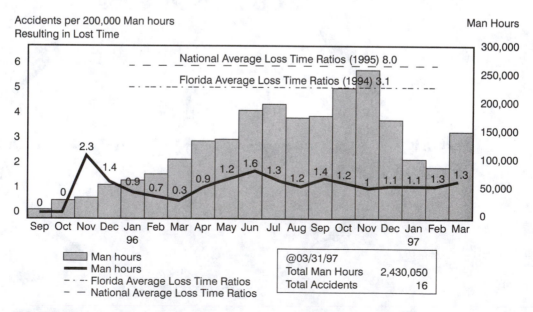

FIGURE 9–3
Lost time accident ratios.

asked specifically what their aim would be with regard to job site safety, we predict that it would resoundingly be "to have a safe job site."

We think it not too bold of a contention on our part to suggest that the first goal in *any* enterprise or institution business operation should be to protect human lives and health in the conduct of business. Obvious though it may be, people in business simply do not want to see other people injured or killed. But why? We think that the following are among the primary motivators for job site safety:

- to prevent human suffering
- to promote job site morale and productivity
- to reduce costs of project insurance coverage
- to minimize governmental participation in the project
- to minimize increased labor union activity on the project
- to avoid adverse publicity

Prevention of Human Suffering

The Bureau of Labor Statistics has determined that 6.1 million injuries and illnesses were reported in private industry workplaces in 1997 (Bureau of Labor Statistics Workplace Injury and Illness Summary, released 12/17/98). While admittedly obvious and basic, we cannot overstate the significance to an owner of the desire to prevent human suffering and death. Who among us would ask another to give his or her life for the sake of building a department store, a theme park, or even a military base? With rare exception, owners do not intentionally set out to expose construction workers to an unreasonable risk of injury.

We recognize that the project-specific nature of the work is sometimes inherently dangerous to the construction labor force. In other more benign projects, schedule compression is often the culprit resulting in a workplace that is *de facto* hazardous. In any case, however, it is atypical for an owner to disregard safety considerations because no *responsible* owner wills for any person to suffer serious bodily injury or death on any project.

Concerns for Job Site Morale, Decreased Quality, and Productivity

There is no question that job site morale is likely to be diminished when an accident occurs. To the coworkers of a victim who is seriously injured or killed in a job site accident, the reality strikes that accidents are something could happen to them as well. To them, serious or fatal accidents and the investigations which follow certainly represent distractions to their work. Frequently, such physical trauma to the injured party poses a secondary emotional impact which directly affects productivity and quality of work.

When workers feel their safety and health are endangered by the work environment, they become reluctant to perform their tasks. Burdened by these concerns, workers are not going to be productive and the decreased work quality is immediately predictable. While difficult to quantify, the "dollars and cents" of such an impact are certainly significant.

Insurance Cost Reductions

Most of the states within the U.S. and the federal government have adopted legislation by which employee injuries are governed through "workers' compensation" or a similar means by which common law rules are overridden. (See, for example, Chapter 440, *Florida Statutes*, 1997.) The essential premise of such legislation is that *fault* on the part of an injured or deceased employee is not considered in determining how that person (or his or her estate) will be compensated for the loss or how the medical bills will be paid. While there are exceptions to this "no-fault" approach (such as drug or alcohol abuse), worker carelessness or even intentional violations of safety standards are not typically a basis on the part of the employer or its insurance carrier to avoid liability for payment.

Premiums charged for workers' compensation insurance are normally based in some fashion upon the payroll of the employer (the theory being that payroll is an indication of volume of work and volume is an indication of exposure).

Each employer develops an Experience Modification Ratio (EMR) which results in an adjustment of the standard premium for an injury-free employer based upon that employer's track record. In some cases, workers' compensation premiums are retrospectively adjusted, again based upon the insured's actual loss experience in "time and materials" and "cost plus" construction projects. The increased costs of project insurance can serve as a very real motivation for the promotion by the owner of job site safety.

On larger projects with multiple prime contractors, owners will frequently opt for an owner-controlled insurance program (OCIP) or "wrap-up" policy of insurance. In an OCIP, owners view it more economical to purchase a single insurance program for all contractors involved in the project than to require each contractor to acquire individual insurance (a cost which is passed through to the owner in any event, usually with a significant mark-up). While a contractor's EMR will most likely be affected in an OCIP, depending upon the structure of the insurance premiums established in the program, the premiums ultimately charged to the owner are affected by an adverse claims experience.

Minimization of Governmental Participation

For all that can be said critically about interference from governmental agencies, involvement by local building officials and federal OSHA representatives in employee safety is largely reactive. Job site inspections and reviews of safety plans are initiated only upon the occurrence of a serious accident or through a complaint of an unsafe condition. Nevertheless, when such interest is generated, governmental officials become understandably interested in both the cause of the unsafe conditions and the owner's plans to avoid similar occurrences. While the better view is to fully cooperate with state and OSHA inspectors once they arrive on-site, the far more preferred approach is to give them no reason to come to the job in the first place.

Concerns for Strikes and Pressure from Labor Unions

The popularity of organized labor unions was generated more than anything else by critically unsafe working conditions in our nation's factories. Although the percentage of employees participating as union members has declined in the last several years (particularly in the southeast United States), aggressive union intervention to assure employee safety remains an effective tool to address hazardous conditions. Recent strikes initiated by labor unions of employees of General Motors and Northwest Airlines reminds the public—and the parties to the construction contracting process—that organized labor still holds a strong position in the United States and cannot be disregarded. Again, avoidance of safety issues remains the best hedge against union involvement in this area.

Concerns for Adverse Publicity

High profile owners generate high profile publicity. Most owners relish the opportunity to have the latest four-color photograph of the progress of their construction project appear "above-the-fold" on page 1, section 1, of the morning newspaper—but not if the accompanying headline reads: "Construction Worker Falls to Death at Construction Site."

Accidents and serious injuries often lead to widespread association of the owner as "guilty by association" with the troubled project. It is inconsequential that the accidents are rarely due to owner's actions or inactions. The public will usually know less about the general contractor or subcontractor with direct supervision over the affected worker than they will about the owner. When the project is complete, chances are good that the injury or death will be more likely allocated in the public's memory to the owner, rather than any other participant in the process.

Another concern here is that owners are traditionally worried that the public will believe that construction job site safety violations equate to operational safety problems. While this may be a sort of myopic paranoia, it is nevertheless a real motivator in the owner's desire to maintain a safe workplace.

THOUGHTS AND TRENDS REGARDING THE ALLOCATION OF RESPONSIBILITY FOR SAFETY

Although general contractors are primarily responsible for job site safety, the responsibility is often shifted (in part) by them to subcontractors. Owners, design professionals and government officials traditionally adopt a "hands-off" approach. We believe that while perhaps desirable when viewed strictly from the legal perspective, this approach may be ill-advised if the concerns of the owner as discussed above are to be satisfied.

Subcontractors, especially small, thinly capitalized proprietorships, often do not have competent or trained persons to take on safety management responsibilities. They may be the best at achieving the desired look when applying stucco to a wall or completing area development, but woefully lacking in any formal, programmatic approach to ensuring job site safety. Common sense, though an ally of safety, is inadequate to meet the challenges to safety presented by a busy project where various trades are jockeying to occupy the same space to get their work done.

As asserted somewhat more aggressively by personal injury attorney William F. Conour:

> In my experience, most construction workers are injured as a direct result of the negligent failure of their employer to follow basic well-known and often required safety practices. Construction injuries are not generally the result of fluke accidents. Workers are hurt because owners, general contractors and subcontractors will not take the time or spend the money to do the job safely and correctly. Most serious construction injuries could be avoided by simply following OSHA or other industrial safety practices. However, the owner doesn't want to pay for a safe job and, therefore, does not include safety specifications in the bidding instructions.

> . . . Only when the owner and general contractor face liability for the injured worker will they retain safety engineers to incorporate safety specifications in the plans, require subcontractors to quote safety equipment in their bids and hire inspectors to monitor the construction to insure compliance with all safety regulations (Conour, 1990).

We disagree with Conour's suggestion that the owner's desire to save money is, in essence, the "root of all evil" as the primary responsibility for construction accidents. However, his advocacy should serve as a wake-up call for any owner who callously dismisses job site safety as someone else's responsibility. In fact, in an article written for *The Indiana Lawyer* (Vol. 7, No. 3; 1996), Greg Kueterman discusses trends in Indiana law which suggest imposition of greater legal responsibility upon owners and prime contractors for injuries to subcontractor employees.

In discussing the 1995 Indiana Supreme Court decision in *Bagley v. Insight Communications*, Kueterman (quoting Indianapolis attorney Richard Dick) contends that the state of the law (at least in Indiana) has been made clear: "Now, because of *Bagley*, if work is hazardous, a worker may have a claim against a general contractor or owner, even though there is no specific statute that creates a duty of safety." As suggested in the article, there seems to be an increasing inclination on the part of the courts to find that "a general contractor or owner may have a *non-delegable duty of safety*." (Emphasis supplied.)

Similar to the recent trend in "partnering" (where the parties to the construction process move from the outset of a project to form a cooperative, non-adversarial working relationship), we believe that a collaborative, cooperative commitment to worker safety and health is both appropriate and necessary. Through such an effort, the ever-important primary objective of preserving human life and avoiding serious injury will more likely be achieved.

FOSTERING A TOTAL SAFETY CULTURE

According to the Bureau of Labor Statistics, since the early 1970s incidences of injuries and illnesses accompanied with time off from work within the construction industry have typically exceeded the rates for industry within the United States overall by more that sixty percent (60%) annually (U.S. Department of Labor, Bureau of Labor Statistics, Summary 95-3, January, 1995). Despite improvements in the frequency of such accidents in recent years, the construction industry remains ripe for a revolutionary approach to change in this arena.

In recent years, some safety professionals have brought forward a new concept about safety management—Total Safety Culture (TSC), a theory incorporating the principles of Total Quality Management (TQM) into the safety arena. In a TSC, everyone acknowledges responsibility for safety and pursues it on a daily basis (Geller 1994). This new perspective brings a paradigm shift in the management of the safety process. As Earl Blair says, "[T]his shift demands that traditional management and safety cultures be abandoned, and requires movement toward a philosophy that embraces total involvement, true empowerment, viewing safety as a 'value rather than a priority,' and improved and recurrent training methods . . . " (Blair 1996).

The involvement of the owner in job site safety is, we believe, nothing more than a recognition of the inherent moral responsibility that the owner, as *the* major stakeholder in the construction process, naturally possesses. The TSC philosophy generates the added benefit of improved awareness pre- and post-operationally. This is highly beneficial in promoting a long-term commitment to safety culture for the owner's organization. In a TSC, safe work practices are supported via rewarding feedback from peers and managers; people "actively care" on a continuous basis for safety (Geller 1994).

In her excellent discussion of "Behavior-Based Safety," published in the August, 1998, issue of *Professional Safety*, Betty Loafmann offers some key factors to consider in attempting to establish a Total Safety Culture:

> . . . [N]o matter how much money the firm spends on equipment, people's behavior plays a major role in their safety. Safety devices help prevent injury, but if accidents continue to occur, employees may be routinely overriding or circumventing these mechanical solutions.

> . . . What is missing [in traditional safety programs] is consistent, frequent, positive reinforcement—the crucial factor in changing human behavior.

> To manage safety, one must know how to reinforce people so they will use safe behaviors, even though risky behaviors are much more rewarding. This skill depends on a working knowledge of systematic measurement, feedback, and the power of positive reinforcement.

Providing Authentic Care to Workers

The provision of authentic care is imperative in an owner organization in a TSC. The most effective way to express the genuine care to employees by management is to establish the safety and health of employees at the workplace as the highest priority. Extending this genuine care to the construction workers for its project, an owner will reinforce with its own employees the importance of employee safety within the organization. As Blair states, management and employees must be convinced that this "caring attitude" is the foundation that foster success (Blair 1996).

Benefits for Continued Safety Management Effort to Operation Period

Through early involvement in the construction process, owners' *operational* safety personnel become familiar with the constructed facility. Through this involvement, they may identify some areas to be addressed during the operational period. This process facilitates future safety efforts and reduces the chances of accidents after the project has become operational.

Richard Hislop contends that the objective of business is not the maximization of income, but the minimization of losses (Hislop 1993). While we may not agree that such minimization is *the* objective of business, as discussed, *supra* avoidance of serious personal injury and death to employees is clearly among the primary objectives of any responsible business owner. It is highly desireable for owners to adopt a proactive position in this matter rather than to rely on contractors to be solely responsible for worker safety and health on the construction site. Certain duties, whether legal or moral, are simply non-delegable; and, in a TSC, it just does not make good business sense to abdicate this responsibility to others.

WHAT OWNERS CAN DO TO PROMOTE JOB-SITE SAFETY

Prequalification of Contractors

Absent serious disciplinary sanction against a contractor's license, past safety experience is rarely a consideration in awarding a project. The safety records of bidders should be incorporated and weighted by owners as a significant criterion in the contractor selection process. Through this practice, owners can disqualify habitually unsafe contractors from bidding.

James E. Roughton (1995) suggests that (at least) four questions should be answered in order to evaluate a contractor's safety performance:

1. What measurable results, such as OSHA recordable accidents, experience modification rate and other performance statistics, are being achieved?
2. Is senior management committed to the program?
3. Is safety an integral part of project management?
4. Is ongoing training and improvement a key program component?

Owner-Sponsored Safety Incentive Programs

One important part of any safety program is to *encourage* safe work practices and achievement. Although much has been said in other discussions about contractor-sponsored incentive programs, fewer owner-sponsored incentive programs are recorded. Typically, owner-sponsored incentive programs include three types of incentive awards:

Safe Worker Award and Recognition

In an environment where employees assume that hazard identification is the function of safety professionals, motivating employees to participate in the hazard identification process is one element of a rewarding safety program (Roughton 1995). According to Kuhn, the most influential person in creating and maintaining a safe work environment is the individual employee (Kuhn 1992). Identification of non-punitive, positive reinforcement techniques in this respect can generate substantial benefits.

Some construction workers tend to believe they can take risks and shortcuts without fear of failure (the "hero mentality"). Employees must be genuinely motivated to accept their responsibilities for safety and to follow safe work practices (Blair 1996). Therefore, workers following safe work practices and voluntarily identifying potential safety hazards should be encouraged and rewarded.

Individual recognition can take many forms. Cash awards, gift certificates, in-kind gifts, paid time off, plaques, and letters of recognition given by the owner's representative before one's peers serve as great motivators. Even OSHA has adopted a program which rewards exemplary performance, both through certificates and cash awards, to its employees (OSHA Administrative Directive No. ADM 2.1, November, 1978).

Supervisor incentives

The crew supervisor is one of the most important individuals in any organization's hierarchical structure in terms of promoting safe work practices (Hislop 1993). The supervisor usually controls the way work is performed and exerts the single greatest influence on employee attitudes. Yet supervisors can be the people having the least motivation to make safety their first priority. Getting the work done within the schedule is their main goal—production results are often the determining measure of a supervisor's job performance.

As Hislop says, a meaningful award program for the supervisor is one tied to the estimated savings achieved following implementation of safe work practices. Alternatively, a supervisor might receive a percentage of the awards earned by work crew members. Through giving supervisors recognition and awards for prioritizing safety and advocating safe work practices by their crew, they can make a meaningful contribution to job site safety and health.

Contractor Incentives

Contractors are also candidates for safety incentive programs (Hislop 1993). Recognition for good safety practices and programs and being awarded by owners is an effective motivator to contractors. By implementing the philosophy that *"safety is a competitive advantage,"* contractors who earn awards can use them as marketing when bidding jobs. (See, for example, Appendix A, reflecting an example of a contractor's touting of its record in safety as a part of its web site.) Perhaps even more effective to motivate contractors in a TSC is the practice of setting aside significant cash awards to the contractor(s) with the best safety record on a project. In the case of a single prime, comparisons to national or state averages for worker injuries may form the basis for an award.

Owner Observation and Corrective Program

Geller suggests that there are three major determinants directly linked to job site safety: environmental factors (i.e., equipment, tools, physical layout, and temperature); personal factors (attitudes, beliefs, and personalities); and behavioral factors (safe and unsafe work practices, exceeding the call of duty to protect another person's safety) (Geller 1994). Although personal factors which are prone to cause accidents are hard to identify, environmental and behavioral factors that are potential safety perils are easier to discover.

The owner's safety personnel can easily identify both contractors and workers with safe or unsafe work practices and adopt corrective or awarding measures accordingly. This safety commitment and enforcement can effectively establish a well-founded safety culture on the construction site.

Attached as Appendix B is an example of a summary of a Contractor Incentive Program for a recent major construction project.

OTHER OWNER CONSIDERATIONS

Establish a Reasonable Schedule

When selecting a contractor, an owner should also take into consideration the reasonableness of the schedules presented by bidding contractors. Although it is normally desirable to get the project finished in the shortest period of time, owners should also be aware that when multiple trades work on a compressed schedule, over-crowding and an unsafe environment frequently exist. By carefully evaluating and challenging contractors' construction schedules, owners can eliminate some of this kind of risk.

Ensure Having Well-Prepared Design Documents

The quality of the design documents directly determines how much change work will take place in the construction stage. Whenever there is change work, the originally planned work schedule often is disrupted and contractors have to keep on schedule by accelerating work. Coordination between multiple trades becomes a challenge and the risk of having accidents increases. Through well-developed owner design intent and the engagement of experienced designers, this risk can be reduced.

Provide for Adequate Safety Staffing

If it is genuinely good business to provide for a safe job site (and we believe it is), funding positions for safety professionals to design, implement, and administer a targeted accident prevention program is essential. The ranks of genuine Safety Professionals with industry-recognized certification, such as the *Certified Safety Professional* designation, are developing behavioral scientists trained and experienced in identifying and eliminating hazards. Designating a "Clerk of the Works" to also serve as the safety representative misses the mark if a truly safe environment is the objective of the project's owner.

Consider OSHA Partnership Programs

OSHA has recently joined forces with various public agencies and private businesses and owners to positively promote safety initiatives. As correctly observed in a recent OSHA National News Release published by the U.S. Department of Labor, Office of Public Affairs:

> In the early years of the Occupational Safety and Health Administration (OSHA), it seemed unlikely that employers, labor unions and OSHA would willingly join forces in coordinated efforts to reduce injuries and illnesses. Today, however, . . . working together with business and labor has become a key strategy for the federal safety and health agency.

The results of such efforts are impressive: $2.0 million saved in direct costs in a Fort Worth, Texas, undertaking; a reduction in injury rates to more than seventy percent (70%) below the national average for a petrochemical manufacturer; and "significant reductions" in a number of other recent programs (U.S. Department of Labor, Office of Public Affairs, November 12, 1998). Whether such endeavors are beneficial must be determined on a case-by-case basis.

ADDITIONAL CONCERNS OF OWNERS

Safety Incentive Programs

Incentive programs are not safety programs nor should they be substituted as such. An incentive program itself will not improve safety if employees do not know how to work safely (Roughton 1995).

Although most safety incentive programs effectively bring job site safety *awareness* to a higher level, there are also negative aspects associated with some safety incentive programs. Many current incentive programs are *outcome-oriented* instead of *process-oriented*. There are limitations on outcome-oriented incentive programs.

First of all, the timing of occurrence of accidents is unpredictable and is wholly a matter of luck. A contractor may work unsafely without having an accident if it is lucky. Looking at results alone can obscure the reality of a hazardous job site.

Secondly, using incident occurrence rates as the only criterion to evaluate job safety performance may discourage the reporting of some incidents which are otherwise reportable. This concern is also recognized by Geller, as "incentives to reduce negative statistics (i.e., everyone wins a prize after one month with no OSHA recordables) will more likely influence injury reporting (employees will not want to ruin the safety record) than continuation of safe work practices (Geller 1994)."

Wayne Pardy, in an article in *ENR* that was published in September, 1989, examined some of the disadvantages of safety incentive programs (Pardy 1997). Quoting workers interviewed for the article who expressed concerns for negative retribution if an accident was reported, Pardy states:

> No doubt these comments were perhaps made in a half joking manner, but I can't help believe that they also reflected a great deal of truth in how the safety award system of this company operated.

They are, in my opinion, a serious reflection of the dysfunction which characterize *(sic)* many safety incentive programs in North America, and indeed entire safety philosophies.

An incentive program must concentrate on rewarding safe work practices or worker achievement in voluntarily identifying safety hazards. These are examples of work process-related safety performance indicators. Yet, statistical tracking of incentive/disincentive contracts within the construction industry have yielded inconclusive results (Arditi and Yasamis 1998).

Prequalification Safety Evaluation

Determining whether a contractor can perform a job safely is difficult (Roughton 1995). A low total in a contractor's OSHA recordable accidents rate does not necessarily imply that a contractor practices good safety processes that will be transferable to the project under consideration. Experience in the type of construction for the subject job is essential for past experience to be an indicator of a commitment to a safe job site.

CONCLUSION

We opened this discussion inquiring whether we who are cast in the role of an owner are, as the pirate looking at forty in the Buffett song, mere "victims of fate." The conclusion must be, we think, that owners have traditionally taken a very passive role in construction safety, thereby perhaps unwittingly becoming "victims of fate," just as the pirate in the song. Yet, unlike the would-be buccaneer who "arrived too late" in history to find that his "occupation [was] just not around," owners of construction projects have a self-determinant option to shed the mantle of victim.

Owners have both a legal and moral responsibility to adapt proactive measures to aggressively promote construction job site safety. If we are to acknowledge the responsibility with which we are laden, commitment to a Total Safety Culture must follow. The benefits in terms of avoidance of human suffering and in the realization that safety is good business will far outweigh the perception of increased risk through undertaking to act responsibly.

REFERENCES

Arditi, David, and Yasamis, Firuzan. "Incentive/Disincentive Contracts: Perceptions of Owners and Contractors," *Journal of Construction Engineering Management*, September/October, 1998.

Blair, Earl H. "Achieving a Total Safety Paradigm Through Authentic Caring and Quality," *Professional Safety, Journal of American Society of Safety Engineers*, Volume 41, 5 May, 1996.

Brycon Corporation. "Our Commitment to Safety," http://www.brycon.com/safe-ty.html.

Conour, William F. "Prime Contractor Vicarious Liability for Injuries to Employees of Subcontractors at Construction Sites," March, 1990, http://www.conour.com/prime_contractor_vicarious_liability.htm.

Geller, Scott E. "Ten Principles for Achieving a Total Safety Culture," *Professional Safety, Journal of American Society of Safety Engineers*, Volume 39, 9 September, 1994.

Hislop, Richard D. "Developing A Safety Incentive Program," *Professional Safety, Journal of American Society of Safety Engineers*, Volume 38, 4 April, 1993.

Kueterman, Greg. "Attorneys Say Construction Law Becoming Clear, Recent Decisions Key on Contractor, Owner Liability," *Indianapolis Business Journal*, Vol. 7, No. 3, May, 1998, http://www.conour.com/attorneys_say-constructon*(sic)*_law.htm.

Kuhn, Todd A. "A Paradigm for Safety," *Professional Safety, Journal of American Society of Safety Engineers*, September, 1992.

Loafmann, Betty. "Behavior-Based Safety: Power & Pitfalls," *Professional Safety, Journal of American Society of Safety Engineers*, August, 1998.

Occupational Safety and Health Administration. "Accident Investigation," http://www.osha-slc.gov/SLTC/smallbusiness/sec6.html.

Occupational Safety and Health Administration. "Employee Recognition Program," OSHA Administrative Directive No. ADM 2.1, November 30, 1978.

Pardy, Wayne G. "Safety Incentive, Recognition and Awareness programs: One Company's Experience & an Industry Perspective," 1997, http://hazard.com/library/npincprog/npincent.html.

Roughton, James E. "Contractor Safety," *Professional Safety, Journal of American Society of Safety Engineers,* Volume 40, 1 January, 1995.

U.S. Department of Labor, Bureau of Labor Statistics. "Workplace Injury and Illness Summary," *Safety & Health Statistics,* December 17, 1998, http://www.bls.gov/news.release/osh/news.htm.

U.S. Department of Labor, Bureau of Labor Statistics. "Safer Construction Workplaces Evident During the Early 1990s," Issues in Labor Statistics, January, 1995, http://www.bls.gov/oshwc/ossm0004.txt.

U.S. Department of Labor, Office of Public Affairs. "OSHA to Highlight Partnerships with Public and Private Groups at Nov. 13 Conference," November 12, 1998, http://www.osha.gov/media/oshnews/nov98/partner.html.

info@brycon.com

Services

Company History

Clients/ Projects

Safety First

Inquiry Form

Contact Us

BRYCON has an exceptional safety record. Aggressive safety programs and employee satisfaction have led to more than 2 million safe man hours at Brycon.

During 1996, we performed 363,000 man-hours of field craft work with only 8 OSHA recordable accidents and no lost time. When compared with the national construction industry average, this is an exemplary record.

Lost Workday Cases	1996 BRYCON Rate per 200,000 MH	1995 BRYCON Rate per 200,000 MH	Bureau of Labor Statistics Rate per 200,000 MH
Lost Workday Cases	0	0.50	3.91
OSHA Recordable Cases	4.06	4.02	8.95

BRYCON is committed to an INJURY FREE ENVIRONMENT (IFE) and meets daily with it's crews to discuss safety and any concerns they may have.

BRYCON has also established a system of incentive to promote safety awareness and to reward employees for practicing safe work habits..

Through our Safety Incentive Program, the company pays safety bonuses to all field employees when the company's total work force meets the expected standards. This program motivates the workers, the leads, and the supervisors to take responsibility for safe performance and enforcement of safety procedures.

Through these policies, **BRYCON's** Workers Compensation Experience Modifier has steadily improved and is now at 0.59

Services | Company History | Clients/Projects
Safety First | Inquiry Form | Contact Us

The 1998 Contractor Safety Incentive Program is comprised of three parts: the Monthly Individual Safety Incentive Awards; the Quarterly Individual Safety Bonus Incentive Awards; and the Best Overall Contractor Management Safety Awards.

MONTHLY INDIVIDUAL SAFETY INCENTIVE AWARDS

On a monthly basis, all participating contractors will submit a list of "qualified employees" to the Safety Department for a random drawing. The list must be submitted by the 8th day of the following month and must be completely filled out to be included in the drawing. The official form will act as a certification that all qualified employees are truly "qualified." If it is determined that a contractor falsifies any documentation in this program, they will be disqualified from all future participation in the entire incentive program.

A "qualified employee" is one who meets all of the following criteria:

1. Any contractor employee who works directly on the project and is under the direct reporting line of a Contractor Superintendent. In addition, all Designated Safety Representatives are included.

2. An employee who works directly for the project, on the site, for a minimum of 120 hours in the monthly period.

3. An employee who DOES NOT sustain an accident or injury during the period. (An employee is not disqualified due to a minor first aid incident.)

On the 10th of each month (or next business day), 25 winners will be randomly chosen for a $500 cash award. In addition, a drawing will be used to randomly award the following prizes:

February:	50 (Approx. a $50 gift)
March:	75 (Approx. a $75 gift)
April:	100 (Approx. a $100 gift)
May:	50
June:	75
July:	100
August:	50
September:	75
October:	100
November:	50
December:	75
January:	100

EQUATES TO APPROXIMATELY $222,500 FOR THE 12-MONTH PERIOD

QUARTERLY INDIVIDUAL SAFETY BONUS INCENTIVE AWARDS

These awards will be a bonus incentive for individuals that qualify consistently in the monthly program. For each quarterly drawing, the contractor must submit a list of all employees who qualified for ALL THE THREE PREVIOUS MONTHLY DRAWINGS—(i.e., the employee has to be under the direct line of reporting to a Contractor Superintendent, including the Designated Safety Representatives; has to have worked at least 120 hours in each of the past three months for the project, on the site; and must not have sustained an accident or injury in the period (with the exception of minor first aid incidents).

The lists must be submitted to the Safety Department by the 8th of the following month (May, August, November, and February) listing all of the names of the qualified employees. The drawing will be held on or about the 15th of the month at a time and place to be posted. The target prizes for the four quarters is as follows:

1st Quarter: A voucher for a vacation trip to anywhere the winner chooses, costing up to $10,000, can be arranged through a local travel agent. In addition, a cash award of $5,000 will be added. TOTAL VALUE—$15,000.

2nd Quarter: A mid-size car, valued at $15,000, plus a $6,000 cash award. TOTAL VALUE— $21,000.

3rd Quarter: A mid-size pick-up truck, valued at $20,000, plus an $8,000 cash award. TOTAL VALUE—$28,000.

4th Quarter: A full-size pick-up truck, valued at $25,000, plus a $10,000 cash award. TOTAL VALUE—$35,000.

TOTAL INCENTIVE VALUE FOR BONUSES: $99,000

APPENDIX D

BEST OVERALL SAFETY MANAGEMENT AWARD

This award will be presented to the contractor with the best overall safety record in each of the following groups:

A.	General Contractors	$200,000 award
B.	Prime Contractors	$125,000 award
C.	Subcontractors	$ 75,000 award

A. The Best Overall Safety Performance for the General Contractor category will be determined after all participating General Contractors submit a summary of the year's total person hours for the project, by contractor/subcontractor, and a copy of all the OSHA 200 Logs for each contractor/subcontractor that worked under the GC, including the GC's own log.

B. The Best Overall Safety Performance for the Prime Contractor category will be determined after all participating Prime Contractors submit a summary of the year's total person hours for the project, by contractor/subcontractor, and a copy of all the OSHA 200 Logs for each contractor/subcontractor who worked under the Prime, including the Prime's own log.

C. The Best Overall Safety Performance for the Subcontractor category will be determined after all participating Subcontractors submit a summary of the year's total person hours for the project and a copy of their OSHA 200 Log.

The best performance will be awarded to the contractor who has the lowest combined frequency and severity rates. Any tie scores will result in the award being split among the winners.

MONTH OF: _____ , 1998

FORM COMPLETED AND CERTIFIED BY:

Print Name: _____   Signature: _____

Title: _____   Contractor: _____

Date: _____ , 1998

This form must be submitted to the Safety Office by the 8th of the following month. Any late forms will **not** be included in the drawing.

Program Qualifications:

1. Any contractor employee who works directly on the project and is under the direct reporting line to a Construction Superintendent. This will include any Designated Safety Representative.

2. The employee must work directly on the project for at least 120 hours in the monthly period.

3. An employee is NOT ELIGIBLE if he or she has sustained an accident/injury. Minor first aid incidents will not disqualify an employee.

QUALIFIED EMPLOYEE   **CONTRACTOR**

_____   _____

_____   _____

_____   _____

_____   _____

_____   _____

_____   _____

_____   _____

HEALTH CONSEQUENCES OF WORKING IN CONSTRUCTION

Marie Haring Sweeney

National Institute for Occupational Safety and Health, Cincinnati, Ohio, U.S.A.

David Fosbroke

Division of Safety Research

National Institute for Occupational Safety and Health, Morgantown, West Virginia, U.S.A.

Linda M. Goldenhar

Division of Surveillance, Hazard Evaluation, and Field Studies

National Institute for Occupational Safety and Health, Cincinnati, Ohio, U.S.A.

Larry L. Jackson

Division of Safety Research

National Institute for Occupational Safety and Health, Morgantown, West Virginia, U.S.A.

Kenneth Linch

Division of Respiratory Disease Studies

National Institute for Occupational Safety and Health, Morgantown, West Virginia, U.S.A.

Boris D. Lushniak

Division of Surveillance, Hazard Evaluation, and Field Studies

National Institute for Occupational Safety and Health, Cincinnati, Ohio, U.S.A.

Carol Merry

Division of Behavioral and Biomedical Sciences

National Institute for Occupational Safety and Health, Cincinnati, Ohio, U.S.A.

Scott Schneider

Laborers' Health and Safety Fund of North America

Mark Stephenson

Division of Biomedical and Behavioral Science

National Institute for Occupational Safety and Health, Cincinnati, Ohio, U.S.A.

ABSTRACT

In the United States, compared to other industries, the rate of work-related injuries and illnesses among construction workers ranks as one of the highest. Falls are the most common events leading to work-related injury deaths in the construction industry, followed by contact with objects and equipment, motor vehicle or transportation incidents, and exposure to harmful substances and environments, primarily electrocutions. Construction workers also die at a greater rate than the general public from chronic diseases, such as chronic lung diseases (asbestosis, silicosis, chronic bronchitis, and emphysema). Furthermore, construction workers are at high risk for musculoskeletal disorders, particularly of the back and shoulder, noise-induced hearing loss, dermatitis and other skin disorders, and eye injuries. All these problems are preventable when the right information and preventive strategies are available and utilized.

KEYWORDS

eye injuries, musculoskeletal disorders, hearing loss, silicosis, skin disorders, traumatic injuries

INTRODUCTION

This chapter provides a brief overview of the many health problems caused by working in the construction environment. The examples and discussions that follow clearly illustrate why safety and health concerns on the construction site should be a focal point for each construction manager.

In the United States, more than 7.5 million workers (about 6.5% of the total labor force) are currently employed in construction. In this industry, high rates of work-related injuries and illnesses have always been considered part of the job. For many years, construction workers experienced much higher rates of occupational injuries and illnesses resulting in more lost work days than workers in the manufacturing sector. Although these rates have decreased nearly threefold in the last 40 years, construction still ranks in the top three industries for workplace deaths and injuries (BLS 1996). In 1996, 16.9% (or 1,039) of all work-related deaths occurred among construction workers. That is, approximately three construction workers died *each day* from injuries sustained on the job. Falls caused nearly a third of these deaths (31%), and ironworkers and roofers accounted for 75% of fall-related deaths (CPWR 1998). Nonfatal injuries also occur frequently among construction workers. In 1995, construction workers experienced more than 182,000 illnesses and injuries causing lost work days (BLS 1998). Contact with or being struck by an object together with musculoskeletal disorders account for more than 50% of all compensable traumatic injuries; backs, hands/fingers, and eyes are the parts of the body most often affected (Lipscomb *et al.* 1996).

Work-related illnesses among construction workers are much less dramatic than traumatic injuries or fatalities, but they are no less harmful or costly. Many of these conditions have slow or late onset, and thus, are under-reported. Chronic low-back pain and other musculoskeletal conditions cost millions of dollars in medical expenses, lost wages, and workers' compensation payments. Occupational skin diseases are the most common occupational illness, second only to musculoskeletal disorders. In 1996, more than 2,000 construction workers (4.5 per 10,000 full-time workers) reported a work-related skin disorder (BLS 1998). Work-related chronic lung diseases such as silicosis, asbestosis, and bronchitis usually take many years to develop and are often diagnosed after the construction worker has retired. In addition, despite the high prevalence of noise-induced hearing loss among construction workers, it has not been recognized until recently as a significant safety and health problem. Finally, with the increasing proportion of tradeswomen entering the construction industry, issues relating to reproductive health, sexual harassment, and appropriately sized personal protective equipment (PPE) are now considered safety and health issues. This chapter briefly covers each of these health consequences of employment as a construction worker and prevention strategies to reduce them.

ILLNESSES, INJURIES, AND MORTALITY AMONG CONSTRUCTION WORKERS

Mortality Experience

The Bureau of Labor Statistics (BLS) usually records work-related deaths from traumatic events as "occupationally related." But the illnesses and deaths construction workers experience from chronic diseases are often not reported as related to their occupations—even though they suffer and die from these chronic conditions at a much greater rate than the general public. For example, workers in skilled construction trades who died before age 65 between 1984 and 1986 had significantly greater proportionate mortality from cancers of the respiratory system (including the lung, larynx, and pleura or peritoneum) and from chronic lung diseases (such as asbestosis, silicosis, and chronic bronchitis and emphysema) than did the general public (Robinson *et al.*, 1995). Past workplace exposures to silica, asbestos, welding fumes, coal tar pitch, solvents, and other substances contribute to these diseases; but this contribution is often unrecognized because although some deaths occur before retirement, many of these deaths are due to diseases which occur many years after the exposures end and the workers are retired.

Construction workers are also more likely to die at proportionately greater rates than the U.S. population from falls, chronic liver disease, homicides, and alcohol-associated diseases (Robinson *et al.*, 1995). When examined by trade in separate studies, union laborers, ironworkers, carpenters, and sheet metal workers had elevated mortality risks for transportation injuries (Stern *et al.*, 1995; Stern and Sweeney 1997; Robinson *et al.*, 1996; Alterman *et al.*, 1996). Operating engineers had excess proportionate rates of death from injuries such as being crushed by machinery (cranes, tractors, etc.) (Stern and Sweeney 1997).

Traumatic Injuries—Overview

Despite great strides in reducing work-related injury rates, U.S. construction workers continue to face significant risk of on-the-job injury. Although construction represents only 6.5% of the U.S. labor force, it represents 18% of fatal injuries (Ore and Fosbroke 1997) and 8% of nonfatal injuries to U.S. workers (BLS 1998). From 1992 through 1996, nearly 5,000 construction workers were fatally injured (BLS 1994–1998). In terms of fatal injury risk, the construction industry ranks 13th of 50 high-risk industries (Fosbroke, *et al.*, 1997). Workers in six construction-related occupations (structural metal workers, operating engineers, electrical power installers and repairers, construction laborers, roofers, and construction supervisors) were among the 20 occupations that had the highest fatal injury risk.

In terms of nonfatal injury risk, the construction industry has the second highest case rate overall and the highest case rate for days away from work in the United States (BLS 1998). From 1992 through 1996, 2.5 million workers suffered an Occupational Safety and Health Administration (OSHA) recordable injury, and nearly 1 million spent 1 or more days away from work due to on-the-job injuries (BLS 1994–1998). During a 4-month period in 1995, an estimated 97,460 construction workers were treated for work-related injuries in hospital emergency departments throughout the United States (Layne *et al.*, forthcoming).

Fatal Injuries

Two major data collection systems exist for the recording and analysis of work-related fatal injuries. As part of the National Traumatic Occupational Fatalities (NTOF) Surveillance System, the National Institute for Occupational Safety and Health (NIOSH) has collected death certificates covering the years 1980 through 1994. Since 1992, BLS has maintained the Census of Fatal Occupational Injuries (CFOI), a data collection system based on multiple source documents (e.g., death certificates, workers' compensation records, newspaper clippings). The NTOF system uses cause-of-death codes (WHO 1977), but the CFOI system uses event or exposure codes to describe the circumstances leading to injury (ANSI 1996).

In both systems, falls are the most common events leading to work-related injury deaths in the construction industry, accounting for nearly one-third of construction worker deaths (Pollack *et al.*, 1996; Chen and Fosbroke 1998). Although fall injuries are certainly not unique to construction, this industry accounts for approximately half of all work-related fatal falls (Kisner and Fosbroke 1994; Cattledge *et al.*, 1996). The CFOI data report that transportation (including motor vehicle events) is the second leading fatal-injury event—followed by contact with objects and equipment and exposure to harmful substances and environments (primarily electrocutions) (Table 10–1). The leading NTOF cause-of-death categories in construction are falls, motor vehicles, electrocutions, and machinery (NIOSH 1998a).

The Construction industry is divided into three major industry groups:

1. Building Construction—General Contractors and Operative Builders (Standard Industrial Classification [SIC] 15)
2. Heavy Construction Other Than Building Construction—Contractors (SIC 16)
3. Construction—Special Trades Contractors (SIC 17) (OMB 1987)

From 1992 through 1995, an average of 991 construction workers died from fatal injuries each year. During the same period, 175 workers were fatally injured each year in SIC 15; another 247 workers per year died in SIC 16; and 565 workers died per year in SIC 17.

In a recent study of fatal injury by occupation and cause of death, Chen and Fosbroke (1998) found that the highest death rates were among electrical power installers and repairers (96.6 deaths/100,000 workers), structural metal workers (864/100,000), operating engineers (410/100,000), drillers—earth (348/100,000), supervisors—painters and paperhangers (345/100,000), and construction laborers (340/100,000). Specific fatal injury hazards vary by occupation. For those occupations with at least 150 deaths over a 5-year period, structural metal workers and roofers were most at risk of fatal falls; operating engineers were most at risk of machinery incidents; and truck drivers were most at risk of motor vehicle incidents.

Separate NTOF publications provide additional details for each of the four leading cause-of-death groups (falls, motor vehicle, machine, and electrocution) in the construction industry. Key results from these papers are described below.

Falls

From 1980 through 1989, 2,798 construction workers died of fall-related injuries (Cattledge *et al.*, 1996). These workers represented 49.6% of all occupational fall-related fatalities in the

TABLE 10–1

Fatal work-related injuries in the U.S. construction industry from 1992 through 1996, based on the CFOIs.

| | | Event or Exposure Leading to Death[1] | | | | | |
Year	All Construction (N)	Transportation (%)	Assault or Violent Act (%)	Contact with Object or Equipment (%)	Falls (%)	Exposure to Harmful Substances (%)	Fire & Explosion (%)
1992	919	24.5	3.0	19.7	29.2	18.8	3.0
1993	924	25.2	4.0	20.2	29.5	17.2	3.5
1994	1027	25.8	2.7	17.8	32.1	19.6	3.3
1995	1048	25.1	3.1	18.2	32.0	16.3	2.0
1996	1039	25.3	2.1	20.8	32.4	18.0	2.8

[1]Percentages within each year do not total 100% because event types representing a small number of deaths are not included in the table.

Source: Bureau of Labor Statistics

United States during that period. In 40.8% of these cases, the victim fell from a building or structure. Scaffolds (18.6%) and ladders (11.0%) were the other leading surfaces from which workers fell. The average age of fatally injured workers was 40.3 years and ranged from 16 to 89 years. Rates were highest for workers aged 20–24 and more than half of the victims were 39 years of age or less.

In a study of fatal falls from roofs, Suruda *et al.* (1995) supplemented the NTOF data with data from OSHA's Integrated Management Information System to examine the circumstances associated with falls from roofs. Over a three-year period, 288 workers from all industries died in fatal falls from roofs. Construction workers accounted for 80% of these deaths. Special trades contractors (SIC 17) (especially those in the roofing, siding, and sheet metal [SIC 1761] and the structural steel erection industries [SIC 1799]) had the highest rates of fatal falls from roofs. Seventy-four percent of fatal falls from roofs in the construction industry were among the special trades contractors. Very few fall deaths occurred among workers of the heavy construction sector (SIC 16) of the industry. Fatal falls occurred from heights of 9 to 175 feet. Details on what part of the roof the worker fell from was missing for 43% of the cases, but clearly the roof edge, roof openings, non-supportive roof structures, and skylights were all important risk factors. Of that 288 cases, the height was known for 148 cases. The mean height of these 148 cases was 34.75 +/-23.9 feet, the range was 9 to 175 feet, and approximately one-third of the deaths for which the height was known were from heights of 30 feet or less.

Motor Vehicles

Workers in the construction industry are twice as likely as the average worker to be killed by a motor vehicle (Ore and Fosbroke 1997). While the number of construction worker deaths declined for each of the leading causes-of-death between 1980 and 1992, the number of deaths caused by motor-vehicle incidents declined at a slower rate than other causes-of-death. The result of this differential decline was that motor vehicle incidents became the second leading cause of death among construction workers in 1988. Analysis of 2,144 deaths indicates that most of these motor vehicle incidents were traffic related (87%)—that is, they occurred on a public highway. A large portion (40%) of these fatally injured construction workers were struck as pedestrians by motor vehicles.

Machine

Nearly 2,000 machine-related deaths in the construction industry occurred from 1980 through 1992 (Pratt *et al.*, 1997). Forty-six percent of these deaths involved three types of machines—cranes (16 %), excavating machines (15%), and tractors (15%). Other machines involved in construction worker deaths were loaders, paving machines, forklifts, and elevators. In nearly one-third of the cases, the worker was struck by a moving mobile machine. Another 17% were killed by overturning machines, and 8% were struck by a machine boom, bucket, or arm. The mean age of construction workers killed in machinery incidents was 40.5, with a range of age of 16 to 90 years. More than 25% of the victims were between the ages of 25 and 34 years old. Two occupations, construction laborers (23.5 percent) and operating engineers (22.6%), accounted for nearly half of machine-related deaths in construction. Based on a subset of data from 1990 through 1992, most deaths were to workers in SIC 16 (204/330) and SIC 17 (100/330).

Electrocution

More than 2,000 construction workers were electrocuted between 1980 and 1991 (Ore and Casini 1996). These deaths represent 40% of electrocutions in all sectors of private industry and 15% of deaths in the construction industry. The median age of death was 26.5 years. The electrocution rate peaked in the 20-to-24-year age group and declined through age 60. Electricians and laborers had the highest number of electrocutions (41.8% and 23.2% of construction electrocutions respectively). Electricians, structural metal workers, laborers, electrical power installers, and painters had rates above the construction industry average. Of the 2,015 electrocutions in construction, 1,153 (57.2%) were associated with wiring, appliances, and electrical machinery. Twenty-three percent were related to electric power generating plants, distribution stations, and transmission lines.

Nonfatal Injuries

Workers' Compensation files, OSHA logs, and hospital data have been used to assess nonfatal injuries among construction workers in the United States. In contrast to fatal injuries, overexertion/bodily reaction is the most common cause, and sprains and strains are the most common diagnosis.

Workers' Compensation

Kisner and Fosbroke (1994) reported an analysis of Workers' Compensation claims data from 15 states. During the study period of 1981–86, the construction industry (101/100 workers) had the highest claims rate of any industry division. Overexertion was the leading cause of injury (23.9%), followed by being struck by an object (22.4%) and falls from elevations (12.8%).

In a study of 182 nonfatal occupational fall injuries in the West Virginia construction industry (Cattledge *et al.*, 1996); ladders (61 cases); scaffolds (39 cases); and roof truss, wall beam, or other structure (25 cases) were the most common surfaces from which workers fell. Most injured workers were using tools (44 cases), handling materials (41 cases), or climbing or descending ladders (19 cases) before the fall. The distance of the fall was known for 178 of the 182 nonfatal fall injuries in the study. In approximately 70% of these cases for which fall distance was known (125/178), the fall distance was less than 10 feet. Sixty-three percent of the injured workers had received some type of training about fall protection, usually in the form of on-the-job training or company pamphlets, posters, or written rules. However, very few of the injured workers used fall protection devices. Some of these fall-related injuries were quite severe, resulting in 0 to 391 lost work days. More than a year after the fall incident, 13.7% of the injured workers reported being temporarily disabled, and 2.2% reported being permanently disabled.

OSHA Recordable Injuries

Each year BLS surveys employers to obtain information about occupational injuries and illnesses. In response to this survey, employers provide data on worker injuries and illnesses from their OSHA 200 logs. National estimates of the number and rate of injuries by industry are published annually. From 1992 through 1995, an estimated half million construction workers annually suffered a work-related injury that was recorded on the OSHA 200 log (BLS 1994–1998). Each year, nearly 200,000 of these workers had an injury that was severe enough to involve at least one day away from work. Special trades contractors (SIC 17) had slightly higher injury rates than building contractors (SIC 15) and heavy and highway contractors (SIC 16). Special trades contractors also accounted for more than 319,000 construction injuries per year compared with 109,000 injuries among residential building contractors and 73,000 injuries among heavy and highway contractors per year. Approximately one-third of cases involving days away from work are due to overexertion and bodily reactions and one-third were due to events involving contact with objects. Falls account for another 20% of injuries with days away from work. Within these broad groupings, the event leading to the greatest number of cases involving days away from work is overexertion while lifting objects or equipment. This single event accounts for an average of 27,144 days away from work cases per year. Falls to a lower level account for nearly as many cases (24,002 per year).

Construction laborers, the largest occupational segment of the construction industry, have the largest number of cases involving days away from work (50,885 per year). Carpenters are the second most frequently injured (27,422 per year) and electricians third (12,274 cases per year). Other types of workers with frequent injuries requiring days away from work include plumbers and pipefitters, construction trade helpers, roofers, truck drivers, painters, heating and air conditioning mechanics, drywall installers, operating engineers, structural metal workers, insulation workers, sheet metal duct installers, and brickmasons.

Hospital records

Studies of construction workers treated in hospitals suggest that hospital-treated injuries consist of a higher proportion of fractures and lacerations than injuries that are recorded on OSHA logs and in Workers' Compensation databases (Layne, *et al.*, 1998; Husberg, Fosbroke, and Conway 1988). Researchers from George Washington University (GWU) collected data on 592 injured construction workers treated at GWU emergency department during a two-year period (Hunting, *et al.*, 1994). Many of these workers were employed in the construction of a large federal building in Washington, D.C. Carpenters represented 23.8% of injuries, followed by laborers (17.1%) and construction workers not otherwise specified (10.8%). Thirty-eight percent of injuries were lacerations, mostly to the wrist, hand, and finger. Sprains and strains (17.9 %), contusion and abrasion (15.7%), and eye injuries (12.3%) were the next most common types of injury. Cutting and piercing objects (e.g., sheet metal, hand tools) and falls were the leading causes of injury. Almost one-third of falls were from scaffolds, while one-quarter of falls were from ladders. Sixty-four percent (18/28) of hospital admissions were due to falls. The National Institute for Occupational Safety and Health conducted a pilot study of injuries to construction workers treated in hospital emergency departments using a stratified random sample of emergency departments from throughout the United States (Layne *et al.*, 1988). During a four-month period, July 15, 1995 through November 15, 1995, approximately 1,500 cases were reported in the 65 sample hospitals, yielding a national estimate of 97,461 (CI$_{95}$ 65,900–129,200) injuries to construction worker who were treated in a U.S. hospital emergency department. Of these 97,461 construction worker injuries, an estimated 3,350 resulted in the worker being hospitalized. Workers in the youngest age groups (16 to 19 and 20 to 29 years of age) had the highest injury rates. Lacerations, contusions (including abrasions and hematomas), and sprains and strains were the leading injury diagnoses, 24.9%, 19.9%, and 18.7%, respectively. Sixty-three percent of the injuries were to the extremities. Contact with objects and equipment was the most frequent injury event, representing two-thirds of injuries treated in emergency departments. Seventeen percent of the cases involved falls and 13% involved bodily reaction or overexertion injuries. Laceration of the hand was the most common type of injury, while fractures that resulted from falls accounted for most hospitalized cases.

In another NIOSH study, a data base of injuries recorded in a statewide trauma registry was analyzed for the construction industry (Husberg, *et al.*, forthcoming). From 1991 through 1995, 365 workers were hospitalized for injuries received while working in the Alaskan construction industry. The length of hospitalization ranged from 1 to 26 days. The main causes of injury were falls (48%) and machinery (17%). Thirty-five percent of falls were from a building or structure, 24% were from a ladder, and 19% were from scaffolds. Over half of these hospitalized patients had fractured bones. Most injuries occurred to the extremities.

Preventing Injuries

Prevention of fatal and nonfatal injuries in the construction industry is more difficult than for many other industries because of the transient nature of the workforce, the constantly changing work environment, economic and time pressures, and the complexity of the construction process (Ringen, *et al.*, 1995). However, safety management on construction sites is possible, and many employers have been successful at greatly reducing injury rates (CPWR 1998). Detailed prevention strategies for the leading fatal and nonfatal injuries are beyond the scope of this chapter. However, several books address construction safety planning and provide practical prevention strategies (MacCollum 1995; Levitt and Samelson 1993; Hinze 1997). Information on controlling specific hazards is contained in the OSHA regulations under CFR (Code of Federal Regulations) Part 1926, CFR Part 1919 and the U.S. Army Corps of Engineers Manual EM–385–1–1. The keys to preventing injuries on construction sites are to make safety planning a part of the construction planning process; assure that workers, foremen, and project managers have the required knowledge and skills to complete the job safely; provide those on the construction site with the tools, equipment, time, and protective technologies needed to assure worker safety; and develop clear lines of responsibility for safety and health among owners, designers, contractors, subcontractors, supervisors, and workers.

To prevent injury, hazards need to be recognized, eliminated where possible, and minimized when elimination is not possible, or when elimination of one hazard creates another, greater hazard. There is a hierarchy of injury control strategies. First, eliminate the hazard through changes in work practice (e.g., modular construction of components on the ground rather than on roofs and trusses), substitution (e.g., using prefabricated materials instead of site-assembled materials), or redesign (e.g., double insulated tools). When a hazard cannot be eliminated, the next control strategy is to reduce exposure to the injury hazard through the application of engineering and administrative controls, such as machine guarding and job rotation. As a last resort, control strategies that require the active participation of employees, such as the use of PPE and the implementation of special procedures, can be used to prevent injuries (MacCollum 1995). These basic concepts of injury control underline the prevention of construction injuries.

Recognizing potential injury hazards is a critical step in preventing construction injuries. Assessing potential hazards has to be a part of the project management process and must continue throughout the life of the project. Each construction site must be assessed since site-specific conditions greatly influence the hazards faced during the construction process. It is not enough for project safety managers to inspect the site only for compliance with OSHA regulations (MacCollum 1995; Levitt and Samelson 1993). Safety management is a proactive approach in which hazards are anticipated; workable solutions are developed; and necessary modifications, work procedures, and precautions are implemented to assure that injuries will not occur (MacCollum 1995).

EYE INJURIES

BLS reported that in 1995 construction had the highest industrial rate of eye injuries involving one or more lost work days (208/10,000 full-time workers) (BLS 1998). Each of the estimated 9,500 eye injuries resulted in an average of two lost work days. Many additional eye injuries required medical treatment but did not result in the loss of a full work day. NIOSH estimates that more than 40,000 U.S. construction workers were treated in emergency rooms for work-related eye injuries in 1996 (Jackson *et al.*, 1998). But since not all work-related eye injuries are treated in emergency rooms, the total number of construction worker eye injuries requiring medical treatment probably exceeded 105,000 in that year. What these statistics do not reflect is the loss of vision that results from these eye injuries.

Although the eye injury events vary widely among the trades and sectors of the construction industry, about three-fourths of the injuries result when a foreign body scratches or becomes embedded in the eye. Other common injuries result from chemical splashes and welding light radiation burns, which typically affect both eyes. Often the injured worker was not wearing appropriate eye protection at the time of the injury. Eye protection is required when a worker is exposed to potential eye or face injury from flying particles, molten metal, liquid chemicals, acids or caustic liquids, chemical gases or vapor, or potentially injurious light radiation (29 CFR 1910.133 and 1926.102). Side protection is required when there is a hazard from flying particles.

Preventing Eye Injuries

Eye and face protection must conform to the requirements of the American National Standards Institute, ANSI Z87.1, Practice for Occupational and Educational Eye and Face Protection (ANSI 1998). All eye protection purchased after July 5, 1994, must comply with the most recent revision.

New eye protection with improved technical characteristics and more up-to-date styles are constantly coming into the marketplace. New antiscratch and antifog coatings have significantly improved the longevity and usability of modern eye protection in certain environments. No longer is a worker limited to the traditional styles. Wrap-around spectacles and more fashionable eyewear are also available to foster compliance with eyewear requirements. Goggles have also had obvious improvements and style changes. Perhaps the newest innovations in eye protection are the products that offer the comfort and vision of a spectacle along with the superior protection provided by goggles. These spectacle/goggle products typically involve some form of foam around the lens to fill the gaps between the spectacles and the face and provide better comfort and protection from low-energy particles. When high-energy impact is possible (at most construction sites, for example), polycarbonate lenses should be used in eye protection, including in prescription spectacles. However, only through appropriate training and ready availability of safety eyewear can we hope to eliminate eye injuries in the construction industry—especially injuries that occur because the worker did not think he or she needed safety eyewear.

The price of protective eyewear is minuscule compared with the cost of any eye injury. According to the National Society to Prevent Blindness (1991), the direct cost (sum of lost wages, medical expense, and insurance administration cost) of an eye injury that requires only first-aid treatment is about $350. But the average direct cost of a disabling injury is $3,666. The direct cost of disabling injuries totals more than $500 million annually. If the indirect costs such as time lost by uninjured workers and production slowdowns are factored in, the total exceeds $1 billion annually.

NOISE-INDUCED HEARING LOSS

A walk through any construction site makes it clear that exposure to hazardous noise (85 decibels or greater, A-weighted [dBA]) is a reality for most construction workers. Consequently, the typical construction worker already has or is acquiring a debilitating, permanent hearing loss. However, no construction worker needs to lose his or her hearing as a result of their occupation. In fact, noise-induced occupational hearing loss is 100% preventable.

Despite the seeming omnipresence of hazardous noise at construction sites, few data exist to quantify construction workers' noise exposures and their associated risk of occupational hearing loss. Unlike the hearing loss prevention services required for workers in the manufacturing sector, OSHA regulations do not require these services for construction workers, thus construction workers are neither monitored for noise exposures nor provided with baseline and monitoring audiometry.

Currently, there is plenty of evidence that construction workers are at risk of occupational hearing loss (NIOSH 1998b). In nearly every construction trade (e.g., highway, residential, non-residential, concrete work, etc.), substantial numbers of workers are exposed to hazardous noise (Hattis 1998). These data are corroborated by recent studies of sheet metal workers (Stephenson 1995), roofers (Tennenbaum and Schneider 1998), and carpenters (Merry and Stephenson 1998). These researchers found a higher rate of hearing loss among construction workers than in similar groups of workers who were not exposed to noise on the job.

Figures 10–1 and 10–2 show why there is cause for concern. Figure 10–1 (from a study of carpenters) illustrates how hearing level increases as a worker ages. The hearing level is a measure of hearing loss. The higher the hearing level (in decibels), the greater the hearing loss.

Figure 10–2 compares the hearing levels of carpenters with those of workers not exposed to noise on-the-job. As Figure 10–2 shows, it will take only five years for the construction worker but 25 years for the worker with no occupational noise exposure to develop the same amount of hearing loss.

Unfortunately, the loss for carpenters continues to worsen throughout the working lifetime. In fact, the average carpenter's hearing loss approximates the hearing loss that would be expected if he/she received a daily exposure of 95 dBA of continuous noise exposure for 8 hours each day! The OSHA limit is 90 dBA. The NIOSH recommended exposure limit (REL) is 85 dBA. The data in Figures 10–1 and 10–2 also indicate that by age 55, many (if not most) construction workers will need hearing aids. Note, however, that unexposed workers still have normal hearing after 35 years of working.

The economic impact of this hearing loss is staggering. In the carpentry sector alone, the cost of providing *one pair* of hearing aids for each worker who needs them exceeds half a *billion* dollars. This cost does not include potential workers' compensation costs or other social and economic considerations.

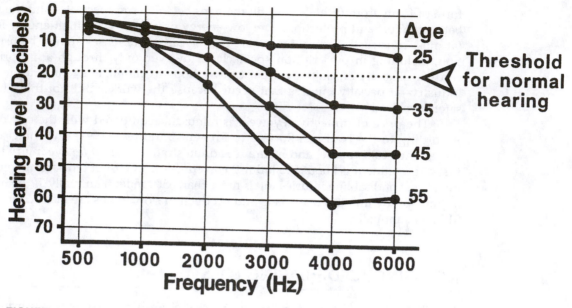

FIGURE 10–1
Hearing levels among carpenters as a function of age.

According to Dobie (1997), the economic burden of occupational hearing loss is greater than the burden of all other sources of hearing loss combined.

Preventing Noise-Induced Hearing Loss

What needs to be done to prevent hearing loss? The traditional criteria for protecting workers from occupational hazards are unquestionably applicable to hearing loss: (1) remove the hazard, (2) remove the worker, and (3) protect the worker.

The best approaches ensure that workers are not exposed to hazardous noise using either engineering controls or administrative controls (such as "buy quiet equipment" policies) to limit worker exposures. Whenever these options are not feasible, hearing protectors can be an effective tool for preventing noise-induced hearing loss. Unfortunately, unlike the manufactur-

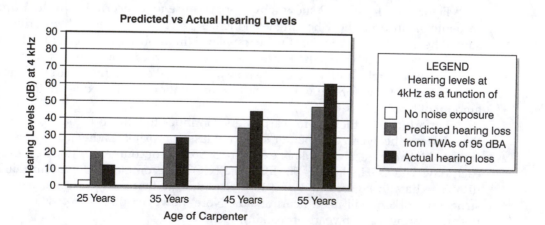

FIGURE 10–2
Comparison of carpenters' Hearing levels at 4 kHz with the hearing of non-noise exposed workers. Also shown is the amount of predicted hearing loss from daily 8-hour exposures to continuous noise levels of 95dBA.

ing sector, the construction industry is not required to provide annual training in the proper use and care of hearing protectors. Hearing protectors will *only* be effective when workers *are taught how to select, fit, and wear them*. Without such training, workers may think they are getting the protection listed on the package; but in reality, they are very likely to get only a fraction of the labeled protection (Berger 1980; Berger *et al.,* 1996).

The best hearing protector is the one that fits well and is worn. Failure to fit hearing protectors properly and to wear them consistently is probably the leading cause of occupational noise-induced hearing loss. It cannot be overemphasized that hearing protectors are effective only when workers are properly motivated to use them. No magic formula exists for training workers effectively, but such training must be relevant to each worker and focus on his or her tasks and needs in the following areas:

1. Risk of hearing loss
2. Self-efficacy
3. Barriers to the use of hearing protectors

Risk
Workers must be informed about their individual risk of hearing loss on jobs that involve hazardous noise exposures. Each exposed worker must be given (1) periodic audiograms to catch temporary hearing loss before it can become permanent, and (2) counseling about the consequences of hearing loss.

Self-efficacy
Workers must be trained how and when to use hearing protectors, and they must believe that they can effectively prevent occupational hearing loss. This training must involve individual or small-group (no more than 6) practice in fitting the hearing protectors they will use. No substitute exists for this individualized approach.

Barriers
Barriers to the use of hearing protectors involve the four C's—comfort, convenience, communication, and culture.

Comfort and convenience.   If a hearing protector is not comfortable and convenient to use, it simply will not be worn. Construction workers need to be aware of the many types of hearing protectors available (NIOSH 1995). Choosing a hearing protector is like trying on shoes: no single device will suit everyone. There are more than 200 different hearing protectors available, so everyone can find at least one hearing protector that is comfortable and convenient to use.

Communication.   Workers are often reluctant to use a hearing protector if they believe it will impair their ability to hear important sounds. Some devices have built-in communication circuits, but most devices simply need to be checked to assure they are not reducing sound more than necessary for the situation. Protectors are also available that muffle background noises but amplify nearby speech. Other new hearing protectors are designed to activate only when noise levels become hazardous (especially useful when noises are intermittent).

Culture.   Training and education must be used to change the current construction culture so that wearing PPE such as hearing protectors is as acceptable as wearing hard hats. Such acceptability can be changed by peer trainers and testimonials from well-respected coworkers who have suffered hearing loss or tinnitus (ringing in the ears).

Preventing hearing loss among construction workers is best achieved when a partnership exists between labor and management. At a minimum, the construction industry should provide its workers with the same hearing loss prevention services that the manufacturing industry provides its workers. These services include: (1) a hearing loss prevention program that includes feasible engineering controls (including "buy quiet" policies), (2) audiometric monitoring (hearing evaluations), and (3) regular worker education and training. Industry should provide workers with a selection of hearing protectors from which to choose and should encourage workers to use them whenever they are around loud noise (not just at work). Labor should buy into a safety culture that supports good hearing. Workers should use and help maintain engineering controls, and they should wear hearing protectors whenever they are in hazardous noise—not just at work. Finally, workers need to participate in audiometric monitoring programs and be proactive in preventing hearing loss or protecting the hearing they still have. Working together, all sectors of the construction industry can ensure that no worker must give up his or her hearing to earn a living.

SILICOSIS

As previously noted, construction workers develop and die from respiratory or lung diseases at a higher rate than the general population. Silicosis is a respiratory disease that affects construction workers at a high rate. Silicosis, a nonreversible fibrotic lung disease, results from breathing crystalline silica dust that is deposited deep in the lungs. Crystalline silica is a naturally occurring mineral in the crust of the earth. The three major forms of crystalline silica are quartz, cristobalite, and tridymite. Quartz is by far the most common form of crystalline silica (sand, for example, can be nearly pure quartz). Only the very small particles (less than 10 microns in diameter), created when crystalline silica is fractured, can be inhaled deeply into the lungs and cause silicosis. In addition to silicosis, studies in humans indicate that inhaled crystalline silica from occupational sources (in the form of quartz or cristobalite) may cause lung cancer, as well as some forms of immunologic disorders (IARC 1997). The time from first exposure to disease onset can range from weeks to several decades, depending on how much and how often the worker was exposed to silica.

Because silicosis often causes death, it is possible to examine its effect on the death rate of construction workers through a systematic examination and analysis of the cause of death noted on death certificates. In a study conducted by NIOSH, silicosis caused more than twice the number of expected deaths among construction workers who died between 1984 and 1986 (Robinson et al., 1995). In this population, only asbestosis caused proportionately more deaths. NIOSH also conducted a study that analyzed the industry recorded on the death certificate of workers with silicosis. The construction industry is recorded on the workers' death certificates that mention silicosis more often than any other industry but mining (NIOSH 1996a).

With few exceptions, silicosis occurs almost exclusively among occupationally exposed populations. The NIOSH National Occupational Exposure Survey (NOES) estimates that 700,000 construction workers are potentially exposed to crystalline silica (NIOSH 1996b). Construction workers may be exposed to crystalline silica in many ways (NIOSH 1996c). Common construction activities that generate dust from earth moving (such as rock drilling and hauling and dumping rock and soil) can generate respirable dust particles. Since sand and rock are used to make concrete, a respiratory hazard may exist whenever concrete is disturbed. Also, masonry items such as common bricks and concrete blocks contain varying amounts of crystalline silica. In addition, the mortar used to build with bricks and blocks contains silica sand. Therefore, whenever concrete or masonry is sawed, ground, chipped, hammered, drilled, bored, or abraded, dust controls must be used to reduce the hazard. Abrasive blasting is a very important source of exposure for construction workers, especially when silica sand is the abrasive.

Despite the fact that we know what causes silicosis, even today construction workers face the possibility of being exposed to high levels of crystalline silica. In a study of silica dust compliance data from OSHA (Linch, et al.), five industry segments were identified in which workers were exposed to at least 10 times the NIOSH REL for respirable crystalline silica (0.05 mg/m^3 [50 ug/m^3] as a time-weighted average for up to 10 hours per day during a 40-hour workweek) (NIOSH 1974). Three of these industry segments were construction:

- SIC 174: Masonry, stonework, tile setting, and plastering (13,800 workers exposed)
- SIC 162: Heavy construction, except highway and street construction (6,300 workers exposed)
- SIC 172: Painting and paper hanging (3,000 workers exposed)

Preventing Silicosis

Since 1974, NIOSH has recommended against the use of silica sand for abrasive blasting (NIOSH 1974). If good dust controls are not used, exposures greatly exceeding the NIOSH REL of 0.05 mg/m^3 can occur in any of the exposure situations discussed (NIOSH, 1996c). Studies have also determined that even if crystalline silica exposure is kept below the OSHA permissible exposure limit (PEL), up to 35% of exposed workers will develop silicosis (Steenland and Brown 1995). Therefore, proper PPE and dust controls must be used, and workers should be well trained to prevent exposure.

To prevent silicosis, airborne dust containing crystalline silica must be eliminated. The main methods for eliminating this dust involve engineering controls such as local exhaust ventilation, wet sawing and drilling, and substitution of less hazardous building materials and blasting abrasives. Respirators should not be the primary means of reducing worker exposures. However, if dust controls cannot keep concentrations below the NIOSH REL, they should be supplemented with the use of respirators. Respirators should be used as part of a comprehensive respiratory protection plan including environmental monitoring, training, selection and fit-testing of the proper NIOSH-approved respirator for the conditions of use, and maintenance and care of the respiratory protection equipment (29 CFR 1910.134 and 1926.103).

MUSCULOSKELETAL DISORDERS IN CONSTRUCTION WORKERS

Substantial evidence indicates that musculoskeletal disorders are a major cause of compensable injuries in the construction industry (Schneider 1997). Musculoskeletal disorders among construction workers account for 22.5% of injuries resulting in lost work days (BLS 1998). The lost-time injury rate for sprain and strain injuries in construction is about 50% higher than that for manufacturing and is second only to the rate for the transportation industry. In 1995, the rate for construction was 158.7 lost work day cases per 10,000 full-time workers—or about 1.6 cases per 100 workers (BLS 1998). The rate in private industry overall was 107.5 cases per 10,000 workers. Although this rate dropped in 1995 by almost 12% from 1994, the rate is still very high and much higher than for other industries.

Surveys of musculoskeletal symptoms among construction workers also show different prevalence patterns for different construction trades (Cook *et al.*, 1996a; Engholm and Holmström 1997; Holmström *et al.*, 1995; Rosecrance *et al.*, 1996; Zimmermann *et al.*, 1997a). Knee injuries are highest among plumbers, roofers, floorlayers, and sheet metal workers whose jobs require a lot of kneeling. Shoulder problems are common among scaffold erectors, insulators, and painters, who often work with hands and arms overhead.

Low-back problems are common among most trades, but they are highest among roofers, floor layers, and scaffold erectors, who must do considerable heavy-materials handling and stooping. Bricklayers have high rates of elbow and shoulder symptoms, apparently because of the awkward postures they maintain while working (Cook *et al.*, 1996b). Operating engineers who operate heavy equipment had the lowest rates of musculoskeletal symptoms because of the nature of their work, primarily sedentary (Zimmermann *et al.*, 1997b).

Substantial bodies of information exist about the types of musculoskeletal injuries occurring in most trades. For many of the trades, researchers have identified construction tasks more likely to be associated with a high risk of developing musculoskeletal disorders. The characteristics of the tasks include one or more of the following:

- High repetition (such as the continuous use of nail guns)
- Working in awkward postures (such as frequent overhead work)
- Forceful movements (such as lifting heavy objects)

Other risk factors include exposure to hand-arm vibration from powered hand tools and cold temperatures that cause loss of feeling and the need to hold onto tools more tightly.

Preventing Work-Related Musculoskeletal Disorders

Interventions or possible changes to work tasks to reduce musculoskeletal disorders have been identified for some trades. Interventions have been developed for the following:

- Concrete reinforcement workers (rodmen)—alternative methods for wiring rebar together (Saari and Wickström, 1978, Wakula *et. al.*, 1997)
- Bricklayers (Cook *et al.*, 1996b; Schierhorn 1996)
- Carpet layers—new carpet stretching device (Tdhun *et al.*, 1987)
- Operating engineers—retrofit of cabs and chassis of heavy equipment with ergonomically correct devices such as seats, roll bars, and steps (Zimmermann 1997b).

Interventions to reduce the risk of musculoskeletal disorders in construction can be classified as follows:

- New materials
- New tools and equipment
- Improved work practices
- Improved work organization and planning
- Education and exercise
- PPE

New materials, such as fiberglass ladders and lighter-weight concrete block, can reduce the risk of injury from materials handling. New tools designed to fit the user's hand and provide more protection with padding to reduce the pressure from hard surfaces can reduce the risk of hand and wrist injuries. Better work practices include using more carts and dollies to minimize the amount of manual materials handling, using scissors lifts to get closer to work overhead, and encouraging workers to bring the work up to waist level by providing sawhorses or work platforms. Better job planning is critical by making sure that worksites are kept clean and free of debris and that materials are delivered where and when they are needed and stored at waist height. Prework stretching programs are also increasing, and some evidence shows they can be a helpful adjunct to a good ergonomics program (Hecker and Gibbons 1997). Protective equipment such as kneepads, gloves, shoulder pads, and shoe inserts are also an important supplement to a comprehensive ergonomics program in construction. Back belts have become more common, but so far little evidence supports their effectiveness in preventing injuries (NIOSH 1994a).

Recently, several participatory ergonomic projects have been tried in construction and other industries with great success (Bronkhorst *et al.*,1997; van der Molen, *et al.*, 1997; Moir and Buchholz 1996; NIOSH 1994b). Workers have been included in the process of identifying high-risk tasks and potential solutions. Projects have led to the development of successful interventions for scaffold erectors, glaziers, and other trades. By including workers in each phase of the process, acceptance of interventions and changes is much easier.

Ergonomic training programs are increasing in the construction industry. They teach workers, designers, and managers how to recognize hazards, how to lift to prevent low-back injuries, and how to implement protective ergonomics changes on their sites. Steps for developing training materials include symptom surveys of workers and worksite assessments to identify and quantify risk factors associated with musculoskeletal disorders. Detailed discussions with retired and current workers, supervisors, trainers, and other knowledgeable individuals detail job activities, stresses, and possible solutions to identified job and task-related problems and concerns. A variety of approaches are being taken in the development of course work and training materials. Most of these approaches encourage participatory training and include sections on the identification of musculoskeletal disorders and the associated risk factors and methods on prevention. These programs include addition of ergonomic awareness modules to apprenticeship programs, creation of toolbox talks on ergonomics, development of trade-specific training modules that demonstrate how different tasks or equipment can be modified to prevent musculoskeletal injuries, and finally, the use of on-site ergonomic walk-throughs to identify potential problems on a day-by-day basis. The latter program, if preceded by ergonomic awareness training, is designed to deal with the ever changing environment of the construction site. Each of these programs have been immensely successful in that they, by default, increase the awareness of workers and management regarding musculoskeletal disorders and associated risk factors. However, more work is needed to evaluate the effectiveness of the various approaches in the long-term prevention of work-related musculoskeletal disorders among construction workers.

OCCUPATIONAL SKIN DISEASES

Although common among construction workers, occupational skin diseases and disorders (OSDs) are not well-recognized as health problems associated with construction work. There are many types of OSDs including contact dermatitis (which includes both irritant contact dermatitis [ICD] and allergic contact dermatitis [ACD]); skin cancers; skin infections; skin injuries; and many other less common skin diseases (Adams 1990; Hogan 1994; Marks and DeLeo 1992). The many causes of OSDs include the following:

1. Physical insults such as friction, pressure, trauma, vibration, heat, cold, variations in humidity, ultraviolet/visible/infrared radiation, ionizing radiation, and electric current
2. Biologic hazards such as plants, bacteria, fungi, protozoa, and insects
3. Chemicals including water, inorganic acids, alkalis, salts of heavy metals, aliphatic acids, aldehydes, alcohols, esters, hydrocarbons, solvents, metalorganic compounds, lipids, aromatic and polycyclic compounds, resin monomers, and proteins

Contact dermatitis is the most common OSD. Epidemiologic data show that contact dermatitis makes up 90% to 95% of all occupational skin diseases (Fregert 1975; Keil and Shmunes 1983; Mathias 1988). About 80% of all cases of contact dermatitis are due to irritation caused by chemicals (ICD) and 20% are caused by allergic reactions (ACD). Both ICD and ACD are inflammations of the skin caused by direct contact with materials. Lists of irritants and allergens are available in reference books (Adams 1990; Fisher 1986). The most frequent causes of ICD include soaps/detergents, fiberglass and particulate dusts, food products, cleaning agents, solvents, plastics and resins, petroleum products and lubricants, metals, and machine oils and coolants (Mathias 1988; 1990). Only certain chemicals cause allergic reactions, and, usually, only a small number of people are susceptible to them. Causes of ACD include metallic salts (nickel, chromate, cobalt), organic dyes, plants, plastic resins, rubber additives, and germicides (Mathias 1990). Construction workers in particular may be exposed to a variety of irritants and allergens. The irritants include dirt, wet cement, solvents, fiberglass, resins, and cleansers (Adams 1990; Marks and DeLeo 1992). A variety of chemical allergens may be found in such sources as rubber products including rubber gloves and boots, leather gloves and boots, protective hand creams, paints and adhesives, wet cement, soldering flux, woods and wood preservatives, and metal or rubber tool handles (Adams 1990; Marks and DeLeo 1992). Complete reviews of ICD and ACD are available (Adams 1990; Marks and DeLeo 1992; Fisher 1986; Rycroft et al., 1992).

In dermatitis, the skin initially turns red and can develop small, oozing blisters (vesicles), and bumps (papules). Stinging, burning, and itching may accompany the rash. The rash usually disappears in one to three weeks after the exposure ends. However, if exposure continues over a long period, the skin may develop deep cracks, scaling, and discoloration. Areas of the skin, such as hands and forearms, which usually have the greatest contact with irritants or allergens, are most commonly affected. If the chemical gets on clothing, it can produce rashes at areas of greatest contact, such as thighs, upper back, armpits, and feet. Dusts can produce rashes at areas where the dust accumulates and is held in contact with the skin, such as under the collar and belt line, at the tops of socks or shoes, and in front of the elbow or back of the knee. Mists can produce a dermatitis on the face and the neck. Irritants and allergens can be transferred to other areas of the body (such as the trunk or genitalia) by unwashed hands or from areas of accumulation (such as under rings or between fingers).

In addition to contact dermatitis, construction workers may be exposed to excessive ultraviolet radiation exposure from sunlight. This exposure can have health effects on the skin, including increasing the risk of skin cancers.

The public health importance of a disease can be measured several ways, using statistical, clinical, and economic measures. In 1996, BLS estimated 58,100 cases of OSDs in the U.S. workforce or 69 cases per 100,000 full-time workers (BLS 1998). Due to limitations of the data, it is estimated that the total number of OSDs may be on the order of 10–50 times higher than reported by BLS (NIOSH 1975). This would potentially raise the number of OSD cases to between one-half million and 2.9 million per year. In 1996, of the 58,100 cases, 1,600 (2.8%) were in the construction trades, for an annual incidence rate for OSDs of 33 per 100,000 construction workers (BLS 1998). The highest rates were seen in heavy construction, concrete work, and residential building construction.

The results of the 1988 National Health Interview Survey (NHIS) estimated that for the 30,074 individuals participating in the NHIS, the period prevalence rate for occupational contact dermatitis was 1.7% for all workers and 2.6% for construction trade workers (Behrens *et al.*, 1994). Projecting these results to the total U.S. working population resulted in an estimate of 1.87 million people with occupational contact dermatitis (Behrens *et al.*, 1994).

Skin cancer (which includes melanoma, basal, and squamous cell cancer) is the most common cancer diagnosed in the United States, with up to 1 million Americans affected each year (and more than 9,000 deaths) (American Cancer Society 1998). Although outdoor workers may be at increased risk for some types of skin cancers, no specific information is available on skin cancers and sun damaged skin in construction workers.

The economic impact of a disease can be measured by the direct costs of medical care and workers' compensation or disability payments and the indirect costs associated with lost workdays and loss of productivity. Although economic data specific to the construction trades are not available, an analysis of 1984 data for OSDs estimated annual medical costs for all private industry of more than $4.7 million and workers' compensation awards of more than $6.3 million (Mathias 1985). The estimated annual indirect cost of lost productivity due to OSDs in 1984 was $11 million ($700 per case) (Mathias 1985). Thus, in 1984 the estimated annual direct and indirect costs exceeded $22 million. However, considering that the actual annual incidence figures may be 10 to 50 times greater than reported in BLS data, the total annual cost of occupational skin diseases may range from $222 million to $1 billion (Mathias 1985). These estimates do not include costs of occupational retraining or costs attributable to the effects on the quality of life.

The data show that OSDs are relatively common diseases in the construction trades, with a noteworthy economic impact. These factors, along with the potential chronicity of some of the disorders and the fact that they are preventable, make OSDs a health effect of public health importance.

Preventing Occupational Skin Diseases

In general, using a combination of strategies and understanding their limitations will contribute to the prevention of OSDs. These strategies include the following:

1. Identifying irritants and allergens in the workplace
2. When feasible, and considering systemic as well as dermatologic toxicity, substituting chemicals that are less irritating/allergenic
3. Establishing engineering controls to reduce skin exposure
4. Using appropriate PPE such as gloves and special clothing
5. Emphasizing personal and occupational hygiene

6. Establishing educational programs to increase employee and employer awareness of workplace irritants and allergens and the suitable means to prevent exposure

7. Providing a system for the evaluation, reporting, and surveillance of dermatologic diseases (Mathias 1988; 1990; NIOSH 1988)

8. Substitution of chemicals in products used by construction workers; for example, the addition of ferrous sulfate to cement to reduce the content of an allergen (chromate) was effective in reducing occupational contact dermatitis in Europe—over a 6-year period, the prevalence of chromate allergy in cement workers fell from 11% to 3% (Avnstorp 1989)

Not all remedies are perfect in reducing occupational contact dermatitis. Skin should be protected from contact with irritants and allergens with proper PPE such as clean gloves, protective coveralls, and sleeve protectors. The effectiveness of PPE depends on the specific exposures and the types of gloves used. PPE selection should be based on information in the specific Material Safety Data Sheets (MSDS) and other guidelines. Use of PPE must be considered carefully since it may create problems by enhancing contact of the irritants or allergens to the skin or by directly irritating the skin or causing ACD from PPE components.

Irritants and allergens that have come in contact with exposed skin should be washed off with soap and water as soon as possible. Soap should be completely rinsed from the skin. Special attention should be directed toward soaps and skin cleansers since they also may be irritants. Excessive hand washing may lead to misuse of soaps and detergents and result in irritation (Mathias 1986). Certain components of the soaps or moisturizers (e.g., lanolin and fragrances) are known allergens and may cause ACD in sensitive individuals. Clothing contaminated with irritants or allergens should be removed and laundered prior to re-use.

The effectiveness of barrier creams is controversial (Orchard 1984), and at times workers using barrier creams may have higher prevalence rates of occupational contact dermatitis compared to those who do not use the creams (Varigos and Dunt 1981). Other interventions, which included providing advice on PPE and educating the workforce about skin care and exposures, were beneficial for workers constructing the English Channel tunnel (Irvine *et al.*, 1994).

Workers should be encouraged to report all possible work-related skin problems. These problems should be investigated on an individual basis by the company and consulting health-care providers. Because the work-relatedness of skin diseases may be difficult to prove, each person with possible work-related skin problems needs to be fully evaluated by a physician, preferably one with expertise in occupational/dermatological conditions. A complete evaluation would include a full medical and occupational history, a medical exam, a review of exposures, possibly diagnostic tests (such as skin patch tests to detect causes of ACD), and complete follow-up to note the progress of the individual. Individuals with definite or possible OSDs should be protected from exposures to presumed causes or exacerbators of the disease. In some cases, workers may have to be reassigned to areas where exposure is minimized or nonexistent.

Measures to prevent skin cancers and sun-damaged skin in outdoor workers include the following:

1. Whenever possible, avoid the sun and seek shade between 10 A.M. and 4 P.M., when the ultraviolet rays are strongest and do the most damage.

2. Wear protective clothing such as a wide-brimmed hat, tightly woven clothes that protect sun-exposed areas of the body, and ultraviolet blocking sunglasses.

3. Liberally apply sunscreen against ultraviolet A and ultraviolet B radiation with a sun protection factor (SPF) of at least 15, apply at least 15 minutes before going outside, and reapply every 2 hours, or every hour after getting wet or sweating profusely.

4. Refer to the daily ultraviolet index (available through the National Weather Service in 58 cities) when planning outdoor activities.

5. Examine your skin regularly and bring new moles or non-healing spots or areas that are changing in size, shape, or color to the attention of a health care provider (American Cancer Society 1997).

WOMEN IN CONSTRUCTION

In 1978, an effort was begun to recruit more women into the construction industry. Twenty years later, only 10% of all workers in the construction industry are women (CPWR 1998), and only 2.5% of those women actually work as skilled tradeswomen. The current labor shortage in the construction industry creates a perfect opportunity to increase this percentage. However, as more women enter the trades, certain gender-related safety and health issues need to be addressed. (Goldenhar and Sweeney 1996).

In 1996, the HASWIC workgroup (Health and Safety of Women in Construction) of the OSHA Advisory Committee on Construction Safety and Health released a report about the unique safety and health issues of women in construction (HASWIC 1997). Much of the information in the HASWIC report was excerpted from a number of previously published studies and reports. This section briefly summarizes the findings of the HASWIC report. The complete report can be obtained from OSHA's Construction Directorate.

Recent studies of tradeswomen suggest that safety and health issues arise primarily from six areas (Goldenhar and Sweeney 1996; Goldenhar, *et al.*, 1998). The primary areas are:

- Ill-fitting PPE and clothing
- Lack of adequate sanitary facilities
- Ergonomic concerns
- Reproductive hazards
- Workplace culture
- Lack of proper health, safety, and skills training

These issues are clearly important both for female and male construction workers.

PPE and Clothing

Women in nontraditional jobs such as construction often find it difficult to obtain well-fitting protective clothing or equipment. In a survey of 200 tradeswomen, approximately half of the respondents reported difficulty in finding appropriately sized safety shoes and gloves (Goldenhar, *et al*, 1998). In interviews, tradeswomen report that ill-fitting clothing and PPE, such as gloves and coveralls, pose safety hazards because they can get caught in machinery. It is important to note that smaller male construction workers also benefit from having smaller sized clothes available

Sanitary Facilities

The availability and cleanliness of toilet facilities is a major concern for most female (and some male) construction workers. Although not having proper sanitary facilities is an OSHA violation, in a recent study, 80% of tradeswomen surveyed reported being at worksites with no toilets or dirty toilets (LeBreton and Loevy 1992). In some court cases, the lack of appropriate sanitary facilities at a worksite has been determined to constitute gender-based discrimination. The health risks associated with the lack of adequate sanitary facilities includes an increased risk of bladder infections from holding urine too long (Foxman and Frerichs 1985) and the transmission of illnesses from unwashed hands. Hand washing facilities are often not available on construction sites. The availability of adequate sanitary facilities and washing facilities allows a worker to clean up after using materials that may cause dermatitis. It also prevents the worker from carrying home potentially toxic substances, such as lead.

Ergonomics and Musculoskeletal Disorders

Similar to the concerns voiced by male construction workers, back injuries are often mentioned by tradeswomen as a major concern. As previously discussed, preventing musculoskeletal disorders among construction workers requires a multifactorial approach. One solution suggested by female workers is to have tools, materials, and equipment available in sizes and designs appropriate for women (Goldenhar and Sweeney 1996). However, most construction tools and equipment are designed for the average-size man. This suggests that alternative work methods could prevent musculoskeletal problems. For example, rather than assuming a tradesperson should be able to lift heavy loads, perhaps construction workers of both genders should be encouraged to ask for help or use assistive devices when heavy lifting is required. Discussions with tradeswomen revealed that many of them felt that "working smarter, not harder" was key to staying safe and uninjured (Goldenhar and Sweeney 1996).

Reproductive Hazards

A reproductive hazard is a chemical, physical, or biological agent that can cause reproductive impairment such as low sperm count or change in the menstrual cycle or have an adverse developmental effect on fetuses. The vast majority of all construction workers (both male and female) are of reproductive age and therefore need to be careful of several chemicals and conditions at the construction site that are considered to be reproductive hazards.

Although few agents or conditions are known to produce birth defects, several that might are common to construction sites: chlorobiphenyls, hyperthermia, and ionizing radiation. Several agents—lead, solvents, and pesticides—are known to affect sperm development. Some of these agents (such as lead) could be carried home on contaminated clothing or other materials. Lead is also known to cause developmental delays in children exposed *in utero* and during the early years of life. More research is needed to determine the extent to which construction workers are exposed to reproductive hazards at the job site.

Workplace Culture

Interviews with tradeswomen reflect the stress of individuals who are the first to break down barriers of longstanding societal or cultural mores. Harassment and verbal abuse by coworkers and isolation on the job have been reported by tradeswomen. Many of these situations have forced them to endure uncomfortably or find other employment (CWIT 1994). To reduce the incidence of complaints and potential for litigation, some segments of the industry are beginning to act through training and enforcement of federal laws (ENR 1998).

Safety, Health, and Skills Training

Learning to work safely involves the combination of learning how to do the job, understanding the hazards of the job, and learning how to do the job safely. In construction, some of this information is learned through formal apprenticeship or vocational programs. Most, however, is learned on the job from coworkers. Many tradeswomen felt that "on-the-job" training was lacking: supervisors did not want to spend the time training; other workers were less than enthusiastic to teach them the secrets of how to do a job better and, perhaps, more safely. A potentially dangerous cycle is created when tradeswomen are asked to do jobs for which they are not properly trained, and when they are unable to do it, they are seen as being incompetent, or worse, they are injured.

Addressing Safety and Health Issues of Tradeswomen

While these issues may have been raised by tradeswomen, some of them likely affect tradesmen as well. It does not matter who is more or less affected by them. What matters is that safety and health hazards exist on the construction site. It appears that, like other industries, the construction workforce will become more diversified in the next 10 years. Collaborative efforts by owners, business agents, contractors, supervisors, foremen, and tradesmen and tradeswomen are necessary to reduce safety and health hazards such that the work is accomplished with dignity and respect for all.

CONCLUSION

In the United States, construction ranks with mining and agriculture as an industry with the highest rate of workplace fatalities and injuries. Occupational illnesses (including lung diseases and cancers, musculoskeletal disorders, noise-induced hearing loss, dermatitis, and other conditions) reduce the overall quality of construction workers' lives and impose the burden of medical costs on the worker, employers, and society at large. In addition, increasing numbers of tradeswomen cause the industry to take note that safety and health concerns raised by tradeswomen apply to all construction workers and, if remedied, would benefit the industry as a whole. Awareness of the need to prevent further illnesses and injuries among construction workers is steadily increasing with the collective understanding that prevention requires interaction among all sectors of the industry.

REFERENCES

Adams, R. M. (1990). *Occupational Skin Disease*, 2nd edition. Philadelphia, PA: WB Saunders.

Alterman, T., Salg, J. A., Lalich, N. R., Petersen, M. R., and Robinson, C. F. (1996). "Proportionate Mortality Ratio Study of Sheet Metal Workers." Proceedings of the American Public Health Association Convention, New York, December 1996.

American Cancer Society. (1997). "Facts About Skin Cancer." American Cancer Society, Inc., Pamphlet 9–200M–No. 2049–CC.

American Cancer Society. (1998). "Cancer Statistics 1998." *CA-A Cancer Journal for Clinicians*, Jan/Feb.

ANSI. (1996). American National Standard for Information Management for Occupational Safety and Health. Itasca, IL: American National Standards Institute, Inc., ANSI Z16.2–1995.

ANSI. (1998). American National Standard for Occupational and Educational Eye and Face Protection. DesPlaines, IL: American National Standards Institute, Inc., American Society of Safety Engineers, ANSI Z87.1–1998.

Avnstorp, C. (1989). "Follow-up of workers from the prefabricated concrete industry after the addition of ferrous sulfate to Danish cement." *Contact Dermatitis*, 20, pp. 365–371.

Behrens, V., Seligman, P., Cameron, L., Mathias, C. G., and Fine, L. (1994). "The prevalence of back pain, hand discomfort, and dermatitis in the U.S. working population." *American Journal of Public Health*, 84, pp. 1780–1785.

Berger, E. H. (1980). EARLOG monographs on hearing and hearing protection: Hearing protector performance: how they work—and—what goes wrong in the real world. Indianapolis, IN: Cabot Safety Corporation, EARLOG 5.

Berger, E. H., Franks, J. R., and Lindgren, F. (1996). "International review of field studies of hearing protector attenuation." In Axelsson A., Borchgrevink, H., Hamernik, R. P., Hellstrom, P., Henderson, D., Salvi, R. J., eds. *Scientific basis of noise-induced hearing loss*. New York: Thieme Medical Publishers, Inc., pp. 361–377.

Bureau of Labor Statistics. (1994). Fatal workplace injuries in 1992: A collection of data and analysis. U.S. Department of Labor, Bureau of Labor Statistics, Report 870.

BLS. (1994). Survey of Occupational Injuries and Illnesses, 1992. U.S. Department of Labor, Bureau of Labor Statistics, Summary 94-3.

BLS. (1995). Fatal workplace injuries in 1993: A collection of data and analysis. U.S. Department of Labor, Bureau of Labor Statistics, Report 891.

BLS. (1995). Survey of Occupational Injuries and Illnesses, 1993. U.S. Department of Labor, Bureau of Labor Statistics, Summary 95-5.

BLS. (1996). Fatal workplace injuries in 1994: A collection of data and analysis. U.S. Department of Labor, Bureau of Labor Statistics, Report 908.

BLS. (1996). Survey of Occupational Injuries and Illnesses, 1994. U.S. Department of Labor, Bureau of Labor Statistics, Summary 96-11.

BLS. (1996). Occupational Injuries and Illnesses in the United States. U.S. Department of Labor, Bureau of Labor Statistics, published annually since 1972; data for 1993 published August 1996 in Bulletin 2478.

BLS. (1997). Fatal workplace injuries in 1995: A collection of data and analysis. U.S. Department of Labor, Bureau of Labor Statistics, Report 913.

BLS. (1997). Survey of Occupational Injuries and Illnesses, 1995. U.S. Department of Labor, Bureau of Labor Statistics, Summary 97-7.

BLS. (1998). Bureau of Labor Statistics Homepage [http://stats.gov/oshhome.htm] Occupational injuries and illnesses: counts, rates, and characteristics—1995. Date accessed: 1998.

BLS. (1998). Fatal workplace injuries in 1996: A collection of data and analysis. U.S. Department of Labor, Bureau of Labor Statistics, Report 922.

BLS. (1998). Survey of Occupational Injuries and Illnesses, 1996. U.S. Department of Labor, Bureau of Labor Statistics, Summary 98-1.

Bronkhorst, R. E., Vink, P., and Koningsveld, E. A. P. (1997). "Ergonomic improvements for the glazier–new working methods and tools do improve the working conditions," presentation to the 13th Triennial Congress of the International Ergonomics Association, Tampere, Finland, June 29–July 4, 1997.

Cattledge, G. H., Hendricks, S., and Stanevich, R. (1996). "Fatal occupational falls in the U.S. construction industry, 1980–1989." *Accident, Analysis, and Prevention*, 28(5), pp. 647–654.

Cattledge, G. H., Schneiderman, A., Stanevich, R., Hendricks, S., and Greenwood, J. (1996). "Nonfatal occupational fall injuries in the West Virginia construction industry." Accident Analysis and Prevention, 28(5):655–663.

CFR. Code of Federal Regulations. Washington, DC: U.S. Government Printing Office, Office of the Federal Register.

Chen, G-X, and Fosbroke, D. E. (1998): "Work-related fatal-injury risk of construction workers by occupation and cause of death." *Human and Ecological Risk Assessment*, 4(6), pp. 1371–1390.

Cook, T. M., Rosecrance, J. C., and Zimmermann, C. L. (1996a). The University of Iowa construction survey. The University of Iowa and the Center to Protect Workers' Rights, Washington, DC, April 1996.

Cook, T. M., Rosecrance, J. C., and Zimmermann, C. L. (1996b). "Work-related musculoskeletal disorders in bricklaying: a symptom and job factors survey and guidelines for improvement." *Applied Occupational and Environmental Hygiene*, 11 (11), pp. 1335–1339.

CPWR. (1998). The construction chart book: the U.S. construction industry and its workers. 2nd edition. The National Institute for Occupational Health and The Center to Protect Workers' Rights, Washington, D.C.

CWIT. (1994). *Tools for Success: A Manual for Tradeswomen.* Chicago, IL: Chicago Women in Trades.

Dobie, R. A. (1997). *Medical-Legal Evaluation of Hearing Loss.* New York: John Wiley and Sons, Inc., p. 1.

Engholm, G., and Holmström, H. (1997). "Physical exposures, psycho-social factors and patterns of prevalence of musculoskeletal disorders in various groups of Swedish construction workers," presentation to the 13th Triennial Congress of the International Ergonomics Association, June 29–July 4, 1997, Tampere, Finland.

ENR. (1998).

Fisher, A. A. (1986). *Contact Dermatitis*, 3rd edition. Philadelphia, PA: Lea and Febiger.

Fosbroke, D. E., Kisner, S., and Myers, J. R. (1997). "Working lifetime risk of occupational fatal injury." *American Journal of Industrial Medicine*, 31, pp. 459–467.

Foxman, B., and Frerichs, R. R. (1985). "Epidemiology of urinary tract infection: II. Diet, clothing, and urination habits." *American Journal of Public Health*, 75, pp.1314–1317.

Fregert, S. (1975). "Occupational dermatitis in a ten-year material (sic)." *Contact Dermatitis*, 1, pp. 96–107.

Goldenhar, L. M., and Sweeney, M. H. (1996). "Tradeswomen's perspectives on occupational health and safety: a qualitative investigation." *American Journal of Industrial Medicine*, 23, pp. 516–520.

Goldenhar, L. M., Swanson, N. G., Hurrel, Jr., J. J., Ruder, A., and Deddens, J. (1998), "Stressors and adverse outcomes for female construction workers." *Journal of Occupational Health Psychology*, 3(1), pp.19–32.

HASWIC. (1997). "Women in the construction workplace: providing equitable safety and health protection." Working paper of the Health and Safety of Women in Construction Workgroup, A Workgroup of the Occupational Safety and Health Administration.

Hattis, D. (1998). "Preliminary assessment of occupational noise sources and exposures in construction industries." *Human and Ecological Risk Assessment Journal*, 4(2), pp. 1417–1441.

Hecker, S., and Gibbons, B. (1997). Evaluation of a Prework Stretching Program in the Construction Industry: 1st International Symposium on Ergonomics in Building Construction. Helsinki, Finland, June 20–July 2, 1997, Book of Abstracts, p. 152.

Hinze, J. W. (1997). *Construction Safety.* Upper Saddle River, NJ: Prentice-Hall, Inc.

Hogan, D. J. (1994). *Occupational Skin Disorders.* New York: Igaku-Shoin.

Holmström, E., Ulrich, M., and Engholm, E. (1995). "Musculoskeletal disorders in construction workers." In: *Occupational Medicine: State of the Art Reviews*, 10(2), pp. 295–312.

Hunting, K. L., Nessel-Stephens, L., Sanford, S. M., Shesser, R., and Welch, L. S. (1994). "Surveillance of construction worker injuries through an urban emergency department." *Journal of Occupational Medicine*, 36, pp. 356–364.

Husberg, B., Fosbroke, D. E., Conway, G. (Forthcoming). Surveillance for Non-Fatal Construction Injuries in Alaska.

IARC. (1997). "IARC monographs on the evaluation of carcinogenic risks to humans." Vol. 68, Silica, some silicates, coal dust and para-aramid fibrils. Geneva, Switzerland: World Health Organization, International Agency for Research on Cancer, p. 210.

Irvine, C., Pugh, C. E., Hansen, E. J., and Rycroft, R. J. G. (1994). "Cement dermatitis in underground workers during construction of the Channel Tunnel." *Occupational Medicine*, 44, pp. 17–23.

Jackson, L. L., Long, D. J., Layne, L. A., and Johnston, J. J. (1998). "Acute eye injury in the construction industry: a perspective from a national sample of emergency department admissions." 4th World Conference on Injury Prevention and Control. Amsterdam, The Netherlands, May 17–20, 1998, Book of Abstracts, 2, p. 934.

Keil, J. E., and Shmunes, E. (1983). "The epidemiology of work-related skin disease in South Carolina." *Archives of Dermatology*, 119, pp. 650–654.

Kisner, S. M., and Fosbroke, D. E. (1994). "Injury hazards in the construction industry." *Journal of Occupational Medicine*, 36(2), pp. 137–143.

Layne, L. A., Fosbroke, D. E., Ore, T., and Sniezak, J. (forthcoming). "A pilot study of nonfatal injuries among construction workers treated in emergency departments in the United States."

LeBreton, L. W., and Loevy, S. S. (1992). *Breaking new Ground: Worksite 2000*. Chicago, IL: Chicago Women in Trades.

Levitt, R. E., and Samelson, N. M. (1993). *Construction Safety Management,* 2nd edition. New York: John Wiley & Sons, Inc.

Linch, K. D., Miller, W. E., Althouse, R. B., Groce, D. W., and Hale, J. M. (1998). Surveillance of respirable crystalline silica dust using OSHA compliance data (1979–1995). *American Journal of Industrial Medicine*, 34, pp. 547–548.

Lipscomb, H. J., Kalat, J., and Dement, J. M. (1996). "Workers' compensation claims of union carpenters 1989–1992: Washington State." *Applied Occupational Environmental Hygiene*, 11(1), pp. 56–63.

MacCollum, D. V. (1995). *Construction Safety Planning*. New York: Van Nostrand Reinhold.

Marks, J. G., and DeLeo V. A. (1992). *Contact and Occupational Dermatology*. St. Louis, MO: Mosby Year Book.

Mathias, C. G. T. (1985). "The cost of occupational skin disease." *Archives of Dermatology*, 121, pp. 332–334.

Mathias, C. G. T. (1986). "Contact dermatitis from use or misuse of soaps, detergents, and cleansers in the workplace." In: *Occupational Skin Disease: State of the Art Reviews—Occupational Medicine*. Philadelphia, PA: Hanley and Belfus.

Mathias, C. G. T. (1988). "Occupational dermatoses." *Journal of the American Academy of Dermatology*, 6 pp. 1107–1114.

Mathias, C. G. T. (1990). "Prevention of occupational contact dermatitis." *Journal of the American Academy of Dermatology*, 23, pp. 742–748.

Merry, M., and Stephenson, M. (1998). Case studies on education and motivation for hearing loss prevention. Seminar presented at the 23rd Annual Meeting of the Hearing Conservation Association, Albuquerque, New Mexico, February 19–21.

Moir, S., and Buchholz, B. (1996). "Emerging participatory approaches to ergonomic interventions in the construction industry." *American Journal of Industrial Medicine*, 29, pp. 425–430.

National Society to Prevent Blindness. (1991). *Guide to Controlling Eye Injuries in Industry*. Schaumburg, IL: National Society to Prevent Blindness.

NIOSH. (1974). "NIOSH criteria for a recommended standard: occupational exposure to crystalline silica." Cincinnati, OH: U.S. Department of Health, Education, and Welfare, Public Health Service, Center for Disease Control and Prevention, National Institute for Occupational Safety and Health, DHEW (NIOSH) Publication No. 75–120:, pp. 54–55, 60–61.

NIOSH. (1975). "National Occupational Survey—Pilot study for development of an occupational disease surveillance method." Rockville, MD, U.S. Department of Health, Education, and Welfare, Healthy Services and Mental Health Administration, National Institute for Occupational Safety and Health, DHEW Publication (NIOSH) 75–162.

NIOSH. (1988). "Proposed national strategy for the prevention of leading work-related diseases and injuries—Dermatological conditions." Cincinnati, OH, U.S. Department of Health and Human Services, Public Health Services, Centers for Disease Control, National Institute for Occupational Safety and Health, DHHS Publication (NIOSH) 89–136.

NIOSH. (1994a). "Workplace use of back belts: review and recommendations." Cincinnati, OH: U.S. Department of Health and Human Services, Public Health Service, Centers for Disease Control and Prevention, National Institute for Occupational Safety and Health, DHHS (NIOSH) Publication No. 94–122.

NIOSH. (1994b). "Participatory ergonomic interventions in meatpacking plants." Cincinnati, OH: U.S. Department of Health and Human Services, Public Health Service, Centers for Disease Control and

Prevention, National Institute for Occupational Safety and Health, DHHS (NIOSH) Publication No. 94–124.

NIOSH. (1995). "The NIOSH compendium of hearing protection devices." Cincinnati, OH: U.S. Department of Health and Human Services, Public Health Service, Centers for Disease Control and Prevention, National Institute for Occupational Safety and Health, DHHS (NIOSH) Publication No. 95–105.

NIOSH. (1996a). "Work-related lung disease surveillance report 1996." Cincinnati, OH: U.S. Department of Health and Human Services, Public Health Service, Centers for Disease Control and Prevention, National Institute for Occupational Safety and Health, DHHS (NIOSH) Publication No. 96–134.

NIOSH. (1996b). "National occupational exposure survey (1981–1983), Unpublished provisional data." Cincinnati, OH: U.S. Department of Health and Human Services, Public Health Service, Centers for Disease Control and Prevention, National Institute for Occupational Safety and Health, Division of Surveillance, Hazard Evaluations and Field Studies.

NIOSH. (1996c). "NIOSH Alert: request for assistance in preventing silicosis and deaths in construction workers." Cincinnati, OH: U.S. Department of Health and Human Services, Public Health Service, Centers for Disease Control and Prevention, National Institute for Occupational Safety and Health, DHHS (NIOSH) Publication No. 96–112.

NIOSH. (1998a). "National Traumatic Occupational Fatalities surveillance system. Internal data analysis for the years 1980 through 1992." Division of Safety Research, Morgantown, West Virginia.

NIOSH. (1998b). "Criteria for a recommended standard: occupational noise exposure—revised criteria 1998." Cincinnati, OH: U.S. Department of Health and Human Services, Public Health Service, Centers for Disease Control and Prevention, National Institute for Occupational Safety and Health, DHHS (NIOSH) Publication No. 98–126.

OMB. (1987). *Standard Industrial Classification Manual, 1987.* Washington, DC: U.S. Government Printing Office, Office of Management and Budget.

Orchard, S. (1984). "Barrier creams." *Clinics in Dermatology, 2,* pp. 619–629.

Ore, T., and Casini, V. (1996). "Electrical fatalities among U.S. construction workers." *Journal of Occupational and Environmental Medicine,* 38, pp. 587–592.

Ore, T., and Fosbroke, D. E. (1997). "Motor vehicle fatalities in the United States construction industry." Accident Analysis and Prevention, 29(5), pp. 613–626.

Pollack, E. S., Griffin, M., Ringen, K., and Weeks, J. L. (1996). "Fatalities in the construction industry in the United States, 1992 and 1993." *American Journal of Industrial Medicine,* 30, pp. 325–330.

Pratt, S. G., Kisner, S. M., and Moore, P. H. (1997). "Machinery-related fatalities in the construction industry." *American Journal of Industrial Medicine,* 32, pp. 41–50.

Ringen, K., Englund, A., Welch, L., Weeks, J. L., and Segal, J. L. (1995). Why is construction different? *Occupational Medicine: State of the Art Reviews,* 10(2):255–259.

Robinson, C. F., Alterman, T., Burnett, C. A., Kisner, S. M., Roscoe, R. J., and Sestito, J. P. (1995). "Mortality patterns among construction workers in the United States." In *Occupational Medicine: State of the Art Reviews,* 10(2) April 1995, pp. 269–283.

Robinson, C. F., Petersen, M., Sieber, W. K., Palu, S., and Halperin, W. E. (1996). "Mortality of Carpenter's Union members employed in the U.S. construction or wood products industries, 1987–1990." *American Journal of Industrial Medicine,* 30, pp. 674–694.

Rosecrance, J. C., Cook, T. M., and Zimmermann, C. L. (1996). "Work-related musculoskeletal symptoms among construction workers in the pipe trades." *Work,* 7, pp. 13–20.

Rycroft, R. J. G., Menne, T., Frosch, P. J., et al., eds. (1992). *Textbook of Contact Dermatitis.* New York, Springer-Verlag.

Saari, J., and Wickström, G. (1978). "Load on back in concrete reinforcement work." *Scandinavian Journal of Work, Environment, and Health,* 4(suppl 1), pp. 13–19.

Schierhorn, C. (1996). "Jobsite ergonomics." *Masonry Construction,* 9(5), pp. 202–207.

Schneider, S. (1997). "Musculoskeletal Injuries in Construction: Are They a Problem?" Proceedings of the 13th Triennial Congress of the International Ergonomics Association, Tampere, Finland, June 29–July 4, 1997, Vol. 6, pp. 169–171.

Steenland, K., and Brown, D. (1995). "Silicosis among gold miners: exposure-response analyses and risk assessment." *American Journal of Public Health,* 85(10), pp. 1372–1377.

Stephenson, M. (1995). "Noise Exposure Characterization via Task Based Analysis." Proceedings of the Hearing Conservation Conference/National Hearing Conservation Association Meeting III/XX, Cincinnati, OH: March 22–25.

Stern, F., Schulte, P., Sweeney, M. H., Fingerhut, M., Vossenas, P., Burkhardt, G., and Kornak, M. (1995). "Proportionate mortality among construction laborers." *American Journal of Industrial Medicine,* 27, pp. 485–509.

Stern, F., and Sweeney, M. H. (1997). "Proportionate mortality among unionized construction operating engineers." *American Journal of Industrial Medicine*, 32, pp. 51–65.

Suruda, A., Fosbroke, D., Braddee, R. (1995). "Fatal work-related falls from roofs." *Journal of Safety Research*, 26(1), pp. 1–8.

Tennenbaum, S., and Schneider, S. (1998). "Hearing loss among roofers." Submitted to the *American Journal of Industrial Medicine*.

Tdhun, M., Tanaka, S., Smith, A. B., Halperin, W. E., Lee, S. T., Luggen, M. E., and Hess, E. V. (1987). "Morbidity from repetitive knee trauma in carpet and floor layers." *British Journal of Industrial Medicine*, 44, pp. 611–620.

Van der Molen, H. F., Vink, P., and Urlings, I. J. M. (1997). "A Participatory Ergonomic Approach to the Redesign of Scaffolders' Work." Proceedings of the 13th Triennial Congress of the International Ergonomics Association, Tampere, Finland, June 19–July 4, 1997, Vol. 1, pp. 450–452.

Varigos, G. A., and Dunt, D. R. (1981). "Occupational dermatitis—An epidemiological study in the rubber and cement industries." *Contact Dermatitis*, 7, pp. 105–110.

Wakula, J., Wimmel, F., Linke-Kaiser, G., Hoffman, G., and Kaiser, R. (1997). "Ergonomic Analysis of Load on the Back in Concrete Work." Proceedings of the 13th Triennial Congress of the International Ergonomics Association, Tampere, Finland, June 29–July 4, 1997, Vol. 6, pp. 191–193.

WHO. (1977). *International Classification of Diseases: Manual on the International Statistical Classification of Diseases, Injuries and Causes of Death*, ninth revision. Geneva: World Health Organization.

Zimmermann, C. L., Cook, T. M., and Rosecrance, J. C. (1997a). "Trade-Specific Trends in Self-Reported Musculoskeletal Symptoms and Job Factor Perceptions among Unionized Construction Workers." Proceedings of the 13th Triennial Congress of the International Ergonomics Association, Tampere, Finland, June 29–July 4, 1997, Vol. 6, pp. 214–216.

Zimmermann, C. L., Cook, T. M., and Rosecrance, J. C. (1997b). "Work–related musculoskeletal symptoms and injuries among operating engineers: a review and guidelines for improvement." *Applied Occupational and Environmental Hygiene*, 12(7), pp. 480–484.